THE LIBRARY OF CHRISTIAN CLASSICS

THE LIBRARY OF CHRISTIAN CLASSICS

Volume

I. *Early Christian Fathers.* Editor: CYRIL C. RICHARDSON, Washburn Professor of Church History, Union Theological Seminary, New York.

II. *Alexandrian Christianity.* Editors: HENRY CHADWICK, Regius Professor of Divinity and Canon of Christ Church, Oxford; J. E. L. OULTON, late Professor of Divinity, Trinity College, Dublin.

III. *Christology of the Later Fathers.* Editor: EDWARD ROCHIE HARDY, Professor of Church History, Berkeley Divinity School, New Haven, Connecticut.

IV. *Cyril of Jerusalem and Nemesius of Emesa.* Editor: WILLIAM TELFER, formerly Master of Selwyn College, Cambridge.

V. *Early Latin Theology.* Editor: S. L. GREENSLADE, Regius Professor of Ecclesiastical History and Canon of Christ Church, University of Oxford.

VI. *Augustine: Earlier Writings.* Editor: J. H. S. BURLEIGH, Professor of Ecclesiastical History, University of Edinburgh, and Principal of New College, Edinburgh.

VII. *Augustine: Confessions and Enchiridion.* Editor: ALBERT COOK OUTLER, Professor of Theology, Perkins School of Theology, Southern Methodist University, Dallas, Texas.

VIII. *Augustine: Later Works.* Editor: JOHN BURNABY, Fellow of Trinity College and formerly Regius Professor of Divinity, University of Cambridge.

IX. *Early Medieval Theology.* Editor: GEORGE E. MCCRACKEN, Professor of Classical Languages, Drake University, Des Moines, Iowa.

X. *A Scholastic Miscellany: Anselm to Ockham.* Editor: EUGENE R. FAIRWEATHER, Associate Professor of Dogmatic Theology and Ethics, Trinity College, University of Toronto, Toronto, Canada.

XI. *Nature and Grace: Selections from the Summa Theologica of Thomas Aquinas.* Editor: A. M. FAIRWEATHER, Lecturer in Philosophy, University of Edinburgh.

XII. *Western Asceticism.* Editor: OWEN CHADWICK, Master of Selwyn College and Dixie Professor of Ecclesiastical History, University of Cambridge.

XIII. *Late Medieval Mysticism.* Editor: RAY C. PETRY, Professor of Church History, The Divinity School, Duke University, Durham, North Carolina.

XIV. *Advocates of Reform: From Wyclif to Erasmus.* Editor: MATTHEW SPINKA, Waldo Professor Emeritus of Church History, Hartford Theological Seminary, Hartford, Connecticut.

VOLUME XIX

MELANCHTHON AND BUCER

THE LIBRARY OF CHRISTIAN CLASSICS

Volume XIX

MELANCHTHON
AND
BUCER

Edited by

WILHELM⌐PAUCK
Distinguished Professor of Church History
The Divinity School, Vanderbilt University
Nashville, Tennessee

Philadelphia
THE WESTMINSTER PRESS

Published simultaneously in the United States of America and in Great Britain by The Westminster Press, Philadelphia, and the SCM Press, Ltd, London

Standard Book No. 664-22019-3

Library of Congress Catalog Card No. 69-12309

Printed in the United States of America

GENERAL EDITORS' PREFACE

The Christian Church possesses in its literature an abundant and incomparable treasure. But it is an inheritance that must be reclaimed by each generation. THE LIBRARY OF CHRISTIAN CLASSICS is designed to present in the English language, and in twenty-six volumes of convenient size, a selection of the most indispensable Christian treatises written prior to the end of the sixteenth century.

The practice of giving circulation to writings selected for superior worth or special interest was adopted at the beginning of Christian history. The canonical Scriptures were themselves a selection from a much wider literature. In the patristic era there began to appear a class of works of compilation (often designed for ready reference in controversy) of the opinions of well-reputed predecessors, and in the Middle Ages many such works were produced. These medieval anthologies actually preserve some noteworthy materials from works otherwise lost.

In modern times, with the increasing inability even of those trained in universities and theological colleges to read Latin and Greek texts with ease and familiarity, the translation of selected portions of earlier Christian literature into modern languages has become more necessary than ever; while the wide range of distinguished books written in vernaculars such as English makes selection there also needful. The efforts that have been made to meet this need are too numerous to be noted here, but none of these collections serves the purpose of the reader who desires a library of representative treatises spanning the Christian centuries as a whole. Most of them embrace only the age of the church fathers, and some of them have long been out of print. A fresh translation of a work already translated may shed much new light upon its meaning. This is true even of Bible translations despite the work of many experts through the centuries. In some instances old translations have been adopted in this series, but wherever necessary or desirable, new ones have been made. Notes have been supplied where these were needed to explain the author's meaning. The introductions provided for the several treatises and extracts will, we believe, furnish welcome guidance.

JOHN BAILLIE
JOHN T. McNEILL
HENRY P. VAN DUSEN

CONTENTS

MARTIN BUCER: DE REGNO CHRISTI

De Regno Christi, translated by Wilhelm Pauck in collaboration with Paul Larkin

BOOK ONE

ABBREVIATIONS

CR	*Corpus Reformatorum: Philippi Melanchthonis Opera quae supersunt omnia,* ed. by C. G. Bretschneider and H. E. Bindseil (Halle, 1834 ff.) .
GCS	*Die griechischen christlichen Schriftsteller der ersten drei Jahrhunderte* (Berlin, 1897 ff.) .
LW	Luther's Works, American edition, ed. by Jaroslav Pelikan and Helmut T. Lehmann, 55 vols. (St. Louis and Philadelphia: Concordia Publishing House and Muhlenberg Press, 1955 ff.) .
LCC	The Library of Christian Classics, ed. by John Baillie, John T. McNeill, and Henry P. Van Dusen, 26 vols. (Philadelphia: The Westminster Press, 1950 ff.) .
MPG	J. P. Migne, ed., *Patrologiae cursus completus, series Graeca.*
MPL	J. P. Migne, ed., *Patrologiae cursus completus, series Latina.*
WA	*Luthers Werke* (Weimar Ausgabe, 1883 ff.) .
WA Tr	Table Talk
WA Br	Letters

EDITOR'S PREFACE

This volume contains two highly important writings of the period of the Protestant Reformation. Melanchthon's book *Loci communes theologici,* the first Protestant dogmatics, as it is sometimes called, represents the work of a young man writing at the very beginning of the Lutheran Reformation. Bucer's work *On the Kingdom of Christ,* the first Protestant treatise on social ethics, is the product of a mature man standing on the verge of old age. It reflects the experience of a lifetime in manifold labors for an actual reformation of the Church as well as of society.

Bucer and Melanchthon, next to Luther the two most influential German Reformers, deserve to be better known in English-speaking lands. Only a very few of their voluminous writings are available in English translations.

The present translation of Melanchthon's first important theological work is based on the edition of Hans Engelland, published in *Melanchthons Werke in Auswahl,* edited by Robert Stupperich (Gütersloh, 1952), Vol. II, Pt. I, pp. 3–163. The translation is the work of Prof. Lowell J. Satre of Luther Theological Seminary, St. Paul, Minnesota. It has been revised in several places by the editor.

Bucer's *De Regno Christi* was the first of his works to be published in the modern edition of his collected writings now in process of publication in Germany and France. It has been splendidly edited by François Wendel in *Martini Buceri Opera Latina* (Vol. XV, Paris and Gütersloh, 1955). For the present volume a first draft of a translation was prepared by Paul Larkin. It was revised by Lowell Satre and then fully reworked and redrafted by the editor. (It may here be remarked that Bucer, who worked

xix

hastily and produced much in an astonishingly short time, wrote in an extraordinarily prolix, wordy, and repetitious style, thus causing considerable difficulty for his modern translators). The editor has made liberal use of Professor Wendel's detailed notes but he has added many of his own. The scholarly student is urged to use Wendel's edition in conjunction with the present one.

W. P.

PHILIP MELANCHTHON

Loci Communes Theologici

Loci Communes Theologici

EDITOR'S INTRODUCTION

PHILIP MELANCHTHON'S WORK *Loci communes rerum theo-logicarum* ("Fundamental Theological Themes") was first published in December, 1521, in Wittenberg (a little later another edition appeared in Basel). Melanchthon had begun to work on it in 1520, at a time when Martin Luther, his friend and older colleague at the University of Wittenberg, was deeply involved in the conflict with the Roman Catholic Church that his Ninety-five Theses of October 31, 1517, had aroused. On June 15, 1520, Pope Leo X published the bull *Exsurge Domine,* which threatened Luther with excommunication unless he recanted his views. On December 10, 1520, Luther publicly burned a copy of the papal bull in order to demonstrate that he would defy papal authority to the end. Throughout this decisive year, in the course of which the role and responsibility of a reformer were forced upon him, he published the programmatic treatises that summed up his criticisms of the Roman Catholic Church, his conception of the Christian gospel, and his proposals for a reformation of the Church. Through these writings he definitely established himself as the leader of the quickly growing movement of the Reformation. Indeed, his power and influence were then so great that when he went to Worms in the early spring of 1521 in order to be given a hearing before the Diet of the Holy Roman Empire, presided over by the new emperor, Charles V, he was the hero of the German nation, despite the fact that in the meantime the papacy had placed the ban upon him.

During all this time, Melanchthon had been at work on his own compendium of theological fundamentals. Indeed, his printer sent him the galleys of the first parts of his work in April, 1521, when

3

Luther was at Worms awaiting the imperial decision about his case after he had once more and with heroic clarity refused to recant his views. Before the Edict of Worms, which declared him an outcast, was published, Luther was secretly put in safety at Wartburg castle and thus removed from Wittenberg. He did not cease to write and, indeed, he composed some of his most influential works in his isolated retreat, including the German translation of the New Testament, but he could no longer exercise a direct, personal influence upon the affairs either of the town or the University of Wittenberg, though he was in lively touch by correspondence with his friends there. Thus, Melanchthon, who had become one of the staunchest defenders of Luther against his critics and enemies, was drawn into active participation in the first actual efforts for the realization of a reformation in the church. It was under these circumstances that, with considerable strain and difficulty, he completed his *Loci* and finally published the work.

Luther, who had been kept informed by Melanchthon about the progress of his work, hailed it with great enthusiasm, believing that it was one of the clearest statements of the Christian religion ever written. His judgment was to be shared by many, for, as we shall see, it proved to be a great success.

I. The Career of Melanchthon, 1497–1521

In 1521, Philip Melanchthon was a widely respected scholar who enjoyed a great reputation, but he was still a young man in his early twenties.

He was born the son of an armorer, on February 16, 1497, in Bretten in the Palatinate. His father died (probably as a result of having drunk poisoned water) when his son Philip was only eleven years old. Philip, who had received elementary education in the schools of his hometown, then was sent to Pforzheim where his maternal grandmother, a sister of the famous Humanist John Reuchlin, lived. There he completed his preparatory education at the well-known Latin school under the supervision and inspiration of his great-uncle Reuchlin. It was probably at Reuchlin's suggestion that he then adopted the Greek form of his family name Schwarzerd—namely, Melanchthon—as a sign that he wanted to become a Humanist scholar.

By October 14, 1509, he had matriculated at the University of Heidelberg and in less than two years he obtained the degree of Bachelor of Arts (June 18, 1511). It is said that because of his extreme youth he was denied the right to continue his studies at

Heidelberg. But on September 17, 1512, he was registered at the University of Tübingen and there, again after an astonishingly short time, he was given the degree of Master of Arts (January 25, 1514). By then he had become an enthusiastic Humanist. Interested in all branches of knowledge, including mathematics and the natural sciences as well as philosophy and theology, he cultivated ancient languages and particularly Greek language and literature, always in the circle of like-minded friends, e.g., John Oecolampadius and Ambrose Blaurer, the later Reformers of Basel and Constance respectively, and always under the influence of Reuchlin. He edited and translated ancient authors and became an expert Greekist. In May, 1518, when he was twenty-one years old, he published a Greek grammar that was to remain in constant demand as a textbook for many decades. He then planned to prepare a reliable Greek edition of the works of Aristotle.

In the meantime, the University of Wittenberg, founded at the beginning of the century on the frontier of German civilization and not at all famous like the older schools of Heidelberg and Tübingen, was becoming prominent—because of Martin Luther, who, even before he became widely known as the author of the Ninety-five Theses on Indulgences, had played a major role in the reform of theological studies on the basis of Biblical theology. In 1518, the Wittenbergers wanted to introduce the study of Greek and Hebrew into their curriculum. The founder and chief sponsor of the University of Wittenberg, Frederick the Wise, Duke of Saxony, turned to Reuchlin for advice, with the result that Melanchthon was recommended to him. "Among Germans," Reuchlin wrote about his grandnephew, "I know of none who is superior to him, except Erasmus." [1]

Thus Melanchthon was appointed the first professor of Greek at Wittenberg. On August 25, 1518, he arrived in the small town on the river Elbe that was to remain his home for forty-two years, or throughout the rest of his life. Four days later, on August 29, 1518, he delivered his inaugural lecture in the castle-church that served the university as the main assembly hall. He spoke on curriculum reform (*De corrigendis adolescentiae studiis*). Over against the methods of the Scholastics, he demanded the renewal of the old disciplines of dialectics and rhetorics according to the standards of humanistic learning. He made a plea for the study of Greek philosophy, particularly of Aristotle, and expressed the hope that true, authentic learning would bring about a broad moral reform

[1] Robert Stupperich, *Melanchthon*, German Edition (Berlin, 1960), p 22; English translation (The Westminster Press, 1965), p. 30.

of life. The audience, which included Luther, responded enthusiastically. Luther was full of admiration for Melanchthon's wide knowledge of languages and for the sharpness of his mind. Melanchthon, on his part, quickly came under the spell of Luther's powerful thought and person. In a short time he, the Humanist in whose eyes Erasmus was the greatest of scholars, identified himself with Luther's cause and supported him wholeheartedly.

In June, 1519, he accompanied Luther to Leipzig in order to give him support in his disputation with John Eck. Almost immediately after his return to Wittenberg from Leipzig he wrote and published a report on the discussion in the form of a letter addressed to his friend Oecolampadius—which was highly favorable toward Luther. Eck responded quickly in a tract that was full of contempt for the "grammarian" from Wittenberg. Its title was *Eck's Defense against what Philip Melanchthon, a grammarian from Wittenberg, has falsely ascribed to him concerning the Theological Disputation at Leipzig.*[2] Melanchthon immediately refuted the attack in a brief treatise entitled *Philip Melanchthon's Defense Against John Eck.*[3] It was eloquently written. Full of a biting sharpness, it contained a defense of Luther's rejection of papal authority as well as a forthright assertion of the supremacy of Scripture over all authorities in the church, including the fathers, an assertion that culminated in the exclamation *"Patribus enim credo, quia scripturae credo."* [4]

Melanchthon, who in the meantime had become not only an ardent admirer but also a personal friend of Luther, thus showed himself to be a Biblical theologian who had adopted Luther's views, and as such a critic of Roman Catholicism and an advocate of the Reformation. He, the Humanist, chose to demonstrate his theological position publicly by preparing himself for the degree of Bachelor of Divinity. On September 9, 1519, he defended twenty-four theological theses [5] which again proved that he was a convinced "Lutheran"; he won the desired degree and with it the marveling plaudits of his friends.

In the same year, he edited Luther's commentaries on The

---

[2] *Excusatio Eckii ad ea quae falso sibi Philippus Melanchthon grammaticus Wittenbergensis super Theologica Disputatione Lipsica adscripsit* (Leipzig, 1519).

[3] *Melanchthons Werke in Auswahl,* ed. by Robert Stupperich, Vol. I (Gütersloh, 1951), pp. 13–22.

[4] "For I believe the fathers because I believe the Scripture." (*Ibid.,* pp. 19, 34.)

[5] *Ibid.,* pp. 24 f.

Psalms and on the letter to the Galatians, providing each of them with a preface of his own. Then he began to direct his attention to the letter to the Romans and, in connection with this, to Pauline doctrine. On January 21, 1520, he delivered the oration at the annual academic feast in honor of the apostle Paul [6] (who was the patron of the theological faculty), and from then on he was a Paulinist. He hailed Paul as superior to all philosophers and theologians because, Melanchthon said, he gave the true understanding of Christ and his "benefits" and because his teaching would lead to a right "order of life" (forma vitae). In the summer semester of 1519 and in the summer and winter semesters of 1520, Melanchthon taught courses on the letter to the Romans and he wrote treatises on Pauline theology. It was his purpose not only to understand as clearly as possible Paul's theological tenets but also to set them over against and to compare them with the teachings of philosophers and the Scholastic theologians.

The earliest of these writings was A Theological Introduction to Paul's Epistle to the Romans.[7] It was characterized by a blanket rejection of philosophy, particularly Aristotelianism. "All philosophy," Melanchthon wrote, "is darkness and untruth" (tenebrae et mendacia). It also contained a summary (summa) of Paul's argument in Romans that was set over against the doctrines and statements in which Peter Lombard had attempted to summarize the Christian religion (in his Four Books of Sentences, which for centuries had been used in the schools as the basic textbook of theology). In 1520, some of Melanchthon's students published, without his knowledge, a "theological summary" that Melanchthon apparently had presented in the classroom as the result of his Pauline studies on the basis of the letter to the Romans. It bore the title Rerum theologicarum capita seu loci [8] ("themes or basic topics of theological matters").

Melanchthon was disturbed by this unauthorized and premature publication of what, in his judgment, represented merely a preparatory study or, as he put it, lucubratiuncula, i.e., lucubrations, i.e., "studies undertaken by lamplight." He decided, therefore, to publish a revised and enlarged version of such a summary of theology. Thus, after having written still another introductory piece, De studio doctrinae Paulinae (1520), he turned to the preparation of Loci communes.

[6] Declamatiuncula in Divi Pauli doctrinam. (Ibid., pp. 27–43.)
[7] Theologica Institutio Phil. Mel. in Epistulam Pauli ad Romanos (1519) (CR, Vol. 21, cols. 49 ff.).
[8] Ibid., cols. 11 ff.

It is clear that all these labors, pursued as they were in the context of the deep excitement which Luther's conflict with the authorities and spokesmen of the Roman Catholic Church had aroused, represented Melanchthon's attempt to explain his conversion to "Lutheran" thinking. In all his writings, he demonstrated that he had decided to abandon Scholastic theology in any form and he also gave clear indications of the fact that he had turned away from Humanism, especially its program of intellectual and moral reform, which before his coming to Wittenberg had commanded all his loyalty.

Yet it is an exaggeration to say this. It is true that, during this period of his life, he was as sharply critical of humanistic ideas as he was of Scholastic teachings. But, nevertheless, he continued to be engaged in peculiarly humanistic studies. This seems to prove that though he had transcended his earliest intellectual outlook, he had not given it up entirely. To be sure, he now rejected Aristotle, whose works he had planned to edit just a few years earlier and whose thought, as he stated in his inaugural lecture, he wanted to restore to its pristine power. But, precisely while he was steeped in Pauline studies, he was also involved in efforts to renew the disciplines of dialectics and rhetorics according to the ancient patterns that the leading Humanists, and especially Erasmus, had rediscovered. During the same years that he worked and lectured on Paul, he prepared and published texts on *Dialectics* (1519) and on *Rhetorics* (1520); also, *Institutiones Rhetoricae* (1521).[9] In his dialectical studies he relied chiefly on Aristotle and Cicero, and in his work on rhetorics he was dependent upon Cicero and Quintilian. He believed that the methods of these disciplines had to be applied to literary texts so that they could be properly understood.

As we shall see, in composing his *Loci* he made ample use of these conclusions and thus he remained attached to Humanism after all. We should not be surprised at this, for when he wrote his *Loci,* he was still a very young man, twenty-four years old. His learning and his intellectual accomplishment were amazing,[10] but his thinking was still in flux.

[9] Cf. Wilhelm Maurer, *Melanchthons Loci communes von 1521 als wissenschaftliche Programmschrift* in *Lutherjahrbuch* 27 (1960), p. 29.
[10] Luther wrote to his mentor and friend Staupitz about Melanchthon's performance in defending his B.D. theses: "He responded in such a way that it seemed to all of us to be a miracle." (*Ita respondit, ut omnibus nobis esset id quod est scilicet miraculum*). Cf. *WA Br.* I, p. 514; also, Stupperich's introduction to the theses in *Melanchthons Werke*, Vol. I, p. 23.

II. The Purpose and Method of Melanchthon's
Loci communes

In several places in his work, Melanchthon makes quite clear what purposes he had in mind in writing his *Loci*. He says, for example, that he does not want to present a detailed commentary on theological doctrines but is, rather, "sketching a common outline of the topics that you can pursue in your study of Holy Scripture" (p. 70). His major purpose is to "summon" students to the Scriptures and to supply them with "a list [or nomenclature] of the topics to which a person roaming through Scripture should be directed" (p. 19).

However, this purpose is coupled with another one, namely, to demonstrate "how corrupt are all the theological hallucinations of those [i.e., the Scholastics] who have offered us the subtleties of Aristotle instead of the teachings of Christ" (p. 19). Melanchthon is persuaded that the "nature of Christianity" (*forma Christianismi*) can be established only by an analysis of the Scripture for the purpose of finding its "main substance" and "scope" (p. 19) and not by a reliance upon "the judgment of human reason" (p. 19) or upon philosophy. "I think," he writes in concluding his work, "that the commentaries of men on sacred matters must be fled like the plague, because the teaching of the Spirit cannot be drunk in purity except from the Scripture itself" (p. 152). He is persuaded that Christianity has been greatly harmed by the fact that "philosophy has gradually crept" into it: Early Christianity "was weakened by Platonic philosophy" and later the Church "embraced Aristotle instead of Christ" (p. 23). Thus "Christian doctrine" gradually "degenerated into Scholastic trifling" (p. 20).

The fundamental themes that the Bible offers to men for their consideration are "sin, law, and grace" or simply "the law and the gospel." They cannot be dealt with philosophically and they must not be put into a philosophical context. This is what the fathers and the Schoolmen did — with the result that the true understanding of Christ was lost. According to Melanchthon, earlier theologians attempted to state fundamentals, but they failed. For example: Origen tended to allegorize and then developed a "philosophical jargon"; John of Damascus "philosophizes too much" and Peter Lombard "piles up the opinions of men" instead of setting forth "the meaning of Scripture" (p. 20). By contrast, Paul does not "philosophize about the mysteries of the Trinity, [and] the mode of the incarnation" (p. 22).

From all this, Melanchthon derives the conclusion that it is "better" for a theologian "to adore the mysteries of the Deity than to investigate them" (p. 21), and that if one wants to know Christ, one must "know his benefits" (pp. 21 f.).

Thus it can be understood why Melanchthon adopted such a negative attitude toward the Scholastics. It must be noted that he had a wide acquaintance with their writings. As his exposition of the *loci theologici* shows, he had read Peter Lombard and he had also studied such diverse theologians as Thomas Aquinas and Gabriel Biel. While he was engaged in the preparation of *Loci communes,* he twice undertook to defend Martin Luther against spokesmen of the Roman Catholic Church and advocates of Scholasticism. In each case, he affirmed a Scriptural theology over against the philosophical tradition of the Schools. In February, 1521, he published a reply [11] to an attack that the Roman Dominican Tommaso Rhadino had directed against Luther under the title *Oration to the princes and people of Germany against Martin Luther who violates the glory of his nation.*[12] In October, 1521, Melanchthon spoke up once more in defense of Luther against Scholastic authorities. He wrote a spirited *Defense of Luther against the mad decree of the Parisian theologians,*[13] a condemnation of Luther chiefly directed against Luther's statements in *The Babylonian Captivity of the Church.* Melanchthon vigorously set the authority of the Scripture against that of the tradition which the theologians of Paris had invoked.

Melanchthon's anti-Scholastic attitude, so one must realize, was inspired by his identification with Luther. Hence it is not astonishing that Luther's ideas reverberate throughout the *Loci communes.* Melanchthon's Paulinism was Lutheran, i.e., inspired by Luther. One may legitimately raise the question whether Melanchthon did not depend also upon Augustine.[14] Now, it is charac-

---

[11] *Didymi Faventini adversus Thomam Placentinum pro Martino Luthero theologo oratio (Melanchthons Werke,* Vol. I, pp. 56–140). It was at first believed that the author of the Roman writing was the Leipzig theologian Jerome Emser, an old foe of Luther's, and that he had chosen to hide his identity under a pseudonym. Hence, Melanchthon too used a pseudonym, Didymus Faventinus.

[12] This is reprinted in *CR,* Vol. 1, cols. 212–262.

[13] *Adversus furiosum Parisiensium theologastrorum decretum Phil. Melanchthonis pro Luthero apologia (Melanchthons Werke,* Vol. I, pp. 142–162). The declaration of the theological faculty of Paris, entitled *Determinatio theologorum Parisiensium super doctrina Lutheriana,* is reprinted in *CR,* Vol. 1, cols. 366–385.

[14] Cf. the highly suggestive essay by Wilhelm Maurer, "Der Einfluss Augustins auf Melanchthons theologische Entwicklung," in *Melanchthon-Studien* (Gütersloh, 1964), pp. 67–102.

teristic of him that while he sharply criticized Origen, Ambrose, and Jerome, he upheld Augustine. However, he did this because, in his thinking, Luther's authority was coupled with Augustine's. In the latter part of the *Loci,* for example, he refers to Augustine's tract *On the Spirit and the Letter* (which had been so important in Luther's theological development) and he remarks in this connection that he would prefer his readers to consult both Augustine *and* Luther!

It is noteworthy that when Melanchthon refers in the *Loci* specifically to Luther, he quotes from or points to Luther's most recent writings, namely, the treatises (of 1520) on *The Babylonian Captivity of the Church,* on *Good Works,* and on *The Freedom of the Christian Man.* While he was completing his book he became acquainted with the defense that Luther had written of his own teaching on justification, *Against Latomus.* It is apparent that this writing made a deep impression upon Melanchthon, especially because it restated Luther's thesis about the Christian as *simul peccator ac iustus,* which, as we shall see, caused him considerable difficulty.

In this connection, we should remark that it would be an error to assume that because Melanchthon was so closely attached to Luther, he agreed with him on everything. The differences between the two, which developed later but which, to be sure, were never allowed to bring about a separation, were indicated as early as the first edition of the *Loci,* despite the fact that this work as a whole was conceived as an enthusiastic endorsement of Luther's thought.

This difference of Melanchthon from Luther is due chiefly to the fact that Melanchthon was so deeply concerned with the problem of the right theological method. He was fascinated by the task of developing a "theology of definitions." [15] This interest enabled him to write *Loci communes,* an outline in which the basic teachings of the Lutheran Reformation were summarized and by the influence of which he became and remained for centuries *the* theological teacher of Lutheranism.

Now, this preoccupation with a "theology of definitions" was the result of his humanistic studies and particularly of his admiration for Erasmus and his dependence upon him. It was from Erasmus and other Humanists, perhaps including Rudolf Agricola,[16]

[15] Cf. Ernst Troeltsch, *Vernunft und Offenbarung bei Johann Gerhard und Melanchthon* (Göttingen, 1891), p. 58.
[16] Cf. Paul Joachimsen, *Loci communes. Eine Untersuchung zur Geistesgeschichte des Humanismus und der Reformation,* in *Lutherjahrbuch* 8

arose from love of self and love of praise, they ought not to be considered real virtues but vices. Socrates was tolerant, but he was a lover of glory or surely was self-satisfied about virtue. Cato was brave, but because of his love for praise. . . . Cicero in his *De finibus* thinks that all motivation for virtue lies in love of ourselves or love of praise. How much pride and haughtiness are to be found in Plato! In my opinion a temperament lofty and forceful in itself could hardly escape taking on some vice from Plato's ambition if it chanced to read him. The teaching of Aristotle is in general a passion for wrangling, so that it is not appropriate to number him among the writers of hortatory philosophy, not even in the last place" (p. 34).

Such sentences, we must judge, were written in utter deviation from Erasmus. It is understandable why Erasmus turned away from Melanchthon and why in his *Diatribe on Free Will* he sharply attacked him (without, to be sure, identifying him by name).[21]

In the first version of the *Loci*, Melanchthon expressed the conviction that only the forgiveness of God as it is promised in the gospel, and of which one can become assured only through Christ by the Holy Spirit, is the sole source of man's renewal. This is why for him only a Scriptural theology was the true theology, for, as far as he could see, the Scripture alone was the "source" (p. 49) and "standard" (p. 63) of the truth by which men live and must live, and in it the "Holy Spirit expresses himself most accurately and most simply" (p. 46).

III. THE THEOLOGICAL CONTENT OF THE *Loci communes*

In this Introduction we must not discuss the entire content of Melanchthon's work, for our purpose should be not to prejudge it for the reader but to help him in understanding it. We shall therefore point out merely those features of Melanchthon's thought which give his work a special character.

Anyone can plainly see that he let Pauline thought as it is expressed mainly in the letters to the Romans and the Galatians determine his teaching. His chief themes are sin and grace and the law and the gospel. Specific doctrines of God and of Christ are not presented (in contrast to later versions of the *Loci* where they reappear). The discussion lacks a certain unity and does not always follow a clearly organized outline. What is offered is not really a "systematic" theology, as it is often asserted.

---

[21] Cf. Wilhelm Maurer, *"Melanchthons Anteil am Streit zwischen Luther und Erasmus"* in *Melanchthon-Studien,* pp. 137–162, particularly pp. 151 ff.

As we have already indicated, in its constructive as well as its polemical parts the work was inspired by Luther. However, Melanchthon is much less profound and paradoxical, but generally much clearer, than Luther, not only when he deals with justification "by faith and not by works" but also when he is engaged in argument with the "Sophists."

There are some emphases in Melanchthon's teaching that give it a special character. They do not represent anything new or original but they lend a distinctive flavor to his thought. In his discussion of sin and the unfree will, he makes much of the "affections," "the emotions," or "the inner disposition" (*affectus*) (pp. 23, 27 ff.), and he asserts that they are not in the power of either intelligence or will and that they can be changed only by a divine action.

Grace is defined as "God's favor" (*favor Dei*) and as God's goodwill toward us. The Roman Catholic teaching, according to which it is or can be seen as a "quality" in (or infused into) the human soul, is vigorously rejected.

Faith is described as a personal trust in God's promise of forgiveness. As such, it is distinguished from any historical knowledge (p. 91) or opinion. It is seen as the sense of "the mercy of God" (p. 92), indeed, as "an affection of the heart" (p. 90).

What is most characteristic is that in Melanchthon's view the life of the Christian is pointed toward renewal. Hence he tends to see justification, which occurs when one knows that he is forgiven (p. 105), as regeneration under the living power of the Holy Spirit (p. 123). Thus the Christian is seen as being in the process of becoming sanctified (p. 130). The following passage may perhaps be regarded as representative of the basic teaching of Melanchthon as it is expressed in the first edition and version of the *Loci communes*: "Christianity is freedom. . . . Those who have been renewed by the Spirit of Christ now conform voluntarily even without the law to what the law used to command. The law is the will of God; the Holy Spirit is nothing else than the living will of God and its being in action (*agitatio*). Therefore, when we have been regenerated by the Spirit of God, who is the living will of God, we now will spontaneously that very thing which the law used to demand" (p. 123; cf. p. 127). This conception led him to affirm a certain perfectionism: A Christian must not go to court or litigate (p. 128); Christians ought to hold their property in common with all (p. 60). Indeed, Melanchthon regarded as "unhealthy" the view that "public affairs cannot be administered according to the gospel" (pp. 58 f.).

He later changed some of these ideas. Indeed, he was in process of changing them when he completed the writing of the first edition of the *Loci,* for then he was involved in the very practical difficulties and the great diversity of opinion concerning the course of action to be followed which attended the first attempts to actualize a reformation of the church in Wittenberg.

IV. The Publication of the Work and Its Impact

The printing of *Loci communes* was begun in April, 1521, but due to the fact that Melanchthon found himself unable to finish the writing of the text as soon as he had planned, it was not completed until September. Two printings appeared in Wittenberg and another one in Basel. In 1522, a new printing became necessary. Melanchthon introduced several changes into the text. By 1525, eighteen different printings of this edition had been made. A German translation, by Georg Spalatin, was also reprinted several times. A second edition of the work, now much revised and enlarged, appeared in 1535, in Wittenberg; it too was published in several printings by 1541; it was translated into German by Justus Jonas. In the early forties, Melanchthon went to work to rewrite his book completely. The new edition, which was almost four times the size of the first one, was first published (again in Wittenberg) in 1543–1544. It was issued in several printings during Melanchthon's lifetime, the last one of which appeared in 1559. Melanchthon himself translated this third and final version of his main work into German (1555).[22] The book remained alive after Melanchthon's death (1560). The last separate printing of it (apart from editions of Melanchthon's complete works and from modern editions) appeared in 1595.

As these many editions and printings of the *Loci communes* show, it was an extraordinarily successful and influential publication. It gained its great reputation from the first edition, for this was marked by a spirit of immediate enthusiasm, eloquence, and great clarity of diction reflecting the moving power that went forth from the person of Martin Luther.

It is remarkable how highly Luther throughout his life praised the book of his collaborator and friend. In his treatise against Erasmus, he hailed it as a work of immortal significance that de-

[22] Melanchthon's German version of the *Loci* has been translated into English by Clyde L. Manschreck. It was published in The Library of Protestant Thought under the title *Melanchthon on Christian Doctrine: Loci Communes, 1555* by the Oxford University Press in 1965.

served to be included in the canon of the church.[23] And, in order
to give just one more example, in his Table Talk he said once at
the end of his life: "You cannot find anywhere a book which treats
the whole of theology so adequately as the *Loci communes* do. . . .
Next to Holy Scripture, there is no better book." [24]

[23] *Invictum libellum, meo iudicio non solum immortalitate, sed canone
quoque ecclesiastico digno (WA* 18, 601,3) .
[24] *WA Tr,* Vol. V, No. 5511.

Loci Communes Theologici

THE TEXT

DEDICATORY LETTER

To Dr. Tileman Plettener,[1] as godly as he is learned: Greetings from Philip Melanchthon!

Last year while expounding Paul's letter to the Romans,[2] I methodically arranged its varied contents under the most common theological topics. This study[3] was prepared for the sole purpose of indicating as cogently as possible to my private students the issues at stake in Paul's theology. Nevertheless, it was made public by persons unknown. Whoever finally published it, I approve their zeal more than their judgment. I say this because I had so composed it that the plan I had followed in the whole work could not be adequately understood apart from Paul's letter.

Because it is not now in my power to suppress a book that has become almost public property, I have decided to review and revise it, for much of it needed more precise argument, much of it needed revision. But most important, in this book the principal

[1] Tileman Plettener, a teacher in Stolberg, who had studied in Leipzig (1505) and Erfurt (1506), matriculated in the University of Wittenberg in the winter semester of 1520 as the companion of the young counts Wolfgang and Ludwig von Stolberg. In the following year, he became vice-rector of the University (his "ward," Wolfgang von Stolberg, was elected rector). On September 20, 1521, he obtained the degree of Lic. Theol. and on October 14, that of Dr. Theol.

[2] Melanchthon offered a course on the letter to the Romans for the first time in the summer of 1519. A year later he again taught a course on this letter.

[3] Melanchthon uses the term *lucubratiuncula* ("that which is produced by lamplight," a study). This study (published in *CR*, Vol. 21, cols. 11 ff.) must be regarded as a final outline of the *Loci communes*. It was published without Melanchthon's consent under the title: *Rerum theologicarum capita seu loci* ("themes or basic topics of theological matters").

18

topics of Christian teaching [4] are pointed out so that youth may arrive at a twofold understanding:

1. What one must chiefly look for in Scripture.

2. How corrupt are all the theological hallucinations of those who have offered us the subtleties of Aristotle instead of the teachings of Christ.[5]

But I am discussing everything sparingly and briefly because the book is to function more as an index than a commentary. I am therefore merely stating a list of the topics to which a person roaming through Scripture should be directed. Further, I am setting forth in only a few words the elements on which the main points of Christian doctrine [6] are based. I do this not to call students away from the Scriptures to obscure and complicated arguments but, rather, to summon them to the Scriptures if I can.

For on the whole I do not look very favorably on commentaries, not even those of the ancients. Far be it from me to call anyone away from the study of canonical Scripture by too lengthy a composition of my own! There is nothing I should desire more, if possible, than that all Christians be occupied in greatest freedom with the divine Scriptures alone and be thoroughly transformed into their nature. For since the Godhead has portrayed its most complete image in them,[7] it cannot be known from any other source with more certainty or accuracy. Anyone is mistaken who seeks to ascertain the nature of Christianity [8] from any source except canonical Scripture. For how much of its purity the commentaries lack! In Scripture you will find nothing unworthy of honor; in the commentaries how many things depend on philosophy, on the judgment of human reason! And these clash absolutely head on with spiritual judgment. The writers of commentaries did not so suppress their mental faculties [9] as to breathe forth nothing but the spiritual. If you delete from Origen his awkward allegories and his forest of philosophical jargon, how little will remain? Yet with few exceptions the Greeks follow this author as do some apparently distinguished [10] Latin writers, such as Ambrose and Jerome. After their time, one could almost say that the more recent an author is,

---

[4] *Christianae disciplinae praecipui loci.*

[5] Here Melanchthon states quite clearly the twofold purpose of his work: (1) he wants to point out the basic themes of Biblical teaching; (2) he desires to show the irreconcilability between Biblical teaching and Scholastic theology.

[6] *Summa Christianae doctrinae.*

[7] *Cum in illis absolutissimam sui imaginem expresserit divinitas.*

[8] *Christianismi formam.*

[9] Melanchthon writes *to psychikon.*

[10] *Qui videntur esse columnae.*

the less Scriptural he is. In a word, Christian doctrine has degenerated into Scholastic trifling, and one does not know whether it is
more godless than it is stupid.

In conclusion, it is inevitable that human writings often deceive
even the careful reader. But if prophecy, inspiration, and the
knowledge of things sacred are worth anything at all, why do we
not embrace this kind of literature through which the Spirit flows?
Or does not God accomplish all things by means of his Word? For
the Spirit, or, as John says, the "anointing" (I John 2:27), will
teach many things by the use of the Scriptures, things that the
greatest effort of the human mind cannot attain. Surely we have no
other aim than to aid in every way possible the studies of those who
wish to be versed in the Scriptures. If my little book does not seem
to accomplish this, by all means let it perish, for it makes no difference to me what people think about this publication.

BASIC TOPICS OF THEOLOGY, OR CHRISTIAN THEOLOGY IN OUTLINE [11]

In each individual science it is customary to seek out certain fundamentals in which the main substance of each is comprised and
which are considered to be the scope toward which we direct all
studies. We see that in theology even the ancients, with caution and
good judgment, followed this procedure. More recently, however,
John of Damascus [12] and Peter Lombard [13] have both done so in-
eptly, for John of Damascus philosophizes too much, and Lombard
prefers to pile up the opinions of men rather than to set forth the
meaning of Scripture. And although, as I have said before, I should
not like students to tarry too long on summaries [14] of this kind,
nevertheless, I consider it almost necessary at least to indicate on
what basic topics the essence of theology [15] depends in order that
we may understand toward what our studies are to be directed.

The usual main headings in theology [16] are as follows:

---

[11] *Hypotyposes theologicae.* The term *hypotypōsis* here translated "outline"
means in Greek "sketch" or "description." It is used in the New Testament
where it signifies "example" (I Tim. 1:16) or "pattern" (II Tim. 1:13).

[12] John of Damascus, *De fide orthodoxa* (MPL, Vol. 94, cols. 790 ff.).

[13] Peter Lombard, *The Four Books of Sentences* (MPL, Vols. 191–192).

[14] *Hoc genus summis.* The theological systems of the Scholastics were called
summae.

[15] *Rerum summa.*

[16] In this enumeration of the main themes of theology, Melanchthon follows
Rudolf Agricola from whom he may have learned his method. Cf. Quirinus
Breen, "The Terms *Loci communes* and *Loci* in Melanchthon," *Church
History,* Vol. 16 (1947), pp. 197–209, especially p. 202.

God	The Fruit of Grace
Unity	Faith
Trinity	Hope
Creation	Love
Man, the Power of Man	Predestination
Sin	Sacramental Signs
The Fruit of Sin, Vices	The State of Man
Punishments	Public Officials
Law	Bishops
Promises	Condemnation
Renewal Through Christ	Blessedness
Grace	

Just as some of these are altogether incomprehensible, so there are others which Christ has willed the universal body of Christians to know with greatest certainty. We do better to adore the mysteries of Deity than to investigate them.[17] What is more, these matters cannot be probed without great danger, and even holy men have often experienced this. The Lord God Almighty clothed his Son with flesh that he might draw us from contemplating his own majesty to a consideration of the flesh, and especially of our weakness. Paul writes in I Cor. 1:21 that God wishes to be known in a new way, i.e., through the foolishness of preaching, since in his wisdom he could not be known through wisdom. Therefore, there is no reason why we should labor so much on those exalted topics such as "God," "The Unity and Trinity of God," "The Mystery of Creation," and "The Manner of the Incarnation." What, I ask you, did the Scholastics accomplish during the many ages they were examining only these points? Have they not, as Paul says, become vain in their disputations (Rom. 1:21), always trifling about universals, formalities, connotations, and various other foolish words? Their stupidity could be left unnoticed if those stupid discussions had not in the meantime covered up for us the gospel and the benefits of Christ.

Now, if I wanted to be clever in an unnecessary pursuit, I could easily overthrow all their arguments for the doctrines of the faith. Actually, they seem to argue more accurately for certain heresies than they do for the Catholic doctrines.

But as for the one who is ignorant of the other fundamentals, namely, "The Power of Sin," "The Law," and "Grace," I do not see how I can call him a Christian. For from these things Christ is known, since to know Christ means to know his benefits, and not

---

[17] *Mysteria divinitatis rectius adoraverimus, quam vestigaverimus.*

as *they* teach, to reflect upon his natures and the modes of his incarnation. For unless you know why Christ put on flesh and was nailed to the cross, what good will it do you to know merely the history about him? Would you say that it is enough for a physician to know the shapes, colors, and contours of plants, and that it makes no difference whether he knows their innate power? Christ was given us as a remedy and, to use the language of Scripture, a saving remedy (Luke 2:30, 3:6; Acts 28:28). It is therefore proper that we know Christ in another way than that which the Scholastics have set forth.

This, then, is Christian knowledge: to know what the law demands, where you may seek power for doing the law and grace to cover sin, how you may strengthen a quaking spirit against the devil, the flesh, and the world, and how you may console an afflicted conscience. Do the Scholastics teach those things? In his letter to the Romans when he was writing a compendium of Christian doctrine, did Paul philosophize about the mysteries of the Trinity, the mode of incarnation, or active and passive creation? [18] No! But what does he discuss? He takes up the law, sin, grace, fundamentals on which the knowledge of Christ exclusively rests. How often Paul states that he wishes for the faithful a rich knowledge of Christ! For he foresaw that when we had left the saving topics, we would turn our minds to disputations that are cold and foreign to Christ. Therefore, we shall draw up some account of those fundamentals which commend Christ to you, strengthen the conscience, and arouse the mind against Satan. Most people seek in the Scriptures only topics of virtues and vices, but this practice is more philosophical than Christian. You will understand a little later why I say this.

THE POWER OF MAN, ESPECIALLY FREE WILL
(Liberum Arbitrium)

Augustine [19] and Bernard [20] wrote on free will (*arbitrium*), and the former revised his ideas extensively in the books that he later wrote against the Pelagians. Bernard is not consistent. There are certain works on this subject even among the Greeks, but they are scattered. Since I shall not follow the opinions of men, I shall explain the matter both very simply and very plainly. Ancient as well as modern writers have almost obscured this view because they

[18] Cf. Thomas Aquinas, *Summa theol.* I, q. 45, a.3.
[19] Augustine, *On Free Will* (*MPL*, Vol. 32, cols. 1221 f.).
[20] Bernard of Clairvaux, *On Grace and Free Will* (*MPL*, Vol. 182, col. 1001).

were interpreting the Scriptures in such a way that they might at the same time satisfy the judgment of human reason. It did not seem polished enough to teach that man sinned by necessity, and it seemed cruel that the will (*voluntas*) be blamed if it could not turn itself from vice to virtue. Therefore, they attributed even more things to human power than was right, and fluctuated remarkably when they saw that the Scriptures everywhere contradicted the judgment of reason.

Although Christian doctrine on this topic differs altogether from philosophy and human reason, yet philosophy has gradually crept into Christianity. The godless doctrine about free will (*arbitrium*) was taken over and the benefits of Christ were obscured through that profane and earthly wisdom of our reason. The term "free will" (*arbitrium*) was used, a term most incongruous with Scripture and the sense and judgment of the Spirit, and a term that often offended holy men. From the philosophy of Plato was added the equally pernicious word "reason." For just as we in these latter times of the Church have embraced Aristotle instead of Christ, so immediately after the beginnings of the Church Christian doctrine was weakened by Platonic philosophy. So it has come about that apart from the canonical Scriptures, there is no reliable literature in the Church. In general, whatever has been handed down in the commentaries reeks with philosophy.[21]

In the first place, we surely do not need the many divisions of philosophy to describe the nature of man. We divide man into only two parts. For there is in him a cognitive faculty, and there is also a faculty by which he either follows or flees the things he has come to know. The cognitive faculty is that by which we discern through the senses, understand, think, compare, and deduce. The faculty from which the affections (*affectus*) arise is that by which we either turn away from or pursue the things known, and this faculty is sometimes called "will" (*voluntas*), sometimes "affection," and sometimes "appetite." I do not think it greatly matters at this point to separate the feelings from what is called the intellect, and the appetite of the feelings from the higher appetite. For we are speaking of the higher one, that is, not only the one in which are hunger, thirst, and feelings like those of the beasts, but concerning that one in which are love, hate, hope, fear, sorrow, anger, and the feelings which arise from these. One calls this "will" (*voluntas*). Knowledge serves the will (*voluntas*), and thus one calls the will (*voluntas*) joined with the knowledge or with the understanding of

21 The older Melanchthon had a much more positive and appreciative opinion about the theology of the ancient church.

the intellect by a new name, "free will" (*arbitrium*) . For the will (*voluntas*) in man corresponds to the place of a despot [22] in a republic. Just as the senate is subject to the despot, so is knowledge to the will (*voluntas*) , with the consequence that although knowledge gives good warning, yet the will (*voluntas*) casts knowledge out and is borne along by its own affection, as we shall explain more clearly hereafter. Furthermore, intellect joined with the will (*voluntas*) they call "reason." We shall use neither the words "reason" nor "free will" (*arbitrium*) , but we shall call the parts of man the "cognitive faculty" and a "faculty subject to the affections," subject, that is, to love, hate, hope, fear, and the like.

I have felt obligated to warn of these matters in order that hereafter the difference between the law and grace may be more easily indicated, and, what is more, that it also may be known with more certainty whether there is any freedom within the power of man. It is marvelous how industriously both the ancients and the moderns have engaged themselves in this matter. If anyone falsely attacks these things, gladly and bravely we shall defend our position. For I have wanted only to picture man very roughly, and I think I have spoken about the parts of man as much as was necessary.

The law, that is, the knowledge of what must be done, belongs to the cognitive faculty. Virtue and sin belong to the faculty of the affections. Freedom cannot rightly be said to belong to the knowing part; rather, it is subject to the will (*voluntas*) and is driven hither and yon. Now, freedom is the ability to act or not to act, the ability to act in this way or in another. Therefore, the question arises whether the will (*voluntas*) is free and to what extent it is free.

ANSWER: Since all things that happen, happen necessarily according to divine predestination, our will (*voluntas*) has no liberty. Paul says in Rom. 11:36: "For from him and through him," etc. In Eph. 1:11 he writes: "Who accomplishes all things according to the counsel of his will." Matt. 10:29 reads: "Are not two sparrows sold for a penny? And not one of them will fall to the ground without your Father's will." What thought, I ask, could be more clearly stated than this? In Prov. 16:4 we read: "The Lord has made everything for its purpose, even the wicked for the day of trouble." Furthermore, Prov. 20:24 reads: "A man's steps are ordered by the Lord; how then can man understand his way?" Again in Prov. 16:9: "A man's mind plans his way, but the Lord directs his steps." Jer. 10:23: "I know, O Lord, that the way of man is not in himself, that it is not in man who walks to direct his steps." Furthermore,

[22] *Tyrannus.*

the divine historical books teach the same thing. Gen. 15:16: "For the iniquity of the Amorites is not yet complete." I Sam. 2:25: "But they would not listen to the voice of their father, for it was the will of the Lord to slay them." What is more like a fortuitous chain of events than Saul's going away to seek the asses, his being anointed by Samuel, and his inauguration into the kingdom? Again in I Sam. 10:26: "And with him went men of valor whose hearts God had touched." I Kings 12:15: "So the king did not hearken to the people; for it was a turn of affairs brought about by the Lord that he might fulfill his word, which the Lord spake by Ahijah the Shilonite to Jeroboam the son of Nebat." And what else does Paul do in Rom 9:11 but refer all things that happen to divine determination? [23] The judgment of the flesh and of human reason revolts at this thought; the judgment of the Spirit, on the contrary, embraces it. For there is no other way to learn more definitely both fear and trust in God than to imbue one's mind with this thought concerning predestination. Does not Solomon in Proverbs drive this home throughout the book in order that he may teach fear at one time and faith at another? Does he not stress this in the book of Ecclesiastes? For it is very important in repressing and condemning both the wisdom and prudence of human reason to believe constantly that all things are done by God. Or does not Christ comfort his disciples very effectively in the passage where he says (Luke 12:7) : "Why, even the hairs of your head are all numbered"?

"What, then," you will say, "is there no chance in events, no accident, or, to use the word of those fellows, no contingency?" [24] The Scriptures teach that all things take place by necessity. Granted that to you it seems that there is a contingency in human affairs, but right here the judgment of reason must be overruled. So said Solomon when he was engaged in thinking about predestination (Eccl. 8:17) : "Then I saw all the work of God, that man cannot find out the work that is done under the sun." But I may seem foolish to discuss the most difficult point, predestination, at the very outset of my work. And still, what does it matter whether I take up first or last in my compendium that which will intrude into all parts of our discussion? And since free will (arbitrium) had to be discussed in the very first topic, how could I conceal the position of Scripture when it deprives our will (voluntas) of freedom by the necessity of predestination? I think it makes considera-

---

[23] In destinationem divinam referat.
[24] Cf. Thomas Aquinas, Summa theol. I, q. 25, a. 3 and 4; Duns Scotus, In sent., lib. II, d. 25, qq. 1, 22.

ble difference that young minds are immediately imbued with this idea that all things come to pass, not according to the plans and efforts of men but according to the will (*voluntas*) of God. Does not Solomon in those maxims which he wrote for youth warn of this from the very beginning? The fact that the idea concerning predestination commonly seems rather harsh we owe to that godless theology of the Sophists which has so impressed on us the contingency of things and the freedom of our will (*voluntas*) that our tender little ears revolt at the truth of Scripture.

Accordingly, in order that we may also counsel those to whom what we have said about predestination seems rather harsh, we shall more closely consider the very nature of the human will (*voluntas*) so that students may understand that the Sophists are wrong, not only in theology but also in their judgment about human nature.[25] We shall soon speak of predestination under its own heading, and tear to pieces as briefly as is permissible what the Sophists have godlessly commented on this topic. Eck [26] says that Valla wanted to know more than he had learned because he refuted the position of the Schools on free will (*arbitrium*), i.e., that he was a very amusing trifler. Now, if these vampires raise the same objection against us, saying that a professor of languages is dabbling in theology,[27] we can only answer that they should not evaluate a work by its author. For it makes no difference in what field of teaching we are, but whether what we teach is true or false. Nor ought the teachings of theology to be thought foreign to us unless we are not Christians, because Christian teaching ought to be the common task of all.

1. But if you think of the power of the human will (*voluntas*) as a capacity of nature, according to human reason it cannot be denied that there is in it a certain freedom in outward works. For instance, you yourself have experienced that it is in your power to

[25] *In naturae iudicio.*

[26] Melanchthon refers to a piece of writing by John Eck, Luther's earliest critic and his opponent at the Disputation in Leipzig (1519), entitled *Chrysopassus* (1514). Laurentius Valla (d. 1457) wrote a treatise *De libero arbitrio*, first published in Louvain (1483), and then in Basel (1543). (There is a modern translation by Charles E. Trinkaus in Ernst Cassirer, Paul O. Kristeller, and John H. Randall, Jr., eds., *The Renaissance Philosophy of Man* [The University of Chicago Press, 1948], pp. 155–182.) Valla "attacked the Aristotelian and Scholastic reconciliation of free will and divine providence and asserted the irrationality of any attempt to understand the paradox that God by hardening or showing mercy allowed free will to men."

[27] This is an allusion to Eck's attack upon Melanchthon in the tract *Excusatio Eckii ad ea quae falso sibi Philippus Melanchthon grammaticus Wittenbergensis super Theologica Disputatione Lipsica adscripsit.*

greet a man or not to greet him, to put on this coat or not to put it on, to eat meat or not to do so. The would-be philosophers who have attributed freedom to the will (*voluntas*) have fixed their eyes upon this contingency of external works. But Scripture tells nothing of that kind of freedom, since God looks not at external works but at the inner disposition of the heart. The philosophers and more recent theologians, who imagine that character consists of a certain external, counterfeit politeness, teach a freedom of this kind.

2. By contrast, internal affections [28] are not in our power, for by experience and habit we find that the will (*voluntas*) cannot in itself control love, hate, or similar affections, but affection is overcome by affection. For instance, because you were betrayed by the one you loved, you ceased to love, for you love yourself more ardently than anyone else. I shall not listen to the Sophists if they deny that the human affections—love, hate, joy, sadness, envy, ambition, and the like—pertain to the will (*voluntas*). For nothing is said now of hunger and thirst. For what is will (*voluntas*) if it is not the fount of the affections? And why do we not use the word "heart" instead of "will" (*voluntas*)? For the Scriptures call the most powerful part of man the "heart," especially that part in which the affections arise. But the Schools are in error when they imagine that the will (*voluntas*) by its very nature opposes the affections, or that it is able to lay an affection aside whenever the intellect so advises or warns.

3. How does it happen, then, that we men often choose something different from what we are disposed to? First, because in an external act we sometimes choose something different from that which the heart or will (*voluntas*) desires, it is possible for affection to overcome affection. For instance, it cannot be denied that Alexander of Macedon was a lover of pleasures, but because he was more zealous for glory, he spurned pleasures, and chose hard work, not because he did not love pleasures, but because he loved glory with more intensity. For we see that in some characters, some affections rule, and that in other persons, others hold sway. Each is drawn by his own desire. In stingy characters the desire of possessing dominates. In those more liberal, according to human judg-

---

[28] *Affectus*. It is difficult to translate adequately what this term meant for Melanchthon. Instead of "affections," we should perhaps say "disposition" or "state of mind" or "attitude." However, the term itself was of great importance for Melanchthon's entire thought. Cf. Heinrich Bornkamm, "Melanchthons Menschenbild" in Walter Elliger, *Philipp Melanchthon. Forschungsbeiträge zur vierhundertsten Wiederkehr seines Todestages* (Göttingen, 1961), pp. 76–90.

ment, the zeal for fame and popular acclaim predominates.

4. Therefore, it can well happen that something is chosen which is entirely contrary to all affections. When this happens, insincerity takes over, as when, for example, someone treats graciously, amicably, and politely a person whom he hates and wishes ill to from the bottom of his heart, and he does this perhaps with no definite reason. And even if the man involved does not realize that he is being overcome by some other affection (for there are some characters so polite that they flatter even those whom they hate), that man, I say, pretends friendliness in an external act, and in this there seems to be a certain freedom, according to natural reasoning. And this is that will (voluntas), which the stupid Scholastics have imagined for us, namely, that power which, no matter what affection fills you, can nevertheless check and govern this affection. Their false teaching on penances depends on this position. However you may be disposed, they think that your will (voluntas) has the power to evoke good acts.[29] If you hate someone, they think your will (voluntas) can decide that it does not wish to hate this person anymore. Thus, although we are by nature godless and downright despisers of God (I do not say merely "without love of God"), those fellows teach that the will (voluntas) can cause nature to love God. I ask you, dear reader, do you not think those insane who have imagined such a will (voluntas) for us? And would that the Sophist who falsifies these matters might meet me that I could refute that godless, stupid, so-called philosophical opinion about the will with a full-fledged book and a thoroughgoing disputation! For when the man who hates decides to lay aside his hatred, unless he has really been overcome by a more vehement affection, it is plainly a fictitious thought of the intellect, and not a work of the will (voluntas). If Paris decided to put away his love for Oenone,[30] the thought of his intellect would have been false and counterfeit had he not been overcome by an affection that was actually more vehement. It is possible that your heart and intellect govern your external members, your tongue, hands, and eyes, in a way which does not coincide with the spirit of your affection because we are all liars by nature. For instance, Joab was controlling his tongue and eyes that he might appear to confront Amasa as politely as possible, but he could not command his heart to put away the

---

[29] Cf. Duns Scotus In sent., lib. II, d. 29, q. 1; and Gabriel Biel, In sent., lib. II, d. 27, q. unica, concl. 4; ibid., d. 28, a. 1, dub. 1. This is the Scholastic teaching against which the young Luther argues so passionately, especially in his Lectures on Romans.

[30] Oenone, a nymph, was the first wife of Paris; he abandoned her for Helen of Troy.

affection it had conceived (II Sam. 20:9 f.). But when he had been overcome by a more vehement affection, he put aside the affection with which he had been occupied.

5. The Schools do not deny the existence of affections, but they call them a "weakness of nature." This is accurate enough if the will (*voluntas*) actually has the power to evoke various acts. But I deny that there is any power in man which can seriously oppose the affections, and I think the acts which are evoked are nothing but a feigned thought of the intellect. For since God judges hearts, the heart and its affections must be the highest and most powerful part of man. Otherwise, why should God judge man by the weaker part and not rather by the better if there is any will (*voluntas*) aside from the heart which is better and stronger than the part which is the seat of the affections? What will the Sophists answer to this? But if we had preferred to use the word "heart," which the Scripture uses, instead of the Aristotelian word "will" (*voluntas*), we should easily have avoided errors so thickheaded and stupid. Choice of things in external matters Aristotle calls "will" (*voluntas*), and this choice is generally deceitful. But what place do external acts have in Christian teaching if the heart is insincere? Furthermore, Aristotle himself did not discuss those "elicited acts"; Scotus dreamed them up. However, now I am not writing to refute them, but to teach you, Christian reader, what you ought to follow. I confess that in the external choice of things there is some freedom, but I deny altogether that internal affections are in our power. Nor do I acknowledge that there is any will (*voluntas*) which seriously opposes the affections, and I say these things, of course, about man as he is by nature. For in those who have been justified by the Spirit, good affections struggle with bad, as we shall teach below.

6. Further, why boast of freedom in external acts when God requires purity of heart? All that stupid and godless men have written about free will (*arbitrium*) and justification by works is nothing but a Pharisaic tradition. When an affection has become a little too vehement, it cannot but break forth, as the saying goes: "Although you drive out nature with a fork, yet it will always come back." [31] Yes, and how many things we do which we ourselves judge good, and which have the best appearance because we do not see the shameful affections from which the acts originated! "There is a way which seems right to a man," says Solomon (Prov. 14:12), "but its end is the way to death." And Jeremiah the prophet says that the heart of man is "deceitful . . . and desperately corrupt"

[31] Horace, *Epistles* 10, 24.

(Jer. 17:9). And David says (Ps. 19:12): "Who can discern his errors?" Also (Ps. 25:7): "Remember not the sins of my youth." Then, too, affection drives blind men to many things that we cannot clearly judge. Therefore, the Christian mind must observe not merely the appearance of an act, but what sort of affection there is in the spirit, not what kind of freedom there is in works, but whether there is any freedom of the affections. The Pharisaical Scholastics will preach the power of free will (*arbitrium*). The Christian will acknowledge that nothing is less in his power than his heart. May the stupid Scholastics see how many thousands of souls they have slain with their Pharisaical double-talk on free will (*arbitrium*)! We shall soon speak more on the affections, however, when we discuss original sin.

Summary

If you relate human will (*voluntas*) to predestination, there is freedom neither in external nor internal acts, but all things take place according to divine determination.

If you relate the will (*voluntas*) to external acts, according to natural judgment there seems to be a certain freedom.

If you relate the will (*voluntas*) to the affections, there is clearly no freedom, even according to natural judgment.

When an affection has begun to rage and seethe, it cannot be kept from breaking forth.

You see, dear reader, with how much more certainty we have written about free will (*arbitrium*) than Bernard or any of the Scholastics. Furthermore, the matters that we have discussed so far will become more clear in the remaining parts of our compendium.

Sin

The Sophists strangely obscured this topic also, disputing about the relations of reason in sin, distinguishing between actual and original sin, and in their treatment of many other things that it is superfluous to record. For why tell everybody's every dream in a compendium? We shall treat the matter in a few words, and use the word "sin" as Scripture does.

What Is Sin?

1. Original sin is a native propensity and an innate force and energy by which we are drawn to sinning. It was propagated from

Adam to all posterity. Just as there is in fire a natural force by which it is borne upward, and just as there is in a magnet a natural force that draws iron to itself, so there is in man the innate force toward sinning. Scripture does not call one sin "original" and another "actual," for original sin is plainly a kind of actual, depraved desire. But Scripture calls both the actual and the original defect (*vitium*) simply "sin" (*peccatum*), although sometimes it calls those sins which we call "actual," the "fruits of sin." Paul commonly does this in Romans; and what we call "original sin," David sometimes calls "transgression," at other times "iniquity." There is no reason why we should dispute here about those stupid relations in sin, mentioned above. Sin is a depraved affection, a depraved activity of the heart against the law of God.

Whence Came Original Sin?

2. When God Almighty had created man without sin, he was near him through his Spirit, who stirred man to pursue the right. The same Spirit would have guided all the posterity of Adam if Adam had not fallen. Now, after Adam fell, God opposed man so that the Spirit of God was not with him as a leader. Thus it happens that the soul, lacking heavenly light and life, is blinded, loves itself most passionately, and seeks its own ends; it desires and wishes for nothing but carnal things. It despises God, and how can I express in words the depravity of the human heart? For it is inevitable that the creature which the love of God has not permeated loves itself most. It is impossible that the flesh love spiritual things. Thus it reads in Gen. 6:3: "My Spirit shall not abide in man forever, for he is flesh." And in Rom. 8:5, Paul writes: "For those who live according to the flesh" (that is, who are without the Spirit of God) "set their minds on the things of the flesh" (for it is evident from that passage in Genesis that the flesh consists of human powers without the Spirit of God). And further: "For the mind that is set on the flesh is hostile to God" (Rom. 8:7). Accordingly, when the Sophists say that original sin is the lack of original righteousness, as they express it, they are right. But why do they not add that where there is no original righteousness or the Spirit, there in reality is flesh, godlessness, a contempt for spiritual things? [32] Therefore, the dominant affection of man's nature is love of self, by which he is swept along, so that he wishes and desires only those things which seem good, pleasant, sweet, and glorious to his own

[32] Cf. Thomas Aquinas, *Summa theol.* II, 1, q. 85, a. 3; Gabriel Biel, *In sent.*, *lib.* II, d. 30, q. 1, a. 3.

nature; he hates and dreads those things which seem against his nature, and he resists the one who keeps him from what he desires or who orders him to pursue what is unpleasant to seek. Oh, how incomprehensible is the misery of mankind! On the one hand, a hatred of divine law and God arises in man, and on the other, God is a consuming fire for man, as we shall soon explain in more detail.

3. But the Pelagians are said to have denied that there is original sin. In several volumes, Augustine brilliantly tore their teaching to bits.[33] For in this controversy he rules as a King so decisively that almost all the other things which he wrote in addition to the Pelagian theme seem rather cold. We shall cite some Scripture passages testifying that there is original sin. And what could be said more clearly than Eph. 2:3: "We were by nature children of wrath, like the rest of mankind"? And if by nature we are the children of wrath, surely we are born children of wrath. For what else does Paul mean than that all our power is born subject to sin, and that there is nothing good at any time in any power of man? In Rom., ch. 5, he carries on a discussion about sin, grace, and law, in which he teaches that sin has been propagated upon all men. In what way is the sin of one propagated unless from that one all are born sinners? Nor can it be denied that Paul is discussing original sin in this passage. For if he were speaking about the sin of each man, he could not say that by the sin of one many died. This is so because anyone can see that this cannot be said about what they call "actual" sin unless one wants to pervert the text. Now, if Adam is not the author of sin, Christ alone will not be the author of justice, but Adam also. Likewise, if he is speaking about the sin of each man, why do children die, who have not committed what they call "actual" sin? And since death does not break in except through sin, it must be that children are guilty of sin and have sin, but what kind? Original sin, certainly! Paul, moreover, speaks of that sin through which all have been condemned to death. To be sure, we are here considering a Pauline figure of speech. In harmony with this passage in Romans, he writes in I Cor. 15:22: "For as in Adam all die, so also in Christ shall all be made alive." The exclamation of the prophet is pertinent here (Ps. 51:5): "Behold, I was brought forth in iniquity, and in sin did my mother conceive me." For David means that he was born a sinner. Furthermore, if "every imagination of the thoughts of man's heart is only evil continually," as is written in Gen. 6:5, it must be that we are born with sin. Now, if

[33] Augustine, *On the Grace of Christ and on Original Sin Against Pelagius and Caelestius* (MPL, Vol. 44, cols. 360 ff.).

we are all being blessed in Christ, we must all have been cursed in Adam. But what is it to be cursed but to be damned because of sin? Uncleanness under the law and the slaughtering of the first-born of Egypt have significance here as types. Why treat the subject loquaciously when Christ says clearly enough in John 3:6: "That which is born of the flesh is flesh." If it is flesh, it therefore seeks its own ends and loves itself, as we have warned above. And if the *first* birth is not subject to sin, what does it mean to be born *again*? And further, if the birth of the flesh is good, of what use is it to be born again of the Spirit?

The Power and Fruit of Sin

4. The ancient Pelagians can be refuted with less trouble than the new Pelagians of our times. Although our contemporaries do not deny the fact of original sin, they nevertheless deny that its power is such that all deeds of man and all human efforts are sin. Therefore, we shall speak a little more at length concerning the power and drive [34] of original sin.

Original sin is an intensely alive force in every part of us, always bearing fruit—vices (*vitia*). For when is the mind of man not seething with evil desires? The worst and most shameful of these are not even detected. Who is there who does not sometimes experience avarice, ambition, hatred, envy, strife, the flame of lustful desire, anger? But few are conscious of their arrogance, haughty pride, Pharisaic hypocrisy, contempt for God, distrust in God, and blasphemy; and these are the chief passions.[35] There are those who live very honorable lives outwardly speaking; Paul says that he lived in such a way before he knew Christ that he could not be blamed. These men have nothing in which to glory, since their minds are subservient to those very disgraceful and wretched affections which they do not sense. What if at some time, as in death, God should open their eyes so that these poor little holy fellows [36] would recognize their vices and diseases? Will they not understand Isa. 40:6: "All flesh is grass and all its beauty is like the flower of the field"? You see how deep, rather, how unfathomable, it is, this wickedness of the human heart. Yet our Sophists are not ashamed to teach works righteousness, satisfactions, and the philosophical [37] virtues.

[34] *Energia.*   [35] *Affectus.*   [36] M. writes ironically *sanctuli.*
[37] Prudence, justice, temperance, and courage, which Thomas Aquinas called the "principal virtues," were called "philosophical" virtues in distinction from faith, hope, and love, which were called the "theological" virtues. Cf. Thomas Aquinas, *Summa theol.* II, 1, q. 61, a. 1 ff., and q. 62, a. 1 ff.

Let it be granted that in Socrates there was a certain constancy, that Xenocrates was chaste, and Zeno temperate. Nevertheless, because these characteristics were in impure minds, and further, because these simulated virtues arose from love of self and love of praise, they ought not to be considered real virtues but vices. Socrates was tolerant, but he was a lover of glory or surely was self-satisfied about virtue. Cato was brave, but because of his love for praise. God pours out these simulated virtues on the Gentiles, on the ungodly, and on whomever you will, just as he bestows beauty, wealth, and similar gifts. And since all human reason marvels at this external mask and ghost of virtue, our pseudotheologians deceived by a blind judgment of human nature have commended to us philosophic pursuits, philosophic virtues, and the merits of external works. But what do most philosophers teach, even the best of them, except trust and love of ourselves? Cicero in his *De finibus* thinks that all motivation for virtue lies in love of ourselves or love of praise. How much pride and haughtiness are to be found in Plato! In my opinion a temperament lofty and forceful in itself could hardly escape taking on some vice from Plato's ambition if it chanced to read him. The teaching of Aristotle is in general a passion for wrangling, so that it is not appropriate to number him among the writers of hortatory philosophy, not even in the last place. But we shall speak of philosophy later, under the heading of law.

5. To summarize briefly, through the powers of nature all men are truly and always sinners and they commit sins. Gen. 6:5: "Every imagination of the thoughts of his heart was only evil continually." This same idea is repeated in Gen. 8:21: "The imagination of man's heart is evil from his youth." Although the translation "prone to evil" does not differ much from the thought that his imagination is evil, nevertheless I have preferred to use the genuine reading because it is clearer, simply affirming that man is evil. I say this lest any Thomist escape Moses by saying that since the tendency or inclination is not the act, it cannot be sin; for thus the stupid Sophists philosophize.[38] Isa. 9:17: "For every one is godless and an evildoer, and every mouth speaks folly." Again in Isa. 41:29: "Behold, they are all a delusion; their works are nothing; their molten images are empty wind." Likewise, in Isa. 53:6: "All we like sheep have gone astray; we have turned every one to his own way; and the Lord has laid on him the iniquity of us all." In this passage the prophet has set forth in a brilliant prophecy both the story of Christ's passion and its fruit by predicting that Christ

[38] Cf. Thomas Aquinas, *Summa theol.* II, 1, q. 85, a. 5.

would suffer such things that he could seem the most debased of all men, but that he would suffer with the purpose of justifying many, since all of us really are sinners and are not justified otherwise than through faith in Christ. And concerning those who wish to be justified by their own strength and works and not through faith in Christ, he says: "And they made his grave with the wicked and with a rich man in his death" (v. 9). Likewise: "He shall divide the spoil with the strong" (v. 12). For the ungodly, the rich, and the strong are plainly those advocates of human justice, free will (*arbitrium*), and the philosophic virtues, in a word, of human powers, but they are unacquainted with Christ. You see how Isaiah has described the whole power of the gospel in a brief discourse. But Thou, O Christ, bestow Thy Spirit to open and explain these mysteries to us.

Now we shall listen to David also. He gives voice to this same idea in many passages, as when he says: "Men are all a vain hope" (Ps. 116:11). But in the whole of Ps. 14 he thunders this forth when he says (vs. 1 ff.): "The fool says in his heart, 'There is no God.' They are corrupt, they do abominable deeds. There is none that does good. The Lord looks down from heaven upon the children of men, to see if there are any that act wisely, that seek after God. They are all gone astray, they are all alike corrupt; there is none that does good, no, not one," etc. Notice that he does not accuse man of simple vices but of the most atrocious crimes—of impiety, unbelief, foolishness, hatred and contempt for God—vices which no one can detect but the Spirit.

What will you say to this, hypocritical theologians? What works of free will (*arbitrium*) will you preach to us, and what power of man? Do you imagine that you are not denying original sin when you teach that a man is able to do something good in his own strength? A bad tree cannot bring forth good fruit, can it? Or do you not see that here the prophet has described the tree and fruit together, speaking not only of the heart of the fool, but also of all the pursuits, counsels, desires, works, and attempts of man? You see, moreover, what a great difference there is between Scripture's view of man and that of philosophy or human reason. Philosophy looks at nothing except the external masks of men; the Holy Scriptures look at the deepest, incomprehensible affections. Since a man is governed by these, the Scriptures judge the acts according to the motivation behind the affections. And since we seek our own advantage in all acts, these acts must really be sins.

I shall not mention now the crassest kinds of desires. And as far as those who live outwardly good lives are concerned, is not one man drawn to these ways by an aversion for human affairs, another because of the fear of fate, another by ambition, and another by a love of tranquillity? For these have been the causes for a better outward life formerly in the case of philosophers and they are now for many men. Still another is restrained by a feigned fear of divine punishment. Some, then, hold back for one reason, and others for another. For who is able to penetrate the labyrinth of the human heart, especially since the diversity of the affections is as great as the diversity of natural talents? But who is there of all men who, according to nature, does not prefer to be permitted to indulge his appetite, and who does not bear with bitterness being coerced by law? If you do not now sense this, it makes no difference; the time will come when you will most certainly realize how the mind hates to have its desires curbed by law. Furthermore, John 1:12 f. says: "But to all who received him, who believed in his name, he gave power to become children of God; who were born, not of blood nor of the will of the flesh nor of the will of man, but of God." You see that blood is damned, as are the will of man, the will of flesh, that is, every last aspect of the power of nature. But from God sons are born again. And to pass over many passages that a studious reader will note by himself, John 15:4 says: "As the branch cannot bear fruit by itself, unless it abides in the vine, neither can you, unless you abide in me."

In passing, I must refute what those godless Sophists growl at when they weaken the clear passages just cited. For they say it is true that man according to nature cannot do good *meritoriously*.[39] Accordingly, they invent a twofold good, meritorious and not meritorious.[40] This they do only so that they may not be compelled to prove defective the philosophical virtues of free will (*arbitrium*) and those external simulated virtues. Oh, what godlessness! Is not this word-juggling, to invent a good that is at one time worthy of eternal life and at another time not worthy? I hope you are definitely convinced that nothing good nor meritorious can be done by men through the power of nature, since Scripture certainly says that every imagination of the thoughts of the human heart is vain and depraved (Gen. 6:5). Surely what is vain and depraved does not only not merit eternal life (for it is appropriate that I use their words), but is also not good. Thus David writes in Ps. 116:11: "Men are all a vain hope." Isa. 9:17: "Every one is godless and an evildoer, and every mouth speaks folly." Why, not only does he say that man is not meritorious, but plainly that he is evil.

[39] *Ibid.,* q. 109, a. 2.
[40] Gabriel Biel, *In sent., lib.* III, d. 19, q. *unica,* a. 2, concl. 5.

Furthermore, both from these things which we have discussed so far and from those things which we shall note a little later, each one by himself will easily refute this nonsense of theirs. The ungodly Sophists did not think that works have their source in the affections of the heart, but they judged them in a philosophical manner. This was the reason for their idle talk.

Now, Paul in nearly all his letters, but especially in Romans and Galatians, does hardly anything but teach that all works and all efforts of human power are sins or vices (*peccata* or *vitia*). You have Rom. 3:9, where he says: "All men . . . are under the power of sin." And he teaches this in a magnificent and splendid manner from the testimonies of the prophets. In the eighth chapter, after he has stated that we cannot keep the law, he compares the flesh and the Spirit. He teaches that the flesh is altogether subservient to sin, but that the Spirit is life and peace. At this point the Sophists, having forgotten the diction and figurative use of language in Scripture, call the "flesh" a "sensitive appetite." [41] For by the word "flesh" the Scripture means not just the body as a part of man, but it means the whole man, soul as well as body. And whenever flesh is compared with Spirit, it signifies the best and most excellent powers of human nature apart from the Holy Spirit. "Spirit" means the Holy Spirit himself and his activity and his workings in us. So John 3:6: "That which is born of the flesh is flesh, and that which is born of the Spirit is spirit." And John 8:15: "You judge according to the flesh." And Gen. 6:3: "My Spirit shall not abide in man for ever, for he is flesh."

We must therefore understand that the word "flesh" is used concerning all the powers of human nature. Otherwise, Paul's arguments in the entire letter to the Romans will not stand. For he continually carries on his argument as follows: "The flesh could not fulfill the law; therefore there is need of the Spirit to fulfill it." If we should here use the word "flesh" for only a part of man, how will Paul's argument stand? For it could be eluded in this way: "Even if the flesh could not keep the law, yet some better part of man could have done so, and thus there would have been no need for the Spirit to fulfill the law."

But we have unlearned, not only the sense of Scripture, but also

---

[41] Cf. Duns Scotus, *In sent., lib.* II, d. 29, 4; and Gabriel Biel, *In sent., lib.* II, d. 30, q. 2, a. 3, *dub.* 2: *Fomes est qualitas inordinata, inclinans appetitum ad actum deformans et vitiosum in habente iudicium rationis* ("The 'tinder' is an inordinate quality of the flesh that inclines the sensitive appetite to an act which in relation to the judgment of reason is deforming and defective").

its language, under these so-called doctors of philosophy.⁴² As we read in Ezra 10:2: "We have married foreign women" and we have used their language instead of our own. Therefore, use the word "flesh" both for the highest powers of human nature and for its best efforts. The fruits of the flesh are both that splendid virtue of a Socrates or a Cato and the parricides of a Caesar as well. The fruits of the flesh are both the very fine virtues that Paul possessed before he knew Christ and the adulteries of a Claudius as well.

Now, what we here call "flesh," we usually call at other times the "old man," which likewise signifies whatever power there is in human nature. That is the meaning which the word itself plainly declares. For he would seem to lack common sense who would hold that only a part of man is meant by the term "old man." For who when he hears the word "man" would think of only the body? Paul uses the terms "old man," "flesh," and "body of sin" interchangeably. Now, "outer man" also means just what "old man" or "flesh" means, that is, not only the outer parts of man, but all his natural powers. I shall say more on the parts of man below when I discuss the topic "Grace." Let it suffice now to have called attention to what "flesh" means. For they are deceived who think that in a man whom the Holy Spirit has not renewed and cleansed there is anything at all which cannot be called "flesh" or "corrupt."

Precisely that we may examine the Pauline position concerning the natural powers of man, I submit his words in Rom. 8:3 f.: "For God has done what the law, weakened by the flesh, could not do: sending his own Son in the likeness of sinful flesh and for sin, he condemned sin in the flesh, in order that the just requirement of the law might be fulfilled in us, who walk not according to the flesh but according to the Spirit." Paul has stated the summary of his argument to this point, namely, that since it is impossible for us to keep the law because we are carnal, God sent his Son that he might satisfy the law for us who are dead to the flesh, but alive in the Spirit. Here I ask, "What does he call 'flesh'?" For, since it is evident that the "Holy Spirit" is called "Spirit," his movements as well as his impulses, it necessarily follows that you call "flesh" whatever in us is foreign to the Holy Spirit. Furthermore, the apostle gives an explanation of his stated position: "For those who live according to flesh set their minds on the things of the flesh, but those who live according to the Spirit set their minds on the things of the Spirit. To set the mind on the flesh is death, but to set the mind on the Spirit is life and peace" (Rom. 8:5 f.) . Take note why the law cannot be satisfied through the flesh: "Those

⁴² *Doctoribus philosophrastris.*

who live according to the flesh, set their minds on the things of the flesh," as if he were to say: "You Pharisees and hypocrites, you think you can fulfill the law in your own strength. You appear to do well on the outside, and seem endowed with the most noble virtues. But all those things are camouflage. For since you are flesh, you seek your own ends and either because of fear of punishment or love of convenience or some other carnal affection, you do well in the eyes of men. Nor can it be that there is in you any sense of God, because you are flesh. Therefore, you cannot desire nor seek after those things which are of God." For who is there, however good he seems to be outwardly, who loves God in such a way that if God wished, he would gladly bear death and hell?

It cannot be stated how many great things the apostle has comprehended in such a brief verse as Rom. 8:5: "Those who live according to the flesh set their minds on the things of the flesh." On the contrary, "those who live according to the Spirit set their minds on the things of the Spirit." This means that those on whom the Holy Spirit has been poured out have in them a sense of God, a trust in God, and the love of God. On the other hand, in the flesh are nothing but contempt and hatred for God. This is what the apostle means when he says in Rom. 8:6: "To set the mind on the flesh is death, but to set the mind on the Spirit is life and peace." And this verse follows: "For the mind that is set on the flesh is hostile to God; it does not submit to God's law, indeed it cannot." Consider, I beg you, Paul's conclusion: he finishes by saying that all power of our flesh is hostile to God and that it cannot submit to God's law. If it cannot submit to the law of God, why do we doubt as to what kind of fruits it bears? Now, he not only says that it does not submit to God's law, but also that it cannot submit to that law. It follows, therefore, that all works of men, however praiseworthy they are externally, are actually corrupt and are sins worthy of death. Let the Sophists, if they please, bring up their foolish little distinctions concerning the flesh and the Spirit, concerning the good and the meritorious, and all similar trifles which they have concocted to wrest away from us this thought of Paul. For what is clearer than that Paul says that the righteousness of the law is not fulfilled except in those who live according to the Spirit? Therefore, those who are not filled with the Holy Spirit do not satisfy the law. But not to do the law, what else is that than to sin? For, indeed, every motion and impulse of the mind against the law is sin.

Therefore, when the Sophists teach that original sin is to have fallen out of the favor of God and to lack original righteousness,

they ought to add that we are accursed because we lack the Spirit
and blessing of God. Since the light is gone, there is nothing in us
but darkness, blindness, and error. Since truth is absent, there is
nothing in us but falsehood. Since life is lacking, there is nothing
in us but sin and death. In Eph. 2:3, Paul sets forth why he calls
us children of wrath: "Among these we all once lived in the passions of our flesh, following the desires of body and mind, and so
we were by nature children of wrath." Below, when we discuss
"The Power of the Law," much more material can be used to supplement this passage; therefore, we need not be delayed here now.
What the power of sin is, then, is finally discerned when the law is
revealed, which accuses all men of sin. "But the Scripture con-
signed all things to sin," as the apostle writes to the Galatians,
"that what was promised to faith in Jesus Christ might be given to
those who believe" (Gal. 3:22). And from what we have discussed
under this topic, you can gather what we must think concerning
human powers. You can see whether there is any freedom, which
the theologians boast of as that of a truly free will (*arbitrium*),
since for their theory of the will (*arbitrium*) they decide whatever
they please when they leave out Scripture. For what freedom is
there without the Spirit when that tyrant of ours, sin in our flesh,
makes trouble even for men overflowing with the Spirit? For which
of the saints has not deplored this servitude, rather, this captivity?
And Paul in Rom. 7:23 says that he sees a law in his members war-
ring against himself and taking himself captive. This law of the
members, this tyranny of sin, is the ferocious attack made by that
sin with which we are born. I shall write below concerning those
who are righteous according to the Spirit while sinners according
to the flesh.

From this it likewise follows that what is commanded cannot
be fulfilled, as we shall discuss more at length below. This is clear
from the passage cited above, Rom. 8:7: "The flesh cannot submit
to God's law." Likewise, from that same context comes the following thought: "It was impossible for the law to justify" (Rom. 8:3).
In other words, the law was not enough, since it merely showed us
what we should do, but it was also necessary that through Christ
the Spirit should be given to inflame us to love the law. And at this
point there rushes in that godless and stupid tenet of moral philosophy and of the theologians of free will which the Scotists never
cease to blare out with puffed cheeks. They say that the will (*voluntas*) can conform itself to every recommendation of right reason, that is, that the will (*voluntas*) is able to will (*velle*) whatever right reason and proper counsel of the intellect prescribe.

Paul says on the contrary that it was impossible for the law to justify, that is, that it was not enough that the law prescribe what we
should do, since the flesh was weak and turned itself away from the
law. But here they have struck upon something by postulating a
certain new kind of will (*voluntas*) which can call forth acts into
whatever sphere affection draws it. But if they had observed the
speech and diction of Scripture, they would easily have detected
the lies and the vain thoughts of the intellect which they have
fastened together concerning these elicited acts. The external
members can sometimes be forced in a direction different from
that in which affection drives, but when this takes place, it is by
simulation and deceit.

Although I shall say more later on "The Power of the Law," I
cannot in passing restrain myself from indicating to the Christian
reader the foolish, insipid, and godless subtleties of the Sophists
with which they prove that we can love God by our natural powers.
For they argue as follows: "A lesser good can be loved—for example, any creature—and therefore also a greater good can be loved." [43]
This certainly is the speech of Christians which Paul wants sea-
soned with salt, is it not? Surely this is both droll and truly Aristotelian, a comment worthy of Aristotelian theologians. First, it is
the nature of love that we love nothing except that which seems
good, pleasant, and convenient for us. Therefore, whatever we
love, we love with a view to our own advantage. You love wealth,
you love money, not because the thing is good in itself, but because you think it will be useful for the necessities of life. In like
manner, you do not love God no matter how good he is, unless you
think that he is useful for your plans and for yourself. Now, even
if you did love God out of regard for your own convenience, you
would be loving in a servile way and with a depraved and perverse
natural passion, and obviously you would be committing sin. But
not even in this way do you ever love God, because no conve-

[43] This is directed chiefly against Gabriel Biel, *In sent., lib.* III, d. 26, q. 26,
unica, a. 3, *dub.* 2: "From his knowledge of and love for himself man
ascends to the knowledge and love of God, for by nature (*naturaliter*)
man loves himself with a friendly love (*amore amicitiae*), but he loves
everything that is good for him with a covetous love (*amore concupi-
scentiae*) and thus also God, the highest good." In another passage (*ibid.,*
d. 28, q. *unica,* a. 1, *dub.* 1) Biel goes so far as to say of man that "by his
natural powers he can elicit [bring forth] the act of loving God above
everything." Against this position, Luther argued at the beginning of his
professional career with great insistence. Cf., for example, his "Theses
Against Scholastic Theology" of September, 1517 (LW, Vol. 31, pp. 9–16;
also, *Luther: Early Theological Works,* ed. and tr. by James Atkinson, LCC,
Vol. XVI [1962], pp. 266–273).

niences are thought to be from him unless the heart has already been purified by the Holy Spirit and the kindness of God has been engraved on a pure and pious heart.

Moreover, what of the time when your conscience shows you the angry God, threatening everlasting death, and the horrible instant of his glance, as David says (Ps. 21:9 f.) . When it is grasped not by a sense of good things, but only of evil, namely, punishments that are inflicted by God—in this situation, I ask, can human nature so dispose the mind that it loves God and readily bears even the punishment of hell? And what of the occasion when the conscience strikes the mind, and presently it turns away from God and dreads him as a cruel murderer, as an avenger, and, what is most atrocious, as being wicked? In this situation, O Sophists, what will those elicited acts of which you prate accomplish, and what will that wonderful will (*voluntas*) which you have imagined bring about? Or will not that wrathful day of fire declare that those human acts of righteousness by the free will (*arbitrium*) are nothing but lying and deceit, and that all the glory of the flesh is as the glory of the field? Did not Israel quake in dread at the fire and the smoke, yes, and even at the very face of Moses when the law was being given? Did not the earth tremble, and was it not moved, and were not the foundations of the mountains disturbed and shaken because God was angry with them? But on this matter I hope that we shall speak adequately below when "The Power of the Law" is discussed. You have, dear reader, the first point here: nothing is loved except what is advantageous for us. But God does not wish to be loved for the sake of any advantage; he wants to be loved freely. The man who loves something advantageous does not love God but himself, and the Scriptures warn everywhere against such depraved love.

Another subtle argument, not entirely different from the above, must be injected here. Our opponents hold that it ought not to seem absurd that they teach that apart from the work of the Holy Spirit, it is possible to love God more deeply than we love ourselves, since often even for perishable things, for men, for lovers, for children, or for spouse, we undergo death. What we must answer to this must be deduced from the argument about the affections. For, in the first place, no one naturally rejoices to die, and those whose lives are risked for the state or for their property would themselves prefer to live. Curtius [44] would have preferred to live and Lu-

---

[44] An ancient Roman legend says that in 362 B.C. a deep gulf opened in the Forum of Rome; some seers declared that it would not close until Rome's most valuable possession was thrown into it. Then Marcus Curtius, believing

cretia [45] too. But because human nature flees adversity, we would prefer to die rather than to live in a wretched state, for example, to freeze. Pyramus would have preferred to live, but because he thought that life without Thisbe would be miserable, he wished to put an end to this evil and to his own life at one and the same time.[46] Saul would have preferred to live, but because of wrath, desperation, and fear of disgrace, he committed suicide to finish all his troubles and his life, once for all.[47] But why do I labor to give such a precise argument about the affections when remarkable deaths, such as those of Lucretia, Saul, and similar ones, are marvelous examples of divine majesty?

Now, as for those things which the Sophists hand out about the merit of congruence (*meritum congrui*), namely, that by moral works which we do in the strength of our own nature, it is congruous (for thus they speak) that we merit grace,[48] you yourself, dear reader, understand that these are false blasphemies dishonoring the grace of God. Further, since the power of human nature without the inspiration of the Holy Spirit cannot do anything but sin, what shall we deserve for our efforts but wrath? Those elicited acts, those counterfeit propositions, those intentions which they falsely call good, in a word, all those things which the Sophists put forth, are lies and misrepresentations. It is so farfetched that we obtain grace through these good intentions that we say there is nothing that resists grace in such a manner as do those Pharisaic preparations. Paul opposes this impiety very persistently. Although

---

that the city possessed no greater treasure than a brave man, sacrificed himself, leaping into the chasm on horseback and in full armor. The gulf immediately closed.

[45] At about 500 B.C., Lucretia, a famous beauty, the wife of Lucius Tarquinius Collatinus was raped by Tarquinius Sextus. After having obtained the promise from her father and her husband that they would avenge her, she stabbed herself to death.

[46] According to an ancient Babylonian legend, the lovers Pyramus and Thisbe chose a tomb as their trysting place. Thisbe, arriving first, came upon a lion that had just killed an ox. She fled, losing her garment, which the lion smeared with blood. Pyramus found her clothing and, believing her dead, killed himself. Later, Thisbe followed him in death.

[47] Cf. I Sam. 31:3-4.

[48] Cf. Duns Scotus, *In sent., lib.* II, d. 28, q. 1B. Gabriel Biel, *In sent., lib.* II, d. 27, q. *unica,* concl. 4, writes: *Anima obicis remotione ac bono motu in deum ex arbitrii libertate elicito primam gratiam mereri potest de congruo. Probatur, quia actum facientis quod in se est, deus acceptat ad tribuendam gratiam primam* ("When the hindrance [*obex*] is removed and a good motion toward God has been elicited from a free decision of the will, the soul can merit [earn] *de congruo* the first grace. This is proved because God accepts the act of one who does what is in him so that he can be given the first grace").

he does this in other places also, he does so especially in the entire letter to the Romans. His whole point is that grace is not grace if it is granted for works. What place is there for mercy if there is consideration of our works? What is the glory of grace, to use Paul's phrase (Eph. 1:6), if it is bound to our works? Paul plainly teaches in Rom., ch. 3, both that all men are under sin and that those who believe are justified by grace. What of his statement in Rom. 9: 31: "But Israel, who pursued the righteousness based on law did not succeed in fulfilling that law"? He means that those who were advancing in the strength of their own free will (*arbitrium*) to do the law never kept the law but only pretended outwardly to do so. The prophet Isaiah freely invites to Christ any and all buyers (ch. 55:1-3): "Come, buy wine and milk without money and without price. Why do you spend your money for that which is not bread, and your labor for that which does not satisfy?" (that is: "Why are you trusting in good works? They will disappoint you"). "Hearken diligently to me, and eat what is good, and delight yourselves in fatness. Incline your ear" (that is, "Believe") . . . "that your soul may live; and I will make with you an everlasting covenant, sure love for David" (that is, "To David I shall promise mercy which is faithful," which means, "established"). Jer. 17:5-8: "Cursed is the man who trusts in man and makes flesh his arm, whose heart turns away from the Lord. He is like a shrub in the desert, and shall not see any good come. He shall dwell in the parched places of the wilderness, in an uninhabited salt land. Blessed is the man who trusts in the Lord, whose trust is the Lord. For he is like a tree planted by water, that sends out its roots by the stream, and does not fear when heat comes," etc. Look at the remainder of the chapter. For that one chapter of the prophet has proved incontestably that moral works are nothing but the pretenses and the lies of our flesh.

What Scholastic theology has fabricated about the beginning of repentance and attrition [49] is pertinent at this point. For nature does not grieve about anything it has done except because of love of self or fear of punishment, and these motives are plainly sins. It is impossible that men not bear with them a hatred for the One who inflicts punishments, namely, God. But in a peculiar way this

[49] According to Scholastic teaching, penance consisted of *contritio cordis* ("contrition of the heart"), *confessio oris* ("oral confession") and *satisfactio operis* ("satisfaction of the [good] work"). Alexander of Hales (d. 1245) was the first to make the distinction between *attritio* and *contritio*. *Attritio* was henceforth understood as regret induced by the fear of punishment and *contritio* as regret inspired by the love of God.

hatred, as well as the recognition of our sin, is the work of God. As Hannah says in I Sam. 2:6 f.: "The Lord kills and brings to life; he brings down to Sheol and raises up. . . . He brings low, he also exalts." In Jer. 31:19 we read: "After I had turned away I repented," etc. But why waste time when it was said by Christ very clearly in John 6:44: "No one can come to me, unless the Father who sent me draws him." Simply because the Sophists are ignorant of the figurative language of Scripture, they bring up the thought of the Lord in Zech. 1:3: "Return to me, . . . and I will return to you." [50] This does not mean that the beginning of repentance is placed in us. Augustine refuted this error more than once, and it is not obscure except to the Sophists, who have mastered nothing but their puny little manuals of logic.[51]

There is a twofold turning of God to us: one precedes our repentance, and the other follows it. The one that precedes takes place when God causes us to repent by the inspiration of his Spirit, when he terrifies and disturbs us by showing us our sin. But God's turning to us following repentance takes place when he puts a stop to our punishments, consoling us and declaring openly that he favors us. Concerning the latter, Zechariah speaks when he says (ch. 1:3) : "Return to me . . . and I will return to you," that is, "Repent, and I shall end your punishments." For the prophet urges those who have already returned from the Assyrian exile to Judea to repent, warned by the example of their fathers, unless they wish to experience again similar divine wrath and punishments. From this it cannot be deduced that the beginning of repentance is in our hands. God himself invites us and draws us to himself, and when he has drawn us, he takes away our punishments and declares that he is pleased with us and reconciled to us. And because he commands, "Return to me," it does not follow that it is in our power to repent or to turn. In the same way, just because he commands that he is to be loved above all, it does not follow that this is in our strength merely because he enjoins it. On the contrary, because of the very fact that he orders it, it is not in our power. For he commands the impossible that he may commend his mercy to us as we shall state below when discussing the law. And why have the Sophists not observed what is stated in Zech. 10:6: "I will bring them back because I have compassion on

---

[50] This was the Scriptural passage which the Scholastics most liked to refer to in support of their view. Cf. Gabriel Biel, *In sent.*, lib. II, d. 27, q. *unica*, concl. 4.
[51] *Parva logicalia.*

them, and they shall be as though I had not rejected them." Note that here God himself says that he will convert Judah, not because of their good deeds, but because of his own mercy. I commend similar passages to your industry, Christian reader. For when you become a little more familiar with the use of Scripture, you will be able to dispose of all the subtleties of the Sophists without any difficulty.

You have here, dear reader, as much concerning the power of innate corruption as I thought ought to be said. Those who wish to be shaped by the meditation and reading of Holy Writ rather than by human commentaries will not require more. For no commentary can satisfy those whose minds are confused by uncertain disputations and various ideas and opinions of men; they understand nothing but the carnal. The Holy Spirit is the one and only teacher, the most simple and the most definite, who expresses himself most accurately and most simply in the Holy Scriptures. When your mind has been transformed, as it were, into these Scriptures, then you will comprehend absolutely, simply, and exactly what is behind this fundamental point and other theological matters as well. Those who depend not on the Spirit, but on the judgment and opinion of men, do not see things as they are, but only some vague shadows of things, and hardly that, just like those in Plato's cave (*Republic* VII, 1). For which of the philosophers or Scholastic theologians has seen the real nature of virtue or vice? The so-called theologians [52] have measured original sin only by outward acts while they did not see the wickedness of the mind and the disease which is under the skin, so to speak. And although they have very well comprehended the wickedness of certain affections, nevertheless, reason has not shown all, nor those which are most at war with the divine Spirit, namely, blasphemy, hatred for God, love of self, distrust of God, and innumerable passions of this kind which are so imbedded in man that they are clinging not only in some one part of him, in his sensitive appetite, as they teach, but they have seized his entire nature and hold it captive. They call those affections a "weakness," but such a weakness as can be overcome by human power. Scripture, on the contrary, denies that the affections of the flesh can be conquered except by the Spirit of God, because "if the Son makes you free, you will be free indeed" (John 8:36). Therefore, do not let the fancies of those fellows about external works move you at all, nor similar things which they have to say about the elicited acts of the will (*voluntas*). God judges the heart, and not the external work. "For the

[52] *Theologastri.*

Lord sees not as man sees," as we read in I Sam. 16:7. We can judge from this how much damage philosophy has done to Christianity, since our so-called theologians, having pursued philosophy, have invented good works and that mask of external deeds. That lone parable in the Gospel about the foolish virgins (Matt. 25:1-13) teaches that good works merit nothing. For the virgins denote nothing but Pharisaic righteousness, that is, the pretense of external works. And what else do the philosophers teach but external works? When they discuss the virtues, do they not relate all things to external works and those fictitious, elicited acts? But they are blind leaders of the blind. Therefore, it is to be hoped that God will change our minds from the judgment of human reason and from philosophy to spiritual discernment. For the blindness of human reason is such that we cannot recognize the full nature of sin or righteousness without the light of the Spirit. All the capacities of human reason are mere shadows. The Spirit of Christ is light, and he alone teaches all truth. The flesh or human reason cannot fix its eyes on the glowing countenance of Moses, and therefore a veil shields the law. The flesh judges only concerning external works, counterfeit propositions, so-called "intentions," or "the letter," to use Paul's term. The Spirit, however, scrutinizes and penetrates the depths (I Cor. 2:10). To indicate in a few words a summary of what we have written on original sin, I shall add some theses, a kind of epitome, of what has been written above:

1. Sin is a state of mind contrary to the law of God.

2. Because we are born sons of wrath, it follows that we are born without the Spirit of God.

3. Since the Spirit of God is not in man, he knows, loves, and seeks nothing but the carnal.

4. For this reason, there is in man a contempt for and an ignorance of God, and whatever faults Ps. 14 describes: "The fool says in his heart, 'There is no God,'" etc.

5. Thus it follows that man by his natural powers can do nothing but sin.

6. For not only a part of man, which they call the "sensitive appetite," is in the power of sinful affections.

7. Since Scripture testifies that the heart is unclean, it follows that all human powers are impure.

8. For the "heart" signifies not only the "sensitive appetite," as they call it, but it means the seat of all affections—love, hate, blasphemy, and incredulity.

9. Just as "heart" signifies the seat of all human affections, so "flesh" means all the natural powers of man.

10. The "carnal" is whatever exists by the power of nature. The constancy of Socrates and the temperance of Zeno are nothing but carnal states.

11. At one place, in I Cor. 2:14, Paul called the work of the reason "natural" (*psychikon*). The philosophical virtues, for instance, are the work of reason.

12. In the same passage it is obvious that the "natural" (*psychikon*) is condemned as being sin.

13. In other passages he sometimes calls "flesh" whatever takes place in us without the work of the Holy Spirit, however good it may seem on the surface. This is apparent in Rom. 8:3 where Paul says that the requirements of the law could not be fulfilled through the flesh. Who does not see that the word "flesh" here means the most powerful resources of man, which seem, in the judgment of men, able to comply with the law? II Cor., ch. 3, also teaches the same thing.

14. I wanted to warn about this distinction which the Scholastics make lest they deceive anyone. They distinguish between the "appetite of the intellect" and the "sensitive appetite" (the appetite related to the senses), and they attribute depraved affections to the appetite of the senses, whereas they maintain that the appetite of the intellect is free of any defect (*vitium*).

15. The passages of Scripture which we have cited above adequately refute this idea of the Scholastics. Nor can they be helped by Origen, as they wish it to seem, when he discusses the soul, the flesh, and the Spirit. But what is the opinion of Origen to us, since we are discussing the position of Scripture, not the ideas of Origen?

16. The reason why the Scholastics deny that all works of men are sins is that they fix their eyes only on the external works and on the veiled countenance of Moses. They do not judge the affections. But God judges the heart and the affections.

17. For the same reason they have inverted free will (*arbitrium*), for they have seen that in certain spheres of external works there is a kind of freedom. For thus the flesh judges external works. On the contrary, the Spirit teaches that all things come to pass necessarily according to predestination.

18. Experience teaches that there is no freedom in the affections.

19. As soon as all things in the Scriptures were related by them to external works, the whole Scripture was obscured, and it was not understood what sin is, what grace is, what the law is, what the gospel is, what Moses is, and what Christ is. And we owe this darkness, worse than Egyptian, to that godless, accursed philosophy of the Scholastic "theologians."

20. What that impurity innate in the heart is, that depravity and wickedness which we call original sin, will become clear when the law is revealed. All holy men deplore original sin, and reason does not understand it. It will become clear when God has opened the eyes of your conscience, as we shall discuss below under "The Law."

We ought to discuss here the fruits of sin also, that is, the classes of vices. Paul has enumerated the fruits of the flesh in his letter to the Galatians, but each man will detect those for himself. It is enough for the Christian to know that all the works of his nature and all the affections and efforts of human power are sins. Now, who is able to enumerate all the affections if we are to derive the kinds of vices from the affections, as we should? Proceeding otherwise, those who have derived the types of virtues and vices from the outward appearance of works have often put forth vices for virtues and virtues for vices. Therefore, we shall leave the judgment of these things to the individual spirit.

THE LAW

The topic "The Law" will reveal much more clearly the power and nature of sin, since the law is said to be the knowledge of sin. Therefore, if anything seems to be lacking in the preceding topic, the one that now follows will make up this deficiency unless I am mistaken. We do not aim to pile up here, however, all that can be said under every single heading, but we give the list of only the most common fundamentals so that you may see on what a summary of Christian doctrine depends and why we must refer to Scripture in preference to everything else. And I want you to learn these fundamentals while I act merely as your prompter and not as a schoolmaster, with Scripture as your source, not my commentary. For, believe me, it makes a lot of difference whether you seek the material about such all-important questions from fountains or from stagnant pools.

Not only are sweeter waters drunk from the fountain, as the poet has said, but they are also purer. For how much more certain is that which the Scriptures prescribe than that which is gleaned from commentaries!

Law is a judgment by which the good is commanded and the bad forbidden. Legal right [53] is the power of acting according to the law. Many things have been said for and against laws by the an-

53 *Ius.*

cients, and we shall try to indicate a little later from what fount they have flowed.

Some laws are natural laws, others divine, and others human. Concerning natural laws, I have seen nothing worthily written either by theologians or lawyers. For when natural laws are being proclaimed, it is proper that their formulas be collected by the method of human reason through the natural syllogism. I have not yet seen this done by anyone, and I do not know at all whether it can be done, since human reason is so enslaved and blinded—at least it has been up until now. Moreover, Paul teaches in Rom. 2:15 in a remarkably fine and clear argument that there is a law of nature. He comes to the conclusion that there is in the Gentiles a conscience which either defends or accuses their acts, and therefore it is law. For what is conscience but a judgment of our deeds which is derived from some law or common rule? The law of nature, therefore, is a common judgment to which all men give the same consent. This law which God has engraved on the mind of each is suitable for the shaping of morals. For just as there are certain common principles in the theoretical branches of learning, in mathematics, for instance (they might be called "common thoughts" or "a priori principles," such as "The whole is greater than its parts") , so there are certain common axioms and a priori principles in the realm of morals; these constitute the ground rules for all human activity. (We must use these terms for pedagogical reasons.) These rules for human activity are rightly called "laws of nature." M. Cicero in his work *On Laws* imitated Plato by deriving the standards for laws from the nature of man.[54] I do not condemn this, but I consider it done with more cleverness than precision. But many godless things have crept into Cicero's disputation, and this usually happens when we follow the methods and shortcuts of our reason rather than what is prescribed in Holy Scripture. For in general the judgment of human comprehension is fallacious because of our innate blindness, so that even if certain patterns of morals [55] have been engraved on our minds, they can scarcely be apprehended. When I say that the laws of nature have been impressed on our minds by God, I mean that the knowledge of these laws consists of certain so-called "concreated attitudes" (*habitus concreati*) . This knowledge is not the product of our own mental powers, but it has been implanted in us by God. I am not concerned to make this agree with the philosophy of Aristotle. For what do I care what that wrangler thought? I pass over those things

[54] Cicero, *De legibus* I, 5, 15 ff.; 6, 18 ff.
[55] *Formae morum.*

which we have in common with the beasts, the instinct of self-preservation, of giving birth, and procreating another from self. The lawyers relate these things to the law of nature, but I call them certain natural dispositions [56] implanted commonly in living beings.

Of the laws that pertain properly to man, however, the principal ones seem to be the following:

1. God must be worshiped.

2. Since we are born into a life that is social, nobody must be harmed.

3. Human society demands that we make common use of all things.

We get the first law, concerning the worship of God, from Rom., ch. 1. There is no doubt that in this chapter the apostle singles out this natural law when he says that God has declared his majesty to all men by founding and administering the universe. But it is more characteristic of a curious than of a pious man to conclude by way of a human syllogism that God is,[57] especially since it is not safe for human reason to argue about such great matters, as I have warned at the beginning of this compendium.

Undoubtedly, the second law, which enjoins us to take care that no one be harmed, can be derived from the common necessity that all of us are born bound and joined to all other men. The Scripture indicates this when it says in Gen. 2:18: "It is not good that man should be alone; I will make him a helper fit for him." Accordingly, the law commands that no one be harmed, that is, that we should all earnestly love one another in order that all may experience our benevolence with zeal and kindness. This law therefore includes the divine commandments that we should not kill anyone, that we should not steal another's property, and similar laws.

If you ask why then do the magistrates kill the guilty, I answer, Fallen Adam branded all of us with the mark of sin. Since the resultant condition of man is such that the good are often harmed by the bad, the human race must see to it that the law about not doing harm should be especially observed. Therefore, those who disturb the public peace and harm the innocent must be coerced, restrained, and taken away. The majority must be preserved by the removal of those who have caused harm. The laws stands: "Harm no one!" But if someone has been harmed, the one who is responsible must be done away with lest more be harmed. It is of more importance to preserve the whole group than one or two individuals.

[56] *Affectus.*　　　　　　　　　[57] *Esse deum.*

Therefore, the man who threatens the whole group by some deed that makes for a bad example is done away with. This is why there are magistracies in the state, this is why there are punishments for the guilty, this is why there are wars, all of which the lawyers refer to the law of nations (*ius gentium*).

The third law, about the common use of things, obviously arises from the very nature of human society. For if the saying "Friends have all things in common" ought to be valid when a few friends are involved, why should it not hold among all men? It should, since all are supposed to cling together as brothers do with brothers, children with parents, and parents with children. For the law not to inflict harm has commanded this. But because human avarice does not allow that we use all things in common, this law had to be corrected by the one above, the law that no one be harmed. Things must be shared to the extent that the public peace and the safety of the group permit. For as a rule inferior laws are corrected by higher ones, and public sharing must be regulated according to some limit.

Therefore, another law must be subjoined to the third, namely, that property must be divided, since the common welfare of the multitude so demands. Furthermore, since it is a condition of human affairs that there is need of at least some sharing of property because by nature things ought to be in common, it has been decided that their use be shared, for instance, through contracts, buying, selling, leases, rents, etc. And here you discern the origin of contracts. Plato sees this when, in the fifth book of his *Laws*,[58] he says that that state is best administered in which the popular saying, "Friends have all things in common," is realized as nearly as possible, where not only the possessions of citizens are held in common, but where even the limbs, eyes, hands, feet, and mouth of each serve the common good of all. One must not look for any other model of a well-constituted state than that state in which it is possible to observe the rule that friends must share. Thus contracts have been devised through which the goods of each are shared by the many so that there may be at least some sharing of things.

So much for the general rules of the laws of nature, which can be condensed in the following way:

1. Worship God!

2. Since we are born into a life that is social, a shared life, harm no one but help everyone in kindness.

3. If it is impossible that absolutely no one be harmed, see to it that the number harmed be reduced to a minimum. Let those who

[58] Plato, *Laws* V, 10.

disturb the public peace be removed. For this purpose let magistracies and punishments for the guilty be set up.

4. Property shall be divided for the sake of public peace. For the rest, some shall alleviate the wants of others through contracts.

He who wants to do so may add to this particular ideas from the poets, orators, and historians that are generally related to the law of nations (*ius gentium*), such as one can read about here and there concerning marriage, adultery, the returning of a favor, ingratitude, hospitality, the exchange of property, and other matters of this kind. But I thought it adequate to mention only the most common forms. And do not rashly consider just any thoughts of the Gentile writers to be laws, for many of their popular ideas express the depraved affections of our nature and not laws. Of this sort is this thought from Hesiod [59]: "Love him who loves you, and go to the one that comes to you. We give to the one who gives to us, and do not give to him who does not give to us." For in these lines friendship is measured by utility alone. Such also is that popular saying: "Give and take." The statement that "force must be repelled by force" is pertinent here, like that which appears in Euripides' [60] *Ion:* "It is fine for those who are prosperous to honor piety, but whenever anyone wishes to treat his enemies badly, no law stands in the way."

Also, so-called civil law contains many things which are obviously human affections rather than natural laws. For what is more foreign to nature than slavery? And in some contracts that which really matters is unjustly concealed. But more about these things later. A good man will temper civil constitutions with right and justice, that is, with both divine and natural laws. Anything that is enacted contrary to divine or natural laws cannot be just. So much about the laws of nature. Define them with more exact and subtle reasoning if you can.

DIVINE LAWS

Divine laws are those which have been established by God through the canonical Scriptures. They have been divided into three categories: moral, judicial, and ceremonial. The moral laws are those which are prescribed in the Decalogue; the student will relate to them all laws concerning morals that are given forth in the entire Scripture. For how often is the same law repeated in the Scriptures! We must beware here, however, of explaining the Deca-

[59] Hesiod, *Works and Days* 353–354.
[60] Euripides, *Ion* 1045–1047.

logue with regard to external acts only and of dividing the commandments into precepts and counsels in the Scholastic fashion. Therefore, I shall run through the principles of the laws in a few words.

The first three commandments are:

"You shall have no other gods before me."

"You shall not take the name of the Lord your God in vain."

"Remember the Sabbath Day, to keep it holy." (Ex. 20:3, 7, 8.) Undoubtedly, Christ explained them by this law: "You shall love the Lord your God with all your heart, and with all your soul, and with all your mind" (Mark 12:30) . There seem to be the following differences in these three laws, however, although they all pertain to the same thing, namely, to the true worship of God. The first, "You shall have no other gods before me," refers particularly to the affections. We are not to love nor fear anything but God, nor are we to trust in our own wealth, virtue, prudence, righteousness, or any creature, but solely in the goodness of God. Since these affections are not in our power, there can be no understanding of what trust, fear, or the love of God is except in a very spiritual sense. Many things in the prophets pertain to this law concerning the fear of God, trusting in him, and similar things. In a remarkable way the words of this law commend to us both trust and fear. For when he says, "I, the Lord your God am a jealous God, visiting the iniquity of the fathers upon the children," etc. (Ex. 20:5) , he terrifies by threatening and declares that the power of his wrath is to be feared. Again when he adds that he shows mercy to those thousands who love him, does he not commend his goodness, and demand that we love him, trust his goodness, etc.? Vastly greater things are demanded, however, than I can express in human words. The Scholastics taught that to love God is the same as to wish that God exists,[61] to believe that he hears, not to begrudge him the Kingdom, and many things like this. They taught this in words more obscure than those which they themselves could understand in their Schools. For unless the Spirit teaches, you cannot know what it is to love God, that is, unless you actually experience it inflamed by the Spirit himself. You have now the contents of the First Commandment, to trust God, and to love and fear him. This is the worship of which Christ says: "True worshipers will worship the Father in spirit and truth" (John 4:23) . An acceptable external worship will naturally follow such an internal state as this.

The Second Commandment warns that the name of God is not to be used rashly. It teaches plainly that we are to demonstrate our

---

[61] *Velle deum esse.*

very faith as well as our fear and love of God by our use of the divine name. Just as the First Commandment is affirmative, demanding faith and love, this one is also, since it demands that we celebrate the name and glory of God, that we invoke his name, and flee to it as to a very well fortified haven, and that we swear by God's name (Deut. 6:13). According to David we are to "sing praise to his name" (Ps. 68:4), and we should acknowledge that saying of Solomon in Prov. 18:10: "The name of the Lord is a strong tower." Let us praise and celebrate God's kindness toward us. Let us give thanks and let all things be done for the praise of the Lord, as the apostle says (Col. 3:23). From this you see that the Second Commandment proceeds from the first.

The Third Commandment orders that the Sabbath be dedicated to God and that we be free from our labors. This means that we should permit and endure God's work in us, the mortification of ourselves. The First Commandment demands faith; the Second, praise of God's name; the Third, submitting to God's work in us. Those who especially violate this commandment are the ones who preach moral acts and the power of free will (*arbitrium*). For this demands the mortification of free will (*arbitrium*), and the people of the new covenant are made alive by the Spirit, since they have a perpetual Sabbath in that their flesh is continually mortified. For they who assert free will (*arbitrium*) know nothing of either the Sabbath or Christianity, and they are enemies of the cross of Christ, justifying themselves by their own works and their own efforts. They follow the example of the man who gathered wood on the Sabbath (Num. 15:32).

You see, then, that the three commandments that God must be trusted, that God must be praised, and that his work in us must be permitted are comprehended in this sentence: "Love God with all your heart," etc. For the one who so loves really trusts, fears, praises, and endures with a most ardent spirit. I have decided not to elaborate on law, for this could not be done properly in a compendium. But I have wished to warn you of these things that you might know how wrong they are who think that nothing that exceeds human powers is demanded of us. One who desires a fuller exposition of the commandments may seek it in Luther's booklet in German, *On Good Works*.[62]

On this point the Sophists err in two ways. First, they think that the highest love of God is not required or demanded in this life, and this is their opinion also in regard to the other affections. But

[62] Martin Luther, *Sermon von den guten Werken* ("On Good Works") (1520) (*WA* 6, 196 ff.; LW, Vol. 44, pp. 21–114).

this text refutes their position clearly enough: "You shall love the Lord your God with all your heart, with all your soul, and with all your mind" (Mark 12:30). For if God demands the whole heart for himself, he never entrusts a part to the creature. Would that an Elijah would meet up with these fellows! He would teach these men who think that a part of the heart belongs to the creature and a part to God how grotesquely their ideas limp along. This commandment cannot be fulfilled while we live in the flesh, but it is not on that account dismissed. But we are all guilty as long as we do not pay what we owe. This is the reason why we said above that all men are always real sinners and always commit sin. And hereafter when we talk about grace, we shall again have to inquire to what extent we are justified and to what extent sinners.

Secondly, the Sophists are under an illusion because they think that both these and other commandments can be fulfilled in our own strength. For they think that we are enjoined only in regard to outward acts that we not worship false gods, idols, etc., with external ceremonies and forms. The very words of the law compel us to explain the law as having to do with dispositions: "You shall love the Lord your God with all your heart." Now, the flesh loves itself most of all, and trusts in its own goodness, prudence, and righteousness. That is what the apostle says in Rom. 8:5 and 7: "Those who live according to the flesh set their minds on the things of the flesh," and "The mind that is set on the flesh . . . does not submit to God's law, indeed it cannot." It cannot therefore love God, trust in the goodness of God, etc. It is a great and incomprehensible thing to love God, to embrace, with a joyous and grateful heart, the divine will through all things, even when it condemns and mortifies. Accordingly, I ask you, O Sophist, whether nature can wish for hell and eternal punishment. If you say it cannot, say also that God cannot freely be loved by the flesh.

The remaining commandments, which are called the Second Table, Christ explains thus: "You shall love your neighbor as yourself" (Mark 12:31). He further elucidates them in a long discourse in Matt., ch. 5. The apostle enumerates almost innumerable laws of love in Rom., ch. 12. But these also the Sophists have explained as dealing only with external acts, saying that the law is fulfilled if you do not commit murder, if you are not openly an adulterer, etc. Christ, on the contrary, explains the law as concerned with the affections, and deals with it affirmatively. In the commandment "You shall not kill" he commands us to have hearts that are upright, clean, free, and open to all men in all things. We are not to render evil for evil nor have lawsuits about our property. In a word, we are not to resist evil, but we are to love even our enemies, and do so freely and openly. Accordingly, they think that the law "You shall not commit adultery" is satisfied if we do not commit the shameful act by an external deed. But Christ explains it to mean that chastity and purity of heart are demanded so that we do not even desire shameful things. The other commandments in the Gospel the diligent reader will by himself attend to.

COUNSELS

In this realm too the Sophists have erred shamefully and godlessly, for they have made "counsels" from divine law. That is, they have taught that certain things are not necessarily demanded by God, but only recommended, so that if anyone cares to, he may obey, and they absolve the one who does not obey.[63] For the most part, they derive the counsels from Matt., ch. 5: "Love your enemies, do not resist evil, avoid public lawsuits and fights, treat well those who deserve evil, forgive one another, give to anyone who is needy even when there is no hope of repayment."

But we hold that all these things are demanded, and we number them among the commandments. For Christ openly condemns those who love only their friends, and he puts them in the same category as the Gentiles and publicans. In like manner he pronounces that man worthy of judgment who is angry at his neighbor or despises him to the extent of calling him a fool. But if He had merely been counseling that we not become angry, why did he threaten judgment? If one is free to become enraged at an offender or not to do so, why did He threaten punishment? The one who holds out the threat of punishment is not merely giving advice: he is making demands. Furthermore, since it was commanded that we love our neighbors, the question comes whether love does not embrace all the things which those fellows enumerate among their counsels. And Paul in Rom. 13:9 relates all these things to the law: "You shall love your neighbor as yourself." And it is written in I John 3:18: "Little children, let us not love in word or speech but in deed and in truth." That is, let us love from the heart, and let us love sincerely, and let us bear witness to that love of ours by doing favors and performing acts of kindness. Now, if they number among the laws the passage "You shall not covet," etc. (Ex. 20:17), why do they not consider as laws all commandments that it implies? Or is not this the work of concupiscence, to be angry at our enemy, to take revenge, or to be unwilling to risk money on

[63] Thomas Aquinas, *Summa theol.* II, 1, q. 108, a. 4.

the needy? Let them admit, therefore, that these things also are commanded, since it is clear we have been commanded not to covet.

Finally, why do they not interpret the whole law as counsel as long as they abrogate a part of it? But you will object, "If I must give to just anyone, my own personal property is at stake." I answer, "This is alleged as an excuse for your cupidity by the prudence of your flesh." For one's spirit will easily judge how far one should go in bestowing gifts, and it will gladly forego its own, provided that the need of a brother has been obviated. Do you not know that you ought to do to your neighbor what you want to be done to you? "But shall we be subject to injuries from all if we cannot avenge ourselves?" Surely, for this is the way of the cross, to be subject to injury. "But," you say, "will not wicked men take away our property if we cannot seek reclamation in court?" A magistrate will be on hand to look out lest one citizen inflict damage on another. It is your task to bear bravely this kind of happening. But why am I trying to break down the arguments of carnal prudence? This is useless, since none but the spiritual can approve of divine law. You will not understand why Christ has ordered you to do anything unless it pleases you to do it. Carnal arguments of this type deceived the Sophists also, since it did not seem right that the possessions of all should be shared so no one could look out just for his own rights. It was also considered inhuman that the slothful enjoy leisure if they could safely enjoy the possessions of others. From this sort of reasoning, counsels have been made out of commandments, and a most unhealthy view has been promulgated, namely, that public affairs cannot be administered according to the gospel. As if Christ has given to us anything of such a nature that it pertains only to some few little monks and not, rather, to the human race as a whole! For what should be more common than the gospel, which Christ ordered to be preached to the whole world.[64] But Augustine also has something to say on this in his letter to Marcellinus, which is the fifth of the Augustinian letters.[65] He breaks down this kind of sophistry against the law which forbids vengeance. Furthermore, this law does not forbid that crimes be punished by magistrates. No, on the contrary, these officials wield the sword to terrify evil men, as the apostle says in Rom. 13:4, but he forbids that we ourselves, with the zeal of vengeance, privately settle matters with our neighbors. The magistrate's responsibility is to see that the state incurs no loss. It is in your

[64] *Universae naturae.* Cf. Matt. 28:19.
[65] Augustine, Letter 139 (*MPL,* Vol. 33, col. 535).

power to suffer a private wrong and disregard it, but perhaps I shall discuss this more fully below.

As far as I know, in the Gospels there is only one instance of counsel, that on celibacy. Christ says on this: "He who is able to receive this, let him receive it" (Matt. 19:12). And in I Cor. 7:25-27, Paul says: "Now concerning the unmarried, I have no command of the Lord, but I give my opinion as one who by the Lord's mercy is trustworthy. I think that in view of the impending distress it is well for a person to remain as he is. Are you bound to a wife? Do not seek to be free. Are you free from a wife? Do not seek marriage," etc. But is not the issue disputed here whether counsels are higher than commandments? This is the foolishness of the Scholastics, who understood the nature of neither commandment nor counsel. For no unmarried person whatsoever fulfills the commandment about not committing adultery, since it is impossible for concupiscence not to stir him up, however chaste he may be. But concupiscence is forbidden by the commandment, and it is possible that ordinarily a married person comes closer to fulfilling this requirement than the unmarried.

THE VOWS OF MONKS

Now, what shall I say on the vows of monks? First, in regard to the very nature of a vow, Scripture neither commands nor counsels that a vow be made. God approves of nothing, however, except that which he either commands or counsels. Therefore, I do not see that anything is added to piety through a vow. The Mosaic law did not demand that vows be made but permitted them. Since the gospel consists on the whole of a certain freedom of spirit, it ignores completely the slavery of vows. And, as far as I can see, the custom of making vows has been accepted only because faith and evangelical freedom have been ignored. The custom of making vows is at variance with faith and the freedom of the spirit. The Scholastics even teach that a work done under a vow surpasses a work done without a vow. Godless fellows, if they think godliness comes from works rather than from spirit and faith! And why do they prefer a work done because of a vow, since a vow is neither demanded nor counseled in Scripture?

Next, I ask, consider what is vowed. They promise celibacy, poverty, and obedience. I do not deny that celibacy is counseled. But since the weakness of our flesh is such that Christ even denies that all should follow his advice about celibacy, what is the object in broadcasting this doubtful and dangerous doctrine to so many thousands of men? As far as we can gather from history, few indeed were the hermits of old who fought successfully against the flesh, though they zealously emaciated their bodies by hunger and thirst and were fortified against the wiles of the devil by the knowledge of Scripture. In what way shall *we* overcome, in such great luxury and with a very great amount of leisure, so unarmed and ignorant of Holy Scripture and the gospel? For unless you are very well instructed in the gospel, your meeting with Satan will be disastrous. And the result teaches with what discretion we should make vows.

Furthermore, poverty is demanded of all Christians by divine law, and pertains not only to monks. What is meant, however, is evangelical poverty, not that vulgar mendicancy, but to have one's property in common with all, to bestow gifts, to give to all the needy, and to conduct one's business in such a way that you alleviate another's want. It is not evangelical poverty to possess nothing, but to possess in such a way that you feel that you are acting as an administrator of someone else's property, and not your own. This is what Paul teaches in Eph. 4:28: "But rather let him labor, doing honest work with his hands, so that he may be able to give to those in need." At this point we can also refer to that idea in the Gospel: "Go, sell what you possess and give to the poor" (Matt. 19:21) . For Christ desired that man to be poor in such a way that he might nevertheless give. But now *we* call "poverty" only that state when men receive from others. Do you see how far removed from the Gospel the institution of mendicancy is? For both poverty and taking care of our business are demanded not for our own sakes, but for the sake of the brethren. This is a far cry from approving mendicancy.

Finally, they promise obedience. But each and every one of us owes this by divine law to his parents, his teachers, and magistrates. Therefore, there is no peculiar perfection in the institution of monasticism. But I do not care to dispute about monks now. It is obvious here how Christian is the judgment of those who prefer monasticism to every other kind of human existence. They evaluate Christianity not by the spirit but from the appearance of external works. At one time the monasteries were nothing but schools, and the unmarried scholars voluntarily spent their time there as long as they liked. They had all things in common with their fellow students, and they submitted to and obeyed their teachers freely. They sang, prayed, and discussed matters together. The whole manner of life was not regarded as some peculiar type of Christianity or a state of perfection, as they now speak of it, but rather as a discipline and training for the immature. Would that this were the condition of the monasteries today! If it were, we should have schools that would be holier, and we should have less superstition and godlessness. For in what part of Christianity does Antichrist reign more powerfully than in monastic servitude?

JUDICIAL AND CEREMONIAL LAWS

There remain judicial and ceremonial laws; a compendium is not the place to say very much on these. Judicial laws concerning legal decisions, penalties, and especially public court cases were given to the Hebrew people in Scripture. The New Testament knows nothing of this type of laws because vengeance is forbidden for Christian people, but poverty and sharing of goods are commanded. Public court action is also forbidden, as Paul teaches in I Cor. 6:7: "To have lawsuits at all with one another is defeat for you."

Ceremonial laws were given in regard to sacrificial rites, differences in days, vestments, victims, and other like matters. In them there is undoubtedly a shadowing of the mysteries of the gospel as Hebrews and some passages in Corinthians teach. Prophetic literature bears witness here and there to the same fact. The prophets for the most part have adapted the types of the law to the mysteries of the gospel in an allegorical way. There are many such passages in The Psalms too. Therefore, allegories are to be sought in these laws, but with discretion. For in this realm even the great authors often prattle more absurdly than boys. Only rites and deeds admit of an allegorical interpretation, those made known as signs of other things. For example, the sacrifices of the Levitical priesthood were made known as signs of the priesthood of Christ. Only the man who is thoroughly conversant with all of Scripture will handle allegories successfully. But the spirit will easily judge, and even common sense will tell us how far and in what particulars allegories may be used. And they add not a little to the understanding of the power both of the law and of the gospel, provided that they are handled in an appropriate way. Hebrews shows us this when it compares Aaron with Christ (Heb. 5:4). It is remarkable how clearly it puts Christ before our eyes, how appropriately it teaches what benefits the world has received through Christ and what the priesthood of Christ confers on the human race, that we are not justified in any way except through the priesthood of Christ.

I still must speak on the power and the abrogation of the law, topics especially relevant here. But since this discussion cannot be understood unless the law is compared with the gospel, I shall take up the power and the abrogation of the law below when I speak on the gospel. I shall now add to this topic what ought to be held about human laws.

HUMAN LAWS

Human laws, finally, are the laws established by men. And, as human affairs now are, some of the human laws are civil, and others are pontifical. Civil laws are those which magistrates, princes, kings, and cities sanction in the state. The authority of this type of laws which ought to be acknowledged Paul teaches in Rom. 13:1-3 when he says: "Let every person be subject to the governing authorities. For there is no authority except from God; and those that exist have been instituted by God. Therefore, he who resists the authorities resists what God has appointed; and those who resist will incur judgment. For rulers are not a terror to good conduct, but to bad." For the duty of civil magistrates and laws is nothing else than to punish and prevent wrongs. For this reason, laws are passed concerning the division of property, forms of contract, and penalties for crimes. For the magistrate is a minister of God, a wrathful avenger of the one who has committed a crime. Furthermore, a magistrate is not permitted to make decrees contrary to divine law, and he ought not to be obeyed contrary to divine law, as Acts 5:29 says: "We must obey God rather than men." And from this passage a wise reader will easily judge to what extent we are subject to human laws. But I shall perhaps say more about magistrates below when I treat of the condition of mankind.

What shall I say about pontifical laws? Insofar as priests pass judgment in lawsuits and trials they obviously act as rulers of the world. As for the rest, in that which pertains to lawsuits and trials, the divine law subjects priests themselves to civil magistrates, kings, and rulers. But now with the connivings of the rulers, they have established laws for themselves which are both godless and tyrannical to an outstanding degree, laws concerning immunities of churches, their own revenues, etc. In this matter the duty of love demanded that the wealthiest alleviate the public need by sharing money and expenditures. For they outlaw and curse with dire threats anyone who demands from a priest tribute or tax or any of the other things which are collected from all for the public need. But of this I shall speak at another time. Let it suffice that I have warned that the laws of the priests in civil affairs have been founded contrary to the principles of love and by sheer tyranny.

Neither the universal Church nor priests nor councils have the right to change or decree anything about faith. Articles of faith must be judged simply in accordance with the canon of Holy Scripture. What has been put forth outside Scripture must not be held as an article of faith. In the first place, Paul orders that nothing at all be changed when he says in Gal. 1:9: "If anyone is preaching to you a gospel contrary to that which you received, let him be accursed." Likewise, how can he who differs from Scripture be a spiritual prophet? Rather, he is a lying spirit who makes pronouncements against the truth. I Tim. 6:3 f. says: "If anyone teaches otherwise and does not agree with the sound words of our Lord Jesus Christ, he is puffed up." Furthermore, many things have been godlessly decreed against Scripture; of these I shall speak a little later.

In the next place, Paul in II Tim. 3:14 testifies that nothing beyond Scripture which men, the Church, or a priest has decided must be held as a doctrine of faith: "As for you, continue in what you have learned and have firmly believed, knowing from whom you learned it." He thinks it important to know the source of our learning. Now, how shall we know the source of what men decree if it cannot be accurately weighed according to Scripture? For it is surely agreed that what the Scriptures confirm originated in the Holy Spirit. It is doubtful whether that which has its origin outside Scripture is from the Spirit of God or from a false spirit. Paul enjoins the Thessalonians (I Thess. 5:21): "Test everything; hold fast what is good." And elsewhere he orders that the spirits be tested to see whether they are from God. I ask you how we shall test the spirits unless they are measured against a definite standard, surely that of Scripture; for Scripture alone is definitely agreed to have been established by the Spirit of God. It is unsound to attribute authority to councils in establishing articles of faith, for in the whole assembly of the council there may be no one who has the Spirit of God.

The prophets of Baal were prophesying in Samaria, and the kings of Israel were doing everything in accordance with their oracles. What wonder that ungodly men without the Spirit of God prophesy now also? The priests in Judah were claiming authenticity when they fought against Jeremiah and the Spirit of God saying (Jer. 18:18): "Come, let us make plots against Jeremiah, for the law shall not perish from the priest, nor counsel from the wise, nor the word from the prophet." What difference is there between that and what the Church of the pope says today: "The authority of making decrees is in our power. A council is ruled immediately by the Holy Spirit, and it cannot err. Holy Scripture is ambiguous and obscure; the right and power of interpreting it are ours, along with many such prerogatives." But it was clearly predicted that the rulers of the Church would err (Ezek. 7:26) : "The Law perishes from the priest, and counsel from the elders." And Matt. 24:24 says: "For false Christs and false prophets will arise and show great signs," etc. Furthermore, Scripture indicates that a body of councils having the Spirit of God to a great degree can yet err (Ezek. 14:9) : "And if the prophet be deceived and speak a word, I, the Lord, have deceived that prophet." In I Kings 22:22 we read: "I will go forth, and will be a lying spirit in the mouth of all his prophets." Why say more? Paul says (Gal. 1:16) that he did not confer with flesh and blood. Should we trust in flesh and blood?

Why, I ask, do you believe in the Nicene Synod rather than the one of Ariminum? [66] Is it not true that you do because the authority of the Roman pontiff approved it? By this reasoning you put the authority of the pontiff above both council and Scripture, which is not only godless but also stupid. For why do you approve of the Synod of Antioch [67] which condemned Paul of Samosata because he denied the deity of Christ when the whole condemnation took place without the authority of the Roman pontiff? In the Council of Alexandria,[68] where the question of the three divine Persons was decided against Sabellius, there was not even a mention of the Roman pontiff. The Roman pontiffs are nowhere said to have been present at the Council of Nicaea. The Greek writers on the Synod of Constantinople and that of Ephesus have made no mention of a Roman pontiff, so it is very likely either that none was present or certainly that none presided.[69]

And not rarely mistakes have been made in those synods over which Roman pontiffs have presided. Stephen VI rescinded the acts of Pope Formosus by the authority of a council. John X in turn condemned the decision of Stephen at the Synod of Ravenna.[70] When synods disagree, one must be in error. The Council of Lyons [71] ought to be considered godless, since it approved the books of decretals in which so many cruel, evil things were de-

---

[66] Melanchthon has in mind the synods of Seleucia and Rimini (Ariminum) of 359. Cf. Carl F. Hefele, *Conciliengeschichte*, 2d ed. (Freiburg, 1873), Vol. I, pp. 679 ff.

[67] These Antiochene synods (264–269) dealt with teachings of Paul of Samosata. Cf. Hefele, Vol. I, pp. 135 f.

[68] This synod convened in 362. Cf. Hefele, Vol. I, pp. 727 ff.

[69] Constantinople, 381 (cf. Hefele, Vol. II [1875], pp. 1 ff.) and Ephesus, 431 (cf. Hefele, Vol. II, pp. 178 ff) .

[70] Cf. Hefele, Vol. IV (1879) , pp. 565 ff.

[71] Held in 1245; cf. Hefele, Vol. V (1886) , pp. 1105 ff.

cided. Furthermore, we see that in papal councils almost nothing has been accomplished except what furthers the cause of Roman tyranny: subjugating emperors, maintaining the patrimony of Peter, increasing the wealth of priests, and oppressing the Greek Church. The decree *Ad abolendam*,[72] which deals with heretics, is obviously heretical itself, for it curses all who think or teach otherwise about the sacraments than the Roman Church teaches or practices. For the Greeks are not heretics, and they differ in very many things from the rites and traditions of the Roman Church. Godless decrees have been made about indulgences in many of the councils. The Council of Constance condemned among other things that strongly evangelical teaching of Scripture about the difference in works, namely, every work is either good or bad, not indifferent: "Either make the tree good," etc. (Matt. 12:33).

But why continue thus, since there are extant the abominable codices of pontifical laws from which you may glean as much as you like? We have made note of these things simply to warn you that the common opinion which boasts that councils cannot err has been accepted without proper consideration. Therefore, since it is certainly clearer than the noonday sun both that councils can err and that they have often erred, I ask you, dear reader, why should anything be held as an article of faith which has been decreed by a council without the approval of Scripture? Since it is obvious that councils can err, why are their decrees not scrutinized in the light of Scripture? Far be it from the Christian mind to think that an article of faith is established by a person about whom there is uncertainty as to whether he cannot deceive or err! Peter denies that the interpretation of Scripture is of private, that is, of human, exposition. Shall we permit men to establish the articles of faith? Why not follow the passage of Scripture just cited, and, as Peter says, take heed of the "lamp shining in a dark place" (II Peter 1:19 f.), especially since the prophet denies that the light of dawn will shine for those who do not depend on the judgment of the law and the testimony. This well-known teaching is to be found in Isa. 8:20. A passage of Paul also belongs here, I Cor. 3:11, where he is discussing Christian doctrine: "For no other foundation can anyone lay than that which is laid." This means that no doctrine and no articles are necessary for salvation except Scripture. He says the Day of the Lord will prove the work built on this foundation (vs. 12 f.). But if this must be tested in the Day of the Lord, why is it accepted not only as doctrinal coin of the realm, but even as

[72] This decree was issued by Pope Lucius II against the Waldenses at the Council of Verona, 1184.

necessary for salvation? Decrees have been made about the transubstantiation of the bread into the body of Christ in the Sacrament, and about the primacy of the pope, and all this in contradiction to the decisions of ancient synods. Why should traditions handed down without the definite approval of Scripture be accepted as unquestioned dogmas? In Paul's letters and in the book of Acts the apostles prove their doctrine with the authority of Scripture. Christ evokes faith in himself through the Scriptures when he commands that we search the Scriptures which bear witness to Him (John 5:39) and when he says that the Father supports him, that the testimony of two must be received, and many things of this kind (John 8:16-18). In Deut. 12:32, the Lord commands that nothing should be added to nor taken from his word. This passage clearly teaches that it is wrong for anyone to teach as an article of faith anything that he does not definitely know is the divine word. The prophets, Christ, and the apostles surely knew that what they were teaching was the word of God. Therefore, they wanted themselves, no, rather, what they said, to be believed.

These arguments fully persuade me that nothing must be held as an article of faith which Scripture does not clearly teach. I say this to blast the theologians of Paris, who, in their foolish, godless condemnation of Luther, call the dogmas of the councils and the Schools "The Principles of Faith." [73] I believe the Council of Nicaea concerning the deity of the Son because I believe Scripture, which so clearly proves to us the deity of Christ that not even the Jews, however blind they be, can controvert the fact that Scripture attributes deity to the Messiah. One of many clear passages is Jer. 23:6: "And this is the name by which he will be called, 'The Lord is our righteousness.'" I hold that the other synods also must be evaluated in the light of Scripture.

But shall the Church make decisions on morals and ceremonies? I do not see what either pontiffs or synods have decided about morals unless the papal laws about wars, lawsuits, and celibacy pertain to morals. If these should be measured by the standard of the Gospel, what could have been decided even by the Scythians that would be less pious?

But we shall speak about ceremonies, although the papists think this is their very own domain. In the first place, to include both morals and ceremonies in one bundle, the bishops do not have the right to demand anything beyond what has been handed down in

[73] See *Melanchthons Werke*, Vol. I, pp. 141 ff., for Melanchthon's defense of Luther against the declaration of the theological faculty of the University of Paris.

Holy Scripture. For Christ sent his apostles to teach what he himself had given them. Matt. 28:20 says: "Teaching them to observe all that I have commanded you." He therefore takes away the power of establishing new laws and new rites. Christ commands his apostles to teach nothing but the gospel. How, then, will the bishops prove their right to establish laws? Would it be from the passage where he says: "He who hears you hears me" (Luke 10:16)? But in Matt. 10:41 he wants a prophet to be received because he is a prophet. He does not, therefore, want a false prophet to be received, one who teaches human comments and the traditions of men.

Scripture calls these fellows "dreamers." But I ask you, solons and legislators of the papacy, produce one syllable from the Scriptures which gives you the authority to establish laws. Scripture, on the contrary, takes away that authority when it enjoins that nothing is to be added to nor taken away from the law of God. Paul also denies this power when he calls the bishops of the new covenant "ministers of the Spirit" (II Cor. 3:6). For a minister of the Spirit is one who condemns all hearts through the law of God, and then consoles them again through the gospel; he is powerful because of the Spirit of God. To this function what do human traditions, which judge external works only, contribute? Scripture condemns traditions too often to be considered obscure in its opinion of them. Jeremiah (ch. 23:28) calls them "straw": "What has straw in common with wheat?" He likewise calls them "lying" and "dreams" (v. 32). Isaiah calls them "vomit" and "filthiness" (Isa. 28:8). Ezekiel calls them "harlotries," "asses' members" and "issue from horses" (ch. 23:2-20). Some prophets call them by one name, others by another. Paul calls them "fair and flattering words" (Rom. 16:18). To give here only one more passage from Paul, he indicates the source of human traditions in I Tim. 4:1-3: "In later times some will depart from the faith by giving heed to deceitful spirits and doctrines of demons, through the pretensions of liars whose consciences are seared, who forbid marriage and enjoin abstinence from foods which God created," etc. You see that a deceitful spirit is the author of the traditions about celibacy, the difference in foods, etc. And what are the papal canons but traditions about celibacy, the difference in foods, and similar trifles? Matt. 15:9 says: "In vain do they worship me, teaching as doctrines the precepts of men." Christ's source for this is Isa. 29:13.

What then? How do traditions of men bind consciences? Do they sin who violate the decrees of men? I answer that papal laws must be endured as we endure any injustice or tyranny, in accordance with Matt. 5:41: "If anyone forces you to go one mile, go with him two miles." They are to be endured, however, only insofar as conscience is not endangered by them. Acts 5:29 says: "We must obey God rather than men." When traditions hinder faith, and when they are an occasion for sin, they must be violated. He who violates them without offending his spiritual judgment does not sin. We shall say more of offense later, however. But you have unequivocal passages of Scripture which teach that consciences are not to be bound by human traditions. I Cor. 3:21 f.: "All things are yours, whether Paul or Apollos or Cephas"; that is, neither Paul nor Cephas has the authority to bind your consciences. It says clearly in the same letter (ch. 7:23): "You were bought with a price; do not become slaves of men." But those whose freedom of conscience has been snatched away by traditions become slaves of men. For as Christian freedom is freedom of conscience, so Christian slavery is the enslavement of conscience. Col. 2:20 is a very clear passage: "If with Christ you died to the elemental spirits of the universe, why do you live as if you still belonged to the world? Why do you submit to regulations?" Then he goes on to mimic and repeat their traditions in vs. 21-23: "'Do not handle, Do not taste, Do not touch' (referring to things which all perish as they are used), according to human precepts and doctrines? These indeed have an appearance of wisdom in promoting vigor of devotion and self-abasement and severity to the body, but they are of no value in checking the indulgence of the flesh." In Jer. 23:16 the Lord forbids that false prophets be heard, which doubtlessly must refer to that situation wherein consciences are endangered: "Do not listen to the words of the prophets who prophesy to you, filling you with vain hopes; they speak visions of their own minds, not from the mouth of the Lord." On this point I can refer also to some rather recent authorities who hold my position, especially Gerson. We agree that consciences are not bound by human traditions; that is, he who violates a human tradition does not sin unless he gives occasion for offense. I wish Bernard were a little more liberal on this point in his *De praecepto et dispensatione*.[74] But the Spirit will very definitely judge, according to II Cor. 3:17: "Where the Spirit of the Lord is, there is freedom." I Cor. 2:15 says: "The spiritual man judges all things, but is himself to be judged by no one."

I could review the sort of things which have been established by councils and pontiffs only if I were willing to retrace not only all of canon law but also the whole of church history. But we shall re-

[74] Cf. *MPL*, Vol. 182, cols. 859 ff.

call a few examples of this type of traditions. From these we can come to an understanding of what Scripture so often warns us to be on guard against, that nothing goes so counter to piety as the doctrines of men. At the Council of Nicaea certain kinds of penance were established. I do not want to judge in what spirit the fathers made this decree, but I do see a good part of the gospel, nay rather, the real power of the gospel, obscured by this tradition. For that was the birthplace of "satisfactions." They were perhaps tolerable at first when the understanding of the gospel within the Church was still rather pure. But a little later, what a torture of consciences did those satisfactions become! Grace was obscured. What the gospel attributes to faith began to be attributed to satisfactions, and what is more godless or pernicious? And the Council of Nicaea certainly gave occasion for these evils. How much better it would have been to follow the example of Paul in the forms of penance. Without any "satisfaction," he accepted that Corinthian adulterer when he came to his senses, simply warning him that reproof is sufficient (II Cor. 2:6). Moreover, the so-called theologians of our times, following the ancient tradition of the Council of Nicaea, have made satisfactions a part of penance. Obviously, there is no other error more harmful than this.

What trouble for the consciences even of the pious has that papal confession made? How many thousands of souls has it alone destroyed! Paul wanted to warn the Corinthians that the adulterer not be afflicted with too much remorse. But what do the Roman pontiffs who invented confession do but vex fearful and truly pious consciences in a most miserable and cruel way?

When Christianity is rent into so many ways of living, what do Christian love and simplicity matter? Some are laymen, others are monks, and still others are clerics. Among these are innumerable parties, and they could perhaps be tolerated if there were not such strife in their status-seeking. Then the intolerable burden of celibacy has been added to certain modes of life. Also, this decree on celibacy was enacted at the Council of Nicaea. The results of that tradition need no mentioning, for by no other counsel could common lust be more freely engaged in. In I Cor., ch. 7, where Paul discusses virginity, he does not dare to command anything lest he cast a snare on them (v. 25). He wishes the course to be chosen in which they can give their "undivided devotion to the Lord" (v. 35). But who are less devoted, who are more vehemently torn away from God than those whom the fires of the flesh inflame? Foreseeing this, Paul does not enjoin celibacy. Rather, when writing to Timothy (I Tim. 4:1), he calls the tradition of celibacy a "doctrine of demons." But Satan conquered, and his law has been accepted and promulgated among many thousands of people to the detriment of Christianity.

And now the Eucharist has been relegated to a particular class of people, the priests. Christ, who wishes to be in communion with all the pious, is now usurped by the priests alone; thus the benefits of the Mass and the power of the Eucharist are utterly obscured. The Eucharist is now nothing else than a trafficking of priests. For Satan has discovered that priests ought to sacrifice in place of the people, that Masses can be sold publicly, and other things of this kind. The use of the Mass would not have perished if the conditions of life had not been rent into those of priests and laymen. O the horrible and abominable godlessness that reigns today in the papal Masses!

But why continue? You can see from these examples that there has been no tradition, pious though it be in appearance, which has not wrought great evil for Christianity. For what seems more fitting than that there be in the Church satisfactions for public misdeeds? But those satisfactions have obscured grace. What is more proper than that bishops live in celibacy? But through celibacy lusts have been released. What is more reverent (for thus men judge, not the Spirit) than restricting the use of the Eucharist? But thus the benefits of the Mass have perished. So it happens that traditions have a certain appearance of wisdom, but that very appearance, that rouge used by wicked, disgraceful Jezebel, is the very thing that does the damage (Rev. 2:20).

THE GOSPEL

So far we have discussed the nature of sin and of laws, perhaps too briefly considering their importance. We are not writing a commentary, however, but are sketching a common outline of the topics that you can pursue in your study of Holy Scripture. Now we shall discuss the gospel and grace, and from the treatment of these topics some light will be shed also on what has gone before. For the discussion concerning the abrogation of the law and the power of the law has been reserved for this particular topic. Furthermore, just as one cannot understand the nature of sin apart from explicit laws, neither can the power of grace be understood except by a description of the gospel. Up to this time we have discussed the condemnation and curse of man; now we shall take up the restoration and blessing of man.

Generally speaking, there are two parts to Scripture, law and gospel. The law shows sin, the gospel grace. The law indicates disease, the gospel points out the remedy. To use Paul's words, the law is the minister of death, the gospel is the minister of life and peace: "The power of sin is the Law" (I Cor. 15:56) , but the gospel is the power of salvation to every one who has faith (Rom. 1:16) . Nor has the Scripture so given us law and gospel that you should think that only that is gospel which Matthew, Mark, Luke, and John have written, and that the books of Moses are nothing but law. But the presentation of the gospel is scattered, and the promises are sprinkled throughout all the books of the Old and New Testaments. On the other hand, law also is scattered in all the books of both the Old and New Testaments. Contrary to common opinion, history is not divided up into some periods of law only, other periods of gospel only. Sometimes law has been revealed immediately followed by the gospel; at other times they have been revealed in another way. Every age known to us is a time of law and a time of gospel just as men have been justified in all ages in the same way: sin has been revealed through the law, and grace through the promise of the gospel. Times of revelation vary, for at one time the law was revealed, and at another time the gospel, and from time to time they were revealed in different ways, a fact established from Scripture. For you can see that in addition to natural law, which in my opinion was engraved on human minds, were also disclosed by God to Adam, e.g., that he not taste the fruit of the tree of knowledge of good and evil. To Cain, God gave the command that he not be angry with his brother, and God also told him that whoever killed him would be committing sin. In this way the Spirit of God was restoring the knowledge of natural law by constant proclamation. This knowledge of law was already being so darkened in human minds blinded by sin that I might almost call natural law not some innate judgment, implanted and engraved by nature on the minds of men, but simply the laws received by the fathers and handed down from time to time to posterity. Adam, for instance, taught his descendants about the creation of things, about worshiping God, and warned Cain that he not kill his brother, etc. But let us return to the gospel.

What Is the Gospel?

Just as the law is that portion of Scripture in which upright actions are enjoined and sin is revealed, so the gospel is the promise of the grace or mercy of God, especially the forgiveness of sins and the testimony of God's goodwill toward us. Because of this message, our minds, assured of God's goodwill, believe that all guilt has been pardoned. Encouraged, they love and praise God, rejoice and exult in God, as we shall discuss below under "The Power of the Gospel." Furthermore, Christ is the pledge of all those promises. Therefore, all Scripture promises are to be related to him, who was dimly revealed at first, but more clearly as time went on.

After Adam had sinned and been destined for eternal death, he would undoubtedly have perished had not the Lord consoled him with the promise of grace. The tyranny of sin is described when God says to the serpent in Gen. 3:15: "I will put enmity between you and the woman, and between your seed and her seed." And immediately victory is promised: "He shall bruise your head." For in my judgment the pronoun in this passage is more correctly taken to refer to the seed than to the woman as we read in our texts. This is the first promise, the first gospel; by this Adam was raised up and he conceived a definite hope of his salvation. Moreover, he was even justified. Then the promise was made to Abraham that in his seed all the nations would be blessed (Gen. 12:3). This promise could not be understood, certainly, except as referring to Christ. He is the bosom of Abraham into which those who have been saved are received. In other words, those are saved who have believed the promise made to Abraham. And this is the promise which the writings of the New Testament mention everywhere. The careful reader will be able to group all promises concerning Christ under this topic: they are obviously nothing else than the gospel. Deut. 18:18 f. says: "I will raise up for them a prophet like you from among their brethren; and I will put my words in his mouth, and he shall speak to them all that I command him. And whoever will not give heed to my words which he shall speak in my name, I myself will require it of him." In II Sam. 7:12 f. Christ is promised to David: "I will raise up your son after you, who shall come forth from your body, and I will establish his kingdom. He shall build a house for my name, and I will establish the throne of his kingdom forever." Because of this promise, the prophets call Christ the "Son of David." More than that, Ezekiel even calls him "David" (Ezek. 34:23 f.; 37:24 f.). The prophets in general both repeat the law and promise Christ. And it will profit a pious mind to note the divine promises and have them on immediate call because they are remarkably effective for strengthening and encouraging the conscience.

In the way described, God revealed the gospel immediately after the fall of Adam, and from time to time he disclosed it more fully until he sent forth Christ. That is what Paul writes in Rom. 1:2 f.: "The gospel concerning his Son . . . which he promised beforehand through his prophets in the Holy Scriptures." And our Gospels do nothing but testify that the promises have been fulfilled. This is the reason why Matthew begins thus: "The book of the genealogy of Jesus Christ, the son of David, the son of Abraham." I call the gospel the promise of the grace, blessing, and favor of God through Christ. There are in Scripture besides this promise of eternal blessing also promises of temporal things. Of this kind is the one made to Noah, and there are more of this type in the law, concerning land, wealth, etc. These are not only symbolic of spiritual promises, but are per se testimonies of the grace and mercy of God. They are meant to console and encourage our consciences in such a way that they glorify God. And we shall surely discuss these promises below under "Faith: What It Is and How It Justifies."

You can see the design of the Holy Spirit in Scripture—how sweetly and charmingly he instructs the devout with only one purpose, that we be saved. The whole of Scripture is in some parts law, in others gospel. The books of Moses in some sections propound the law, in others the gospel, and moreover the gospel is concealed in the very law itself. For what can you find more evangelical than that promise which the Spirit of God added as the etiology of the First Commandment: "Showing steadfast love to thousands of those who love me and keep my commandments" (Deut. 5:10)? And see how suddenly Moses is transformed from lawgiver to evangelist, that is, a herald of grace and mercy, when he says in Ex. 34:6 f.: "The Lord, the Lord, a God merciful and gracious, slow to anger and abounding in steadfast love and faithfulness, keeping steadfast love for thousands, forgiving iniquity and transgression and sin, but who will by no means clear the guilty." Try to find a more evangelical passage in the whole New Testament. In this way the books of Moses teach law in one place, gospel in another. I am not talking at all now about figures of speech but about that which the text obviously declares. For figurative language warrants special study. Historical narratives in Scripture are examples sometimes of the law, at other times of the gospel. The terrible case of Saul definitely points to the law. The case of David relates to the gospel, for though he had wronged another man's wife, he nevertheless gained grace. And that declaration of the prophet in II Sam. 12:13 was plainly the voice of the gospel: "The Lord has put away your sin; you shall not die."

One must analyze similar examples in this way. The prophets teach law when they rail at hypocrisy, godlessness, carelessness, and other things of this type. For while they denounce hidden vices or hypocrisy to the utmost, they also proclaim the gospel when they raise up, animate, and fill the tottering conscience with their very lively promises about Christ. This they do in such a way that the apostle's question plainly sounds forth: "Who shall separate us from the love of Christ?" (Rom. 8:35). The Gospels of Matthew, Mark, Luke, and John likewise expound sometimes law, and sometimes gospel, and in them are examples of both the love and the wrath of God. The cases of Zacchaeus, the centurion, and the Syrophoenician woman witness to God's mercy. The blindness and anger of the Pharisees testify to the wrath of God. The narratives of the apostles, however, differ from those of the Old Testament in that they testify of the revealed Christ whom the more ancient authors had merely foretold. Therefore, the New Testament promises of grace, righteousness, and eternal life explain things more clearly than the books of Moses or the writings of the prophets. The apostle Paul instructively compares the gospel with the law and sin with grace, especially in the letter to the Romans, which I think is a touchstone and a measuring stick of all Scripture. Since the other letters are paraenetic for the most part, they pertain to the law, although there is not one in which he does not somewhere touch on arguments for the gospel. A careful reader will notice this for himself.

We have called special attention to these matters in order that we might root out that common error which the godless Sophist professors of theology have spread abroad on the differences between law and gospel, and the Old Testament and the New. They say that Christ has become the successor of Moses and has given a new law, and that this new law is called the gospel; it is found, they say, in Matt., chs. 5 to 6. For them the difference between the law of Moses and the law of Christ is that the former demands external works only, whereas Christ's law makes demands on the inner man also. As if Moses' law teaches some kind of hypocrisy and Pharisaic righteousness! For what else is this pretense of outward works than Pharisaism? Moreover, let even the prophets bear witness that the Mosaic law makes demands on the inner man. Often they enjoin the people to acknowledge God, to fear him, to make a decision, and to do justice. Perhaps the Sophists will grant that the prophets taught these things before the incarnation of Christ and before the men of his times. For what is more obvious than the fact that the following statement of Jeremiah is to be related to the law of Moses, whether the Sophists will it or not? "For the day that I brought them out of the land of Egypt, I did not speak to your fathers or command them concerning burnt offerings and sacrifices; but this command I gave them, 'Obey my voice, and I will be your God, and you shall be my people' " (Jer. 7:22 f.) . Tell me, Thomas, what has entered your mind that you should teach that the Mosaic law exacts nothing but Pharisaism, that is, external works? [75] How can you do this when even Moses so often discusses the inner life in no uncertain terms? To pass over many passages, does he not forbid the coveting of the property of another, etc., in Ex. 20:17? He had already forbidden the deed when he gave the commandments prohibiting stealing and adultery. You will grant, therefore, that he is warning about the inner man in these words: "You shall not covet your neighbor's house; you shall not covet your neighbor's wife or his manservant, etc." (Ex. 20:17) . Deut. 10:12 f. says: "And now, Israel, what does the Lord your God require of you, but to fear the Lord your God, to walk in all his ways, to love him, to serve the Lord your God with all your heart and with all your soul, and to keep the commandments and statutes of the Lord, which I command you this day for your good?" And again (Deut. 10:16) : "Circumcise therefore the foreskin of your heart, and be no longer stubborn." Since you could find six hundred passages like this in the Pentateuch, it is very clear that Moses demands both the heart and works.

In like manner, Christ expounds law, for grace cannot be preached without law. He finds fault with the interpretation of the scribes and the Pharisees when at the beginning of the Sermon on the Mount he says that we shall not enter the Kingdom of Heaven unless our righteousness exceeds that of the scribes and Pharisees (Matt. 5:20) . The Pharisees thought the commandment "You shall not kill" was fulfilled if murder by physical violence was not committed. They held that the commandment "You shall not commit adultery" was kept if one did not wrong the wife of another. Christ teaches that an inner disposition is demanded by the law, not only the external pretense of works, for the law prohibits covetousness. The law also forbade vengeance, and, more than that, it demanded that we love our enemies. Lev. 19:17 f. reads: "You shall not hate your brother in your heart, but you shall reason with your neighbor, lest you bear sin because of him. You shall not take vengeance or bear any grudge against the sons of your own people, but you shall love your neighbor as yourself." I do not know why Jerome preferred to change the word to "friend," for thus our texts read, while the Hebrew word has more the meaning of "relative," and

---

[75] Cf. Carl Mirbt, *Quellen zur Geschichte des Papsttums*, 4th edition (Tübingen, 1924) , p. 112.

the LXX interpreters have changed it to "neighbor." Paul follows them in Rom. 13:9 where he cites this precept from the law. The summary of this passage in Moses is as follows: the Jews are to love each other, both friends and enemies, and they are to treat well even those deserving ill. In this context belongs Isa., ch. 58, which is clearly against vengeance and demands love even for enemies. In Prov. 20:22 we read: "Do not say, 'I will repay evil'; wait for the Lord, and he will help you."

Now, you would never, as far as I know, find in the law these words: "You shall hate your enemy." Therefore, it is sufficiently clear that Christ did not refer to the law as such, but to the Pharisaic tradition, to condemn it. The Jews had received the command to destroy the Canaanites (Ex. 23:23-33). Some think Christ alludes to this passage when he states that a word has previously been given about avenging ourselves on our enemies (Matt. 5:43). If this is true, it looks as if Christ meant the following: now that the gospel had been revealed, and the middle wall of partition had been broken down, as Paul says (Eph. 2:14), and the distinction between Jews and Gentiles had been done away with and erased, there would be changes; just as the Jews had been commanded to love Jews, both friends and enemies, so we were to love both Gentiles and Jews, both friends and enemies. But what of the fact that the command to Israel was about Canaanites only? What of the fact that they are ordered to love foreigners also? Relevant here is the decree concerning interest: interest is to be charged outsiders, but not relatives. Since none are outsiders now, but all are relatives, interest is universally prohibited.

It cannot be denied that Christ changed some things in the law, for instance, the matter of divorce. Moreover, although the Jews were commanded to defend their legal rights with the sword, Christ does not command that the Gospel be defended with arms. On the contrary, he says to Peter: "Put your sword back into its place; for all who take the sword will perish by the sword" (Matt. 26:52). In spite of these examples, it is not the primary or proper office of Christ to establish the law, but to bestow grace. Moses is the legislator and the judge; Christ is the Savior, as he testifies concerning himself in John 3:17: "God sent the Son into the world not to condemn the world, but that the world might be saved through him." The law condemns because we by ourselves cannot satisfy it. On believers Christ bestows grace to forgive sin. Often, to be sure, Christ also preaches law, because without law sin cannot be recognized, and unless we experience sin, we shall not understand the power and fullness of grace. Therefore, both law and gospel ought to be preached at the same time, and both sin and grace ought to be made clear. There were two cherubim placed on the Ark, the law and the gospel; therefore, it is impossible to teach correctly or fruitfully either gospel without law or law without gospel. And just as Christ joined law with gospel, so did the prophets join gospel with law. You have examples of this also in the sermons of the apostles in the book of Acts. The same holds true in a remarkable degree in all the letters of Paul, in which he usually discourses first on the nature of the gospel and later gives exhortations.

The Power of the Law

We have said that gospel is not law, but the promise of grace. Now it is our task to teach what the power of the law is as well as that of the gospel. For from this consideration we shall be able to recognize, to some extent, the difference between law and gospel. In the first place, Scripture differs from human reason in its view of the power of the law. Scripture calls law "the power of anger," "the power of sin," "the scepter of the avenger," "lightning," "thunder." Human reason calls it "a corrector of crimes" and "an instructor in living." For Cicero employs such language when he speaks of laws. And nothing is more commonly celebrated than the praise of laws, so that Paul could seem to the flesh even to be mad when he calls law "the power of sin." Accordingly, the Jews, when they profess themselves disciples of Moses, are unwilling to acknowledge Christ (John 9:28). Therefore, in order to discuss the power of law in precise fashion, let us compare two classes of men.

In the first class are those who understand the law carnally; these blind fellows do not realize that the law demands impossible things, and they see neither sin, law, nor righteousness. These are the hypocrites and Sophists of all ages. Paul calls the righteousness of this class "righteousness by works of law." He means the righteousness of those who, when they hear the law, set out to keep it by their own works. They give over their hands, feet, and head to the law, but their heart they keep back. For actually they would prefer to be without the law, however holy they appear to be in their own eyes. Pleasures, wealth, and honor are still pleasing to them. No one has declared better than the Spirit of God what sort of people they are. In the first place, they lack faith, that is, their heart understands nothing of God, and, as Scripture says, does not seek after God; it does not glorify God, but despises him. Therefore, they go astray, according to Ps. 14:3; that is to say that since they do not fear God nor trust him, they veer away toward their own ideas, by means of which, in their despisal of God, they make a way for themselves either to wealth or positions of dignity. Furthermore, they even try to justify themselves by their own works, and Scripture often berates such workers of iniquity. In Ps. 5:9 David describes the hypocrites in this way: "There is no truth in their mouth; their heart is destruction, their throat is an open sepulcher." For this type of man, the law furnishes no problem. Since they live in a false, carnal interpretation of the law, the law cannot accomplish in them what it ought. But they fashion idols for themselves from the law, images of men,[76] and semblances of the carnal virtues. For they are drawn to simulate good works by some carnal passion, either by fear of punishment or by desire for the convenient; since they do not see the sickness of their soul, they are secure in their stupidity.

The haughtiness, pride, stubbornness, and self-love of this class are incredible. They come so far from satisfying the law that none are farther. Of this class is that Pharisee in Luke 18:11 who says: "I am not like other men." Isa. 28:15 describes the drunkards of Ephraim: "We have made a covenant with death, and with Sheol we have an agreement." Jer. 6:15: "They did not know how to blush." Matt. 7:23: "Evildoers." Paul says he was of this sort before he was converted. Rom. 7:9: "I was once alive apart from the law," that is, there was a time when I thought I fulfilled the law in an outstanding way, when I outstripped all my peers in the hypocrisy of works, for at that time the law did not convict, accuse, or condemn me. And such indeed are all men who attempt, by the powers of nature, to portray the law in accordance with the grasp of reason, since they understand neither the law nor their own strength. And these are the people who contemplate only the back and the veiled countenance of Moses. This is what Paul means in II Cor. 3:13 ff., where he says that evangelical righteousness cannot be understood by the Jews because they look upon Moses with a veiled heart: they do not see by the law what the law demands and how we are nothing but sin and a curse.

So far do I write on those who try fulfilling the law by their natural strength in accordance with the faculty of human reason. Everyone will be able to judge from his heart what sort they are. To such men these sayings of Paul do not properly apply: the law is the power of wrath and of sin, the servant of death, etc. Nevertheless, the law condemns also them because they make of it an idol and do everything with a certain indescribable pride and vexation of heart.

[76] Cf. Ezek. 16:17.

In the other class are those to whom the following passages apply: the law is the power of sin, of wrath, etc. God reveals to them the law, shows them their hearts, and terrifies and confuses them with a realization of their own sin. In a word, these are the ones in whom God works through the law. Among hypocrites the law does nothing, but they fashion a shadowy imitation of the law by their simulated, hypocritical righteousness. The law truly and properly works in those to whom sin is revealed. Because this really takes place, it is done by God, and Scripture calls this work "judgment," "the wrath of God," "the anger of God," his "glance" and "countenance of wrath," etc. Ps. 97:2-5: "Righteousness and justice are the foundation of his throne. Fire goes before him, and burns up his adversaries round about. His lightnings lighten the world; the earth sees and trembles. The mountains melt like wax before the Lord, before the Lord of all the earth." Ps. 76:8: "From the heavens thou didst utter judgment; the earth feared and was still." Zech. 2:13: "Be silent, all flesh, before the Lord." Isa. 11:4: "He shall smite the earth with the rod of his mouth, and with the breath of his lips he shall slay the wicked." Hab. 3:6: "He looked and shook the nations; then the eternal mountains were scattered."

But why pile up many passages, since the law is obviously one part of Scripture, and the work of the law is to kill and to damn, to reveal the root of our sin, and to perplex us? It mortifies not only avarice and desire, but the root of all evils, our love of self, the judgment of reason, and whatever good our nature seems to possess. From this it will be apparent how the moral virtues stink, and how the righteousness of the saints is nothing but dirty, bloody rags. Therefore, it was fitting that even Moses exclaimed in Ex. 34:7 that before God not even the innocent is innocent. Nahum 1:3: "He will by no means clear the guilty." David says in Ps. 143:2: "Enter not into judgment with thy servant." Ps. 6:1: "O Lord, rebuke me not in thy anger." In Isa. 38:13, Hezekiah says: "Like a lion he breaks all my bones." John says with his characteristic succinctness: "The law was given through Moses; grace and truth came through Jesus Christ" (John 1:17). Truth is opposed to hypocrisy, and grace to the anger of God. Through Jesus Christ, grace (that is, the mercy and favor of God) and true righteousness are born in our hearts. Therefore, it follows that the law is the author of hypocrisy only when it forces those who are unwilling and raging against God; it produces wrath when it condemns us as guilty sinners.

In Rom. 7:7, where Paul discusses the power of the law most thoroughly, he writes: "If it had not been for the law, I should not

have known sin. I should not have known what it is to covet if
the law had not said, 'You shall not covet.'" Likewise in Rom.
3:20 he says: "Through the law comes knowledge of sin," as if he
would say that hypocrites are falsely persuaded that righteousness
is wrought by law, since the law simply shows the heart its sin.
Next: "But sin, finding opportunity in the commandment,
wrought in me all kinds of covetousness" (Rom. 7:8). That is,
when I began to realize the burden of the law, nothing positive
was effected by it; as a result, my coveting, stirred up even more,
began to rage against the judgment and the will of God. For "apart
from the law sin lies dead" (v. 8), that is, unless the law had
shown me the sin in my heart, unless a sense of sin had throughly
terrified me, sin would have died and would not have boiled up.
For "I was once alive apart from the law" (v. 9). There was a time
when I seemed righteous to myself, for I did not see the law or
even sin. When I was in that condition, sin was slumbering and
did not openly fight against God. "But when the commandment
came, sin revived and I died" (v. 9). That is, when God had shown
me my sin by means of the law, sin was resuscitated; I was thrown
into confusion, terrified, horror-stricken—in a word, "I died." It
was precisely then that I saw what the power of the law is. Certainly the law was given that we might live, but since we are not
able to keep it, it is an instrument of death. Finally, why is it that
the law slays? The law is spiritual, that is, it demands spiritual
things—truth, faith glorifying God, love for God. But I am carnal,
unbelieving, without knowledge of God, senseless, loving myself,
etc.

Nowhere did the apostle Paul treat of the power and nature of
the law so fully as in the passage we have cited; I see nothing left
out in it. There is no obscurity, nothing entangled, and all things
are plain and open; as to his meaning, there can be no doubt. If
a studious reader of the Scripture wishes, let him add to this passage as supporting evidence those sections which are scattered
throughout the other letters.

I Cor. 15:56 says: "The sting of death is sin, and the power of
sin is the law." For sin would not confound and terrify us unless
it were shown to us by the law. Moreover, sin would not be powerful were it not revealed and stirred up through the law. So neither
would death be powerful unless the law terrified us with the work
and power of sin. II Cor. 3:5 f. distinguishes the law from the
Spirit in this way: "Our sufficiency is from God, who has qualified
us to be ministers of a new covenant, not in a written code but in
the Spirit; for the written code kills, but the Spirit gives life." The

next two verses teach more clearly what is meant by Spirit and written code: "Now if the dispensation of death, carved in letters on stone, came with such splendor that the Israelites could not look at Moses' faces because of its brightness, fading as this was, why should not the dispensation of the Spirit be attended with greater splendor?" (II Cor. 3:7-8). The law is the dispensation of death; after it has revealed and shown sin, it confounds, terrifies, and slays the conscience. The gospel is the dispensation of the Spirit, as we shall show later; it consoles, encourages, animates, and makes alive minds that before were quaking.

In Gal., ch. 3, after the apostle in a long discussion has taught that righteousness is not attained by the help of only the law, he adds the question which seems justifiable: "Why then the law?" (v. 19). That is, if it was of no help in attaining righteousness, I ask what use it was. "It was added because of transgressions," he answers (v. 19), that is, in order that sin might be increased. For knowledge of sin causes sin to increase, both because it rages more implacably when it is restrained, and because nature indignantly bears its being confounded, and rages against divine judgment.

Many of the types in Scripture [77] also teach that this is the power of the law. In Ex., ch. 19, when God was about to give the law, the people were extremely terrified by thunder, smoke, lightning, clouds, the blast of a trumpet, and all kinds of terrible spectacles (Ex. 19:16-18). All of these designate the terrors of a stricken conscience. Or is not the voice of the people the voice of a shaken conscience when they say: "Let not God speak to us, lest we die" (ch. 20:19)? In a remarkable way Moses alleviates the people's consternation, not now as the servant of the law but as an evangelist when he says: "Do not fear; for God has come to prove you, and that the fear of him may be before your eyes, that you may not sin" (v. 20). O voice of Moses, clearly containing the gospel! Unless the conscience hears this, how will it bear that horrible countenance of the Judge? But we shall speak more of the consolation of the gospel hereafter.

Presently that light shone from the face of Moses so that the eyes of the people were blinded. This was the reason that thereafter he did not show himself to the people unless his face was veiled. For human minds or eyes do not endure the splendor of divine light.

In a word, the lightning and flames on the mountain and the splendor in the face of Moses clearly indicate, to speak in Pauline language, the glory of God by which he confounds the human heart. The judgment of God is that knowledge of sin. For

[77] *Typi scripturae* = figurative or symbolical passages.

this reason, let the attritions of the Sophists and their pretended contritions give way, as well as the seared consciences of hypocrites. Here, God looks at the depths of the heart. That human reason sees its own sin is so far from the truth that it is proper even for the saints and those filled with the Spirit to pray confessing their ignorance. David exclaims: "Who can discern his errors?" (Ps. 19: 12). Ps. 25:7: "Remember not the sins of my youth." David says many more things like this elsewhere. In Jer. 17:9 it says that the heart is deceitful and corrupt, and in the following verse we read: "I the Lord search the mind and try the heart." Jer. 31:18 f.: "Thou hast chastened me, and I was chastened like an untrained calf; bring me back, that I may be restored, for thou art the Lord my God. For after I had turned away I repented; and after I was instructed, I smote upon my thigh. I was ashamed, and I was confounded because I bore the disgrace of my youth." And who is there who thinks he has fulfilled the law, since Christ commands in Matt. 16:24 that we should deny our very selves? To sum up, the proper work of the law is the revealing of sin, or, to put it more clearly, the bringing about of a consciousness of sin; Paul calls it the "bond which stood against us with its legal demands" (Col. 2:14). For thus Paul defines conscience both more elegantly and more exactly than the Sophist writers of *Sentences* who conjure up numerous practical syllogisms when they describe the word "conscience." [78] For what else is the consciousness of sin than the judgment of the law revealing the sin in our heart? For that is what Paul says in Col. 2:14: "The bond which stood against us with its legal demands." He means that the conscience is a bond, a bond with legal demands because through legal demands, through the law, it stands against us.

You understand that the work of the law is the revealing of sin. Furthermore, when I speak of sin, I include all kinds of sin— external, internal, hypocrisy, unbelief, love of self, and contempt for or ignorance of God—which are certainly the very roots of all human works. And in the justification of sinners the first work of God is to reveal our sin: to confound our conscience, make us tremble, terrify us, briefly, to condemn us, as the example just cited from Jeremiah indicates. Paul says in Gal. 2:19: "For I through the law died to the law." David, undone by the reproach of the prophet, cries out in II Sam. 12:13: "I have sinned against

[78] *Syllogismus practicus* is a conclusion drawn from an action (practice); for example: God's blessing follows upon a good act. According to Scholastic teaching, "conscience" is a *habitus motivus et cognitivus,* a motivated and cognitive disposition or attitude of mind and, as such, practical intellect (*intellectus practicus*).

the Lord." I Kings 21:27 tells us that "Ahab . . . rent his clothes," etc., "and went about dejectedly" as the Scripture puts it. In II Chron. 33:12 it is written of Manasseh that "he was in distress," for I must use here the term of Scripture. And in Acts 2:37 it says that those who heard "were cut to the heart." Let this suffice to show that the beginning of repentance consists of that work of the law by which the Spirit of God terrifies and confounds consciences. For nature per se cannot even recognize the filth of sin, to say nothing of being able to hate it. "For the unspiritual man does not receive the gifts of the Spirit of God" (I Cor. 2:14). Rom. 8:5: "For those who live according to the flesh set their minds on the things of the flesh." The Sophists discuss the beginning of repentance in the fourth (and last) book of the *Sentences*,[79] but we have done so here in the vestibule, as it were, of our work. For the putting to death, the judgment, and the confounding of the sinner, wrought by the Spirit of God through the law, begin the justification and moreover the genuine baptism of man. And for this reason, just as the Christian life must certainly begin with the knowledge of sin, so Christian doctrine must begin with the function of the law.

It is not worthwhile to argue whether this fear is a servile or a so-called filial fear. Let us leave discussions of that type to idle minds. But many dispute on this question in such a way that it is quite clear they do not know what either servile or filial fear is. Certain it is that no one can be moved to hate sin except by the Holy Spirit; it is likewise sure that those so terrified flee the face of God and the sight of him unless they are so drawn back, recalled, and strengthened by the Spirit of God that they cry out with Paul: "What shall I do, Lord?" (Acts 22:10). That those terrified by the law flee the sight of God, history teaches in Ex. 20:19 when the people call upon Moses, saying: "Let not God speak to us, lest we die." David says in Ps. 139:7: "Whither shall I go from thy Spirit? Or whither shall I flee from thy presence?" The Scriptures abound with many testimonies on this topic; I have deemed it sufficient to have sounded the foregoing warning in order that the distinction between law and gospel may be more definitely maintained. But you can see what a difference there is between a simulated and a true repentance.

[79] In the *Books of Sentences* of Peter Lombard, the last (or fourth) book is devoted to a discussion of the sacraments (including, of course, the sacrament of penance). Accordingly, the Scholastics dealt with the sacraments at the end of their *summae*.

The Power of the Gospel

Those whom conscience has terrified in this manner would most surely be driven to despair, the usual condition of the condemned, if they were not lifted up and encouraged by the promise of the grace and mercy of God, commonly called the gospel. If the afflicted conscience believes the promise of grace in Christ, it is resuscitated and quickened by faith, as the following examples will reveal wonderfully.

In Gen., ch. 3, the sin, repentance, and justification of Adam are described. After Adam and Eve had sinned and were looking for coverings for their nakedness—for we hypocrites have the habit of relieving our consciences by making amends [80]—they were called to account by the Lord; but his voice was unbearable. Under these conditions neither coverings nor pretexts excused their sin. Convicted and guilty, the conscience lies prostrate when it is directly confronted with sin through the voice of God. They flee, and Adam explains the cause of their flight when he says: "I heard the sound of thee in the garden, and I was afraid, because I was naked" (Gen. 3:10). Note the confession and the acknowledgment by the conscience. In the meantime, Adam eats his heart out in grief until he hears the promise of mercy, the word spoken about his wife that her seed would bruise the serpent's head (Gen. 3:15). Even that the Lord clothed them did something to strengthen their consciences, and is unmistakably a sign of the incarnation of Christ. For it is that flesh which in the last analysis covers our nakedness and destroys the confusion of trembling consciences on which the insults of the reproachful have fallen (Ps. 69).

We recalled before how David was undone by the voice of the prophet Nathan. And he certainly would have perished if he had not at once heard the gospel: "The Lord also has put away your sin; you shall not die" (II Sam. 12:13). Some think that only allegories are to be looked for in the narratives of the Old Testament, but here you see how much you can learn from this one example of David if you consider only the literal meaning. In fact this alone is to be considered, for by it the Spirit of God has richly shown us the works both of his wrath and of his mercy. What more evangelical expression can be conceived of than this: "The Lord has put away your sin"? Is this not the sum of the gospel or of the preaching of the New Testament: Sin has been taken away? You may add to these examples many stories from the gospels. Luke 7:37-50 tells of the sinful woman who washes the feet of the Lord;

[80] *Per satisfactiones nostras.*

he consoles her with these words: "Your sins are forgiven" (v. 48).
And what is better known than the story in Luke, ch. 15, of the
prodigal son, who confesses his sin? How lovingly his father receives, embraces, and kisses him! In Luke 5:8 Peter, stunned by
the miracle and, what is more, struck in his heart, exclaims: "Depart from me, for I am a sinful man, O Lord." Christ consoles and
restores him by saying: "Do not be afraid," etc. (v. 10). From
these examples I believe it can be understood what the difference
is between law and gospel, and what the power of the gospel is as
well as that of the law. The law terrifies; the gospel consoles. The
law is the voice of wrath and death; the gospel is the voice of peace
and life, and to sum up, "the voice of the bridegroom and the
voice of the bride," as the prophet says (Jer. 7:34). And he who is
thus encouraged by the voice of the gospel and trusts God is already justified; on this I shall soon say more. Christians well know
how much joy and gladness that consolation brings. And here belong those happy words the prophets use to describe Christ and
the Church. Isa. 32:18: "My people will abide in a peaceful habitation, in secure dwellings, and in quiet resting places." Isa. 51:3:
"Joy and gladness will be found in her, thanksgiving and the voice
of song." Jer. 33:6: "I will . . . reveal to them abundance of
prosperity and security." Jer. 33:9: "And this city shall be to me a
name of joy, a praise and a glory before all the nations of the
earth." Zeph. 3:9: "I will change the speech of the peoples to a
pure speech, that all of them may call on the name of the Lord."
Ps. 21:6: "Thou dost make him glad with the joy of thy presence,"
etc. Ps. 97:11: "Light dawns for the righteous, and joy for the upright in heart."

But why heap up arguments when it is obvious from the promulgation of the law and the advent of Christ what the power of both
law and gospel is? Thus Ex., ch. 19, describes with what a horrifying spectacle the law was given, and we have just reviewed this
above. For just as the Lord terrified Israel at that time, so the consciences of individuals are tormented by the voice of the law, and
they exclaim along with Israel: "Let not God speak to us, lest we
die" (Ex. 20:19). The law demands the impossible, and the conscience, convicted of sin, is assailed from all directions. In this condition, dread and confusion so trouble the conscience that no
remedy appears anywhere unless the very One who cast it down
raises it up. Some seek consolation by their own strength, efforts,
works, and acts of appeasement. But these do not accomplish any
more than Adam accomplished with his fig leaves. So are those who
array themselves against sin in the power of their own will (*arbi-*

trium). The actual facts teach that they soon fall even more miserably. "The war horse is a vain hope for victory; and by its great might it cannot save" (Ps. 33:17). "O grant us help against the foe, for vain is the help of man" (Ps. 108:12)!

On the other hand, the advent of Christ is described by the prophet Zechariah as follows in ch. 9:9: "Rejoice greatly, O daughter of Zion! Shout aloud, O daughter of Jerusalem! Lo, your king comes to you; triumphant and victorious is he, humble." First, when the prophet gives the order to rejoice, he teaches that the word of this King is different from the law; moreover, he expresses the gladness in the conscience of one overjoyed at hearing the word of grace. Next, there is nothing tumultuous, but all is calm, that you may understand he is the author of peace, not of wrath. This is that characteristic which elicits Zechariah's term "humble," which the Evangelist, as if in explanation, has made "meek." Isaiah has the same idea in ch. 42:3: "A bruised reed he will not break, and a dimly burning wick he will not quench."

In a similar vein the apostle contrasts the face of Moses with that of Christ in II Cor. 3:13 ff. Moses terrified the people with a glance of his countenance, as we have stated above. For who could bear the majesty of divine judgment when even the prophet deprecates it: "Enter not into judgment with thy servant" (Ps. 143: 2)? When the disciples see the glory of Christ on Mt. Tabor, such a new and wonderful joy floods their hearts that Peter, forgetting himself, exclaims: "Lord, it is well that we are here; if you wish, I will make booths here" (Matt. 17:4). Here is a view of the grace and mercy of God. Just as a glance at the bronze serpent saved men in the wilderness, so are they saved who have fixed eyes of faith on the cross of Christ (John 3:14 ff.). Therefore the apostles most fittingly called their joyful message *euangelion,* or "good tidings." For the Greeks also commonly designate their announcements and public commendations of deeds well done as *euangelion,* ("good tidings"). For example, in Isocrates we read: "Twice already have we brought good tidings."

GRACE

Just as the law is the knowledge of sin, so the gospel is the promise of grace and righteousness. Therefore, since we have spoken of the word of grace and righteousness, that is, the gospel, the principles of grace and justification should be included here. For in this way the nature of the gospel can be more fully understood.

At this point one may rightly remonstrate with the Scholastics.

They have shamefully misused that sacred word "grace" by using it to designate a quality in the souls of the saints. The worst of all offenders are the Thomists who have placed the quality "grace" in the nature of the soul,[81] and faith, hope, and love in the powers of the soul. How old-womanish and stupid is the way they dispute about the powers of the soul! But let these godless men demean themselves and pay the penalty for their trifling with the gospel and despising it. You, dear reader, pray that the Spirit of God may reveal his gospel to our hearts. For the gospel is the word of the Spirit which cannot be taught except through the Spirit. Isaiah says this in ch. 54:13: "All your sons shall be taught by the Lord."

1. In the writings of the New Testament the word "grace" (gratia) is commonly used for the Hebrew word ḥēn. This the translators of the LXX often changed to charis, as in Ex. 33:12: "You have also found favor (gratia) in my sight." But it means plainly what favor means in Latin, and would that the translators had preferred to use the word favor to gratia! For then the Sophists would have lacked the occasion for going foolishly astray on this topic. Therefore, just as the grammarians say that Julius favors Curio when they mean that in Julius is the favor with which he has befriended Curio, so in Holy Writ "grace" means "favor," and it is the "grace" or "favor" in God with which he has befriended the saints. Those Aristotelian figments about qualities are tiresome. Grace is nothing else, if it is to be most accurately defined, than God's goodwill toward us, or the will of God which has mercy on us. Therefore, the word "grace" does not mean some quality in us, but rather the very will of God, or the goodwill of God toward us.

2. Paul in Rom. 5:15 distinguishes "grace" from the "gift of grace." "For if many died through one man's trespass, much more have the grace of God, and the free gift in the grace of that one man Jesus Christ abounded for many." He calls grace the favor of

[81] Thomas Aquinas, Summa theol. II, 1, q. 110, a. 2. Thomas distinguishes between two ways by which God's grace works in man: (1) Anima hominis movetur a Deo ad aliquid cognoscendum vel volendum vel agendum: et hoc modo ipse gratuitus effectus in homine non est qualitas sed motus quidam animae; (2) aliquod habituale donum a Deo animae infunditur: . . . infundit aliquas formas seu qualitates supernaturales . . . et sic donum gratiae qualitas quaedam est . . . et quia gratia est supra naturam humanam . . . est forma accidentalis ipsius animae ("A man's mind is helped by God to know, to will, or to act. Such an effect of grace is not a quality but a movement of the soul. . . . God infuses a habitual gift into the soul. . . . God infuses certain forms or supernatural qualities. . . . The gift of grace, therefore, is a certain quality") . Cf. Nature and Grace: Selections from the Summa Theologica of Thomas Aquinas, tr. and ed. by A. M. Fairweather (LCC, Vol. XI [1954]) , pp. 159 f.

God in which he embraced Christ and, in Christ and because of Christ, all the saints. Therefore, because he favors, God cannot help pouring out his gifts on those on whom he has had mercy. In like manner, men help along with the affairs of those whom they favor, and share with them what they have. But the gift of God is the Holy Spirit himself, whom God has poured out into their hearts. John 20:22: "He breathed on them, and said to them, 'Receive the Holy Spirit.'" Rom. 8:15 f.: "You have received the spirit of sonship. When we cry, 'Abba! Father!' it is the Spirit." Moreover, the works of the Holy Spirit in the hearts of the saints are faith, peace, joy, love, etc., as Gal. 5:22 f. points out. It is strange how superciliously the Sophists treat Peter Lombard [82] because he occasionally identified grace with the Holy Spirit rather than with that fictitious Parisian "quality"; for he thought much more correctly than they on these matters.

3. But we have made the terminology of the word "grace" as simple as possible, following the phraseology of Scripture, which says that grace is the favor, mercy, and gratuitous goodwill of God toward us. The gift is the Holy Spirit himself, whom he pours into the hearts of those on whom he has had mercy. The fruits of the Holy Spirit are faith, hope, love, and the remaining virtues. So much for the term "grace." To sum it all up, grace is nothing but the forgiveness or remission of sins. The Holy Spirit is the gift that regenerates and sanctifies hearts, in accordance with Ps. 104:30: "When thou sendest forth thy Spirit, they are created; and thou renewest the face of the ground." The gospel promises grace as well as the gift of grace. The Scriptures are plain on this, and therefore it seems enough to cite one passage, Jer. 31:33: "After those days, says the Lord, I will put my law within them, and I will write it upon their hearts." These words certainly refer to the gift of grace, and the words following them to grace itself (v. 34): "They shall all know me, from the least of them to the greatest of them, says the Lord; for I will forgive their iniquity, and I will remember their sin no more."

JUSTIFICATION AND FAITH

1. Therefore, we are justified when, put to death by the law, we are made alive again by the word of grace promised in Christ; the gospel forgives our sins, and we cling to Christ in faith, not doubt-

---

[82] Cf. Peter Lombard, *Sent.* I, dist. 17, 2: *Ipse Spiritus sanctus est amor sive caritas qua nos diligimus deum et proximum* ("The Holy Spirit himself is the love by which we love God and the neighbor").

ing in the least that the righteousness of Christ is our righteousness, that the satisfaction Christ wrought is our expiation, and that the resurrection of Christ is ours. In a word, we do not doubt at all that our sins have been forgiven and that God now favors us and wills our good. Nothing, therefore, of our own works, however good they may seem or be, constitutes our righteousness. But FAITH alone in the mercy and grace of God in Christ Jesus is our RIGHTEOUSNESS. This is what the prophet says and what Paul discusses so often. "The righteous shall live by faith" (Rom. 1:17). Rom. 3:22 speaks of "the righteousness of God through faith in Jesus Christ." There has now been made manifest not the hypocrisy of works, which men count as righteousness, but a righteousness has been revealed of such a kind that God reckons it as righteousness. Rom. 4:5: "To one who . . . TRUSTS . . . , his faith is reckoned as righteousness." Gen. 15:6: "And he [Abraham] BELIEVED the Lord; and he reckoned it to him as righteousness." I commend these two passages to you very highly so that you may understand that faith is properly called righteousness. For the Sophists are offended by this kind of speech—when we say that faith is righteousness. But in order to examine the nature and power of faith more closely, we shall have to look a little more deeply into its basis.

2. It is well known that the common run of Sophists define faith as the assent [83] to what is set forth in Scripture; therefore, they say that even the godless have this faith. According to them, even the unrighteous believe, and there is in the soul a neutral quality, common to both godless and godly. That their position may not collapse when they see that Scripture says that "the just shall live by faith" (Rom. 1:17) and likewise that righteousness is by faith (Rom. 9:30; 10:6), they invent another faith which they call "complete" (formata), that is, joined with love. The other kind they call "incomplete" (informis); [84] it is found even in the godless, who lack love. Furthermore, these sharp fellows pretend that the apostle falsely attributed to faith that which is characteristic of love in order that by this bait he might invite as many as possible to faith. Now they have invented "infused," "acquired," "general," and "special" faith also, and strange words of all kinds.

But let us dismiss those trifles, for after a little we shall confute

---

[83] Cf. Thomas Aquinas, *Summa theol.* II, 2, q. 1, a. 1: *Fides . . . non assentit alicui nisi quia est a Deo revelatum* ("Faith does not assent to anything except on the ground that it is revealed by God"). Cf. LCC, Vol. XI, p. 220.
[84] Thomas Aquinas, *Summa theol.* II, 2, q. 4, a. 4.

the Sophists with actual facts so that they must concede that faith is not what they themselves have called it.

3. Well known is the saying of the prophet: "The fool says in his heart, 'There is no God'" (Ps. 53:1). Paul's statement in I Cor. 2:14 is very widely known: "The unspiritual man does not receive the gifts of the Spirit of God." Ezek. 29:9: "The Nile is mine, and I made it." Passages of this kind testify that the flesh neither knows nor recognizes anything except the carnal. The reality of God,[85] the wrath of God, and the mercy of God are spiritual things, and therefore cannot be known by the flesh. Therefore, everything nature knows about God without God's Spirit to strengthen and enlighten our hearts, whatever it may be, is not faith, but frigid conjecture. It is nothing but pretense, hypocrisy, ignorance of and contempt for God. Although carnal eyes do not discern this actual hypocrisy, the Spirit judges all things (I Cor. 2:14 f.). Examples will help us see the truth.

Outwardly, Saul seems to have been faithful, but the outcome of his life shows his hypocrisy. For he did not believe (from the heart, I mean) that the great things he was doing were divinely administered, that they were the gifts and works of the mercy of God, but he thought they all depended on his own designs. I am speaking of an affection of the heart: he neither feared the wrath of God nor trusted in his goodwill. He reveals his contempt of God when he himself makes the sacrifice without waiting for Samuel, lest he be anticipated by the Philistines (I Sam. 13:9). On another occasion he erects a monument for himself in the manner of the Gentiles (I Sam., ch. 15). Saul was of the opinion that God exists,[86] that he punishes sin and is merciful. Otherwise, why would he have sacrificed? But that was not faith; to use a remarkable expression of Scripture, he did not seek after God (Ps. 53:2). He did not honor Him;[87] his heart was ignorant both of the severity and of the goodness of God. What a horrible and wretched spectacle if it is our lot to see with spiritual eyes this godlessness of heart! I ask you to take a look at your life, and from its fruits judge as best you can your uncleanness of heart. Do you not, to use Scriptural terms, go astray and turn your mind to your own desires? Are you not worried about your livelihood, reputation, life, children, and wife because you trust God too little, because you do not weigh the abundance of divine mercy? Do you not afterward rush into other sins because you despair of the grace and mercy of God toward you? You would undoubtedly do and endure

[85] *Esse deum.*   [86] *Deum esse.*
[87] Melanchthon uses the German phrase: *er acht seyn nicht.*

all things with a very grateful heart if you could lay hold of the sure hope of your salvation. Do you not build your estate and aspire to wealth by whatever means possible simply because you do not fear the judgment of God? But you would surely fear if you believed from the heart, if you could conceive in your mind of the power of God's wrath. I mean this foolishness, this ignorance, and this blindness of heart when I state that in human nature there is no faith. Faith is something greater and more certain than what the flesh can comprehend.

Therefore, that faith of the Sophists which they call both "incomplete" and "acquired," [88] by which godless men assent to the gospel history as we commonly give assent to the history of Livy or Sallust, is not really faith; it is opinion, that is, the uncertain, inconstant, and fluctuating deliberation of a mind on the Word of God. You now know how we must evaluate the Scholastic view of faith; the Sophists teach nothing but lying, vanity, and hypocrisy. But if I seem at this point to have said something too severe about their teaching, let them not be angry with me, but with Paul, who calls a faith that is invented "hypocrisy." I Tim. 1:5: "The aim of our charge is love that issues from a pure heart and a good conscience and a FAITH that is not invented." By this he indicates that faith is sometimes counterfeit. And of hypocrites he speaks in Titus 1:15 f.: "To the pure all things are pure, but to the corrupt and unbelieving nothing is pure; their very minds and their consciences are corrupted. They profess to know God, but they deny him by their deeds; they are detestable, disobedient, unfit for any good deed." If the faith of godless men here were truly faith—for he surely speaks here of those who are godly in appearance—he ought not to call them "unbelieving," but simply "lacking in love," as the Paris theologians say. In Timothy he attributes to hypocrites an invented faith, and in Titus he calls them unbelievers.

Therefore, there is no reason why we should distinguish between "complete" and "incomplete" faith. For obviously faith is not that opinion concerning beliefs or divine history which hypocrites have conceived without the Holy Spirit. Nature does not assent to the Word of God, and moreover is not moved by it. For

---

[88] Cf. Gabriel Biel, *In sent.*, lib. III, d. 23, q. 2, a. 2: *Fides acquisita ad credendum fidei articulos est necessaria. . . . Ad credendum articulos necesse est credere ecclesiae; hoc est credere ecclesiam esse veracem. Hoc credimus fide acquisita* ("An acquired faith is necessary in order to believe the articles of faith. In order to believe the articles of faith it is necessary to believe the Church, i.e., that the Church is truthful. This we believe by our acquired faith") .

pedagogical reasons I used to call that which was acquired and incomplete, "historical faith"; now I do not call it faith at all, but merely "opinion." What we have said is pertinent that you may know that Scripture uses the word "faith" very simply. That Parisian quality, which is even in the godless and in despisers of God, cannot be called "faith." But the condemned believe not in order to give glory to the Word of God. They are driven by experience, which certainly cannot be called "faith." The same can be said of the despairing of Cain and Saul, for example. For what is the difference between these and the condemned? What, therefore, is faith? It is constantly to assent to every word of God; this cannot take place unless the Spirit of God renews and illuminates our hearts. Further, the Word of God is both law and gospel. To the law threats are joined. Scripture calls that by which man believes those threats "fear," and calls that by which he trusts the gospel or divine promises "faith." Fear without faith does not justify. For otherwise even the despairing and condemned would be justified. For those who fear God in this way do not glorify God or believe every word of God. For they do not believe the promises. Therefore, faith alone justifies.

4. Accordingly, faith is nothing else than trust in the divine mercy promised in Christ, and it makes no difference with what sign it has been promised. This trust in the goodwill or mercy of God first calms our hearts and then inflames us to give thanks to God for his mercy so that we keep the law gladly and willingly. Otherwise, as long as we do not believe, there is no sense of the mercy of God in our hearts. Where there is no sense of the mercy of God, there is either contempt or hatred for God. Therefore, no matter how many works of the law are done without faith, man sins. And this is what Paul says in Rom. 14:23: "Whatever does not proceed from faith is sin." This passage explains very clearly the power and nature of faith. For whatever happens without faith takes place either by nature or because of the hatred of God. Of this latter type are the deeds of those who do good works unwillingly, because of fear of the law and punishment. For when we feign good works without faith, our hearts think something like this: "Surely I have done what I could, but I do not know whether God approves of my works or disapproves. He is a severe Judge, and I do not know whether he is merciful to me or not." With this kind of thinking, how can we help being infuriated at the judgment of God? In this hypocrisy and great annoyance of heart the greatest part of mankind lives; from the foregoing example we can see how depraved is their judgment. For they ought not to con-

template their own works but the promise of the mercy of God. For what is worse than to judge from our own works the will of God which he himself has declared to us in his Word? And a great part of mankind lives with a contempt for God and will so act and live even if it is displeasing to God. Of this type are the works which are done without faith, that is, which are done either in hatred or contempt for God.

Therefore, the saying of Ecclesiasticus is very fine: "In all your work believe in heartfelt faith, for this is the keeping of the commandments" (Ecclus. 32:23). Whatever works you do, eating, drinking, laboring with your hands, teaching, or even sinning openly, there is no reason you should look at your works. Look at the promise of God's mercy, and with confidence in him do not doubt at all that you have a Father in heaven, not a Judge. You are the object of his care, just as sons are of their human parents. If there were no indication of the divine will toward us beyond the fact that God desired us to address him as "Father" in that prayer which we pray daily, this alone would be a strong argument that nothing but faith is demanded of us. Now, since God so often asks faith of us, so often approves of this alone, and since he has so often commended this to us with the richest promises, and especially through the death of his Son, why is it that we should not commit ourselves to that great mercy of his and trust him? In place of faith, the anchor of the conscience, Scholastic theology has taught works and satisfactions by men. May God utterly destroy that offense to his Church!

5. You now have the way in which Scripture uses the word "faith"; it means to trust in the gracious mercy of God without any respect to our works, whether they be good or bad. For we all receive of the fullness of Christ. Those who so trust now really assent to every word of God, both to the threats and the promises of divine history. Scholastic faith is nothing but a dead opinion. For how can they say they believe every word of God when they do not believe in the promised remission of sins? The Sophists say that the ungodly believe that the remission of sins is not for themselves, but for others; this does not hold. For I ask: "Is not the promised forgiveness of sins for those godless ones also?" But we decided not to argue, content to have shown in a few words what the term "faith" means. There is Luther's treatise *The Freedom of the Christian Man;* in it he who will may find further praise of faith. Now, I think we shall understand the power of faith more clearly by citing Scriptural examples.

In Gen. 15:1, God promises Abraham his mercy in magnificent

words: "Fear not, Abram: I am your shield; your reward shall be very great." A little later he also promises him posterity. Then follow the words: "And he believed the Lord; and it was reckoned to him as righteousness." What, then, did Abraham believe? Did he believe only in the existence of God? No! He believed also the promise of God, and later he showed this faith in a singular way when he was on the verge of sacrificing his son. He did not have a doubt that God would give him posterity even though this son died. Now, since faith is assenting to the word of God, what Abraham believed is also quite evident from the promise God made declaring himself to be Abraham's shield. Therefore, believers are those who consider God their shield and Father, not only their Judge. In Ex., ch. 14, the Israelites groaned in distrust when the waters and the mountains were blocking their flight and the enemy was at their heels. Moses orders them to stand still and behold the mighty works of God; he adds the promise (v. 14) : "The Lord will fight for you, and you have only to be still." What if the Israelites had then disputed about faith in the manner of our Schools? These would have reasoned: "It is enough that they believe history, that they themselves also are evil and that it may be that God wishes to punish both the Egyptians and Israel." But they believed the divine voice and the divine miracles; they trusted in the mercy of God, although they themselves also deserved to die, and thus they entrusted themselves in faith to the bottom of the sea. When they had found out by this experience the will of God toward them, when they saw that they had been saved and that the Egyptians had perished in the waves, "the people feared the Lord," it says, "and they believed the Lord and his servant Moses" (Ex. 14:31) . And these examples have been shown us that we may learn to believe, not with that "faith" of the Sophists, but with the trust in the word of God you see Moses had according to this passage and others.

What kind of faith does God demand in Num., ch. 14, when the people of Israel were despairing about the occupation of Palestine? For the Lord says (v. 11) : "How long will this people despise me? And how long will they not believe in me, in spite of all the signs which I have wrought among them?" In Num. 20:12, he is angry with Moses and Aaron because they had not believed that water would flow from the rock. Certainly, Moses and Aaron believed in the existence of God, but they doubted the divine voice by which water from the rock had been promised. It is this unbelief the Lord censures.

Or of what faith does Moses speak in Deut. 1:31-33: "The Lord your God bore you, as a man bears his son, in all the way that you went, until you came to this place. Yet in spite of this word you did not believe the Lord your God, who went before you in the way," etc.? Those Israelites surely had an "unformed faith" and an "acquired faith," but they did not trust in the promises of God's mercy; their hearts were not encouraged by trust in the mercy of God. They were living in unbelief, despising the word and work of God, disgusted with their return from Egypt. On account of this unbelief they were punished, although in other respects they undoubtedly seemed to be good men. This is the hypocrisy of men who, like the Israelites, have been whitewashed in good works. But their heart has not been strengthened by trust and joy in God, although God requires this trust alone. For he has given his Son for the express purpose that we not doubt his goodwill toward us, but that we place our hope in God, not forget his works, and "keep his commandments" (Ps. 78:7). Likewise, it says in I Chron. 5:20: "For they cried to God in the battle, and he granted their entreaty because they trusted in him." II Chron. 16:9: "For the eyes of the Lord run to and fro throughout the whole earth, to show his might in behalf of those whose heart is blameless toward him." In this passage Hanani, the prophet of Judah, is reproving King Asa for his trusting in the aid of the Syrians. But I do not know of a single instance where Scripture shows a more striking example of the power of faith than in the life of Jehoshaphat. In II Chron. 20:21 ff., we read that when that hero of faith overthrew the Ammonites and the Moabites with only a song, he had commanded his army to do nothing but take a stand in faith. The instance of Hezekiah is also of this kind (II Kings 20:1-7).

Isaiah demanded this faith of Ahaz when he forbade him to seek aid from the Syrians and promised him divine aid, saying, "If you will not believe, surely you shall not be established" (Isa. 7:9).

All the sacred historical books are full of examples of this kind. Therefore, it will be the task of the pious and studious reader to gather these examples, both for the sake of learning more about the nature of faith and also for the strengthening of his conscience. But we shall cite some passages from the writings of the New Testament also that it may be understood that the spirit in the stories of both Testaments is one and the same.

I shall begin with Acts, ch. 15, where Peter says that the fathers were not justified by the works of the law, although they were living in the era of the law, but they were justified by faith; he adds that their hearts were purified by faith (vs. 9 ff.). Unless you understand trust in the grace and mercy of God as he explains it, you are entirely wrong. For how could Scholastic faith possibly purify hearts? Peter therefore means that all the works of the fathers, of David, Isaiah, and Jeremiah, were sin, but that they were justified by trust alone, trust in the mercy of God promised in Christ, as the prophets often testify about themselves. This faith in the goodwill of God permeates the whole life, all works, all physical and spiritual trials.

6. It is one and the same faith that trusts God and his goodness, whatever testing may come. That was a spiritual testing which the woman who was a sinner had (Luke, ch. 7). Jesus encouraged her, saying, "Your sins are forgiven" (v. 48). Likewise, he says (v. 50): "Your faith has saved you; go in peace." There were many instances of physical testing when Christ healed diseases, and he often reproved the unbelief of the disciples in material things. This was the case in Matt., ch. 16, when they were worried about bread. For he rebukes them thus: "O men of little faith, why do you discuss among yourselves?" (v. 8). And how often he emphasizes the care of the Father for his own in material things! Matt. 6:32: "Your heavenly Father knows that you need them all." Matt. 10:31: "You are of more value than many sparrows." Corporeal testings of this sort constitute the beginnings in the exercise of faith that must not be despised.

7. I give this warning lest we trouble ourselves in distinguishing between the divine promises. For some are of material things, as are all those of the Old Testament. Others are spiritual, which properly pertain to the New Testament. For I think that none but the righteous believe from the heart the material promises and that God has declared his mercy by his promise of material things. For the saints could easily conclude that if their bodies have been objects of God's concern, much more are their souls, and that he who has acted as a Father for their bodies does not cease to be a Father of their souls. This is what I said before, that even the promises of material things consist per se in a promise of grace, a promise faint, to be sure, but nevertheless sufficiently known to those who have the Spirit of God. Now, even to Moses praying about the sin of the people in Num. 14:19 ff. forgiveness for the sin of the people is granted. And the law itself was given with a promise of grace. Ex. 20:5 f.: "For I [am] the Lord your God . . . showing steadfast love to thousands of those who love me and keep my commandments." Sacrifices were offered for sin, and we must confess that these sacrifices were signs of the forgiveness of sins for the faithful. I am not looking for allegories, but I mean that the Biblical narrative promises mercy in the very fact that material bene-

fits have been promised. Many Biblical narratives square very beautifully with this. Jacob says in Gen. 28:20 f.: "If God will be with me, and will keep me in this way that I go, and will give me bread to eat, and clothing to wear . . . then the Lord shall be my God." By his examples of deeds and material promises, Moses has very effectively commended to us faith in the mercy and goodness of God. Deut. 8:3: "He let you hunger and fed you with manna, which you did not know, nor did your fathers know; that he might make you know that man does not live by bread alone, but that man lives by everything that proceeds out of the mouth of the Lord." Therefore, anything by which the human heart recognizes the mercy of God is a word of life. Examples of this type of faith are rehearsed in Heb., ch. 11; many of these instances pertain to material things. And why do we not include that whole chapter under this point?

At the outset it defines faith as follows: "Faith is the assurance of things hoped for, the conviction of things not seen." This sketch of genuine faith the Sophists have twisted in their glosses to suit their own dreams and have turned it into that puny carnal opinion which they call "faith," so that the apostle's meaning is entirely misunderstood. Therefore we shall choose the simplest words with the simplest meaning: "Faith is the conviction of things not seen." What conviction is this? I ask. Human nature certainly comprehends nothing in divine and spiritual things unless enlightened through the Holy Spirit. The author of Hebrews calls faith also "the assurance of things hoped for." Therefore, it is not faith to believe nothing but threats; in fact, Scripture instead calls this "fear." But to have faith is to believe the promises, that is, to trust the mercy and goodness of God against the wickedness of the world, sin, death, and even the gates of hell. You see, then, that "the assurance of things hoped for" is called "faith." Therefore, those who do not hope for the promised salvation do not believe. "But," you will say, "I believe that salvation was promised, but that it will come to others." For thus the flesh thinks. But listen! These promises are made to you also, are they not? Has not the gospel been preached to all the nations? You do not really believe, therefore, unless you believe that salvation has been promised to you also. It is definitely godlessness and unfaithfulness not to believe every word of God or not to be able to believe that the forgiveness of sins has been promised to you also.

The letter to the Hebrews moreover adds examples to illustrate its definition. Heb. 11:3: "By faith we understand that the world was created by the word of God" so that visible things, that is, works, are understood to come from invisible, that is, his divinity, virtue, and divine power. So interpreted this passage agrees with the one in Romans (ch. 1:20). At this point the Sophists raise a howl, foolishly saying that there is required of us another faith beyond historical faith, since the letter to the Hebrews speaks here only of history, that of the founding of the world. But listen! How will this example square with the definition of faith given above if it pertains to historical faith only? Therefore, by this faith in the history of the creation of the world the author means not only that common opinion of which even the Gentiles and Saracens have been persuaded, but a knowledge of God's power and goodness derived from the work of creation. This faith is not different from that of Peter or Paul. For Peter understands the power of God in the resurrection of Christ as well as his goodness and mercy when he believes that Christ was a sacrifice and satisfaction for him. Furthermore, he did not trust at all in any work of his own, but simply in the mercy of God which he promised in Christ. In like manner, he who by the Spirit judges creation sees both the power of God, the author of such mighty works, and his goodness when he feels that he accepts everything from the hands of the Creator, including his life, support, and offspring; these gifts he entrusts to the Creator to regulate, govern, administer, and supply as he pleases in his goodness. This faith concerning creation is no frigid opinion, but a very lively recognition of both the power and the goodness of God, pouring itself out on all creatures, ruling and governing them all. Could I explain it as the importance of the matter demands, how many pages would I take for this one point alone! Yet he who truly believes will in the Spirit easily judge what faith about creation really is.

Perhaps the Sophists will laugh, but just let them laugh as long as they cannot refute the things which I know are so firm that they cannot be torn loose, not even by the gates of hell. Paul calls faith in creation something more noble and lively than the Sophists' "opinion" when he says in Rom. 1:20: "His invisible nature, namely, his eternal power and deity, has been clearly perceived in the things that have been made." What is the power or deity of God but his omnipotence and goodness? Acts 14:17: "Yet he did not leave himself without witness, for he did good and gave you from heaven rains and fruitful seasons." And how pleasantly David delights in meditating on creation in Ps. 104:24: "In wisdom thou hast made them all; the earth is full of thy creatures." Likewise, in vs. 27 f.: "These all look to thee, to give them their food in due season. When thou givest to them, they gather it up;

when thou openest thy hand, they are filled with good things."
I ask you whether the flesh is able to treat the mysteries of creation
in this way. Or is philosophy, that chaos of carnal dreams, able to
do so, since it clearly denies the work of creation when it says that
things happen by contingency?

Likewise, the people of the law recognized the power and goodness of God in his freeing them from the bondage of Egypt. For
thus it says in Ex. 20:2: "I am the Lord your God, who brought
you out of the land of Egypt, out of the house of bondage"; before
the law was promulgated, the fathers knew among themselves the
things God had done with Abraham, Isaac, and Jacob. Therefore,
they call him the God of Abraham, etc. Even before the patriarchs,
creation was a definite sign and condition from which God was
recognized. In this way, Abel and the other saints believed, although the promise that the head of the serpent would be bruised
through the seed of Eve also evoked faith in them. Therefore, it
is added: "By faith Abel offered to God a more acceptable sacrifice
than Cain" (Heb. 11:4). Undoubtedly, both had a knowledge of
history, for otherwise why would Cain make an offering? Therefore, when the author of Hebrews attributes faith to Abel and
not to Cain, he does not mean some historical opinion, but faith
which glorifies God, thinks well of God, trusts in the divine mercy,
etc. By this faith, Abel overcame, and through this faith "he received approval as righteous." This the author of the letter carefully notes in order to establish that it is faith which is imputed for
righteousness, and not a sacrifice nor any work.

"By faith Enoch was taken up so that he should not see death"
(Heb. 11:5). That is, because Enoch believed, he pleased God, and
in such a way that in him God showed to the fathers both a reason
and a hope for a better life when He took him up. Why seek to
discover to what place he was taken up, provided that we understand that he was shown to the fathers as a model of life and a most
certain argument for immortality for the strengthening of their
faith? Now, for the verse following (Heb. 11:6): "And without
faith it is impossible to please him. For whoever would draw near
to God must believe that he exists and that he rewards those who
seek him." You see how this cannot be understood as applying to
the "faith" of the Scholastics because it is well established that
hypocrites do not trust that God has been merciful to them, that
he wishes them well, that he will save. For if you ask their hearts,
will they not answer thus: "I do not know whether God has accepted my works, nor do I know whether I can be saved. Surely I
know salvation has been promised, I know God is merciful, but

perhaps he will not treat me in accordance with his mercy. The majesty of God has no concern for me." They say this and many godless things of this sort. Yet even these things which the ungodly say about the judgment of God they do not say from a true heart. For they despise God's judgment and do not fear it until God confounds them. But we would be completely subdued if the heart could conceive of the greatness of God's goodness and the fullness of his grace, and if it could trust in this way: "God has not forgotten you; so great is his mercy that if you believe him, he will preserve, guard, and save you. Trust therefore." Hearts which have been thus strengthened by a sense of the goodness of God, which believe that the things that God has promised will happen to *them,* these hearts, I say, truly believe that God is their Rewarder. More than that, these hearts also really believe God. For the ungodly do not believe, but hold to a frigid opinion but not from the bottom of the heart.

"By faith Noah, being warned by God concerning events as yet unseen, took heed and constructed an ark for the saving of his household" (Heb. 11:7). See how the faith of Noah embraces two things, threats and promises. And this bears out what I said before, that the ungodly believe no word of God, neither threats nor promises; Noah attributed true glory to God, and therefore feared the threats and trusted in the promise of salvation, especially in God's mercy. Undoubtedly also many hypocrites lived in those times. They pretended to believe in God's existence, that he is the Avenger of the wicked and the Preserver of the good. But the threats of God did not budge them at all. Why not? Because they would not believe with a true heart, and the promise of salvation through the ark did not move them because they would not trust God's mercy toward them. Likewise, the "faith" of the Sophists is nothing but sheer pretense, a mere mockery of souls, and yet the impious and godless Sophists teach that this feigned faith of theirs can qualify as a good work. I call them impious and godless to say this because that is not a good work which is done in hatred and contempt for God. But whatever is not done in trust in the mercy and goodness of God is done in hatred and contempt for God. It is as Paul says in Rom. 14:23: "Whatever does not proceed from faith is sin." In Heb. 11:7 we read: "By this [the ark] he condemned the world." It is true that because faith saved one, unbelief destroyed the rest. Note the deep concern with which the author of Hebrews admonishes us that faith in the mercy and grace of God is the perfection of righteousness when he adds (v. 7): "He became an heir of the righteousness which comes by faith." I speak not at all of

figures of speech, and I am not looking for allegories, but I refer
to the very simple narrative itself. Noah was not justified by any
good work of his own, but by faith alone in the mercy of God.
His faith had been evoked both by the promise that he would be
saved from the waters, and by the prophecy handed down by his
ancestors that the head of the serpent, that is, the sting of death,
would be crushed.

"By faith Abraham obeyed when he was called to go out to a
place which he was to receive as an inheritance; and he went out,
not knowing where he was to go" (Heb. 11:8). Abraham was trusting in the mercy and goodness of God, not doubting at all that
wherever he was in the world, he would have God as his Protector
and Preserver. Therefore, he entrusted himself to God's voice,
deserting his fatherland, just as the Israelites entrusted themselves
to the voice of Moses when they entered the waters of the Red Sea.
And how great was this faith of Abraham! Although he wandered
about all his life without a definite dwelling place, yet his faith
did not waver. He considered himself sufficiently powerful and
wealthy, and felt he was living in a safe enough place because he
was spending his time under the shadow of God's wings. Because of
the very fact that he saw neither his son nor himself definitely set-
tled in Canaan, he knew that he was a stranger on this earth, and he
hoped to be a citizen of an eternal city. "By faith Sarah herself
received power to conceive" (v. 11). For the Word of God makes
alive and creates all things, and when Sarah trusted in it, that is,
in the promise of progeny, she could not help becoming fertile,
though she had been sterile and effete. "ALL THINGS are possible to him who believes" (Mark 9:23).

But how Abraham's faith was assaulted when it was put to the test
by a veritable battering ram! I mean the time when he was ordered
to sacrifice Isaac in whom he knew his posterity had been promised.
How constant in faith was young Isaac when he did not delay at
all in obeying the command of his father nor the divine will! Do
you think that a father could have carried out such a harsh command against his son, and a son to whom posterity had been
promised? Do you think that the son would have obeyed the father
unless each had trusted in the divine mercy and entrusted himself
to it? Nor did faith deceive. The son was saved, he was restored to
his father, and the obedience of the father was praised. Do you see
that here was rehearsed the whole drama of sin, death, justification,
and resurrection, and indeed of the whole New Testament? Or can
we not say that not only Abraham and Isaac, but all the faithful
who lived before the gospel was revealed, learned from this the hope

God offers in the face of death. Indeed, did not the fathers perceive the victory over death by this example, and did they not see here a prelude to Christ who was to crush the head of the serpent, the sting of death?

"By faith Isaac invoked future blessings on Jacob and Esau" (Heb. 11:20). He believed that at some future date they would occupy the Promised Land. Now, it is quite remarkable that he wished the blessing of Jacob confirmed, for Jacob had snatched this blessing away from his older brother prematurely; the blessing was really Esau's by law. But Isaac blessed them with faith in the divine word: "The elder shall serve the younger" (Gen. 25:23). "By faith Jacob . . . blessed each of the sons of Joseph" (Heb. 11:21). Although they were then exiles, he did not doubt at all that they would yet return to Canaan, nor that they were the progenitors of very great nations. Nor did the parents of Moses doubt that they would return to Palestine; it was for this reason that they hid their babe, the hope of the race. That was also the reason that they entrusted him to divine mercy, exposed though he was, in preference to killing him.

Add, if you wish, still other examples. We have described and dealt with representative examples, and we have not taught anything about Sophistic hypocrisy. Rather have we shown that the author of Hebrews is speaking about faith, that is, about trust in the mercy or grace of God.

Here you see that there is no difference in the divine promises, but the word of faith is the promise of the mercy and grace of God whether it is made concerning temporal or eternal things. Although usually the promises of spiritual things can be derived from the promises of temporal things, I do not say that it is so much by allegory as by a clear and manifest argument of the Spirit. The sacrifice of his son taught Abraham clearly what was to be hoped for in death. Now, the fact that all other promises were related to the first promise concerning the seed of Eve, that is, Christ, corroborates my position that we should not distinguish between types of divine promises. Posterity was expected because that seed, Christ, was awaited. And thus the promise made to Eve was renewed in the promise made to Abraham, recorded in Gen. 22:18: "And by your descendants shall all the nations of the earth be blessed." For unless this is about Christ, it cannot be explained. And thus the apostle interprets it in Gal. 3:16: " 'And to your offspring,' which is Christ." The fact that posterity was expected as well as a kingdom, because of the promised Christ, Jacob tells us clearly in Gen. 49:10: "The scepter shall not depart from Judah, nor the ruler's staff from between his feet until he comes to whom it belongs; and to him shall be the obedience of the peoples." What did he mean here but that all the promises of a kingdom, and even of temporal things, are to be related to Christ and consummated in Christ? This is the reason that Paul cites all the promises made to Abraham without distinction. In Gal. 3:8 he records the promise of Gen. 12:3: "In thee shall all the nations be blessed." And in Rom. 4:13 he says that the world was promised to Abraham as an inheritance both because those from every tribe who believe are sons of Abraham, and because all the faithful are kings in Christ the King. Ps. 8:6 speaks in a like vein: "Thou hast put all things under his feet."

Furthermore, those who believe in Christ now that the gospel has been clearly revealed have all temporal blessings in him. "He who did not spare his own Son but gave him up for us all, will he not give us all things in him" (Rom. 8:32)? Likewise, it appears from the very nature of the Kingdom that just as all creatures have been subjected to Christ, so have they been subjected to the brothers of Christ. In other words, death, hunger, the sword, powers, things above, things beneath, sin, and every last thing that human weakness usually fears, are all in our power and have been put under our feet unless we do not believe that Christ reigns. What I said above applies here, namely, that faith enters into all the vicissitudes of our life and death because we use no creature rightly unless we do so through faith, and we abuse all creatures by unbelief, that is, if we do not believe that in using the creature we are pleasing God, and if we do not believe in the mercy and goodwill of God toward us while using the creature. A man has a wrong conception of want, death, and adverse circumstances if he does not believe that they are works of divine mercy. One who lacks faith at this point flees to human help, for he doubts that he is able to conquer in Christ. So Abraham would have reacted wrongly to that exceedingly grim command concerning the slaying of his son unless he had gladly obeyed and entrusted himself to divine mercy, confident that God would treat him with fatherly affection. One who does not recognize that money, life, and favorable circumstances are gifts of divine mercy, and who does not use these gifts faithfully as though they are gifts of Another, misuses them no less than Abraham would have.

In a word, he who has Christ has all things and can do all things, for in him are righteousness, peace, life, and salvation. And you see that in this way the divine promises harmonize. For they are simply individual marks and testimonies of God's goodwill toward us, which he commends and brings home to us at one time with a work, at another time with a gift. God so thoroughly concentrates on this in all of Scriptural history in order to teach us and make us accustomed to trust in his goodness. If anyone beholds this goodness in so many and such varied promises, how can he keep from pouring out his mind and spirit into the bosom of so great a mercy? Furthermore, Christ, whom he gave as Intercessor, Sacrifice, and Satisfaction for us, deserved his goodwill. "For God so loved the world that he gave his only Son" (John 3:16) for the world. Because he favors him, he favors us, and because he has subjected all things to him, he has done so for us. Accordingly, all the promises are to be related to the One who merited the mercy of God for us, and who reconciled the Father for us. Thus John speaks in ch. 1:16: "And from his fullness have we all received, grace upon grace," that is, God favored us on the basis of his favor toward Christ. You will exercise your spirit well by meditation on the promises, since Christ simply cannot be known except through them. Unless you know Christ, you will not know the Father. Here, then, bring all the thoughts of your spirit, lay them down here, that you may know from the promises what has been given you in Christ.[89] But where, I ask, has Scholastic theology remembered the promises even in one word? This omission accounts for the fact that their theology obscures the grace of Christ, and makes of him not a pledge of mercy, but a legislator, and a much more exacting one than even Moses is considered to be.

So far do I write on the promises, all of which ought to be related to that first one which was made to Eve. It signified to Adam and Eve that sin, and death, the penalty of that sin, would at some time be abolished, namely, when the progeny of Eve should bruise the head of that serpent. For what do the head of the serpent and its cunning signify but the kingdom of sin and death? If you should relate all promises to this one, you will see that the gospel is sprinkled throughout the whole of Scripture in a remarkable way; and the gospel is simply the preaching of grace or the forgiveness of sins through Christ. And yet as I said a little while ago, all promises, even those of temporal things, are testimonies of the goodwill or the mercy of God; he who trusts in them is righteous because he thinks well of God and has given praise to him for his kindness and goodness. He who hears the threats and acknowledges the

[89] Ernst Bizer characterizes the teaching of Melanchthon in the first edition of the *Loci* as a "theology of the promise." Cf. his book *Theologie der Verheissung. Studien zur theologischen Entwicklung des jungen Melanchthon (1519–1524)* (Neukirchen, 1964), esp. pp. 50–85.

history does not yet believe every word of God; but he does who, in addition to the threats and the history, believes also the promises. It is not merely a matter of believing the history about Christ; this is what the godless do. What matters is to believe why he took on flesh, why he was crucified, and why he came back to life after his death; the reason, of course, is that he might justify as many as would believe on him. If you believe that these things have been done for your good and for the sake of saving you, you have a blessed belief. Aside from faith of this kind, whatever they call "faith" is deceit, lying, and false madness.

Why is it that justification is attributed to faith alone? I answer that since we are justified by the mercy of God alone, and faith is clearly the recognition of that mercy by whatever promise you apprehend it, justification is attributed to faith alone. Let those who marvel that justification is attributed to faith alone marvel also that justification is attributed only to the mercy of God, and not rather to human merits. For to trust in divine mercy is to have no confidence in any of our own works. He who denies that the saints are justified by faith offends against divine mercy. For since our justification is a work of divine mercy alone and is not a merit of our own works, as Paul clearly teaches in Rom., ch. 11, justification must be attributed to faith alone: faith is that through which alone we receive the promised mercy.

What, then, of works that precede justification, works of the free will (*arbitrium*)? All those of the accursed tree are accursed fruits. Although they are examples of the finest virtues, comparable to the righteousness of Paul before his conversion, yet they are nothing but deceit and treachery because they have their source in an unclean heart. Uncleanness of heart consists of the lack of the knowledge of God, not fearing God, not trusting God, and not seeking after God, as we have shown above. For the flesh knows nothing but carnal things, as it says in Rom. 8:5: "Those who live according to the flesh set their minds on the things of the flesh." I Cor. 2:14 and 16: "The unspiritual man does not receive the gifts of the Spirit of God. . . . 'For who has known the mind of the Lord?'" By nature, man knows, understands, and pursues glory, wealth, tranquillity of life, and dignity. The philosophers enumerate many such things in their definitions of the *summum bonum;* one suggests happiness, and another, lack of pain. It is clear that by nature man pursues nothing divine. For he is neither terrified by the word of God, nor is he quickened to the state of faith. What are the fruits of such a tree but sin?

But although the works that follow justification have their

source in the Spirit of God who has invaded the hearts of the justi-fied, because they are performed in flesh still unclean, the works themselves are also unclean. For justification has begun but is not consummated. We have the firstfruits of the Spirit (Rom. 8:23), but not yet the whole harvest. We are still awaiting with groaning the redemption of our bodies, as we read in Rom. 8:26. There-fore, because there is something unclean even in these works, they do not deserve the name of righteousness, and wherever you turn, whether to the works preceding justification, or to those which follow, there is no room for our merit. Therefore, justification must be a work of the mercy of God alone. This is what Paul says in Gal. 2:20: "And the life I now live in the flesh I live by faith in the Son of God, who loved me and gave himself for me." He does not say: "I live now in my good works," but "I live by faith in the mercy of God." Moreover, faith is the reason that those works which follow justification are not imputed as sin. This we shall discuss a little later.

Therefore, when justification is attributed to faith, it is attrib-uted to the mercy of God; it is taken out of the realm of human efforts, works, and merits. The beginning and growth of righteous-ness are bound to the mercy of God so that the righteousness of the entire life is nothing else than faith. That is why the prophet Isaiah calls the Kingdom of Christ a kingdom of mercy: "And a throne will be established in steadfast love," etc. (Isa. 16:5). For if we were justified by our own works, the kingdom would not be that of Christ, nor of mercy, but it would be our own, a kingdom of our own works. Hos. 2:19 f.: "And I will betroth you to me forever; I will betroth you to me in righteousness and in justice, in steadfast love, and in mercy. I will betroth you to me in faithful-ness; and you shall know the Lord." Ps. 89:14: "Steadfast love and faithfulness go before thee." This steadfast love consists of freely given favor, which has nothing to do with our merit. Faithfulness is a work of God who justifies us truly, and not hypocritically.

What is the use of piling up more evidence when the prophet Isaiah condemns all our righteousness by saying: "All we like sheep have gone astray; we have turned every one to his own way; and the Lord has laid on him the iniquity of us all" (Isa. 53:6)? And he states a little later that not by our works, not by the outstanding efforts of our will (voluntas), not by our plans are we justified, but Christ himself will justify many by the knowledge of himself (v. 11). See, then, that the knowledge of Christ is justification, but that knowledge is faith alone. The careful reader will note by himself other passages of this type. For I do not seem to be able to explain the nature and power of faith satisfactorily in mere words. Those who have come to know the power of sin, whose consciences have been struck by the knowledge of sin, are the ones who delight in hearing this doctrine of faith. But our gospel is veiled among the hypocrites whose unbelieving minds "the god of this world has blinded . . . to keep them from seeing the light of the gospel of the glory of Christ, who is the likeness of God" (II Cor. 4:4).

You will say: "Do we then merit nothing? Why, then, does Scripture use the word 'reward' so often?" I answer that there is a reward, and it is not because of any merit of ours; but because the Father promised, he has now laid himself under obligation to us and made himself a debtor to those who had deserved nothing of the kind. For one can say nothing which is more clearly against the doctrine of our own merits than that which we find in Luke 17:9 f.: "Does he thank the servant because he did what was commanded? So you also, when you have done all that is commanded you, say, 'We are unworthy servants; we have only done what was our duty.'" Paul says in Rom. 6:23: "For the wages of sin is death, but the free gift of God is eternal life." He calls eternal life a "gift," not a "debt," although it is also a debt because the Father promised it and he has pledged us his word.

There is no reason why those passages of Scripture which seem to preach the merits of works should give offense, for instance, Rom. 2:10: "But glory and honor and peace for every one who does good." Matt. 25:35 is similar: "For I was hungry, and you gave me food," etc. For there are many verses of this type in Scripture. In explanation of these passages I say briefly that Scripture speaks not only of the external aspect or the appearance of the work, but of the totality of the work; that is, it speaks both of its external aspect and then too and especially so of the will (*voluntas*) or the disposition behind the deed. By the term "good work" Scripture means not only the external aspect of a deed, but the total work, that is, the good disposition and the fruit of that disposition. It speaks in about the same way a man with common sense usually does. For who considers that a good deed which he knows has its source in an evil heart? Therefore, when Paul says: "Glory and honor for him who does good," I do not see what need we have of an exegesis which keeps us from understanding the words in the simplest way possible, as Paul states them. For Paul does not say: "To him that simulates good," but, "For him who does," from the heart, the disposition of the mind, and with the hands. Therefore, what the apostle says very simply and correctly is perverted by those who explain his words as not referring to the whole work, to the life, and to the spirit of the deed, but to the external aspect of the work. For it is axiomatic in the Schools, and common sense also teaches that there is no goodness in a deed apart from the disposition of the doer. Let them use common sense who interpret Scripture concerning only a part of a work, and not concerning the whole. What of the fact that Paul in this very passage very beautifully relates a life well lived to faith, and teaches that good works have their origin in faith as from a fountain? For he says: "To those who by patience in well-doing seek for glory and honor" (Rom. 2:7). For to seek is nothing else than that which is written in Heb. 11:6: "For whoever would draw near to God must believe that he exists and that he rewards those who seek him." Those who seek are those who believe, those who by trust in the Word of God are drawn to glory. And how can the power and nature of faith be more accurately expressed than by the word "patience"? For no one without great faith would be able to stand fast and be patient in well-doing amid so many allurements of the flesh and the world and in the midst of so many afflictions. Again in the same passage he attributes a life badly spent to unbelief when he says: "For those who are factious and do not obey the truth" (Rom. 2:8). Not obeying the truth is nothing else than mistrusting God. The factious are those who fight against the truth and follow the mind of the flesh. For anyone who sins openly sins either out of contempt for God or because of despair of his mercy.

Because Sennacherib thought God to be nothing, he took up godless arms against Israel (II Kings, ch. 18). Because Cain despaired of mercy, he never dared anything afterward. For there is no one who would not very eagerly align himself with the law of God if he trusted that God would have mercy on him. But because we are factious, we fight even with our own selves, and we think that the fullness of divine wrath and mercy is something more limited than is actually the case. Therefore, in contempt both of the wrath and the mercy of God, we turn to our own desires, and we poor godless, blind, raging creatures with our love for glory, property, and pleasures dare absolutely nothing. What a miserable spectacle it would be if you could see that godless insanity and insane godlessness of your heart! You see how fittingly Paul relates the well-spent life to faith, and the one ill-spent to unbelief. In the same way the contexts explain other passages too so that there is no need for any strange exegesis. I leave the treatment of these passages to the industry of spiritual readers. I do not mean those Sophists who employ their leisure unprofitably, for nothing has been said so well and so simply that they cannot distort, divide,

and dissect it into a thousand shapes. Surely if one rightly understands the matter, there is no obscurity in that passage in Matthew
which we have cited. Not to press the argument, but when Christ
calls them "blessed of his Father," he means that salvation has
come by divine blessing and not by our own merits. It cannot be
denied that Christ is speaking of the works of faith when he says
in Matt. 25:35: "I was hungry, and you gave me food," and a little
later: "As you did it to one of the least of these my brethren, you
did it to me." For because the righteous believe that what they do
for them they are doing for Christ, they are acting properly. This
faith makes the difference between works. Hypocrites do not wine
and dine Christ, but themselves. For they serve their own glory no
matter how much they cover themselves with a coating of the
finest virtues. This exposition must be sufficient to furnish students
a model for the treatment of such passages, for my commentary
must be kept to a moderate size.

The Efficacy of Faith

Now, we must also consider that works as fruits of the Spirit are
marks, testimonies, and signs of his presence. For Christ says in
Matt. 7:16: "You will know them by their fruits." For it is impossible for hypocrisy to deceive forever, and faith cannot but pour
forth from all creatures in most eager service to God as a dutiful
son serves a godly father. For when we have tasted the mercy of
God through faith and have come to know the divine goodness
through the word of the gospel, which forgives sins and promises
grace for sin, the mind cannot help loving God in return; it exults
and witnesses to its own thankfulness for such great mercy by
some form of reciprocated service. Paul expresses this very signifi-
cantly in Rom. 8:15 where he says that by faith we cry, "Abba,
Father." Now, because such a mind has subjected itself to God,
ambition, rivalry, malice, envy, avarice, sensual pleasures, and the
fruits of all these are throttled. It knows humility, hates itself,
and deprecates all its own desires. What Paul so very aptly says
in Rom. 6:21 is found to be true: now we are ashamed of those
things which we used to enjoy. Therefore, faith pours itself out for
each neighbor, it serves him, it offers itself to him to be used, and
it considers his need its own. It does all things with all men in a
candid, sincere manner, without self-seeking and malice.

The efficacy of faith is such that from its fruits it is very evident
in whose hearts it really is. Of such faith Paul writes in Gal. 5:6:
"For in Christ Jesus neither circumcision nor uncircumcision is of

any avail, but faith working through love." He says that faith avails in Christ and then that it is the nature of faith that it pours itself out in love for the need of its neighbor. John expresses this in a remarkable way in I John 4:7 f.: "He who loves is born of God and knows God. He who does not love does not know God; for God is love." II Peter 1:5-8: "Supplement your faith with virtue, and virtue with knowledge, and knowledge with self-control, and self-control with steadfastness, and steadfastness with godliness, and godliness with brotherly affection, and brotherly affection with love. For if these things are yours and abound, they keep you from being ineffective or unfruitful in the knowledge of our Lord Jesus Christ." By this progression Peter grafts into faith as the root the very fine branches consisting of the other virtues, so that excellence, consisting of zeal and an urge to mortify the flesh, accompanies faith. But let knowledge rule this zeal in order that also the body be taken care of. Let there be some plan by which the subjugated body may serve the spirit with constancy, to use the Pauline word (I Cor. 7:35), and still not perish. Again, let the needs of the body be met to such a degree that it does not become wanton but possesses self-control. In addition to self-control let there be also steadfastness in the face of evil circumstances. For many have self-control, but when offended, they are implacable. Let godliness accompany steadfastness, so that we bear adversities calmly, not only before men, but also before God, giving thanks to him who mortifies us. We should not be indignant at the will of God and groan against it as the Israelites did who perished in the desert. Let godliness bring about brotherly affection. This means that we should do good to the very ones who persecute us, that we may attract our enemies by our good deeds. Finally, all this should originate in a sincere heart in order that we may love all men equally and candidly. You have here the sum and substance of the whole Christian life, faith with its fruits. Nor is there any reason why we should divide the types and forms of virtues into moral and theological as the philosophers and Scholastics do. Nor need we distinguish between gifts and fruits in the way Aquinas and his followers foolishly did.[90] Faith is in a class by itself. It is a sense of the mercy of God which is the source, the life, and the director of all good works.

[90] Cf. Thomas Aquinas, *Summa theol.* II, 1, q. 68, a. 2.

LOVE AND HOPE

From the above remarks it is apparent how the love (*amor*) of God and love (*amor*) of the neighbor, which is also called "charity" (*caritas*), have their source in faith. For a knowledge of the mercy of God causes us to love God in return and also to subject ourselves voluntarily to all creatures, and this is love of the neighbor.

Furthermore, hope also is a work of faith. For by faith man believes the Word, and in hope he expects what is promised through the Word. Faith in the Word of God causes us to expect what it promises. Ps. 9:10 expresses it thus: "And those who know thy name put their trust in thee." There is no reason why we should separate faith from hope. Surely Scripture uses the words "hope" and "faith," "expecting" and "enduring," interchangeably. And just as faith is trust in the gracious mercy of God, with no regard for our own works, so hope is the expectation of salvation, with no regard for our own merits. In fact, it is not hope concerning God at all if it is based on merits. For how can he hope for mercy who demands a reward for his own merits as if a reward were due him? The troubled conscience rejoices as does the evangelical sinner that there is no regard for merits. The hypocrite is angry, so that Christ becomes an offense to the Jews, and foolishness to the Gentiles, but salvation and wisdom to those who believe.

I Cor. 13:2 is thrown in the teeth of those who contend for the righteousness of faith: "And if I have all faith, so as to remove mountains, but have not love, I am nothing." But I ask you, Sophists, if all of Scripture does not converge in teaching that justification is a work of mercy? Paul repeats this truth very often in no uncertain terms. For example, he says in Rom. 1:17: "The righteous shall live by faith." He expresses the same thought in Rom. 4:5: "And to one who . . . trusts him who justifies the ungodly, his faith is reckoned as righteousness." Rom. 10:10 likewise: "For man believes with his heart and so is justified," and he has many passages of the same tenor. When you see this, why do you oppose this one passage from I Corinthians to the whole of Scripture and to the entire contents of all Paul's letters in such a way that you dismiss all the other passages with explanations and are unwilling to qualify this one by interpretation? We shall bring out its meaning with no gloss and very simply, just as it was written. In the first place, it is obvious that in this passage Paul is speaking about love toward the neighbor, to which your Schools do not attribute the beginning of justification. For I shall not waste time with the fiction that the love of God and love of the neighbor are the same. Therefore, it cannot be denied that he has here used the word "faith" to designate the gift or faculty of performing miracles. I Cor. 12:9 bears this out: "To another [is given] faith by the same Spirit." It is a generally accepted fact that the charismatic gift of performing miracles can be conferred even on the ungodly, as can the gifts of prophecy, skill in tongues, and eloquence.

It is my opinion that even if you do not precisely distinguish between justifying faith and the gift of miracles, Paul is here, just as in almost the whole of that letter, demanding love in addition to faith. This is what he does elsewhere in all his letters, demanding good works from believers, i.e., the justified. Although faith per se is not without those fruits, he nevertheless demands them because of the weakness of our faith. And when he says that he who has all faith but no love is nothing, he is right. For although faith alone justifies, love is also demanded, which is the other part of the law, as Rom. 13:9 teaches: "[The whole law is] summed up in this sentence, 'You shall love your neighbor as yourself.' " But love does not justify because no one loves as he ought. Faith, however, justifies; it trusts in the mercy of God and not in its own merit.

There is also the passage in James 2:17: "So faith by itself, if it has no works, is dead." He did well to say this, for he was reprimanding those who thought that faith is merely a historical opinion about Christ. For just as Paul calls one type of faith "true," and the other "feigned," so James calls the one kind "living" and the other "dead." A living faith is that efficacious, burning trust in the mercy of God which never fails to bring forth good fruits. That is what James says in ch. 2:22: "Faith was completed by works." Likewise, because his works declared that Abraham had this living faith, Scripture was fulfilled where it says (v. 23): "Abraham believed God, and it was reckoned to him as righteousness." Therefore, the whole point that James is making is that dead faith, that frigid "opinion" of the Parisian theologians, does not justify, but a living faith justifies. But a living faith is that which pours itself out in works. For he speaks as follows (v. 18): "Show me your faith apart from your works, and I by my works will show you my faith." But he does not say: "I shall show you works without faith." My exposition squares most harmoniously with what we read in James: "So faith by itself, if it has no works, is dead." Therefore, it is obvious that he is teaching here merely that faith is dead in those who do not bring forth the fruit of faith, even though from external appearances they seem to believe.

It will not be useless to give some suggestions on a matter which

I see is being debated everywhere, namely, how a man may know whether he is in the grace of God and whether it can be known that faith dwells in our hearts. The question is twofold: for in the first part it concerns the will of God toward us, not our condition; in the latter part, it concerns only our condition. The Scholastics, of course, erring most shamefully, have taught that neither can be known; therefore, it is quite clear from this alone that the Spirit has never been in that whole tribe. For how can the flesh know the divine will toward itself, since it is altogether ignorant of God? And how shall the flesh judge of spiritual affections when it has not even well understood its own? Jer. 17:9 reads: "The heart is deceitful above all things, and desperately corrupt; who can understand it?" Therefore, the Scholastics imagined that in the soul of man some qualities lie snoring which we ourselves do not know. Furthermore, they imagined that God does not even want us to seek these things, with the result that the conscience is left to itself to fluctuate continually in incertitude. What is this but to teach despair? At least that is what I think.

First, as far as the divine will is concerned, faith is nothing else than a sure and constant trust in God's goodwill toward us. The will of God is known but it is known from the promise of the gospel, by faith. For you do not attribute true glory to God if you do not believe that God wills as he has given witness in the gospel. Those who believe the Word of God, and who judge the will of God from his Word, and not from our merits, know that they are in the grace of God, that is, that they have a kind God. So when Paul teaches with many arguments in Rom., ch. 4, that righteousness is through faith, he finally interposes this most effective argument: If justification were from our own works rather than by faith, the conscience would never rest; it would lack now this and now that in our life and in our work so that it could not help despairing. And so we read in Rom. 4:16: "That is why it depends on faith, in order that the promise may rest on grace." And how often the prophets glory in this security! For example, in Hos. 2:18 we read: "I will make you lie down in safety." Also Jer. 23:6: "In his days Judah shall be saved, and Israel will dwell securely." What else do the terms "in safety," "securely," and others like them connote than security? Micah characterizes this security very well (ch. 4:4): "But they shall sit every man under his vine and under his fig tree." Nor is there anything obscure about Isa. 32:17 f.: "And the effect of righteousness will be peace, and the result of righteousness, quietness, and trust forever. My people will abide in a peaceful habitation, in secure dwellings, and in quiet resting places." In this way the prophets point out that the reign of Christ will be a reign of peace. But what security will there be if consciences are perpetually in a quandary as to the will of God? We must be certain about grace, therefore, and about God's goodwill toward us. This is what the Lord says in Jer. 9:24: "But let him who glories glory in this, that he understands and knows me." God wills that his will be known, and that we glory in his will. What is therefore more godless than to deny that the divine will ought to be known or can be known? This is especially true since he has expressed his will in his Word.

And let us ask the Sophists whether they believe what is stated in the Apostles' Creed: "I believe in the forgiveness of sins." Further, do they believe the pronouncement of the priest when they are absolved? If they believe this, they must acknowledge that they are in the grace of God. If they do not believe, why do they confess? Accursed Rome and Eck, the author of the Roman bull, have condemned that particular article of Luther on faith which teaches that one must believe the absolution.[91] Let them answer, therefore, why they listen to the absolution if they do not believe. This is a benighted godlessness and more deadly than one can imagine. I do not doubt that it has slain many souls which have been driven to despair by that carnal, Sophistic doctrine of the Paris theologians.[92] May the Lord destroy all lips speaking falsehood. With experience as its teacher, a Christian mind will easily learn that Christianity is nothing else than a life that is certain of the mercy of God. Rom. 12:2: "That you may prove what is the will of God, what is good and acceptable and perfect." Therefore, the Sophists will say that there is no reason why we should fear. This is right. If fear is without faith, it is godless. Further, when this fear is joined with faith, it is not then ignorant of God's mercy. Job 9:28 says: "I become afraid of all my suffering." The saints fear because

[91] Melanchthon here refers to the bull *Exsurge Domine* (published on June 15, 1520) in which Luther was threatened with excommunication and which condemned 41 statements that had been culled from his writings. The statement to which Melanchthon here refers is the following: "One's sins are not forgiven unless he believes the forgiving priest that they are forgiven; on the contrary, his sin would remain, if he did not believe that it is forgiven; for the forgiveness of sins and the bestowal of grace as such do not suffice; one must also believe that he is forgiven." Cf. Martin Luther, *Assertio omnium articulorum* (*WA* 7, pp. 119 and 370 ff.; LW, Vol. 32, pp. 44 ff.).

[92] Melanchthon has in mind the condemnation by the theologians in Paris of the following statement by Luther: "It is very poor teaching when the theologians say that we do not know when we are in God's love." Cf. Th. Kolde in his edition of the *Loci* (Leipzig, 1900), p. 197.

of their works, but trust in the mercy of God, whereas hypocrites trust in works and know nothing of God's mercy, nor even the fear of God. Thus the prophet has said: "There is no fear of God before his eyes" (Ps. 36:1). This is borne out in Luke 18:10 ff. in the parable of the Pharisee and the publican. The usage of Scripture, however, will teach us the proper relation of faith and fear. For the present, it is enough to point out that fear ought to be related to our own works, and faith to the mercy of God. Faith is the source of a holy fear. That fear which lacks trust in the goodness of God is necessarily godless.

The quotation from Eccl. 9:1: "Whether it is love or hate, man does not know. Everything is kept for the future" does not mean that man is ignorant of whether God has forgiven his guilt or not. If they want to give it that meaning, I could also get out of it that man does not know whether God is angry at sin or not. I cannot wonder enough at the cunning of Satan with this passage when I see with amazement that by its abuse he has driven out of men's hearts not only faith but also fear. What has Paul in mind in Eph. 4:14 by "the cunning of men, by their craftiness in deceitful wiles" if not this Parisian theology which so cunningly undermines Scripture? Solomon is simply stating in this book that God's judgments must not be evaluated according to human arguments, and therefore he refutes the calumnies of godless philosophy against the judgments of God. Would that this book rather than that pestilential philosophy could be put before our youth to be learned! It would strengthen weak hearts in the faith and fear of God. Now, through philosophical godlessness and the godless ideas of poets and orators the godlessness of human nature is aroused, and it must be suppressed and torn out in every way possible through the Word of God.

The meaning, then, of Solomon in Eccl. 9:1 is that there are just men and wise, but there is no reason why they can trust in their righteousness or wisdom. For "their deeds are in the hand of God." See how magnificently Solomon has taught in one verse both fear and faith in that he forbids our trusting either in our own righteousness or wisdom! Again, since the works of just and wise men are in the hand of God, he bids us trust that One who has the spirit of the wise and the just in his power. Afterward comes the thought that there are those who are loved by God and those whom God resists, but men cannot distinguish them by appearance; but all things are reserved for the future. That is, human reason judges that those have been accepted by God whom he gives his gifts, wealth, wisdom, righteousness, and glory. Again, reason thinks that those who lack these things are hated by God and forms wrong conclusions in this way. For God loves most those who are needy, troubled, poor, and lowly. He hates most those upon whom he bestows gifts beyond measure. You have an example of each truth in Pharaoh and the Children of Israel. For this reason we cannot discern between the godly and the godless by external events as human reason thinks. For if you interpret Solomon as to the judgment of each man's conscience, I do not understand how a sinner can be ignorant of the hatred of God, since nothing is more certain than that God is offended with sin. Therefore, even if we should simply grant that Solomon is to be understood as speaking of the judgment of the conscience of the saints, it amounts only to this, that the saints are not yet secure except insofar as they believe. Rom. 8:24 is pertinent here: "For in this hope we were saved." Yes, faith alone is clearly the security of the saints. But as they know mercy by faith, so they permit themselves with trusting fear to be judged and condemned by the divine will so that they may give glory to God. For thus we pray: "Thy will be done." You have the example of David in II Sam. 15:25 f.: "If I find favor in the eyes of the Lord, he will bring me back and let me see both it and his habitation; but if he says, 'I have no pleasure in you,' behold, here I am, let him do to me what seems good to him." For fear cannot be separated from faith. Faith looks on the mercy of God alone. Fear looks on the judgment of God and our works. Thus Paul writes in Rom. 11:20: "You stand fast only through faith. So be not puffed up in your mind, but fear." Furthermore, since this whole book of Solomon has as its purpose to teach that the divine counsels are not to be judged by the flesh, that, denying ourselves, we should both fear and believe God, I think one can see readily why the author reminds us that one cannot know whom God has chosen and whom he has rejected, lest saints be proud and sinners despair.

As for the rest, Solomon's words would convey this meaning, as far as I can understand: Every man is ignorant of love and hate as far as appearances are concerned, for all things befall the righteous and godless alike. From this it is obvious that Solomon is not speaking of the judgment of each man's conscience, but of the matter of distinguishing the godly from the ungodly by external observations, and of making distinctions among the godly by the same means. The reading in the Latin edition, "All things are reserved for the future," seems to have been added by an interpreter for the sake of clarity. This is not in the Hebrew, as far as I know, nor in the Greek texts. But this needs a longer discussion elsewhere. Let it be a very deep conviction that we who are justified are always to be most certain of the forgiveness of sins and of God's goodwill toward us. Therefore, sacraments or signs of God's mercy have been added to his promises to testify very definitely that the grace of God has come upon us, as I shall say hereafter. Just as a creditor is certain he will receive his money from the man whose sealed autograph he has as security, so in order that Christians may be sure their sins are being forgiven, the signs of Baptism and participation in the Lord's Supper have been added to the autographed promises of Christ. And the saints know very definitely by faith that they are in the grace of God and that their sins have been forgiven them. For God does not deceive, and he has promised that he will forgive the sins of those who believe, even if they are uncertain as to whether they will persevere.

I have said so far that we must be certain of God's goodwill toward us. But what are we able to know of the works of the Spirit of God in ourselves? Can we know whether we have received the spirit of God in our hearts? I answer: The fruits of the Holy Spirit witness to us that he dwells in our hearts. Gal. 5:24 reads: "And those who belong to Christ Jesus have crucified the flesh," etc. Each man knows whether he really hates and despises sin from the bottom of his heart, for this is to crucify the flesh. Each knows also whether he fears and believes God. To be sure, hypocrisy emulates the Spirit of God, but trials reveal the difference, since the faithful alone endure. Neither can hypocrisy hate its faults. So no matter how you evaluate yourself, see to it first of all that you believe. For God wills that true glory be attributed to himself.

Let us bring this whole discussion of law, gospel, and faith together under several theses:

1. The law is the doctrine that commands what is and what is not to be done.

2. The gospel is the promise of the grace of God.

3. The law demands impossible things such as the love of God and our neighbor. (Cf. Rom., ch. 8.)

4. Those who try to keep the law by their natural powers or free will (*arbitrium*) simulate only the external works; they do not give expression to those attitudes (*affectus*) which the law demands.

5. Therefore, they do not satisfy the law, but they are hypocrites, "whitewashed tombs," as Christ calls them in Matt. 23:27. Gal. 3:10 says: "For all who rely on works of the law are under a curse."

6. Therefore, it is not the function of the law to justify.

7. But the proper function of the law is to reveal sin and especially to confound the conscience. Rom. 3:20: "Through the law comes knowledge of sin."

8. To a conscience acknowledging sin and confounded by the law, the gospel reveals Christ.

9. Thus John reveals Christ at the very time he preaches repentance: "Behold the Lamb of God, who takes away the sin of the world!" (John 1:29).

10. The faith by which we believe the gospel showing us Christ and by which Christ is received as the one who has placated the Father and through whom grace is given, this faith is our righteousness. John 1:12: "But to all who received him, who believed in his name, he gave power to become children of God."

11. If it is actually faith alone that justifies, there is clearly no regard for our merits or our works, but only for the merits of Christ.

12. This faith calms and gladdens the heart. Rom. 5:1: "Therefore, since we are justified by faith, we have peace."

13. The result of faith is that for such a great blessing, the forgiveness of sins because of Christ, we love God in return. Therefore, love for God is a fruit of faith.

14. This same faith causes us to be ashamed of having offended such a kind and generous Father.

15. Therefore, it causes us to abhor our flesh with its evil desires.

16. Human reason neither fears God nor believes him, but is utterly ignorant of him and despises him. We know this from Ps. 14:1: "The fool says in his heart, 'There is no God.'" Luke 16:31: "If they do not hear Moses and the prophets, neither will they be convinced if someone should rise from the dead." Here Christ points out that the human heart does not believe the word of God. This madness of the human heart is what Solomon railed at in the whole book of Ecclesiastes as can be seen from ch. 8:11: "Because sentence against an evil deed is not executed speedily, the heart of the sons of men is fully set to do evil."

17. Because the human heart is utterly ignorant of God, it turns aside to its own counsels and desires, and sets itself up in the place of God.

18. When God confounds the human heart through the law with a sense of sin, it does not yet know God, that is, it does not know his goodness and therefore hates him as if he were a tormentor.

19. When God comforts and consoles the human heart through the gospel by showing it Christ, then finally it knows God, for it recognizes both his power and his goodness. This is what Jer. 9:24

means: "But let him who glories glory in this, that . . . he knows me."

20. The heart of him who has believed the gospel and come to know the goodness of God is now fortified so that it trusts in God and fears him and consequently abhors the thoughts of the human heart.

21. Peter said very fittingly in Acts 15:9 that hearts are cleansed by faith.

22. Mercy is revealed through the promises.

23. Sometimes material things are promised, and at other times spiritual.

24. In the law, material things such as the Land of Canaan, the Kingdom, etc., are promised.

25. The gospel is the promise of grace or the forgiveness of sins through Christ.

26. All material promises are dependent on the promise of Christ.

27. For the first promise was a promise of grace or Christ. It is found in Gen. 3:15: "He shall bruise your head." This means that the seed of Eve will crush the kingdom of the serpent plotting against our heel, that is, Christ will crush sin and death.

28. This was renewed in the promise made to Abraham: "By your descendants shall all the nations of the earth be blessed" (Gen. 22:18).

29. Therefore, since Christ was to be born of the descendants of Abraham, the promises added to the law about the possession of the earth, etc., were obscure promises of the Christ who was to come. For those material things were promised to the people until the promised seed should be born, lest they perish and in order that in the meantime God might indicate his mercy by material things and might thereby exercise the faith of his people.

30. By Christ's birth the promises to mankind were consummated, and the forgiveness of sins, for which Christ had to be born, was openly made known.

31. The promises of the Old Testament are signs of the Christ to come and also of the promise of grace to be broadcast at some future time. The gospel, the very promise of grace, has already been made known.

32. Just as that man does not know God who knows only that he exists but does not know either his power or his mercy, so also that man does not believe who believes only that God exists but does not believe both in his power and his mercy.

33. He really believes, therefore, who, looking beyond the

threats, believes the gospel also, who fixes his face on the mercy of God or on Christ, the pledge of divine mercy.

So much on faith; we shall add certain things on love a little later after we have dealt with the difference between law and gospel.

THE DIFFERENCE BETWEEN THE OLD AND NEW TESTAMENTS AND THE ABROGATION OF THE LAW

From the things we have said concerning law and gospel and their respective functions one can easily ascertain the difference between the Old and New Testaments. The Schools fail just as miserably in this area as in their distinction between law and gospel; they call the Old Testament a kind of law which demands external works only, and the New Testament a law which demands the heart in addition to external works. From this kind of reasoning the majesty and fullness of grace are obfuscated. But grace ought to be placed in the spotlight where it is perfectly obvious for all to see from every direction, and it alone should be preached. We shall resolve the matter in a few words. What the law and gospel are you can find out from the foregoing chapters. Here we shall discuss the usage of the terms.

It seems to me that those who call the Old Testament simply law are following an inaccurate way of speaking rather than reason. They use the word "testament" generally in the sense of "constitution" or "ordinance." I consider the Old Testament a promise of material things linked up with the demands of the law. For God demands righteousness through the law and also promises its reward, the Land of Canaan, wealth, etc. This we see from Deut. 29:10-13: "You stand this day all of you before the Lord your God; the heads of your tribes, your elders, and your officers, all the men of Israel, your little ones, your wives, and the sojourner who is in your camp, both he who hews your wood and he who draws your water, that you may enter into the sworn covenant of the Lord your God which the Lord your God makes with you this day; that he may establish you this day as his people, and that he may be your God, as he promised you," etc. By contrast, the New Testament is nothing else than the promise of all good things without regard to the law and with no respect to our own righteousness. In the Old Testament good things were promised, but at the same time it was demanded of the people that they keep the law. In the New Testament good things are promised unconditionally, since nothing is demanded of us in turn. And here you see what the fullness of grace is; it is a veritable prodigality of divine mercy. Here you see briefly what the glory of the gospel is; it bestows salvation gratuitously without regard for our righteousness or our works. Should not the human heart cry aloud at such outpouring of grace? Who could believe this report? Jer., ch. 31, indicates this difference between the Old and New Testaments. In order to understand this more clearly, we must discuss the abrogation of the law.

Since there are three parts to the law, we shall take up to what extent each part has been abrogated, especially since they do not seem antiquated to the same degree. The consensus of writers has maintained that the judicial and ceremonial have become obsolete, and that the moral law has been renewed. We shall first speak of the moral law.

That part of the law called the Decalogue or the moral commandments has been abrogated by the New Testament. The proof of this is first of all, the passage of Jeremiah quoted in Hebrews where the prophet contends that the law has been divinely abrogated because the people made it invalid (Jer. 31:31 ff.; Heb. 8:8 ff.). Israel sinned not merely against the ceremonies, but rather against the Decalogue, the highest part of the law, as Christ calls it in the Gospel (Matt. 22:35-40). Likewise, when the prophet calls the gospel a "new covenant," he means that the old is abrogated just as the author of Hebrews argues: "In speaking of a new covenant he treats the first as obsolete" (Heb. 8:13). In I Tim. 1:9 it is written: "The law is not laid down for the just." There are many similar testimonies of freedom, both in Romans and Galatians. Everybody knows that common passage, Gal. 5:13: "For you were called to freedom, brethren; only do not use your freedom as an opportunity for the flesh." No, that would be a very cheap sort of Christian freedom, more like slavery, if it should take away only the ceremonies, for this is the part of the law which is easiest of all to keep. For who could not slay a flock of sheep with less trouble than it would take to curb his anger, love, or other passions? It must be said, therefore, that the Decalogue also has been abrogated.

Can you therefore do what you will, murder the innocent, commit perjury, etc.? Paul puts the same question in Rom. 6:15 when he says: "Are we to sin because we are not under law?" But our freedom consists in this, that every right of accusing and condemning us has been taken away from the law. The law curses those who have not all at once kept the whole law. But does not the whole law demand the highest love toward God and the most intense fear of him? Since such love and fear are very foreign to our whole nature, even though we should cloak ourselves with the finest robe of Pharisaism, we are nevertheless subject to the curse. Christ took away that curse of the law and the right which it had so that even though you have sinned, even though you now have sin (for we must use the language of Scripture), yet you are saved. Our Samson has shattered the power of death, the power of sin, the gates of hell. This is what Paul means in Gal. 3:13: "Christ redeemed us from the curse of the law, having become a curse for us." In Gal. 4:4 f., it is written: "But when the time had fully come, God sent forth his Son, born of woman, born under the law, to redeem those who were under the law." In Rom. 6:14 we read: "For sin will have no dominion over you, since you are not under law, but under grace." And this is the security which the prophets celebrate so vociferously, saying that those who are in Christ are above all power of the law. This means that although you have sinned and although you have sin, you cannot be condemned, according to the passage: " 'Death is swallowed up in victory.' 'O death, where is thy victory?' " etc. (I Cor. 15:55).

These things ought to be inculcated in Christians at all times, especially when they are about to die, since for the dying this is the abiding, truly sacred anchor, as the proverb says. And this is the freedom which Paul preaches almost everywhere. He touches on ceremonies in only one or two places. The New Testament is nothing else than the promulgation of this freedom. This is what the prophet so aptly pointed out in Ps. 2:6: "I have set my king on Zion, my holy hill." Here the Father says that he will designate a king for Mt. Zion. Afterward he shows what kind of kingdom it will be; it is to be one where God reigns by his Word, not with human strength or the power of the world. Therefore, he adds in Ps. 2:7: "I will tell of the decree of the Lord: He said to me, 'You are my son, today I have begotten you.' " What will this new preaching be? Was not the Word of God, the law, preached before on Mt. Zion? But this is abrogated by the new preaching, now that the message concerning his Son Christ is begun. If nothing is preached but that Christ is the Son of God, it follows that the righteousness of the law, or works, are not demanded, nor is anything else; and all that is commanded is that we embrace that Son. He says this more clearly a little later: "Blessed are all who take refuge in him" (v. 12). Your righteousness will not save you, your wisdom will not save you, but this Son will save you; he is your King, your bulwark, etc. In Scripture there are many similar passages which commend this freedom to us. For what else is the gospel in general than the preaching of this freedom?

Finally, Christianity is freedom, because those who do not have the Spirit of Christ cannot in any way perform the law; they are rather subject to the curse of the law. Those who have been renewed by the Spirit of Christ now conform voluntarily even without the law to what the law used to command. The law is the will of God; the Holy Spirit is nothing else than the living will of God and its being in action (*agitatio*). Therefore, when we have been regenerated by the Spirit of God, who is the living will of God, we now will spontaneously that very thing which the law used to demand. It was to express this idea that Paul wrote in I Tim. 1:9: "The law is not laid down for the just." Rom. 8:2 is also relevant: "The law of the spirit of life (that is, the law as the activity of the life-giving Spirit) in Christ Jesus has set me free from the law of sin and death." Augustine discusses Christian freedom at length in this manner in his book *The Spirit and the Letter*.[93] Jer. 31:31-34 says: "Behold, the days are coming, says the Lord, when I will make a new covenant with the house of Israel and the house of Judah, not like the covenant which I made with their fathers when I took them by the hand to bring them out of the land of Egypt, my covenant which they broke, though I was their husband, says the Lord. But this is the covenant which I will make with the house of Israel after those days, says the Lord: I will put my law within them and I will write it upon their hearts; and I will be their God, and they shall be my people. And no longer shall each man teach his neighbor, and each his brother, saying, 'Know the Lord,' for they shall all know me, from the least of them to the greatest, says the Lord; for I will forgive their iniquity, and I will remember their sin no more." In this passage the prophet mentions a twofold covenant, the old and the new; the old, justification by the law, he says, has been made void. For who could keep the law? Therefore, he says that since the demand has been taken away, the law must now be inscribed in men's hearts so that it can be kept. Therefore, freedom does not consist in this, that we do not observe the law, but that we will and desire spontaneously and from the heart what the law demands. This no one could ever do before. Ezek. 11:19 f. has the same thought: "And I will take the stony heart out of their flesh and give them a heart of flesh, that they may walk in my

[93] Augustine, *On the Spirit and the Letter*, XVII, 30 to XXV, 42, (*MPL*, Vol. 44, cols. 209 f.) ; *Augustine: Later Works*, selected and tr. by John Burnaby (LCC, Vol. 8 [1955]) , pp. 217-226.

statutes and keep my ordinances and obey them; and they shall be my people."

You know now to what extent we are free from the Decalogue. We are free first because although we are sinners, it cannot condemn those who are in Christ. Secondly, those who are in Christ are led by the Spirit to do the law and they really act by the Spirit. They love and fear God, devote themselves to the needs of their neighbor, and desire to do those very things which the law demanded. They would do them even if no law had been given. Their will is nothing else than the Spirit, the living law.

In this way the fathers who had the Spirit of Christ were also free even before his incarnation. Peter sees this (Acts 15:10) when he says that they could not keep the law: "Which neither our fathers nor we have been able to bear." But they were justified by faith. That is, although the fathers could not fulfill the law, they knew that they also were free through Christ, and they were justified by faith in Christ, not by the merits of their own works or righteousness. For Peter in that passage in Acts is speaking not only of ceremonies but of the whole law. For you cannot keep the law of the ceremonies without keeping the Decalogue also. For the ceremonies cannot really be performed in the presence of God except by a believing, willing heart. Peter was not trying to say that the external works of the ceremonies cannot be performed. For what is easier than the performance of a few paltry little ceremonies? If you should count them, you would see how many more papal rites there are in the Church today than there were in Moses' time. You could cover most of the Mosaic ceremonies in a few sentences, whereas large volumes of decrees and decretals would not suffice for the papal rites. How different are the Roman pontiffs from Peter, the predecessor in whom they glory! He abrogated those very few ceremonies, handed down by divine right. But these fellows have invented foolish new ceremonies in every age. Therefore, Peter cannot have been speaking only of ceremonies in that passage of Acts, but he was talking about the whole law.

In Romans, the apostle discusses this liberty more fully in chs. 6 to 8, teaching that only the new man is free. Therefore, insofar as we have been renewed by the Spirit, we are free; and insofar as we are flesh and old man, we are under the law. Yet for those who believe, what is left of the old man is forgiven because of faith. In a word, insofar as we believe, we are free, and insofar as we do not believe, we are under the law. In his work *Against Latomus*,[94]

94 Luther, *Rationis Latomianae . . . confutatio* (*WA*, 8, pp. 42 ff.) ; *Against Latomus* (LW, Vol. 32, pp. 137 ff.; also, LCC, Vol. XVI, pp. 311–364) .

Luther has fully discussed the sins of the saints or the remnants of the old man in the regenerate; therefore, it is not necessary for me to treat this matter at length. This is especially true, since Paul says so clearly that he is still a captive of sin (Rom. 7:23). Augustine and Cyprian say the same in many passages. For here our justification is only begun; we have not yet completed it. Thus Paul commands us from time to time to be transformed by the renewal of our mind (Rom. 12:2). And in Phil. 3:12 he says that he has not yet attained, that he is not yet perfect, but that he presses on that he may make it his own. Therefore, in discussing the abrogation of the law, we had to take up to what extent the gospel has abrogated the Decalogue rather than the fact that the ceremonies and judicial laws have been abolished. For from the abrogation of the Decalogue the fullness of grace can perhaps best be comprehended, since it declares that believers are saved apart from the demands of the law with no regard for our works. Therefore, the law has been abrogated, not that it not be kept, but in order that, even though not kept, it not condemn, and then too in order that it can be kept. Would that those who have related freedom to judicial and ceremonial laws only had argued with more precision!

In all this we must closely observe what Paul says in I Cor. 7:19: "Circumcision counts for nothing." In Gal. 5:6 he says: "For in Christ Jesus neither circumcision nor uncircumcision is of any avail, but faith working through love." Likewise, I Cor. 10:26: "The earth is the Lord's, and everything in it." These passages prove that Christian freedom is such that you can either use or not use external observances of this type. Thus Paul circumcises one man and does not circumcise another; at one time he accommodated himself to those who were observing Jewish rites, and at another time he resisted them. Let our freedom be the same. Those who are circumcised do not sin, nor do those who do not submit to circumcision. Therefore, what Jerome has formulated [95] about abrogated ceremonies is too severe, and he is the man most heeded today. But they sin who think that circumcision is necessary and who are circumcised in order to be justified and to do a good work. They also sin who forego circumcision in order to be justified. So Jerome errs when he forbids circumcision just as the Jews erred when they required it. Likewise, a man errs if he commands that pork be eaten just as whoever does who forbids it. This was Paul's view also. He was unwilling to circumcise Titus when he saw that the Jews demanded circumcision and indeed eclipsed the doctrine

[95] Jerome, *Commentary on Galatians*, lib. III, cap. 6:1 (*MPL,* Vol. 26, col. 425).

of faith by attributing justification to circumcision and not to faith. In moral works too we have to be on our guard so that just as you do not eat and drink in order to be justified, you do not give alms for your justification. But just as you eat and drink in order to provide for your bodily needs, you should give alms, love your brother, etc., in order to provide for the common need. You should restrain your appetite in order that your body may be subject to the spirit. As eating, drinking, sleeping, standing, and sitting do not justify, neither does circumcision nor those moral deeds such as chastity, providing for the needs of the brethren, and the like. For faith alone justifies according to Rom. 1:17: "The righteous shall live by faith." Moreover, this freedom in the moral sphere is as necessary to know as it is hard to comprehend; it cannot be understood except by spiritual men.

Therefore, let what we have said stand, that judicial or ceremonial laws have not been so abrogated that one sins if he acts according to any one of them. But because Christianity is a kind of freedom, it is in our power to use this or that or leave it alone, just as it is in our power to eat or drink. As for the rest, I should like Christians to use that kind of judicial code which Moses laid down and many of the ceremonial laws as well. For since in this life we have to have judicial laws, and, it seems to me, ceremonial ones, it would be better to use those given by Moses than either the Gentile laws or papal ceremonies.

To get nearer the facts, there is one and the same reason why the entire law has been abrogated, not only ceremonial laws and judicial codes, but the Decalogue as well: it could not be fulfilled. Peter sets forth this reason for the abrogation of the law in Acts (ch. 15:10) and Jeremiah agrees when he teaches that the new covenant is entered into because we made that old one void (Jer. 31:32). And in this passage he does not exclude any part of the law, so it is obvious that he is speaking of the whole law. It has been abrogated, however, only in the case of those who have believed in the later covenant, namely, the gospel. And so those in whom Christ's Spirit dwells are entirely free from all law.

The reason why the saints keep the Decalogue is that it does not demand definite distinctions of places and times, persons and things, beyond the righteousness of the heart, and also because the Spirit is actually the righteousness of the heart. Now that the law has been abrogated, the Decalogue cannot but be fulfilled. Just as it cannot but be a bright day after the rising of the sun, so the Decalogue cannot help being fulfilled now that the Spirit has been poured out into the hearts of the saints. Furthermore, the spiritual man is so free that unless the Spirit himself were bringing the fulfillment of the Decalogue by virtue of his own nature, we would not even be obligated to keep the Ten Commandments. Now, when the Spirit bestows a will of this kind, which is in itself the fulfillment of the Decalogue, the law is kept not because it is demanded but because the spiritual man cannot do otherwise.

Judicial and ceremonial laws are external observances apart from the righteousness of the heart, and they are circumscribed by things, persons, places, and times. Since the Spirit does not necessarily bring these observances with himself, there is no reason why we should do them. The Spirit of God cannot be in the human heart without fulfilling the Decalogue. The Decalogue is therefore observed by necessity. The Spirit of God can be in the human heart even without those external observances. The ceremonial and judicial laws are therefore not observed by necessity. From this it is evident why the Decalogue contains mostly negative laws. This is in order that it may be clear that no definite work, circumscribed by persons, places, or times is required, but rather the righteousness of the heart. The remaining laws distribute and arrange external matters, but this type of freedom I leave to the meditation of spirits more sublime. I am content to point out that the Decalogue has been abrogated, not in order that it not be kept, but that it not condemn if we fail in anything; then too it has been abrogated that it may be kept. So this freedom is the freedom of a conscience which perceives by faith that sin is forgiven.

Generally speaking, men hold that the ceremonies have been abrogated because they were simply shadows of the gospel and that now there is no need of them since the body, namely, the gospel itself, has come. I have no idea whether Paul has anywhere pursued this argument. In Col. 2:16 f. he says: "Therefore let no one pass judgment on you in questions of food and drink or with regard to a festival or a new moon or a sabbath. These are only a shadow of what is to come, but the substance belongs to Christ." In this passage Paul can perhaps be interpreted as advocating the idea of the type. Certainly in Galatians he rejects ceremonies because they do not justify. This goes for Hebrews too; in the whole letter the author teaches that not only ceremonies are abrogated because they cannot justify, but also the whole law, or, as we said above, it is abrogated because it cannot be fulfilled. Heb. 7:18 expresses this idea: "A former commandment is set aside because of its weakness and uselessness." In its extensive treatment of the priesthood the letter holds that the Levitical priesthood was abrogated because it did not obtain the forgiveness of sin, but Christ, our High Priest, gains this for us. You see how this one reason for the abrogation of the law is thrust forward and urged in Scripture, that the law was abrogated because it did not justify or because it could not be fulfilled. The Schools abolish only the ceremonies because they were allegedly types of the gospel. The Decalogue remains because it does not seem "typical."

But in what sense does this imply the commendation of grace? Scripture so discusses the abrogation of the law that everywhere in the discussion it commends the fullness of grace. It so abolishes ceremonies that it becomes evident that all law has been abrogated. It so rejects ceremonies that it is clear that because the Decalogue has been abrogated, ceremonies are done away with. There is no other commendation of grace and it is also the highest. Therefore, ceremonies have been abrogated, not in order that they be not performed but because they can be performed or omitted with no peril of conscience, because they do not condemn if they are left undone and because they do not justify even if you observe them. Let it suffice to have pointed out these matters; you may seek proof of them in Galatians and Hebrews. In a passage somewhere in which Augustine inquires [96] into the cause of the abrogation of the law, he argues for nothing but types. Scripture abrogates the law for the reason that it does not justify. Why, then, was the law given? It was given to reveal sin or to convict of sin and to demonstrate clearly that we need the mercy of God.

I think the same about judicial codes. They also have been rejected because they are external observations just as the ceremonial laws are. A free spirit can either use them or not use them, as he pleases. The Christian is not allowed to take part in a lawsuit, but this is no reason for doing away with law. For although those who litigate sin in doing so, yet laws and courts are necessary in order to coerce evil men. Nor do they sin who pronounce judgment or give a legal decision. Law was not given to Moses to be a matter of litigation for the citizens but to be a formula of judging for the magistrate. We must not argue, therefore, whether or not anyone who wishes to litigate can use the Mosaic law or any law, for he who litigates is not a Christian. But is not the Christian judge obligated to use only the Mosaic law? I answer that it is within the power of the judge either to use or not to use the Mosaic law. For there is a certain handling of external matters which does not have anything more to do with Christianity than eating and drinking. Paul demands only that a judge be a wise man and one in whom

[96] Augustine, *Against Faustus, the Manichean* XIX, 10 (*MPL*, Vol. 42, cols. 353 f.) .

the Spirit of Christ dwells. He says in I Cor. 6:2: "Do you not know that the saints will judge the world?" He continues (v. 5): "Can it be that there is no man among you wise enough to decide between members of the brotherhood?" From these passages it is clear that he does not require any definite law, but simply the judgment of a spiritual man.

In another passage he approves even of the sword of the Gentiles, of which we shall speak later; he calls this something ordained of God (Rom. 13:1-4). Furthermore, laws are the most powerful part of the sword, and thus Naaman the Syrian, Nebuchadnezzar, and other pious Gentile princes used the sword and the laws of the Gentiles. I do not know at all whether Daniel also did so, as well as other Israelites, among the Assyrians. Certainly the Roman garrison which was imposed upon Judea wielded the sword of the Gentiles, and John approved of this in Luke 3:14: "Rob no one by violence or by false accusation, and be content with your wages." Such a man was Cornelius in Acts, ch. 10, and the proconsul Sergius in Acts 13:7-12. I have mentioned these things that we may understand that the civil and external dispensation of things has nothing to do with the Spirit's righteousness, no more than do plowing a field, building, or cobbling shoes. It is within the power of Christians either to use the Mosaic judicial codes or not. I should like, however, that the Mosaic laws be received in place of those of the Gentiles, which are often stupid. For we are those who have been grafted into the olive tree (Rom. 11:24), and man ought to prefer the Word of God to human constitutions. Today there is scarcely any other use of Roman law than for litigation, so that the shyster lawyers may have a means of making a living. I think that one can determine to some extent from the remarks which we have made how far the law has been abrogated; the Spirit will give a more definite teaching by familiarity with the Scripture. For this freedom can be understood only by spiritual men.

You will say, however, that if those who have the Spirit of Christ are free, were both David and Moses free? Absolutely! For this is what Peter says in Acts 15:10: "Which neither our fathers nor we have been able to bear. But we believe that we shall be saved through the grace of the Lord Jesus, just as they will." He means that the fathers recognized that all their works were sin and that they did not merit salvation by any of their own works; but they knew that they needed the mercy of God. Accordingly, they believed and they were saved by trusting in the mercy of God; when they had received God's Spirit, they realized they were free from the curse of the law, and also from every burden or demand of the law. But the reason they did not cease performing the ceremonies was that freedom had not yet been revealed and the gospel of freedom had not yet been spread abroad. They did not, therefore, bear the law onerously; for they realized that they were justified by faith. You see also that they sometimes used the privilege of freedom properly as in I Sam. 21:6 where we find that David ate the bread of the Presence which it was right for only a priest to eat. David speaks of liberty in a remarkable way when he says (I Sam. 21:5): "The vessels of the young men are holy, even when it is a common journey." That is to say, they were clean because they were faithful, and all things including food, works, etc., are sanctified by the faith of the saints. Paul says the same thing in Titus 1:15: "To the pure all things are pure, but to the corrupt and unbelieving, nothing is pure."

To summarize, we are free through faith from the entire law, but this same faith, that very Spirit of Christ which we have received, puts to death the remnants of sin in our flesh. It does so not because the law demands it, but because the Spirit is such by nature that it cannot but mortify the flesh. This is what Paul means in Rom. 8:1: "There is therefore now no condemnation for those who are in Christ Jesus," that is, for those who believe, because they have already been redeemed from the curse of the law and are saved. These individuals do not walk after the flesh; this means that because the Spirit reigns in them, the remnants of the flesh are being crucified. For believers, laws are prescribed through which the Spirit mortifies the flesh. For freedom has not yet been consummated in us, but it is being appropriated, both while the Spirit is increasing and while the flesh is being slain. The Decalogue is useful in mortifying the flesh, but the ceremonial and judicial laws are not. So it is that believers need the Decalogue, but not the other laws. But the Spirit observes ceremonies and external laws as it pleases.

The Old Man and the New

I have said that our freedom is not yet complete because our sanctification is not yet perfected. For our sanctification begins as an act of the Spirit of God, and we are in the process of being sanctified until the flesh is utterly killed off. So it is that the saints have a twofold nature, Spirit and flesh, new man and old, the inner and outer man. "Flesh" designates not only the body, as I have argued above, but it obviously means the whole "natural" man, in the sense of Paul in I Cor. 2:14. He means by this term one who is governed by the natural affections and emotions. "Flesh," "old man," and "outer man" mean the same thing. By "flesh" are meant the natural human feelings, not only being hungry and thirsty, but loving wealth and glory and other things of this kind. The philosophical virtues and all efforts of free will (arbitrium) are plainly "flesh." On the other hand "Spirit" signifies both the Holy Spirit himself and also his activity in us. "The new man" and "the inner man" are "spirit" because they have been regenerated by the Holy Spirit. John 3:6: "That which is born of the Spirit is spirit." We are saints insofar as we are spirit, insofar as we have been renewed. Sin still adheres in the flesh, the old man, the outer man. In this connection the apostle says (Gal. 5:17): "For the desires of the flesh are against the Spirit, and the desires of the Spirit are against the flesh." The Paris Sophists deny that the concupiscence in the saints' flesh is sin; they say it is "weakness." Luther refuted them quite adequately in his Against Latomus.[97] There is nothing more evident than that sin is everything which resists the law of God. The flesh lusts against the law of God. Why, then, do they not call concupiscence sin? Do not even the saints seek their own ends, and is there not among them love of life, of glory, of security, of tranquillity, and of possessions? The Paris theologians do not call these things sin because they do not have an understanding of the affections; but they think that sin is a matter of outward deeds. They do not see the root of these deeds. This is why they evaluate fruits so foolishly. What work is so good that in it nature does not seek something for itself? Even though you have got rid of the love of vanity, you have certainly not yet put aside the fear of punishment. Therefore, the flesh pollutes works, no matter how good they are. Do we not sin most shamefully and atrociously in our sluggishness and cowardice of spirit even if we commit no other sin? We should rather burn with trust and love of God and quake in fear of him; this is what is commanded in the First Commandment. But who does this?

Let us therefore confess the actual state of affairs: we have sin in our flesh, and it is the glory of God's mercy that he forgives believers their sin. The abrogation of the law means nothing else than that through Christ its right of condemning sinners has been taken away. There are those who have divided man into three parts, spirit, soul, and body. I do not object to this provided that they concede the actual state of affairs, namely, that the spirit is not properly a part of nature but a divine activity. Body and soul,

[97] WA 8, pp. 43 ff.

that is, nature without the spirit, cannot help sinning, nor do the moral virtues excuse it from sin. The apostle Paul says in Phil. 3:8 that he considers as loss and dung all the righteousness which the efforts of his nature had produced in his law-dominated period. Why is it, then, that these blasphemous Sophists boast about the works of nature, even to the point of doing violence to the gospel? For nothing so darkens the fullness of grace as does that godless doctrine of moral works. Paul rejoices to be found in Christ, not having a righteousness of his own based on law, but that which is through faith in Christ, the righteousness from God (cf. Phil. 3:9). The Sophists even see merit in righteousness based on law.

MORTAL AND DAILY SIN

I have spoken of sin above and have advisedly left out a discussion of the kinds of sin, "mortal" and "venial," as they are called. For every work of man is mortal sin if he is not in Christ, because the fruit of a bad tree, the flesh, is bad. Rom. 8:6 reads: "To set the mind on the flesh is death." The following verse says: "For the mind that is set on the flesh is hostile to God," and v. 8: "Those who are in the flesh cannot please God." In these passages it is necessary to interpret "flesh" as the whole nature of man, and especially as the most excellent powers of nature, as we have taught above.

Moreover, no other part of man is more truly flesh than that supreme power, the reason, because strictly speaking it is the seat of ignorance and contempt of God, unbelief, and other deadly pests of this kind, of which all human activities are the fruits and works. On the contrary all the works of the saints are venial sins because, as we know, through the mercy of God they are forgiven to those who believe. Sometimes God takes his Spirit away from the saints so that they fall into open vices which they well call "mortal sins" with no objection from me, provided that they realize that I call them "mortal" in the sense that they are deeds committed by those who lack the Spirit of God. The Sophists [98] used to call these patently evil deeds "crimes," but now they call them "mortal sins." Likewise, what used to be called "daily sins" they now designate as "venial."

I think that what I have said of law and gospel and of the Old and New Testaments is most urgently needed. I see that I have not handled these matters in enough detail to compare with their actual worth, but I do not wish to be called "Rabbi." Familiarity

[98] Cf. Thomas Aquinas, *Summa theol.* II, 1, q. 88, a. 1.

with Scripture will abundantly supply what we have passed over. I thought it was enough to indicate the Scriptural facts which you most urgently need. You will need to understand law and gospel. The law reveals sin and terrifies the conscience. The gospel forgives sin and grants the Spirit, who inflames the heart for keeping the law. If you were to consider the term "testament" more closely, you would find that the Old Testament as a type of the New was in reality not a real testament because the testator did not die. In the New Testament the Testator died. In the Old Testament a flock of sheep were slaughtered in the place of a testator as a type; they signified the death of a testator. But these matters require more words than the plan of this commentary permits. At this point it is usual to dispute of the letter and the Spirit. On these matters I prefer that you consult Augustine or Luther rather than me. Nevertheless, I touched briefly on this question above in the section on "The Law."

SIGNS

We have said that the gospel is the promise of grace. This section on signs is very closely related to the promises. The Scriptures add these signs to the promises as seals which remind us of the promises, and definitely testify of the divine will toward us. They testify that we shall surely receive what God has promised. In the use of signs there have been most shameful errors. For when the Schools argue the difference between the sacraments of the Old and New Testaments, they say that there is no power to justify in the sacraments of the Old Testament. They attribute the power to justify to the sacraments of the New Testament,[99] which is surely an obvious mistake, for faith alone justifies.

You can most easily understand the nature of signs from Paul in Rom. 4:10 ff., where he speaks of circumcision, as I shall here explain. He says that Abraham was not justified by circumcision but before circumcision and without merit of circumcision. But afterward he received circumcision as a seal of righteousness: through this seal God bore witness that Abraham was justified, and He made known to Abraham that he was righteous before God, lest his sorely troubled conscience despair. If you understand this usage of signs, there can be nothing more cheering. It is not enough for signs to remind you of the divine promises. The great fact is that they are a testimony of God's will toward you. Thus Moses calls circumcision a "sign" in Gen. 17:11: "And it shall be a sign of the covenant between me and you." The fact that circumcision is a

[99] *Ibid.*, III, q. 62, a. 6.

sign reminds Abraham and all the circumcised of the divine promise. The fact that circumcision is a sign of the covenant, that is,
that it signifies that this covenant will be ratified, strengthens the
conscience of Abraham so that he does not doubt at all that what
has been promised will come to pass, that God will furnish what
he promised. And what was it that God promised to Abraham?
Was it not that he would be Abraham's God: that he would cherish, justify, and preserve him, etc.? Abraham did not doubt that
these things were certain, since he had been strengthened by circumcision as by a seal.

Run through all Scripture, if you care to, and dig out the meaning of signs from sacred history,[100] not from the godless Sophists.
The Lord prolonged the life of Hezekiah through a revelation of
Isaiah. God strengthened that promise by adding a sign that the
king might know for certain that it would be kept: the shadow on
the sundial went back ten steps (II Kings 20:8-11). Gideon was
strengthened by two signs lest he doubt that Israel would be lib-
erated under his leadership (Judg. 6:33-40). Isaiah rebuked Ahaz
for despising the sign of the divine will toward him (Isa. 7:10-17),
for he did not believe the promise. Why seek many examples, since
Scripture is full of instances of this kind? From them I believe the
function of signs can be learned.

Signs do not justify, as the apostle says: "Neither circumcision
counts for anything nor uncircumcision" (I Cor. 7:19). So Baptism is nothing, and participation in the Lord's Supper is nothing,
but they are testimonies and seals of the divine will toward you
which give assurance to your conscience if it doubts grace or God's
goodwill toward itself. Hezekiah could not doubt that he would
recover when he had not only heard the promise but had also seen
the promise confirmed by a sign. Gideon could not doubt the
promise that he would be victorious, since he had been strengthened by so many signs. In like manner you ought not to doubt that
you have experienced mercy when you have heard the gospel and
received the signs of the gospel, baptism, and the body and blood
of the Lord. Hezekiah could have been restored without a sign if
he had been willing to believe the bare promise of God, and
Gideon would have overcome without a sign if he had believed. So
you can be justified without a sign, provided you believe.

Therefore, signs do not justify, but the faith of Hezekiah and
Gideon had to be buoyed up, strengthened, and confirmed by such
signs. In the same way our weakness is strengthened by signs, lest
it despair of the mercy of God amid so many attacks from sin. If

[100] *Ex historiis sacris.*

God himself were to speak with you face to face or show you some peculiar pledge of his mercy as, for instance, a miracle, you would consider it nothing else than a sign of divine favor. As for these signs, then, you ought to believe with as much certainty that God is merciful to you when you receive Baptism and participate in the Lord's Supper as you would if God himself were to speak with you or to show forth some other miracle that would pertain peculiarly to you. Signs are given for the purpose of stirring up faith. They who call these things into question have now lost both faith and the use of signs. The knowledge of signs is very healthful, and I have no idea whether there is anything else that consoles the conscience and strengthens it more effectively than this use of signs.

Those things which others call "sacraments" we call "signs," or, if you please, "sacramental signs." For Paul calls Christ himself a "sacrament" (Col. 1:27; I Tim. 3:16, Vulg.).[101] If you do not like the term "sign," you may call the sacraments "seals," for by this term the nature of the sacraments is more closely approximated. Those are to be commended who have compared these signs with symbols or military passwords, because signs were only marks by which those to whom the divine promises pertained could be known. Although he had already been justified, Cornelius was baptized that he might be reckoned in the number of those to whom the promise of the Kingdom of God and eternal life pertained. I have given this instruction on the nature of signs that you may understand what a godly use of the sacraments is, lest anyone follow the Scholastics, who have attributed justification to the signs by a terrible error.

There are two signs, however, instituted by Christ in the Gospel: Baptism and participation in the Lord's Table. For we judge that sacramental signs are only those which have been divinely handed down as signs of the grace of God. For we men can neither institute a sign of the divine will toward us nor can we adapt those signs which Scripture has employed otherwise as signifying that will. Therefore, we marvel the more how it ever came into the minds of the Sophists to include among the sacraments things which the Scriptures do not mention by so much as a word, especially when they attributed justification to signs. From what source has their doctrine of ordination been fabricated? God did not in-

---

101 The Vulgate reads "sacrament" for "mystery." Col. 1:27: "To them [i.e., his saints] God chose to make known how great among the Gentiles are the riches of the glory of this sacrament which is Christ in you"; I Tim. 3:16: "Great indeed . . . is the sacrament of our religion; He was manifested in the flesh."

stitute marriage to be a special sign of grace. Extreme unction is more an ancient rite than a sign of grace. Luther disputed at length on this subject in his *Babylonian Captivity*,[102] and from this work you will get a more precise argument. This is the core of the matter: grace is not definitely and properly revealed except by those signs which have been handed down by God. Therefore, nothing can be called a sacramental sign except what has been added to the divine promises. For this reason, it was said by the ancients that sacraments consist of things and words. The thing is the sign and the words are the promise of grace.

BAPTISM

The Sophists have discussed the so-called matter and form of the sacraments at length and with superstition, but they do not point out their function. The sign of Baptism is the immersion into water. The minister who immerses signifies thereby a work of God and also signifies that this immersion is a sign of the divine will when he says that he baptizes in the name of the Father, Son, and Holy Spirit, or in the name of Christ, as the apostles did in Acts. These words plainly mean that you are to receive the fact of your immersion as a definite testimony of divine favor toward you, as definite as if God himself should baptize you. Hezekiah considered it a testimony of divine favor that God made the shadow turn back, a remarkable event. The people of Israel held it a testimony of divine favor that the waves in the Arabian Gulf opened up a way for them. So you shall consider this immersion as a sure pledge of divine grace. For the fact that the words "in the name of the Father, Son, and Holy Spirit" are said means that the Father, Son, and Holy Spirit baptize in turn. Let him who is baptized interpret this to mean that his sins are forgiven by God himself, Father, Son, and Holy Spirit.

It is a fact that by baptism is signified a transition through death to life, and from this can be seen its function. There is a submersion of the old Adam into death, and a revival of the new. That is why Paul calls baptism the "washing of regeneration" (Titus 3:5). This meaning will most easily be understood from a type. Baptism was foreshadowed in the Israelites' crossing of the Arabian Gulf. What else than death did they enter when they entrusted themselves to the waters? By faith they were crossing through the waters, and through death, until they came out. In this story what

---

[102] Luther, *On the Babylonian Captivity of the Church* (*WA* 6, pp. 567 ff.; LW, Vol. 36, pp. 117 ff.).

baptism signifies actually took place. That is, the Israelites crossed over through death to life. So the whole Christian life is a mortification of the flesh and a renewal of the spirit. What baptism signifies takes place until we suddenly rise from the dead. True repentance is the very thing that baptism signifies. Therefore, baptism is the sacrament of repentance, as we shall say hereafter.

The function of this sign is to testify that you are crossing through death to life, that the mortification of your flesh brings salvation. Sins terrify, death terrifies, other evils of the world terrify; but simply trust that because you have received the sign of God's mercy toward you, you will be saved no matter how the gates of hell storm against you. Thus you see both the meaning of baptism and that the use of this sign lasts during the whole life of the saint. I would even go so far as to say that no more effective consolation can be given to those about to die than the mention of this sign if they are reminded that in baptism they received the seal of the divine promise in order that they might definitely know that God would lead them through death into life. There would have been no need of this sign if the crossing could have been made without divine help. Now, the sign has been given that they may believe that with God leading them out they will escape. If Moses had baptized the Israelites before they entered upon their watery road, should he not have in the meantime while they were crossing the sea reminded them of the sign received as to the outcome of the matter, and commanded them to remember that the sign had been given, lest they doubt that they would be saved?

Baptism is also useful in mortification. It reminds the terrified conscience of the forgiveness of sins, and it makes it certain of the grace of God. It sees to it that we do not despair in this mortification. Therefore, the use of the sign lasts as long as does mortification. Mortification is not completed, however, as long as the old Adam is not altogether extinct. Therefore, there is need for this sign from time to time throughout the entire life, for it consoles the conscience in that continual mortification. From this it is evident that signs are nothing but reminders for exercising faith. In this way Paul views baptism in Rom. 6:3: "All of us who have been baptized into Christ Jesus were baptized into his death." This is true in order that they may be mortified just as Christ was mortified and that they may know, with baptism as their monitor, that this mortification is the transition to life. Paul adds: "We were buried therefore with him by baptism into death" (v. 4). This teaches that the saints are not only mortified, but also that they lie resting in mortification, spending this rest period in the sepulcher of Christ. The godless are mortified, but because they do not believe that through Christ there is a transition to life, they despair and utterly perish. The godly are mortified but in such a way that they rest in the sepulcher of Christ, that is, they believe that he is the way to life, and they await consolation through Christ. In the meantime, baptism is the pledge and reminder of that consolation as Paul says: "We were buried therefore with him by baptism into death." Faith causes us to rest, to be quiet, and to await consolation. As a sign of divine grace, baptism kindles faith. In my opinion no one could very easily express how rich a consolation for the troubled consciences this use of baptism is.

There is difficulty over the institution of baptism and about the difference between the baptism of John and that of Christ. The clearest thinkers on this matter have felt that the baptism of John is simply a sign of mortification, whereas that of Christ is a sign of vivification, because to it was added the promise of grace or the forgiveness of sins. Therefore, they call the washing of John a "baptism of repentance" and that of Christ a "baptism for the remission of sins." For John by his preaching of the law prepares the consciences for Christ by getting them to acknowledge their sin. Christ makes alive those whose consciences have been terrified by the law-preaching of John. For the knowledge of sin and the fear of divine judgment constitute the beginning of justification; its consummation is faith and peace of conscience, which the Holy Spirit instills into the heart as we have said above on law and gospel.

It seems to me that these two washings can be distinguished more simply. If you grant that the baptism of John was a sign of the grace to be preached a little later through Christ, and that the baptism of Christ was a sign of grace already bestowed, then each baptism is a sign of the same thing, but with this difference: the baptism of John is the sign of grace to come a little later, and the baptism of Christ is the pledge and seal of grace already conferred. So each baptism signified the same thing, mortification and vivification. For no one is justified unless he has previously been mortified. I am led to this view, first, by the fact that John's office was not only to preach the law, but primarily to testify of Christ, of the gospel, or remission of sin. In John 1:7 we read: "He came for testimony, to bear witness to the light, that all might believe through him." Matt. 11:11: "Among those born of woman there has risen no one greater than John the Baptist; yet he who is least in the kingdom of heaven is greater than he." This means that before the revelation of the gospel no man's office outranks that of

John because he preaches not only the law, as Moses and the other prophets did, but also testifies to the gospel soon to be revealed through Christ. Furthermore, although Christ is the least, he is greater than John. Therefore, the office of the apostles will be greater than that of John. Because John is a witness of the gospel, through him the sign was instituted which was later to be the pledge of the gospel and of grace bestowed.

Then, in Luke 3:3, the baptism of John is called a "baptism of repentance for the forgiveness of sins." John 1:31 states very clearly: "For this I came baptizing with water, that he might be revealed to Israel." In Acts 19:4, Paul says: "John baptized with the baptism of repentance, telling the people to believe in the one who was to come after him, that is, Jesus." In Matt. 3:11, John testifies that his baptism is a sign of the future baptism through the Holy Spirit when he says: "I baptize you with water for repentance, but he who is coming after me . . . will baptize you with the Holy Spirit." He says he is not the Christ but a witness to Christ. For example in John 3:28 he says: "I am not the Christ." Therefore, both baptisms signify the same thing, but with this distinction: the baptism of John was a testimony of grace yet to be proclaimed, whereas the baptism of Christ was a testimony of grace already bestowed. In my opinion the disciples of Christ baptized (John 4:1 f.) with a baptism like John's because Christ had not yet been glorified.

Those who had been washed in the baptism of John had to be baptized again that they might be certain they had now received the remission of sins which they had up to this time believed would come. For signs are added to make the conscience certain. Neither the baptism of John nor that of Christ justified as signs but they strengthened faith. The washing of John had to do with grace yet to be proclaimed. The baptism of Christ testified that grace had already been bestowed and that the promise of grace had been spread abroad. In both it was faith that justified. But John baptized with water because he was not the One in whom man should believe, the One who was to save. Since Christ is the Savior, he baptizes with the Holy Spirit and with fire. Those who had been washed by John were rebaptized even though they were justified, and there were justified Jews everywhere who had not been washed in the baptism of John. For the baptism of Christ gives assurance of grace already bestowed. I do not see any difference between the justified Jews before John and those who were washed by John, for both looked forward to Christ, except that the latter knew the gospel and the forgiveness of sins closer at hand.

Let this brief discussion on these matters suffice lest by a longer treatment we keep someone from reading Scripture, where questions of this sort must be more diligently examined.

REPENTANCE

It is obvious that repentance is not a sign. For repentance is the mortification of our old Adam and the renewal of the spirit. The sacrament or sign of this is simply Baptism, which could most appropriately be called the "sacrament of repentance." For repentance truly is the mortification of our being, followed by life and renewal, and this is what baptism signifies, as I have said before. Paul says in Rom. 6:3: "All of us who have been baptized into Christ Jesus were baptized into his death." In Titus 3:5 he calls baptism the "washing of regeneration." The Christian life is nothing else than this very repentance, that is, the regeneration of our being. Mortification is brought about through the law, as stated above. For the law terrifies and slays our conscience. Vivification takes place through the gospel or through absolution. For the gospel is nothing else than absolution.

What we call "mortification" the Scholastics preferred to call "contrition." I agree to this as long as they are not talking about a sorrow which is feigned through free will (*arbitrium*) or through human powers. For nature cannot hate sin, but to confound and trouble our conscience is a divine work. Jer. 6:15: "They did not know how to blush." Jer. 17:1: "The sin of Judah is written with a pen of iron; with a point of a diamond it is engraved on the tablet of their heart." Jer. 31:19: "And after I was instructed, I smote upon my thigh." Christ says of the Pharisees in Luke 11:39: "Now you Pharisees cleanse the outside of the cup and of the dish, but inside you are full of extortion and wickedness." But we touched on these matters more extensively above when we were discussing the relationship between law and gospel. For repentance is nothing but justification. In the meantime I advise that you avoid like the plague the Scholastic dreams about attrition and about sorrow feigned through free will (*arbitrium*). But your heart will easily judge whether you are really stricken with sorrow or are feigning it. Do not trust in your sorrow, however, as if your sin were forgiven you because you are sorry; rather, as I shall say below, trust in the absolution and in the Word of God.

You will perhaps grant that Baptism is the sign of repentance, that is, of mortification and vivification, for one persevering in repentance. But what is the sign which shows those who have fallen from grace that they are being taken back in again? For the word and sacrament, "repentance," have been related to the fallen only. I answer that just as we have not lost the gospel, though we have sometimes fallen, so we do not lose baptism, the seal of the gospel, when we fall. For it is certain that the gospel forgives sin not only once but again and again. Therefore baptism pertains not less to the second forgiveness than to the first. For baptism is an earnest and a pledge of the gospel, that is, of the forgiveness of sins. In Matt. 18:21, Peter asks how often he ought to forgive his brother. The Lord answers him: "Seventy times seven times." I John 2:1 f.: "But if anyone does sin, we have an advocate with the Father, Jesus Christ the righteous; and he is the expiation for our sins," etc. In II Cor. 2:5-8, Paul commands that the adulterer be reinstated. In the works of Chrysostom and of Clement of Alexandria a story is told of a deed of the apostle John: he called back to repentance a certain youth who had turned his back on Christianity.[103]

Since they have divided repentance into contrition, confession, and satisfaction, we shall briefly give our opinion on these matters. Enough has been said of contrition; if it is real, it is the mortification of our old Adam, as the Scriptures call it. It is an utterly greater sorrow than human reason can even imagine. That we are made contrite or are mortified by free will (arbitrium) without the work of the Holy Spirit is far from the truth.

From one point of view, confession involves acknowledging our sin before God and condemning ourselves. This confession is no different from mortification and true contrition, of which I just spoke. Scripture often reminds us of this fact. I John 1:9: "If we confess ours sins, he is faithful and just and will forgive our sins." David says in Ps. 51:3 f.: "For I know my transgressions, and my sin is ever before me. Against thee, thee only, have I sinned, and done that which is evil in thy sight, so that thou art justified in thy sentence and blameless in thy judgment." Ps. 32:5: "I said, 'I will confess my transgressions to the Lord'; then thou didst forgive the guilt of my sin." Without this confession there is no forgiveness of sins. On the other hand, when we make a confession in which we accuse and condemn ourselves and attribute to God true glory and righteousness, forgiveness must follow.

Viewed from another angle, confession is not only a private acknowledgment of our guilt to ourselves but an accusation of ourselves before others. The following was the kind of confession that formerly existed in the Church: he who was guilty of a crime

[103] Clement of Alexandria, *Can a Rich Man Be Saved?* (GCS, Vol. III, pp. 159 ff.).

was first accused privately by some brother, and then before the
Church. There his guilt was forgiven if he repented. He who did
not heed the Church was put out of the Church. You have the
model of this confession in Matt. 18:15-18, where the office of the
keys is set forth. There is now no example of this in the Church,
although no other method of restraining faults was more appropriate. But this was succeeded by that kind of confession which is
carried on privately and apart before individual priests.[104] Between
that early kind of confession and ours there is this difference: the
earlier one was concerned only with open, public crimes, but the
present kind concerns itself with private sins also. The oldest custom was to make accusation of public crimes before the whole
congregation and to receive absolution by the vote of the entire
congregation. This custom has long since been abrogated. One of
the presbyters was then designated before whom the charges were
privately rehearsed even though they were for public crimes. In
accordance with his judgment this presbyter imposed a penalty for
the public offenders, in the presence of the congregation. They
were not admitted to Communion unless they had paid that public
penalty.

An example of this still remains in the public repentance of our
times when homicides are punished in the congregation. This kind
of repentance is described by the author of what is called the *Historia tripartita;* [105] apparently he is a Greek. He says that it has
been done away with at Constantinople, but persists in the Western Churches and is that type which Cyprian often cites. Yet when
Cyprian speaks of the confession of public crimes, he indicates that
it is made before the priest rather than before the whole congregation. Just take, if you please, that sermon of his, "The Fallen."
But I shall quote some words of the Greek *History:* "It was decided by the ancient pontiffs that sins be bared to the surveillance
of the congregation just like a play in a theater. For this purpose
they designated a presbyter, a wise man of good character who
could keep a secret; to this man came those who had sinned, confessing their sins. He imposed a penalty in accordance with each
person's guilt. This is a custom which is diligently observed in the
Western Churches and especially at Rome even to this day. In
Roman practice, there is even a definite place for the guilty penitents to stand, just as for those who mourn. Moreover, when the
Holy Celebration has been completed, the guilty ones, who have

[104] *Presbyteros.*
[105] Flavius Magnus Aurelius Cassiodorus, *Historia ecclesiastica tripartita* IX,
35 (cf. *MPL,* Vol. 69, col. 1151) .

not participated in Communion, prostrate themselves on the earth with groaning and lamentation. The bishop himself runs to them, and falls down with tears and spiritual groaning, while the whole congregation bursts into tears. Then the bishop gets up first and raises the fallen from the earth. After prayer has been made for the penitents, he dismisses all. In the meantime the penitents torment themselves with various afflictions according to the judgment of the bishop; they await the time of Communion, which the bishop prescribes. At this time they participate in Communion with the rest of the church as if the debt had now been paid in full. The Roman pontiffs have observed these customs right up to our times. But in Constantinople a presbyter presided over the penitents only until a certain woman of the highest nobility, after her confession, had lain several times with a deacon as she was doing penance in the church. When this was noised abroad, the common people rose against the presbyters because they had violated the church. Then it was that Bishop Nectarius ejected the deacon from his office and abrogated the ancient custom of penitents; no presbyter was designated for the penitents. He permitted each person to participate in the Lord's Supper when he pleased according to the judgment of his own conscience." The above is almost a verbatim quotation from the *Historia tripartita*.

From these examples you will gather that the form of public repentance in times past has been twofold. The one kind, that of the early Church, was that in which the matter was carried out before the whole congregation. The offenders who would not repent were ejected from the communion of believers, whereas those who repented were absolved. You have an example of this kind in the incest dealt with in I Cor., ch. 5, and in II Cor., ch. 2. The other type was that in which the penalty was public, but the confession was not. An example of this is current today in the repentance of homicides. Yet penalties are not due by divine right, but they have come about by human traditions as I shall say hereafter. On this type of repentance almost all the old canons speak. The foolish professors of pontifical law clumsily twist these canons in favor of private repentance.

PRIVATE CONFESSIONS

In addition to public repentance there are private confessions. First are those by which we are privately reconciled with those whom we have offended. This is the kind spoken of in Matt. 5:23 f.: "So if you are offering your gift at the altar, and there remember that your brother has something against you, leave your gift there before the altar, and go; first be reconciled to your brother, and then come and offer your gift." James 5:16: "Therefore confess your sins to one another," that is, let one intercede for the offense of the other.

Then there are those ecclesiastical private confessions, the use of which is common today. It appears that they were formerly used in somewhat the following way: those whose consciences troubled them about some matter would consult holy men who were experienced in spiritual things, and would be absolved by them. Basil makes mention of this in his treatise, *The Ordinances of Monks,* if the title does not escape me, a work which one believes was translated into Latin by Rufinus.[106] I have found so many kinds of confessions, some handed down by divine law and others the inventions of man, that they must be carefully distinguished.

It is well established that a confession made before God is demanded by divine law. The passage from I John, ch. 1, cited above proves this. For sin is not forgiven unless we make confession to God, that is, until we condemn ourselves and trust that our guilt is forgiven by the mercy of God.

Why argue about public confession of public crimes where the matter is carried on before witnesses in the presence of the congregation? The very situation compels us to confess our sins if we are accused; it is not only divine law which does so. It compels us likewise to placate our brother.

The remaining confessions are traditions of men. For if you offer yourself voluntarily to the congregation and wish to be absolved, whether you have sinned privately or publicly, divine law does not demand a rehearsal of your acts. Christ forgave many in this way, and the apostles absolved several thousands in the same manner in Acts 2:38 f. They did not demand that a catalog of sins be recited. I say this to counsel the weak consciences of those who can only despair if they have passed over anything in reciting their confession.

Private absolution is thus as necessary as baptism. For although you hear the gospel preached to the whole congregation in general, yet in the end you are certain that it pertains particularly to you when you are privately and individually absolved. He does not thirst for grace who does not desperately desire to hear the divine pronouncement concerning himself. For it is the pronouncement of God and not of men with which you are absolved, pro-

---

[106] Basil of Caesarea, *The Ordinances of Monks* (MPG, Vol. 31, cols. 889 ff.) ; Rufinus, *Church History* 11, 9 (GCS, II, 2, p. 1015).

vided you believe the absolution. How certain was that sinful woman in Luke 7:36-50 that all her guilt was removed when she heard the voice of Christ saying: "Your sins are forgiven" (v. 48)! So certain are you to be also when you are absolved by a brother, whoever he is. But one is not really absolved unless one hopes and believes one is absolved. Therefore, those who are coerced by the pontifical constitution to feign repentance and confession once a year are not absolved. On the contrary, those who seek the absolution by the compulsion of pontifical law and not because of a longing of the spirit simply make a mockery of Christ.

There is no satisfaction outside the death of Christ. Isa. 53:11 says: "He shall bear their iniquities." But those satisfactions now commanded are nothing but the inventions of men. They have their origin in the penitential canons that were established to deal with the public repentance of days gone by. Because of these false satisfactions, Christ's satisfaction and faith in the word of absolution are completely annihilated. Here and there in Scripture penalties for sins are stated, but they do not cover all sins. Therefore, it is inaccurate to call those penalties "satisfactions." From these satisfactions, indulgences—Rome's merchandise—got their start; the indulgences forgave those canonical penalties entailed in public repentance. Godless men decreed that these indulgences be sold rather than that divine forgiveness be declared, and men came to trust in their word rather than God's.

To conclude this section let me say that there are two parts to repentance, mortification and vivification. Mortification takes place when the conscience is terrified by the law, vivification, when one is comforted and strengthened through the absolution. For absolution is the gospel with which Christ forgives your guilt. There is no other sign of repentance but Baptism.

PARTICIPATION IN THE LORD'S TABLE

Participation in the Lord's Table, that is, eating the body and drinking the blood of Christ, is a certain sign of grace. For He says in Luke 22:20: "This cup . . . is the new covenant in my blood," etc. In I Cor. 11:25 we read: "Do this as often as you drink it, in remembrance of me." This means that when you celebrate Communion, you should be reminded of the gospel or the remission of sins. It is not, therefore, a sacrifice if it was given only as a sure reminder of the promise of the gospel. Nor does participation in the Supper destroy sin, but faith destroys it, and faith is strengthened by this sign. The sight of Christ did not justify

Stephen when he was on the point of death, but it strengthened the faith through which he was justified and made alive. Likewise, participation in the Supper does not justify, but it strengthens faith, as I have said above. All Masses are godless, therefore, except those by which consciences are encouraged for the strengthening of faith. A sacrifice is what we offer to God, but we do not offer Christ to God. But he himself offered up himself once for all. Therefore, those who perform Masses in order to do some good work or offer Christ to God for the living and the dead with the idea that the oftener this is repeated, the better they become, are caught in godless error. I think that for the most part these errors must be blamed on Thomas who taught that a Mass benefits others besides the one who partakes.[107]

The function of this sacrament, however, is to strengthen us whenever our consciences totter and whenever we have doubts concerning God's will toward us. These times come often in life, but especially when we are about to die. Particularly those about to die, therefore, must be strengthened by this sacrament. Nor are we living a true Christian life unless we die continually. Confirmation, in my opinion, is the laying on of hands. Unction, I think, is what Mark 6:13 mentions. But I cannot see that these two have been given as sure signs of grace. It is certain that marriage was not instituted for this purpose either. And what came into the minds of those who numbered ordination among the signs of grace? For ordination is nothing else than choosing from the Church those who are to teach, baptize, bless the Supper, and share alms with the needy. Those who taught, baptized, and blessed the Supper were called "bishops" or "presbyters." Those who distributed alms to the needy were known as "deacons." The functions of these men were not so specialized that it was sacrilege for a deacon to teach, to baptize, or to bless the Supper. On the other hand, these duties are for all Christians, for the keys belong to all (Matt. 18:18). But the administration of these things was put in the hands of certain men that there might be those who knew that it was their special duty to superintend ecclesiastical affairs, and that there might be those to whom matters could be duly referred if anything came up.

In passing, I should like to remind you that the words "bishop," "presbyter," and "deacon," have nothing to do with the word "priest." For Scripture uses the word "priest" in connection with sacrifice and intercessory prayer. We Christians are all priests because we offer a sacrifice, namely, our body. Apart from this, there

[107] Thomas Aquinas, *Summa theol.* III, q. 79, a. 7.

is no place for sacrifice in Christianity, and we have the right to pray to God and even to placate him. The thought of Peter is relevant here: "You are . . . a royal priesthood, a holy nation" (I Peter 2:9). For we Christians are kings because through Christ we are free from all created things, we rule over life, death, and sin, as I said above. We are priests because we offer ourselves to God and because we importune forgiveness for our sins. The Letter to the Hebrews discusses this at greater length (ch. 13:15 f.). Bishops, presbyters, and deacons are simply those who teach, baptize, bless the Supper, and distribute alms. The priests of the Mass are prophets of Jezebel, that is, of Rome.

LOVE

So far I have discussed sin, law, grace, gospel, and especially justification. This matter of justification has always been the common question of all mankind, and always will be. For how can a man be justified? Philosophers and Pharisees have taught that a man is justified by his own virtues and efforts. We have taught that he is justified by faith alone, that is, that the righteousness of Christ is ours through faith, and that our works and efforts are nothing but sin. He who holds this has grasped the basic content of Scripture: believers are justified by the MERCY OF GOD. Finally, our theme requires that we say a few words on love.

I pointed out above that love for God is the fruit of faith, for one who grasps the mercy of God in faith cannot help loving God in return. Therefore, love for God is a fruit of faith. Out of love for God is born love for our neighbor also, when we desire to serve God in all his creatures. I certainly cannot give a briefer or more suitable rule in regard to this aspect of love than the following: "You shall love your neighbor as yourself" (Mark 12:31). Augustine devised a system of ranking the things to be loved: first we should love our souls, then our bodies; we should love first our own people, and after them strangers. We always prefer faith to love. Therefore, we usually prefer those things which are of the soul to the necessities of the body. On the other hand, Christ commands that we love strangers and enemies just as we love our friends (Matt. 5:44), and Paul does the same (Rom. 12:13, 17 ff.). Your spirit will easily judge that you ought to do good to your friends as well as to your enemies. Certainly, Paul in his letters to the Galatians (ch. 6:10) and to Timothy (I Tim. 5:8) expressed the wish that a man make special provision for those of his own household. For I do not want freedom of the spirit to be bound by disputations of the sort in which the Scholastics and Book III of Cicero's *De officiis* [108] engage; in this part of his work Cicero discusses the duty of the man who, after being shipwrecked, chances upon the same plank that a certain wise man is holding. Away with such stupid questions which hardly ever arise in actual human affairs!

MAGISTRATES

This section on magistrates I consider very important. For the present I shall follow the popular division for pedagogical reasons. Some magistrates are civil and others ecclesiastical. The civil magistrate is one who bears the sword and watches over the civil peace. Paul approves this in Rom. 13:1 ff. Matters under the sword are civil rights, civil ordinances of public courts, and penalties for criminals. It is the obligation of the sword to enforce the laws against murder, vengeance, etc. Therefore, the fact that the magistrate wields the sword is pleasing to God. The same can be said for lawyers if they render an opinion about law or defend the oppressed, even though litigants commit great sin. On wielding the power of the sword, I have this to say. In the first place, if rulers command anything that is contrary to God, they must not be obeyed. Acts 5:29: "We must obey God rather than men." You have innumerable statements of this principle, especially that very fine one in Amos 7:10-17.

In the next place, if they command anything that is for the public good, we must obey them in accordance with Rom. 13:5: "Therefore one must be subject, not only to avoid God's wrath, but also for the sake of conscience." For love constrains us to fulfill all civil obligations.

Finally, if anything is commanded with tyrannical caprice, we must bear with this magistracy also because of love, since nothing can be changed without a public uprising or sedition. Pertinent is Christ's word: "But if anyone strikes you on the right cheek, turn to him the other also" (Matt. 5:39).

But if you can escape without offense and public disturbance, do so. For example, if you have been unjustly thrown into prison and are able to break away without public disturbance, nothing forbids your escape according to I Cor. 7:21: "But if you can gain your freedom, avail yourself of the opportunity."

As far as ecclesiastical magistrates are concerned, first, we think that bishops are servants and neither powers nor magistrates. Sec-

[108] Cicero, *On Duties* (*De officiis*) III, 23.

ondly, the bishops have no right to establish laws, since they have been enjoined to preach only the Word of God, not that of men, as we have said above. This seems sufficiently clear from Jer., ch. 23.

1. Therefore, in the first place, if they teach Scripture, they are to be heard as if Christ himself were speaking. Luke 10:16 brings this out: "He who hears you, hears me." This refers to Scripture, not to human traditions as is evident when he says in Matt. 10:41: "He who receives a prophet because he is a prophet . . ."; he does not say here "pseudoprophet."

2. Secondly, if they teach anything contrary to Scripture, they must not be listened to. Acts 5:29: "We must obey God rather than men." Matt. 15:6: "So, for the sake of your tradition, you have made void the word of God." In these days the pope has decreed something contrary to divine justice in the bull by which Luther was condemned; in this he must by no means be obeyed.

3. In the third place, if they decree anything that goes beyond Scripture in order to bind consciences, they must not be listened to. For nothing but divine law obligates the conscience. Paul was speaking about this in I Tim. 4:1 ff., where he calls the law of celibacy and of forbidden foods "doctrines of demons." He does this, although these things do not seem to contradict Scripture and although they seem to be things which per se are not bad. For celibacy and abstaining from meat are not evil in themselves. But these rules are ungodly if you think you are committing sin by not keeping them. Those who think a man is sinning who does not observe the canonical hours or who eats meat on the sixth or seventh day are teaching godless things. For a bishop cannot bind a Christian conscience. II Cor. 13:10: "I write this while I am away from you, in order that when I come I may not have to be severe in the use of the authority which the Lord has given me for building up and not for tearing down."

4. In the fourth place, if you do not want to burden the conscience with the law of a bishop but interpret his command only as an external obligation (as spiritual men and those usually do who understand that the conscience can be bound by no human law), you will consider the law of a bishop to be on a par with the tyranny of a civil magistrate. For whatever the bishops command that goes beyond Scripture is tyranny, since they do not have the right so to command. You will bear these burdens because of love according to the passage: "But if anyone strikes you on the right cheek, turn to him the other also" (Matt. 5:39). Moreover, if you can oppose without offense, nothing forbids you. For instance, if

without a public disturbance you can break out of a prison in which you are held bound by a tyrant, nothing prevents it, according to I Cor. 7:21: "But if you can gain your freedom, avail yourself of the opportunity." And Christ dispensed with the Pharisaic traditions in Matt., chs. 9 and 12, but he did not uproot civil laws. Now that Pharisaic laws are dispensed with, we are more free, not only because they are more a concern for each individual than they are common burdens, but also because they easily ensnare the conscience. The rule and direction of all human laws are under faith and love, and especially under necessity. Necessity liberates from all traditions if at any point either the soul or the life of the body has fallen into danger through tradition.

OFFENSE

You ask to what extent we must consider the question of offense. First of all, I point out as I have before, that faith and love are the models of all human activities, but of these faith is the more important.

An offense is an injury by which either our neighbor's faith or his love is harmed. If anything different from Holy Scripture is taught, the faith of our neighbor is hurt. All Scholastic doctrine is an offense of this kind, since it approves of satisfactions and works of free will (arbitrium) and obscures grace. Christ speaks of this type of offense in Matt. 18:6: "But whoever causes one of these little ones who believe in me to stumble, it would be better for him to have a great millstone fastened round his neck, and to be drowned in the depth of the sea."

Love is harmed if one does not help a brother in need or if one disturbs the public peace. Christ speaks of this kind of offense in Matt. 17:26 f. concerning the paying of tribute, when he says: "However, not to give offense to them . . ."

1. As for that which is demanded by divine law, what is so demanded must be obeyed, done, and taught without respect to offense. For faith must always be preferred to love. Acts 5:29 applies here: "We must obey God rather than men." Christ says: "I have not come to bring peace, but a sword" (Matt. 10:34). So Daniel did not obey the law demanding the worship of the golden statue. Neither should we obey godless rulers who condemn the gospel in our time.

2. As for what is in the sphere of human law, so-called intermediate matters such as celibacy and abstaining from meats, human tradition does not obligate in case of necessity. For even

Christ dispenses with the divine law in case of necessity, as in Matt. 12:1, where we read of the disciples plucking the ears on the Sabbath. How much more is it permissible to violate human traditions if the necessity of life demands it! Even more demanding is the case of a soul in danger, as when a priest burns, as they say. II Cor. 13:10 fittingly says: "The authority which the Lord has given me for building up and not for tearing down." Paul in Col. 2:16-23 condemns the laws which unduly burden the body.

3. In the presence of Pharisees who demand the observance of their traditions as if they were necessary for salvation, these traditions should be violated without regard for offense. Paul did this with divine law when he refused to circumcise Titus (Gal. 2:3). How much more should we do this with stupid papal traditions! Christ commands that those who were scandalized be let alone because they were blind leaders of the blind (Matt. 15:12-14).

4. For the sake of freedom we must teach that human traditions may be violated so that the inexperienced understand that they do not sin even if they permit something contrary to the traditions of men. It was evidently in such a situation that Paul reproved Peter (Gal. 2:11 ff.) because he had given in to the inexperienced who were stupidly observing laws, ignorant of evangelical freedom.

5. As over against the weak and those who have not heard the gospel, the duty of love must be performed and human traditions must be kept, provided that we do nothing against divine law. Thus Paul in Jerusalem had himself shaved since there were still only a few in such a great multitude who adequately understood evangelical freedom (Acts 21:24 ff.). And Paul would rather abstain from meat during his whole life than destroy the soul of a brother. Rom. 14:1: "As for the man who is weak in faith, welcome him." In those times, to be sure, it was a question of divine law, but now when we are concerned with human traditions, let us dispense with them rather freely. It is even godless to obey bishops if they demand observance of these traditions in such a way that they wish to burden the conscience with sin if they are violated. When they are thus exacted, they are "doctrines of demons." But if they are not demanded, let Paul's rule be observed: "We are no worse off if we do not eat, and no better off if we do" (I Cor. 8:8).

You now have the most common fundamentals in the field of theology. Seek a more exact account from the Scriptures; we are content to have stated what you here see. I think I have done well to discuss such important topics more briefly than I should have done, lest with misplaced diligence I call someone away from

Scripture to my disputations. For I think that the commentaries of men on sacred matters must be fled like the plague, because the teaching of the Spirit cannot be drunk in purity except from Scripture itself. For who has expressed the Spirit of God more appropriately than he himself?

Οὐκ ἐν λόγῳ ἡ βασιλεία τοῦ Θεοῦ, ἀλλ' ἐν δυνάμει.

"For the kingdom of God does not consist in talk, but in power" (I Cor. 4:20).

MARTIN BUCER

De Regno Christi

De Regno Christi

EDITOR'S INTRODUCTION

I. MARTIN BUCER, AUTHOR OF *On the Kingdom of Christ*

Martin Bucer,[1] for many years the most prominent leader of the Reformation in Strassburg and, indeed, throughout southern Germany, deserves to be better known. Next to Luther, Melanchthon, Zwingli, and Calvin, he was the most influential of the Protestant Reformers. He helped to introduce the Reformation in Strassburg and then became the chief builder and spokesman of the Reformed Church in that city. He represented and defended it at many important political and ecclesiastical meetings during the Reformation period. Because of his accomplishments in Strassburg, he became an organizer of Protestant churches in many places, e.g., in Hesse and in such important cities as Ulm, Augsburg, and Constance. He spent much time and energy in order to obtain unity in the ranks of the Reformers through the reconciliation of Luther and Zwingli. Indeed, he hoped to unite the German and the Swiss movements of the Reformation. At the same time, he was ready to negotiate with Roman Catholic churchmen in order to bring about a reunion between Protestantism and the Roman Catholic Church. He spared no effort in order to overcome differences. He held innumerable "conversations" and was involved in arguments with defenders of all kinds of religious and ecclesiastical causes—Anabaptists and Spiritualists, trained and untrained theologians, clergymen and laymen, political leaders as well as the common people.

Many were suspicious of him because he was so indefatigable in his readiness to settle disputes. They did not trust him, for he

[1] Cf. Heinrich Bornkamm, *Martin Bucers Bedeutung für die europäische Reformationsgeschichte* (Gütersloh, 1952).

seemed not to take seriously the groundings of the positions that he attempted to reconcile with one another, often by proposing a skillfully formulated phrase. But he had definite and strong convictions of his own. He was not shifty, as many have suspected at his own time as well as later, either in his theology or in his churchmanship. In both respects, he displayed great strength and consistency. This was the secret of his wide influence and of the persistency of his leadership in many places, but chiefly in Strassburg, over many years.

He became a follower of Luther at the very beginning of the Reformation in 1518, under the direct impact of the power of critical and constructive theological thought which Luther displayed in defending his teachings before the convent of Augustinian Friars in Heidelberg. Bucer was then a Dominican monk, steeped in the Thomistic traditions of his order and, at the same time, filled with enthusiasm for the humanistic learning of Erasmus. Throughout his career, he never ceased to exhibit certain characteristically Thomistic trends of thought, but he also held theological views distinctive of Erasmian Humanism.

Yet his basic position was that of one who had learned from Luther that the Bible should be the source and center of all theological thinking. To be sure, from the beginning of his career as a defender of the Reformation, he differed from Luther at certain points, particularly insofar as he stressed the agency of the Holy Spirit in the election of individual believers and in the constitution of the church; but he never wavered in his loyalty to Luther and he adhered to Luther's fundamental teachings. In connection with his work as an organizer, he came under the influence of Zwingli and, in the course of his labors for the establishment of the Reformation in Strassburg, he went far beyond Luther in his insistence that not only the church as an institution but the whole of human life, individual and social, must be ordered according to the will of God as revealed in the Bible. He regarded the Reformation as a movement through which the Christianization of all human life was to be accomplished. The Bible was for him the source and pattern of all legislation required to this end. This view was far different from that of Luther, because it did not agree with the latter's distinction between the law and the gospel.

Bucer stated his distinctive conviction and program not only in numerous memoranda, proposals,[2] and letters addressed to

---

[2] Many of these are now published in his *Deutsche Schriften*, ed. by Robert Stupperich (Vols. I, II, III, and VII have appeared to date; Gütersloh, 1960 ff).

princes and magistrates as well as to clergymen and private persons in Strassburg and elsewhere, but also in theological works of a scholarly character. Most of these were Biblical commentaries (e.g., on The Psalms; the Synoptic Gospels; the letter to the Romans; etc.). Others were in the form of theological treatises, chiefly on ecclesiastical themes (e.g., "Of the True Cure of Souls," "Dialogues on the Christian Magistrate," etc.). These works, which were written (or dictated) in the midst of a very active and greatly varied career of practical church leadership, display broad learning as well as original scholarship. They entitle Bucer to a place of honor next to the technical scholars of the Reformation, especially Melanchthon and Calvin. Indeed, theologically he closely resembles these two. There was a kinship between him and Melanchthon because as Protestant theologians both cultivated the methods of Erasmian Humanism and, probably because of this Humanism, they were prepared to engage in constructive discussions with Roman Catholics. There was also a deep affinity between Bucer and Calvin, not only because their outlook, especially on the needs of the Church, was similar (in this connection, we must note that, like Bucer, Calvin also found himself drawn to Melanchthon), but chiefly because Calvin's mind was profoundly shaped by what he learned and took over from Bucer, particularly during the years (1538–1541) when they were associated in common work in Strassburg.[3]

Bucer's most characteristic book was the last one he wrote, entitled *De Regno Christi* (*On the Kingdom of Christ*), which is here published for the first time in an English translation.[4] It reflects his entire career insofar as in it he sets forth that doctrinal and practical understanding of the Reformation which he had achieved in connection with his work and experience. It shows him as an ecclesiastical organizer of unusual practical talent, as a teacher with great power of communication, and as a theologian with deep moral convictions.

It was written in 1550 for the young English king Edward VI, the son and successor of Henry VIII, in the hope that during his reign and under his own auspices, the Reformation would be established in England in such a way that it would shape and penetrate the entire life of the nation.

[3] Cf. Wilhelm Pauck, "Butzer and Calvin," *The Heritage of the Reformation,* rev. ed. (Oxford University Press, Paperback, 1968), pp. 85–99.
[4] Cf. the excellent critical edition of *De Regno Christi* (Vol. XV of *Martini Buceri Opera Latina* [Paris, 1955]) which has been prepared by François Wendel.

Bucer was then in exile from his own country, having been forced to give up his position as superintendent of the church in Strassburg, because he had urged rejection of the terms of the "Interim Peace" which the emperor Charles V had imposed upon the German Protestants after he had defeated them in the Smalcaldic War. At the invitation of Archbishop Cranmer, he had come to England in April, 1549.[5] In the fall of that year, he was appointed Regius Professor of Divinity at the University of Cambridge. Because of much sickness [6] and considerable difficulty in learning to adjust himself to England, he did not take up his duties as a professor until the first part of 1550. He then offered a course of lectures on the letter to the Ephesians, presided at disputations, delivered series of sermons in Latin, and advised Cranmer and the leaders of the English Church on the introduction of the Reformation.

We do not know when he began to work on *De Regno Christi*. He wrote it in response to a plea of his English friends and sponsors who suggested to him that by way of acknowledging the welcome he had received in their country he might present to the king as a "New Year's gift" a treatise in which his own convictions

[5] On Bucer's stay and work in England, cf. next to the very informative Introduction by Wendel in his edition of *De Regno Christi*: Wilhelm Pauck, *Das Reich Gottes auf Erden. Utopie und Wirklichkeit. Eine Untersuchung zu Butzers De Regno Christi u. der englischen Staatskirche des 16. Jahrhunderts* (Berlin, 1928) ; Constantin Hopf, *Martin Bucer and the English Reformation* (Oxford: Basil Blackwell & Mott, Ltd., 1946) (a good summary of those studies is to be found in Hopf's article "Martin Bucer und England" in *Zeitschrift für Kirchengeschichte* 71 [1960], pp. 82–109) ; and Harry C. Porter, *Reformation and Reaction in Tudor Cambridge* (Cambridge: Cambridge University Press, 1958) , pp. 51–67.

[6] On May 15, 1550, he wrote to the Swabian Reformer Brenz (*Original Letters relative to the English Reformation*, ed. by H. Robinson for the Parker Society [Cambridge, 1846–1847], Vol. I, pp. 543 f.) , as follows: "Ever since August [i.e., 1549] it has pleased God to chasten me by severe illness, the remains of which still confine me, namely excessive weakness in my legs, arms, and hands. In my left hand one and in my right hand two fingers, still refuse their office; so that I am not yet able to write. The Lord gave me some respite about Christmas, so that from that time until the middle of March, I was able tolerably to perform my office; but since that time my most painful disorders returned from which the Lord began to relieve me a little more than a month ago, so that I have since then returned to my duty. My disorders consisted of incredibly cold and slow humours in all my muscles and joints; colic pains, gravely severe pains at first in all my limbs, succeeded afterwards by the greatest weakness and prostration of strength, together with a constant obstruction of the bowels. The Lord spared me to my fifty-ninth year without afflicting me with any grievous disease: it is therefore time for me to feel something of what I have deserved by my sins."

and experiences as a Protestant Reformer would be reflected. On October 21, 1550, he sent the completed work (in the form of a first copy made from his manuscript) to John Cheke, the tutor of the king.[7] We must therefore assume that he composed the book during the summer and early fall of 1550. He must have written it quickly (it was his custom, anyway, to produce his written work in haste), and it clearly shows traces of this. There are many unnecessary repetitions in it, and the style of writing is wordy and often rather careless. Nevertheless, the work as a whole represents a considerable achievement. It is well organized [8] and its content is of great variety and solid substance. Certain parts of it were perhaps written before Bucer came to England and were incorporated by him in his treatise in the form in which he had them available. This is almost certainly the case with respect to the long series of chapters on marriage and divorce [9] which occupy more than a quarter of the whole work and which represent a treatment that in comparison with the other topics is disappointingly long.

What deserves special notice is how directly Bucer addressed

[7] Cf. John Strype, *The Life of the Learned Sir John Cheke* (Oxford, 1821), pp. 55 f.: "In the same year [1550], the XII of the month of November, there passed another letter from Bucer to Cheke, styling him therein *his most honoured patron;* herewith sending him up his most famous book that he wrote for the King on reforming religion *De Regno Christi constituendo;* signifying that he had shown it to none but P. Martyr (then teaching at Oxford), who was, as he said, of the same opinion with him. He added that this book should be read by none but such who should read it for their own and the Church's profit. And he desired him to recommend this his labours and pains to the King."

[8] Cf. the detailed Table of Contents.

[9] On account of the inordinate length of this part of the work only a few chapters of it have been included in this translation.

Throughout his career and especially in connection with his work in Strassburg, Bucer was greatly interested in the best ways by which marriage and divorce should be regulated (cf. Wendel, ed., *De Regno Christi,* p. xlix). He does not indicate in any way whatsoever for what purpose and under what circumstances he prepared the twenty-two chapters on marriage and divorce. He pays special attention to the problems of divorce, and the particular question that was in the center of his interest was under what condition divorce with the right of remarriage can be permissible in accordance with the teachings of Christ which must be regulative for all laws. On the basis of a comparison and harmonization of passages of the Old and New Testaments and by references to natural law as stated in Justinian's *Corpus Iuris Civilis,* he comes to the conclusion that (1) divorce should be granted not only in cases of adultery but whenever the nature of marriage (i.e., the living together of a man and woman as husband and wife) has proved to be unrealizable, and (2) that the innocent partner has the right to remarry.

himself to the English situation in respect not only of problems of the Church but also of general cultural questions, especially such as are related to education, economics, social life, and politics. This is surprising, for Bucer did not understand or speak English. He had to rely for his knowledge of English affairs on his own direct observations. Yet, throughout his career as a Reformer, he had been involved in public affairs, not only as an observer but also as a policy maker. He was therefore capable of quickly assessing the English situation. He was introduced to it by Cranmer and his advisers who were intimately acquainted with the problems and issues that required special attention if the Reformation was to be introduced in England so that it would determine the life of the whole commonwealth. From the beginning of his English sojourn, they sought out his judgment and advice on doctrinal and liturgical questions.

In Cambridge he was treated with greatest respect. Shortly after his arrival there, he was given the honorary degree of Doctor of Divinity on the recommendation of Walter Haddon, Master of Trinity College and Vice-Chancellor of the university (a specialist in Roman law), and on the proposal of Matthew Parker, Master of Corpus Christi College (who was to become the first archbishop of Canterbury under Elizabeth).[10] These two remained his close friends. At the request of Bucer, they agreed to serve as the executors of his last will and testament,[11] and they both were the main speakers at his funeral on March 2, 1551 (Bucer died on February 28, 1551). Haddon delivered the Latin eulogy and Parker the English sermon.[12]

We must assume that he was in touch with these men throughout his stay at Cambridge and that he thus obtained direct information about the conditions prevailing in England. It is reported that the circle of his friends also included, next to Haddon

---

[10] Cf. Wendel, ed., *De Regno Christi*, p. xxvi.

[11] Cf. *Original Letters*, ed. for the Parker Society (Cambridge, 1856), pp. 361 f.

[12] It is said that about three thousand persons attended the funeral at St. Mary's Church. If true, this would indicate how highly esteemed Bucer was in Cambridge. Another proof of the high reputation in which he was held is the fact that when, under Queen Mary, the Protestant Reformation was undone, he was posthumously condemned as a heretic at a formal trial; then his bones were taken from his grave and publicly burned on the Market Square of Cambridge (February 6, 1556). At the instigation of Parker and Haddon, who were supported by Edmund Grindal, Bucer's name was rehabilitated in a public ceremony on July 22, 1560. Cf. *Scripta Anglicana* (Basel, 1577), pp. 935 ff.

and Parker, Roger Ascham,[13] the distinguished Humanist; John Cheke, the royal preceptor; Nicholas Carr, a professor of Greek and a recent translator of Plato's *Laws;* Edmund Grindal, the later archbishop of Canterbury (to whom Conrad Hubert, Bucer's secretary and editor, dedicated the volume of Bucer's works written in England, which he published in 1577 under the title *Scripta Anglicana*); Edwin Sandys, then a preacher in Cambridge and later bishop of London; Thomas Lever, a preacher with a great zeal for social reform; and John Bradford, martyred under Mary, who was Bucer's most loyal English disciple. From these persons Bucer probably obtained the detailed information on the burning economic questions relating to agriculture and the wool trade, unemployment and poor relief, which he displayed in his book when he proposed special legislation concerning these issues.[14]

II. THE PURPOSE OF *On the Kingdom of Christ*

Bucer himself says that it was his purpose to describe "the ways and means by which, as we are taught by the eternal and only salutary Word of God," all Christian rulers, but particularly the king of England, "can and should firmly restore for their peoples the blessed Kingdom of the Son of God, our only Redeemer, i.e., renew, institute, and establish the administration not only of religion but also of all other parts of the common life according to the mind of Christ, our Savior and supreme King" p. 384). This book contains proposals for the introduction of the Reformation in England. It also presents outlines of a series of fundamental laws designed to secure the observance of a Christian "discipline" in all private and social life.

Bucer suggests that the king establish a council of religious affairs whose duty it would be to draw up plans for the Reformation. With the approval of Parliament, evangelists would then be sent to all parts of the country in order to inform the people of the plans made and to render them willing to accept them as their own. At the same time, steps should be taken in order to keep church property for the use of the churches and to administer it in such a way as to make funds available for the salaries of ministers, for their training at the universities, for the maintenance of ecclesias-

[13] Cf. the very informative work of Lawrence V. Ryan, *Roger Ascham* (Stanford University Press, 1963).

[14] Wendell suggests (Introduction, *De Regno Christi*, p. liii) very cautiously that Bucer may have adopted as his own proposals worked out by these friends or other experts. On Bucer's English friends, cf. C. Hopf, *Martin Bucer and the English Reformation*, pp. 16 ff.

tical buildings, and for poor relief. Once all these necessities are fulfilled and properly qualified ministers appointed and installed in their posts, the king should proclaim the introduction of the Reformation throughout the realm. Then he should proceed to draw up and declare a series of laws by the observance of which the kingdom would become a "Christian commonwealth," a *respublica Christiana,* as Bucer loved to say.

These laws relate first to the Church and then to the common life. They number fourteen and regulate: (1) religious education; (2) the sanctification of Sundays and holidays; (3) the sanctification of church buildings; (4) the reformation of the ministry; (5) the protection of church property; (6) poor relief; (7) marriage and divorce; (8) public education and the conquest of idleness (through a proper training for the professions and crafts; the supervision of industry, commerce, and agriculture; and the proper ordering of hostelries, inns, theaters, and public entertainment) ; (9) food; (10) civil legislation; (11) the civil service; (12) the courts; (13) the penal system; and (14) penal law and capital punishment.

What Bucer here has to say is a summary of his experience in church leadership in the city of Strassburg as he brought it to bear on the conditions of England. It is interesting to see how he endeavored to adjust his recommendations to the needs of England while maintaining them in substance according to what he had learned in the republic of Strassburg. What is particularly noteworthy is that he made an effort to be as specific as possible in order to address himself concretely to the prevailing situation. This becomes apparent especially in his frequently reiterated concern for the preservation of church property for ecclesiastical use, for it was in peril of being appropriated by secular powers according to the example set by Henry VIII in the secularization of the monasteries. The same concern is even more obvious in relation to his proposals for poor relief and the abolition of idleness and unemployment in connection with his recommendation for the solution of economic problems peculiar to England as they were raised, during the middle of the sixteenth century, by the growth of the sheep-and-wool industry and the social and economic shifts that resulted from this. In regard to poor relief, he relied on practical lessons he had learned in Strassburg, but he endeavored to justify his views by basing them on new principles of social ethics, namely, the sacredness of labor as it is expressed in the idea of work as a divine vocation. Together with other Protestant Reformers, he (and he especially) had developed these principles as a protest against the Roman Catholic teaching on good works; however, we must assume that he also made himself the spokesman of certain English social reformers who had directed his attention to these matters. Thus he was able to deal with them in the specific way that distinguishes his discourse.

Bucer's *De Regno Christi* contains, then, a program that is remarkable because it advocates the reformation of religion not only in the context of worship and the Church but also relates it to the whole common life.

Following the example of Bucer's earlier interpreters, one may be inclined to regard this work as the outline and description of "Christian politics" [15] or of a "Christian government," but this would not be an entirely correct description either of Bucer's purpose or of his achievement, for he refrains from discussing the basic question of politics, i.e., the form of government; the nature of law and the system of laws, including international law; war and peace; etc. He does not seem to have concerned himself with the problem of political power, its origin and nature, its use and limits. He simply took for granted existing conditions and practices. When he came upon questions of principle, which was unavoidable, he dealt with them either in a pragmatic way or he relied on theological doctrines — and these he regarded as absolutely true and binding and therefore as applicable to all situations. He did not ask himself, so it seems, whether they could really be applied practically. As he saw it, doctrinal truth implied the obligation of carrying out whatever action this truth required.

For example: he was convinced that rulers and governments are responsible for the welfare (*salus*) of their subjects. In a somewhat Thomistic way, he understood this to mean that they must procure and secure for them not only happiness in this world but also eternal salvation. In other words: he believed that they are responsible for the introduction and maintenance of true religion. He was persuaded that this was as feasible as it was true. He believed that this was confirmed by the example of the Jewish kings of the Old Testament, particularly Hezekiah and Josiah, and by that of the Christian Roman emperors, especially Theodosius and Justinian. He thought that they all had actually ruled in conformity with divine law. He idealized them and he was not aware of the extent to which his ideas were unhistorical.

Something similar must be said about his conception of law and legislation. He believed that the Great Commandment must

[15] R. H. Tawney, *Religion and the Rise of Capitalism* (London, 1926), p. 142, calls Bucer's book "a manuscript of Christian politics."

be the basis of all laws. He interpreted this commandment in relation to the moral laws of the Old and New Testaments and, fundamentally, in terms of the Decalogue and the Golden Rule: Do to others what you want others to do to you. He had no doubt that all legislation had to follow this norm and he was sure that it was possible to enforce it. He wrote: "Inasmuch as no sanction or constitution made for the regulation of men's life and behavior can sustain the name of law unless it is derived from the principal law of God and received according to the mind of the provident ruler of all things, and so also all the law of God and the entire teaching of the prophets depend on these two headings as our Savior Jesus Christ has affirmed: 'Thou shalt love God Jehovah with thy whole heart, thy whole soul, and all thy strength, and thy neighbor as thyself' (Luke 10:27), certainly all laws, whether divinely handed down or issued by men, must be referred to these two headings. In all things whatsoever, therefore, which are known, commanded, or forbidden, all who give, revise, and institute laws must first of all see to it that only that is prescribed to men which is accommodated to a pure and sincere worship of God and a firm and dutiful love and beneficence toward one's neighbor, and that whatever is contrary to these things is prohibited" (p. 359).

He was conscious of the possibility that his enterprise might be characterized by some as Utopian [16] but, in the conclusion of his work, he rejected this. "Those who think," he wrote, "that what I have presented is too different from present ways of doing things and the thinking of modern men, a matter of wishful thinking rather than practicality, and that I want to design (*architectari*) some so-called Platonic republic, I earnestly ask, for the sake of the Kingdom and coming of our Lord Jesus Christ and the salvation all of us have in common, that they would judge and estimate what I have proffered and suggested not on the basis of the

---

[16] In my book *Das Reich Gottes* I implied (also indirectly through the title) that Bucer's program must be judged to be Utopian. For this I have frequently been criticized by other interpreters of Bucer (cf. Wendel, ed., *De Regno Christi*, p. xxxix). To be sure, Bucer did not *intend* to present in his book a Utopia, as his own words clearly indicate. Yet a critical historian cannot come to any other conclusion about the feasibility of Bucer's program of social reform than that it was largely unrealistic and, in this sense, Utopian. Also Wendel concludes that with the exception of his proposals for the reform of the church, Bucer's program was unrealizable. Indeed, he says that the attitude which Bucer displayed in most parts of his work "inspired as it was by doctrinal considerations" was as "chimerical as that of Petrarch had been when he recommended to the emperor Charles IV the restoration of ancient Rome" (*ibid.*).

judgment of men of this or an earlier age, but by the eternal and immutable Word of God.[17] Those who make an earnest effort to do this will undoubtedly see and acknowledge that all these things are not remote and different from the aims and practices of modern men who glory in the rule of Christ, but rather that they are easy to receive and observe for all who have not decided to renounce Christ as Lord . . . and that they are necessary for the salvation of mankind both now and forever.

"For how can one acknowledge and adore Christ, God and Man, our only Savior, also as one's own Christ, Redeemer, King, and God, and not accept all his words and try to follow them wholeheartedly, just as they are, the words of eternal life? And is it not necessary for those to whom this has been given, that they receive and embrace the salvation which Christ the Lord offers in his gospel as well as in the sacraments and in all the precepts of his discipline, with as much more ardent a desire and greater a gratitude of spirit as the Creator excels every creature, as God excels men, and as the sure, eternal life and happiness excel a false, empty opinion and an imagined semblance of the good?" (p. 385).

Here he states as plainly as possible why he regarded his program as practicable: In his judgment, it was in accordance with "the eternal and immutable Word of God" and therefore as feasible as it was true.

The reformation of the Church and of the common life that he recommended was thus inspired by doctrinal considerations. One cannot understand Bucer's proposals if one does not relate them to his theological views. He himself makes this plain by the manner in which he introduces his ideas of reform, for he prefaces the second book of his work in which he outlines his program, with a first book in which he develops, always on the basis of the Bible,

---

[17] Here a word should be said about Bucer's Biblicism. It was not as pure as he himself appears to have believed it was. In the first place, he regarded the Old Testament and the New Testament as a unity, as the exegetical chapters of De Regno Christi clearly show. Secondly, he considered the teachings of the fathers as Biblical and he was thus able to regard them as authoritative and fit to supplement Biblical laws with lessons derived from them. In De Regno Christi, he quotes mainly Tertullian, Cyprian, Chrysostom, Jerome, Ambrose, and Augustine. He also cites Eusebius but mainly because of what he wrote about Constantine. Bucer regarded the Christian Roman Emperors as authorities that modern Christian rulers should follow. Fourthly, therefore, he quoted from Justinian's Corpus Iuris Civilis in support and supplementation of his Biblicism. Finally, we must note to what an extent he depended upon Plato's Laws and Republic and upon Cicero's treatises on the Offices and the Laws. It is clear, then, that his "Biblical legalism" was constructed on a broad base.

his conception of the Kingdom of Christ, the Church, and Christian government.

III. Bucer's Theological Presuppositions

"The Kingdom of our Savior Jesus Christ is that administration and care of the eternal life of God's elect, by which this very Lord and King of Heaven by his doctrine and discipline, administered by suitable ministers chosen for this very purpose, gathers to himself his elect, those dispersed throughout the world who are his but whom he nonetheless wills to be subject to the powers of this world. He incorporates them into himself and his Church and so governs them in it that purged more fully day by day from sins, they live well and happily both here and in the time to come" (p. 225).

This definition of the Kingdom of Christ may be regarded as a summary of Bucer's theological convictions. It was his basic concern that men should live "well and happily" [18] and his thinking was directed therefore to the ways by which human lives oriented to such a purpose could be so "administered" and "managed" that this purpose would be realized. He was persuaded that the Church and political government were the two institutions designed for the exercise of this administration and management. Hence he was preoccupied throughout his career with the question of how the Church and the State could be so regulated and ordered that they would fulfill their ultimate functions. But he knew that human designing and planning can never obtain foreseeable results and that human actions do not necessarily obtain the success aimed at. Aware of the possibility that the best-organized church and the best-ordered government, as long as they are merely human creations and enterprises, can fail in providing men with a good and happy life, he viewed them also (and primarily) as divine institutions that are meant by God to serve as instruments for the realization of *his* ends. Thus the concept of the Kingdom of Christ, which in his mind was identical with that of the Kingdom of God, assumed great importance for him, and he thought of the Church and the State only in relation to the Kingdom of Christ. In his view, no church or state would be true unless seen as manifestations of the rulership of God, i.e., the rulership of God in Christ.

As Bucer saw it, there can be no good and happy life apart from Christ. He is the Lord, King, and Savior of men. He rules over

[18] *Bene beateque vivere.* This phrase which he had taken over from Cicero occurs throughout his writings.

them and they are his subjects—not all men, only those whom he has chosen for himself. Only they will obtain eternal life and only they are able to live well and happily, because they are guided by the Holy Spirit, the agent of Christ among his elect. Through the Spirit, Christ has revealed in the Bible his design for the lives of men. Human life must be ordered in conformity with the laws and commandments disclosed in the Scriptures. Christ has chosen to bind his rule to the instrumentalities that are established in obedience to his will. Only through them the true life can be obtained. The chief instrumentalities are the church and the political government, i.e., the church that is ordered according to Christ's law manifested in the Bible and the political government that knows itself as subject to Christ and responsible to him. Thus Bucer linked the Kingdom of Christ, the Church, and the State with one another. He never thought of the Kingdom of Christ apart from the Church and the State and he was unable to deal with either Church or State without relating them to the Kingdom of Christ.

According to his understanding, this Kingdom was the expression of the Kingship of Christ. *Regnum Christi* meant for him the reign or rule of Christ as manifested in the life of mankind ordered according to Christ's will as revealed in the Bible. The true life is realizable only in a Christocracy, i.e., no man can live "well and happily," except in a Christocratic society, i.e., a Christian commonwealth (*respublica Christiana*) which is shaped and dominated by the Christian Church and a Christian government.

Under Christ, the Church and the State are responsible for the cultivation of true religion. Both must carry out his will. Bucer went so far as to describe the duty of political rulers as follows: "The kings of this world also ought to establish and promote the means of making their citizens devout and righteous who rightly acknowledge and worship their God and who are truly helpful toward their neighbors in all their actions. For this purpose, the kings of this world ought also to be ready to undergo any dangers, exile, and even death itself" (p. 180).

The political rulers, therefore, must make sure that the Church is ordered according to the law of Christ. If necessary, they must carry out a reformation. In any case, they control the training and appointment of the ministers. They can use coercion in order to bring about conformity with certain requirements of church discipline, chiefly church attendance and the sanctification of the houses of worship and of Sundays and holidays. They share with the Church, and particularly its officers, the clergy, the responsibility for the observance of Christian (i.e., Biblical) laws of marriage and divorce, for the proper administration of poor relief, for the education and training of young and old. In all these respects, but particularly in relation to education, political rulers are the agents of God. For according to Bucer, every person is endowed by God with special capabilities and aptitudes, which, under divine guidance, must be developed for the good of the community. Those who exercise government must see to it that by education and proper training these gifts are developed. "It is the principal function of kings and of governors," he writes, "to search for and explore what function of life has been designed by God for each citizen, and to take care that each one is initiated, prepared, and helped toward this end from childhood" (p. 227). In another place, he expresses the same thought still more forcefully: "Our heavenly King also attends to the details of providing and making abundantly available the necessities of life to his subjects, so that not a single one among his people shall be in need of these things. For he knows what things they need (Acts 6:1-4; Matt. 6:30-32). First of all, and this is also the duty of the kings of the world, he sets each of his citizens, directly from childhood, to encountering and learning the skills and functions for which he himself has fashioned and fitted each individual" (p. 182).

In dealing with the function of the Church, Bucer writes: "It is not enough for the churches of Christ to care for the mere life of their people, they must also make provision so that they live to the Lord by being useful to one another and to the whole commonwealth and the Church" (p. 315).

Bucer could have used the same words for the ultimate purpose of the State! And, indeed, in his view there was no difference between the Church and the State with respect to the nature and final purpose of their responsibility for their members and subjects, for he believed them both to be in the service of Christ in order to bring about his rule among men. The State uses the sword, i.e., coercive force; the Church employs persuasion. The State governs by means of law and its enforcement; the Church provides inspiration (in the literal sense of the word) for life and regulates it by means of the Christ-appointed offices of preaching and teaching the word, administering the sacraments, as well as the discipline of life (*disciplina vitae ac morum*), and poor relief.

The function of the State and the Church coincide in the fields of discipline insofar as they both assume certain responsibilities for the ordering of family life and the care of the poor: political power by enforcing the basic laws, the Church by providing counsel and supervision, and this, in relation to marriage and the family, through the offices of preachers and elders, and in the case of poor relief, through the office of the deacons. Because they both, the Church and the State, are the instruments by which, under God, Christ exercises his rule, they cooperate with one another in pursuit of the same ultimate end. But the Church is subject to the political government insofar as the rulers control the whole of the common life, and the State is subject to the Church insofar as the political rulers must be directed by the ministers as the representatives of Christ and as the spokesmen of the body of Christ, to a constant consideration of the ultimate end of life, namely, the establishment of the Kingdom, i.e., the rule of Christ.

In the understanding of Bucer, this Kingdom, we must note, is to be established here on earth. The sign that it has actually and fully come will be the realization of a community of love among all men. This brotherhood of love and mutual service will come into being in the natural and historical conditions of life. Through the Holy Spirit they are penetrated by the Christian virtues of which the chief ones are industry in the pursuit of one's God-given tasks and mutual usefulness. "For those over whom . . . [Christ] truly reigns seek nothing for themselves, but only what is useful for others (I Cor. 13:5) : they see to it that each one among them can do his job with complete serenity and diligence, keeping his place in the body of Christ. He does not cause disturbance by meddling, nor is he negligent through indolence or laziness. This is true to such an extent that they refuse to associate with those who fail to do their duty and prefer a life of indolence. . . .

"In all this action they can, as God's children, readily accomplish by the Spirit of God what they have begun. For this Spirit distributes his gifts to each individual, so that everyone can contribute something to the common advantage [19] (I Cor. 12:7). Accordingly, because brotherly love really flourishes among them, those who are endowed with an abundance of temporal goods share liberally with those who suffer from a need of these things" (pp. 182 f.) .

Where such a community of love and mutual service exists, there is the Kingdom of Christ—and there also is the truly Christian Church and the Christian commonwealth.

This was Bucer's deepest religious conviction. By it he was guided in his work of practical church leadership as well as in his theological and ecclesiological writings. It is reflected throughout the program which, in *De Regno Christi*, he recommended to Edward VI for the introduction and establishment of the Reforma-

---

[19] *Ad communem utilitatem* (Wendel, ed., *De Regno Christi*, p. 11).

tion in England and for the transformation of the whole national community of England by the power of the Christian faith.

IV. THE EFFECT AND INFLUENCE OF *De Regno Christi*

The immediate outreach of Bucer's book was small. His personal impact upon English affairs was cut short by his death on February 28, 1551. His memory was kept alive by his numerous friends, and the fact that several among them were men of power who, in the course of time, came to occupy important positions, made it possible that his work and his writings were remembered. His book, a copy of which his wife had taken back from England to Strassburg, was printed only in 1557 in Basel through the good offices of his friend and secretary Conrad Hubert. It is impossible to tell how widely this printing was distributed and to what an extent it reached England. It is noteworthy that a year later there appeared in Strassburg a German translation by Israel Achacius [20] and, in Geneva, possibly under the sponsorship of John Calvin, a French translation.[21]

It is unknown how widely these books were distributed and what impact they exercised. Today, they are to be found only in the rare-book rooms of a few libraries.

In England, they could hardly come to immediate influence.[22] Edward VI died in 1553 to be succeeded by Mary, his sister, the oldest daughter of Henry VIII. She restored the Roman Catholic Church and attempted to stamp out all traces of the Reformation in England. As we have stated before, Bucer was officially declared a heretic and his remains were publicly burned. During Edward's reign, the proposals of his book had been ineffective because the Reformation movement had not sufficiently progressed to allow its sponsors to attempt such steps as he had recommended. There prevailed a great lack of adequately trained preachers and teachers, and the social and moral conditions of the country were so unpromising that the enactment of a program of general reform was an impossibility. To be sure, at the beginning of Edward's reign and under the Protectorate of the Duke of Somerset, the anti-

---

[20] It was printed by Wendel Rihel (1558). In 1568, there was published a new edition of this translation (Strassburg: Emmet).

[21] It was printed by Jaques Berthet (1558). In the same year, another French translation appeared in Lausanne (Mendin, 1558). Except for the first four chapters, it is identical with the Genevan French translation (cf. Wendel, ed., *De Regno Christi*, p. lx). Wendel has issued a modern edition of the Mendin translation as Vol. XV *bis* of Bucer's *Opera Latina* (Paris: 1958).

[22] Cf. Pauck, *Das Reich Gottes*, pp. 107 ff.

Protestant statues of Henry VIII had been suspended and the Reformation had been officially introduced. Royal and episcopal visitations had taken place. Catechisms and collections of evangelical sermons had been published. The Book of Common Prayer (1549, 1552) and the Articles of Religion (1552) had been issued. Next to Bucer, several influential Protestant scholars and preachers from the Continent were active in England, especially Peter Martyr. But a real success of the Reformation could not be felt during the period of Bucer's stay in England. Great things were expected of the young king. Ever since Cranmer had referred to him on the occasion of his coronation as a second Josiah, he was called so by many (including Bucer) who set their hopes on him.

It seems that his book found an echo with the young ruler. In the year 1551, Edward wrote an essay entitled "Discourse on the Reformation of Abuses" which may possibly have been influenced by Bucer's work. It deals, first of all, with the tasks of ecclesiastical power, and special emphasis is put on the strict observance of the order of the Book of Common Prayer and on the introduction of church discipline. But the particular interest of the king belonged to the proposals Bucer made on behalf of secular power. In order to "engender friendship in all parts of the commonwealth," Edward recommends that steps be taken: (1) to combat the luxury that had spread in all classes of the population and (2) to check idleness and unemployment which were becoming worse through the lack of adequate education. All the evils are named that had called forth Bucer's program of reform: e.g., the enclosures, the expensive and wasteful import trade, general wastefulness, the corruption of judges and public officials, etc. The king's proposals for the alleviation of these evils seem to breathe the spirit of Bucer's recommendations: good education, good laws, just jurisdiction, exemplary behavior of officials, punishment of beggars and vagabonds, good service to all customers, etc. Also, the overall idea was possibly inspired by Bucer: society must be organized in such a way that everyone fulfills the position in which he finds himself placed, and nobody harms his neighbors or the whole community by selfishly reaching out beyond the boundaries set to him.

It may not have been incidental that, during the years 1551–1553, Edward was much concerned about the founding of schools and that his main interest was directed to a catechism on which all training in grammar schools was to be based. Such a catechism was written by Bishop John Ponet and published in 1553 on royal and episcopal authority, together with the Articles of Religion.

Thus Bucer's book perhaps actually fulfilled, even if only partly,

the purpose for which it was written. But its effect would undoubtedly have been deeper if Edward VI had not died so soon and
if the development of the Reformation in England had not been
interrupted so suddenly.

When, under Elizabeth, Protestantism was reintroduced in 1558,
Bucer's work had no immediate influence chiefly because by then
he had lost the position of authority that he had enjoyed while he
was alive. However, he continued to be respectfully remembered
by such influential personages as Matthew Parker, Edmund Grindal, Edwin Sandys, and John Jewel, all of whom occupied high
positions in the Church of England during the first part of Elizabeth's reign. Grindal, Bishop of London, collected the treatises,
memoranda, and other materials written by Bucer in England and
sent them to Conrad Hubert for inclusion in the *Scripta Anglicana*. They were published in Basel in 1577 [23] and dedicated to
Grindal. He frequently expressed his gratitude and sense of in-
debtedness toward Bucer.

In the Anglican writings of the sixteenth century, Bucer is most
frequently quoted (and almost always in connection with church
polity) in the writings of John Whitgift.[24] But also the latter's
chief opponent, Thomas Cartwright, referred to Bucer.[25] This
proves that he had adherents among Anglicans as well as Presby-
terians.

In view of the close affinity and resemblance of his ideas to those
of Calvin, one might assume that the Puritans would have been
drawn to him, particularly because of his proposals in *De Regno
Christi*. But this was not the case [26] and, indeed, there is very little
evidence to show that Bucer's total program made a deep impression upon any churchmen in either the Anglican or the Puritan
party. There is a letter by the (Presbyterian) Puritan Thomas
Sampson, addressed in 1577 to Lord Burleigh, Elizabeth's Chan-
cellor, in which he pleads that the polity of the Church of England
should be changed. He refers specifically to *De Regno Christi*,
stating that he knew of no one who was more convincing than
Bucer. He writes that during the preceding year, he had urged

[23] This remained the only volume of Bucer's collected works. Hubert planned
others but he never was able to carry out his project.

[24] One may suppose that Whitgift owed his knowledge of Bucer (he cites not
only *De Regno Christi* but most of his main writings) to John Bradford,
Bucer's close friend, who was Whitgift's tutor at Pembroke Hall in Cambridge (John Strype, *Whitgift* [London, 1718], p. 4).

[25] Cf. Scott-Pearson, *Thomas Cartwright* (Cambridge, 1925), pp. 226, 409 f.

[26] August Lang, *Puritanismus und Pietismus* (Neukirchen, 1941), has tried
to show that this was so, but his assertions are not sufficiently substantiated.

Burleigh to read this book. But Burleigh apparently did not heed this advice. Therefore, Sampson prepared for him a resumé of Bucer's book, omitting only the treatise on divorce, which he was unable to approve. He concluded his letter with the statement that in Bucer's book there were set forth as clearly as possible "the Wants of the Things of Christ's Kingdom in this Kingdom." [27] Burleigh sent a friendly reply saying that he personally would welcome a reform of the faults of the Church, but that he was not able to bring them about in the way he wanted to or as others thought he could.[28]

We do not know whether and under what circumstances others read Bucer's work and how they reacted to it. As a curiosum we record the fact that, in 1644, John Milton, personally interested in the liberalization of divorce laws, published a partial translation of the chapters on divorce that Bucer had included in his book, under the title *The Judgment of Martin Bucer concerning Divorce, written to Edward the Sixth, in his second book of the Kingdom of Christ and now Englisht* [by John Milton], *wherein a later book* [by John Milton] *restoring the "Doctrine and Discipline of Divorce," is here confirmed and justified by the authority of Mart. Bucer. To the Parliament of England* [with a postscript and with various extracts prefixed in commendation of Bucer].

Today, Bucer's work is chiefly of historical interest. It demonstrates to us in an excellent way the deep interest in problems of social ethics on the part of one of the most representative Protestant Reformers. It is no exaggeration to say that Bucer's views on moral issues are not only more comprehensive than those of other Reformers but also just as instructive as those of Luther and Calvin, perhaps even more so.

[27] Cf. Pauck, *Das Reich Gottes*, p. 112; Wendel, ed., *De Regno Christi*, p. l; John Strype, *Annals of the Reformation and Establishment of Religion* (4 vols., Oxford, 1820–1840), Vol. II, Part 1, pp. 392 ff.; Strype, *The Life and Acts of Matthew Parker* (3 vols., Oxford, 1821), Vol. I, pp. 56, 177 f.
[28] Strype, *Parker*, p. 448.

De Regno Christi

THE TEXT

DEDICATED TO EDWARD VI, KING OF ENGLAND

BOOK ONE

PREFACE

MAY THE BENEVOLENCE AND KINDNESS OF GOD OUR HEAVENLY Father, through our Savior Jesus Christ, more and more abound toward Your Royal Majesty, O most glorious and devout King.

I have just recently been reflecting on the fact that those who teach Holy Scripture in the schools of higher learning at Your Majesty's appointment and command, are accustomed at the beginning of the year, as do also his other ministers, to wish Your Majesty a successful passage of the entire year, and at the same time to offer some small service appropriate to their profession. I, too, do not wish in any way to be neglectful of my duty, most especially toward Your Majesty, whom God has enlightened with a broad knowledge of his name, inspired with zeal and adorned with all other virtues like some saving star shining in the darkness and turmoil of this disastrous age for the great comfort and restoration of his people, whom the Antichrists have not completely suppressed.

So far as these things are concerned, what would I not do for Your Majesty if only I might accomplish or produce something pleasing to him who has so kindly received as exiles into his kingdom both me and Paul Fagius [1] of blessed memory, that very select vessel of Christ our Savior; in addition to this, he committed to us the sacred trust of explaining Holy Scripture in this illustrious University of his at so very generous a salary, which he even wished us to enjoy during the months when, hindered by ill health, we were able to do nothing at all in the work of our ministry. But Your Majesty's kindness was by no means satisfied with this; he added a splendid gift of twenty pounds with which I might obtain, not so much a convenience as a necessity, a stove to warm my frail body, exhausted as I am by age and broken by sickness. When I am now comfortably warmed by it, I rightly beg the Lord to warm and foster Your Majesty with the fire of His love and the kindling of every blessing, keeping from him everything cold, whether it be a matter of sins or of disasters and sorrows.

The Lord knows how much I want to show myself grateful to Your Majesty for his most generous and noteworthy kindnesses to me. Therefore, if I had known that it was appropriate also for me to make some little effort for him at the beginning of the year, even though at that time I was feeling rather low and indisposed, I would have made some kind of attempt to produce something of my own. I acknowledge, however, that it is not in my power, even if I were in excellent health, to produce anything worthy of Your Majesty and befitting my vocation. I readily understand literary composition is expected of me, some small work giving counsel on some phase of our religion, something that would both please and prove useful to Your Majesty. But I see that to compose a writing of sufficient excellence for Your Majesty with respect to learning and Christ's religion is far beyond the limits of my talents. But just as God our most indulgent Father finds it enough if we have good intentions and do our best, so Your Majesty, who seeks to show forth the image of God, as is the special duty of pious kings, will not despise whatever small attempts I make to please him.

It would seem fitting to write for Your Majesty a little about the fuller acceptance and reestablishment of the Kingdom of Christ in your realm. Thus it may be better understood how salutary and necessary it is both for Your Majesty and all classes of men in his realm, thoughtfully, consistently, carefully, and tenaciously to work toward this goal, that Christ's Kingdom may as fully as possi-

---

[1] Paul Fagius (1504–1549) was a Hebrew scholar. From 1544, he was a professor of the Old Testament in Strassburg. He was dismissed from this post at the same time that Bucer was forced to give up his duties. He accompanied Bucer to England. He was appointed to teach the Old Testament in Cambridge and soon after assuming this chair he died (November 13, 1549).

ble be accepted and hold sway over us. I shall present the ways and means which are proper, sure, and suitable to advance, recommend, and urge effectively and acceptably this cause in which is contained the eternal happiness and salvation of all. Above all, I shall bend my energies to show from Holy Scripture the nature and properties of the Kingdom of Christ among and within us who live in an age in every way perversely opposed to God. I shall set forth what the Kingdom's fellowship and order really are. Very few people today have any solid knowledge of these mysteries of our salvation, although they repeat so many times, "Our Father who art in heaven, . . . thy Kingdom come" (Matt. 6:10).

I shall advise about these few matters from the eternal word of God as the Lord gives me the gift to do so. And first I shall treat of what the Kingdom of Christ among us is and describe its nature, its distinct purpose, fellowship, and order. Then I shall show how salutary and completely necessary it is for all to direct all concerted thoughts and efforts to have this Kingdom fully accepted and restored among us. Finally, I shall indicate how Your Majesty can and should establish, foster, and encourage the full restoration of the Kingdom of Christ among his subjects.

May our Lord and King, Jesus Christ, be present in his Spirit, that I may offer this counsel completely according to his view and Your Majesty may read it with profit. Amen.

CHAPTER I

NAMES OF THE KINGDOM OF CHRIST

To know more fully and surely the nature and properties of the Kingdom of Christ among his people in this world, and the nature of true fellowship and order in this Kingdom, let us consider first by what names it is called in Holy Scripture, and then what properties are attributed to it. Furthermore, we should do this with the confidence that the Lord and Holy Spirit, just as in the naming of other things, so also in the naming of his Kingdom, has used names most appropriate, descriptive, and meaningful, and has explained so clearly and abundantly what the essence, nature, and proper marks of this Kingdom are that only a sincere and firm faith is needed for us to grasp and hold firmly the meaning of these names and the characteristics which the Scriptures attribute to this Kingdom.

We read that this Kingdom is called "the Kingdom of God"

(Matt. 6:33), "the Kingdom of Christ the beloved Son of God" (Eph. 5:5), and "the Kingdom of Heaven" (Matt. 3:2).

Now, we know that a kingdom, if it is rightly and properly so called, is said to be the administration of a people or state by which the one person who excels the others in wisdom and every virtue so arranges and obtains whatever is for the well-being of the citizens that nothing at all is lacking to them, in such a way that from earliest childhood everyone is formed and led toward a responsible and happy way of life.

Since this is the nature and purpose of any kingdom which can really be called a kingdom, let us consider that the kingdom about which we are reading is called the Kingdom of God. Whatever good properties exist in any human kingdom exist and are found in fuller perfection here, inasmuch as God is above all men, both in the wisdom of his governance and in the benevolence of his will for all mankind. Indeed, since God alone is good, wise, and powerful, only in his Kingdom can those things which ought to be done by royal rule be plainly perceived.

We discover the same thing when we read in Holy Scripture that this is the Kingdom of our Lord Jesus Christ, "the beloved Son of God" (Col. 1:13), for he is of the same nature as his Father. But let us furthermore devoutly consider and ponder in what way the Lord as he was made man aided and began to govern his Kingdom in this world, and promised to do so until the world's end. When he came into this world, sent by the Father into his Kingdom, "he emptied himself, and taking the form of a slave" (Phil. 2:7), showed that he was a man of the common people, without worldly wealth or office. Nor did he "have any place to rest his head" (Matt. 8:20); and when he was seized for torment, he was deserted by all his own (cf. Matt. 26:56). He manifested none of this world's wisdom and eloquence, for they who were then held to be the wisest and holiest among the people of God judged him to be insane and unworthy of a wise man's hearing (John 10:20). And so he found no favor among the powerful, I mean the chief priests, the scribes, and the elders of the people, as well as the Pharisees, so that they were not able to satisfy their hatred of him by insult or injury, until they had brought about his nailing to a cross.

And so this our King chose for himself ministers altogether contemptible in the judgment of the world, unsophisticated, inept, inexperienced in the affairs of men. On account of him they were themselves numbered among the lowest class of men; indeed, they were considered unworthy of being tolerated among men (Rom. 8:36). For like men condemned to death, they were sorely afflicted with hunger, thirst, and all manner of injury; they were beaten, hammered with shouts and blasphemies, excluded from hospitality, and were in every way known as the castoffs of the world, rejected by all (I Cor. 4:9-11).

Although the world and, worst of all, his own people, the Jews, paid back only with great cruelty and inhumanity the most wonderful benefits of our King, which both through himself and through his ministers he daily heaped upon them, nevertheless he subjected himself to all and made himself a minister of their salvation, even unto death (Phil. 2:8), and by doing good for all in word and deed, and also by very great miracles, he made an effort to conquer their savage madness. He evaded the kingdom offered by the people (John 6:15), and assumed so little worldly power for himself that, when Pilate, exercising public authority, pronounced that most unjust sentence of death, he accepted it in a tranquil spirit, acknowledging that Pilate's power over him was from heaven (John 19:11).

Furthermore, in his deep humiliation and rejection, our Lord and Redeemer, in that extreme want of worldly things, in contempt, hatred, and most cruel affliction, nevertheless truly reigned and exercised wonderful power, not only over all material and spatial things and bodies, but also over minds. Those true citizens of his Kingdom whom the Father had given to him he moved with his word and Spirit to follow him most eagerly wherever he went, with parents, wives, children, and all things else left behind (Matt. 4:18-22); and they followed him to poverty, shame in this world, and even death itself, but also to holiness, piety, and righteousness. He controlled with a nod his enemies who were furiously intent upon killing him; with a whip he expelled them from the Temple; by means of a word he prostrated them on the ground; the demons, the sea, the winds, and all creatures he held obedient to his will as often as he wished. How? He had received all power from his Father in heaven and on earth (Matt. 28:18). But he wielded and used that power only by his word and Spirit, without the aids, tools, and weapons of this world. And toward the same purpose, he opened his Kingdom to all and established it through his apostles and ministers. Nor was there ever a time that he ruled among men in any other way, nor shall he ever, in this world.

All this we must know, ponder, and think about with a deeply religious spirit as we hear or remember or read anything about the Kingdom of our Lord Jesus Christ, the Kingdom of the Crucified One.

The third name of this Kingdom, the Kingdom of Heaven,

teaches us almost the same things. First of all, when it is called the Kingdom of Heaven, it is clearly expressed that it is not of this world, even though it is within us, who are still involved in this world (John 17:11). It is of heaven, where we have and invoke our Father and Creator, where our King Jesus Christ sits at the right hand of the Father and establishes all things which are in heaven and on earth (Eph. 1:10); we are invited by the gospel and the Holy Spirit into this Kingdom, and we are directed toward eternal life. Therefore our citizenship [2] ought to be in heaven (Phil. 3:20), as God has chosen us from this world (John 15:19), and together with his Son has vivified us, raised us up, and placed us on high (Eph. 2:5-6). That is, he made us, through faith in himself and his Son, participants in a blessed, heavenly life, and certain of our hoped-for resurrection and translation into heaven, where we may fully enjoy this life of God.

In order that we may more clearly and surely realize what the nature and power of the Kingdom of Christ are, and what is necessary for its restoration among us, let us discuss what things are common to this Kingdom and the kingdoms of the world, and what things are specifically different.

CHAPTER II

What the Kingdom of Christ and the Kingdoms of the World Have in Common and What They Do Not

The first point of similarity between the kingdoms of the world and the Kingdom of Christ is that one person exercises the supreme power of government. There is a difference, however, inasmuch as the kings of the world, since they cannot be everywhere present with their subjects, nor recognize and provide for their realms single-handedly, must establish in various places, according to the size of their kingdoms, representatives, vice-regents, and other authorities, and also have in their power men outstanding in prudence and wisdom, whose counsel they may use in their royal administration.

But our heavenly King, Jesus Christ, is, according to his promise, with us everywhere and every day, "to the consummation of the world" (Matt. 28:20). He himself sees, attends to, and accomplishes whatever pertains to the salvation of his own.

[2] Bucer quotes from the Greek text of the New Testament and writes *politeuma*.

Therefore, he has no need of representatives to take his place. He does use ministers, and certain specific kinds of offices for his work of salvation, but their every work and labor is vain unless he himself gives the growth to their planting and watering (I Cor. 3:6-8); he makes them "ministers of the new covenant, not of the letter but of the Spirit" (II Cor. 3:6). For they cannot even think that they of themselves contribute anything to the administration of this Kingdom whenever earthly kings have need of the kind of minister who will help realize the royal decrees by using his own industry and judgment, and perform the king's orders in a more effective way than originally intended.

Secondly, the governance of the kingdoms of the world and of Christ have this in common, that the kings of this world also ought to establish and promote the means of making their citizens devout and righteous who rightly acknowledge and worship their God and who are truly helpful toward their neighbors in all their actions. For this purpose, the kings of this world ought also to be ready to undergo any dangers, exile, and even death itself. For from God on high they have received all power over his people and the sheep of his fold, "for the building" of their faith and salvation, "not for destruction" (II Cor. 10:8 and 13:10). Thus it is necessary for them, as they use their power, to work with "their whole heart, their whole soul, and all their strength" (Luke 10:27), and to leave nothing undone toward their goal.

Further, although earthly kings extend all their concern in this direction and omit nothing pertinent to this matter, nevertheless they themselves are not able to purge the hearts of men of their innate impiety and unrighteousness nor to endow them with true piety and righteousness. They are able to cut down from the field of the Lord, from the people entrusted to them, the useless trees, briars, and thorns, by the suppression of impious wrongdoing of lost men; they are able to prune and nourish the field, that is, the curable element of the people, with good laws, and to some extent to prepare them for the reception of the Word of God. (In this they ought to work with utmost zeal, for they are ministers of God, made so for this very purpose.) But it cannot be expected that this field will bear the fruit of piety and righteousness until Christ our King has breathed his own increase upon the seed of the gospel scattered there (I Cor. 3:7). For it is he himself alone who regenerates his subjects, and leads those dead in their sins to a life of righteousness (John 3:5 and 5:24-25). That he might receive this power from the Father, he underwent a most bitter death for his subjects, even when they were still his enemies, both personally and collectively.

Thirdly, it is common to the kingdoms of this world and to the Kingdom of Christ that they should tolerate the wicked while they lie hidden among the good; but when they have done their impious misdeeds openly, and will not change their ways when corrected, it is proper to remove them from the commonwealth, as Plato indicates in his *Politics*.[3] For the Lord has commanded his people quite strictly that they are to drive criminal and incorrigible men from their midst, and to burn them with fire, and thus to wipe out their offensiveness as completely as possible (Deut. 13:5 ff.; 17:2-5; 19:11-21; 21:18-21; 22:13-28; and 24:7).

There is this difference, however, between the administration of the kingdoms of the world and the Kingdom of Christ, that the kings of the world, for the amendment of vice and the removal of unworthy citizens from the commonwealth, use, by God's command, beatings, whippings, prison, exile, and various forms of execution. "For they do not bear the sword in vain" (Rom. 13:4). But in the Kingdom of Heaven and of Christ, those who have wandered from the way of salvation, if they are curable, are led back to it with the chains of repentance, under the impulse of only the word and the Spirit. It is sufficient for the people of Christ "to treat as heathens and publicans" those who are obstinate and who persist in their evil ways (Matt. 16:19 and 18:15-18; I Cor. 5:1-5; II Cor. 2:5-11 and 12:20-21; II Thess. 3:6).

However, in order to strike his own with the dread of sinning, Christ our King generally seizes those in his churches who sin more seriously, by sending them now and then sickness and various disasters, and those who persist in wickedness he very often takes suddenly from our midst by horrible kinds of death, casting them away into Gehenna. In the exercise of this severity, he sometimes uses the ministry of evil spirits, as he did in chastising and proving his servant Job (Job 1:12), and in punishing the Egyptians (Ex. 12:23). Occasionally he uses the ministry of his own saints, as when by Peter's rebuke he killed Ananias and Sapphira, and through Paul struck a resisting magician with blindness (Acts 5:1-6; and 13:8-11). He delivered Alexander and Hymenaeus over to Satan for punishment for blaspheming his gospel (I Tim. 1:20). And there were not a few of the saints in the early Church who had this gift and this faculty from the Holy Spirit which Saint Paul, writing to the Corinthians (I Cor. 12:10), called "power."[4] Even

---

[3] Plato, *Politics* 308e–309a.   [4] Bucer writes: *dynamin.*

today the prayers of saintly men against wicked enemies of the Kingdom of Christ are not ineffective; just as the curse of Elisha the prophet was not ineffectual against the boys who were mocking him, for she-bears promptly tore them apart (II Kings 2:23-24).

Fourthly, there is a similarity between the kingdoms of the world and of Christ, in that, as do the kings of the world, so also Christ our heavenly King wants his subjects to be received into and sealed for his Kingdom, to be gathered into his congregations, to come together in his name, and to be ruled by his ministries by means of certain covenants and sacraments of an external nature. Our King, however, cleanses his subjects from sins through his sacraments according to the hidden counsel of his eternal election, and he gives a new and eternal life, beyond the power of earthly kings (Rom. 6:4; I Cor. 12:13; Gal. 3:27; Eph. 5:27; Titus 3:5-7). For that same purpose, Christ our heavenly King wants his own to be divided into certain tribes, so to speak, and he wants them to have their holy assemblies so that there they may hear his Word, pray to him, express thanks for benefits received, both in words and in consecrated offerings for Christ's poor, and finally, in the sacrament of his holy communion, so that they may ratify the covenant of eternal salvation both with God and between themselves, in order thus to be more fully united with their head and to grow up in all things into him (John 6:54-58; Eph. 4:15-16).

Thus, toward this end, he ordains and appoints for his own, ministers and pastors (Eph. 4:11-12) to lay his laws externally before them, to administer the sacraments, and to care for each and every one that through their ministry faith may be preserved among his elect, together with an eagerness for the heavenly life, and that it may grow day by day and be perfected.

Fifthly, our heavenly King also attends to the details of providing and making abundantly available the necessities of life to his subjects, so that not a single one among his people shall be in need of these. For he knows what things they need (Acts 6:1-4; Matt. 6:30-32). First of all, and this is also the duty of the kings of the world, he sets each of his citizens, directly from childhood, to encountering and learning the skills and functions for which he himself has fashioned and fitted each individual. And he has so distributed them that only in his Kingdom this end of civil government [5] is achieved.

For those over whom he truly reigns seek nothing for themselves, but only what is useful for others (I Cor. 13:5): they see to it that each one among them can do this job with complete

[5] Bucer adds: *autarkeia* ("through independence").

serenity and diligence, keeping his place in the body of Christ; he does not cause disturbance by meddling,[6] nor is he negligent through indolence or laziness. This is true to such an extent that they refuse to associate with those who fail to do their duty and prefer a life of indolence (I Thess. 2:9-12; II Thess. 3:7-12; I Cor. 12:24-26; Eph. 4:28).

In all this action they can, as God's children, readily accomplish by the Spirit of God what they have begun. For this Spirit distributes his gifts to each individual, so that everyone contributes something to the common advantage [7] (I Cor. 12:7). Accordingly, because brotherly love really flourishes among them, those who are endowed with an abundance of temporal goods share liberally with those who suffer from a need of these things.

Finally, since no one should come empty-handed into the sight of the Lord in solemn assemblies (Ex. 23:15; Deut. 16:16-17), but should with a grateful heart offer something to the Lord for every last one of his blessings, and these things according to the ordinance of the Holy Spirit are to be dispensed by faithful overseers and deacons of the Church among those in need (Acts 6:1-6), it logically follows that no one among the true citizens of Christ is found in need, but to everyone is given as much as he needs in order to live well and happily [8] (Acts 2:44 and 4:35).

The kings of the world also have the duty to obtain all these things in the commonwealth. They use external power and domain toward these goals in such a way that not a single one of their subjects is in need, but rather that enough will be available to each in order to live well and happily. But they cannot give to those who abound in the blessings of this life a willingness to share readily, or to those in need hearts that will accept an unavoidable dependence on the kindness of others, whereas our King, the dis-

---

[6] Bucer again uses a Greek phrase: *polypragmosynei*. Plato, *Republic* IV, 434b, and *Laws* VIII, 846d–847a.

[7] *Ad communem utilitatem*. Wendel points out (*De Regno Christi*, p. 11, n. 6) that this phrase occurs in the translation of Aristotle's *Politics* published by Faber Stapulensis, where Bucer may have read it. This entire passage is a characteristic statement of Bucer's ideal of work and vocation. It was his opinion that a Christian commonwealth is distinguished from other communities by the fact that all who belong to it are mutually useful to one another. This view, which Bucer believed to be an expression of the Biblical faith he shared with the Reformers, is a synthesis of traditionally Christian and humanistic concerns as they were pursued in the medieval town-communities such as Strassburg.

[8] Bucer liked to sum up his conception of the purpose of life in the phrase "to live well and happily" (*bene* [or *pie*] *beateque vivere*). It is frequently to be found in the writings of Cicero; it is mentioned by Augustine; as used by Bucer, it has a humanistic (Erasmian) flavor.

penser of true love and patience, by his word and Spirit renders the minds of his subjects as willing and strong as possible for this salutary sharing of their wealth and patience in poverty.

To establish more securely and to render more fruitful this sharing of things among his own, he likewise brings about by his word and Spirit that each one of his subjects both enters religiously and develops with constancy that mode of life to which he is called. Marriage in his Kingdom, when his rule truly prevails, entails no rash union nor one according to the desire of the flesh, but is entered into with consideration for the advice and authority of parents or other guardians, whether they be appointed by the family or by the State. And these are especially solicitous to accept for their sons wives who are in agreement concerning religion and who will sincerely subject themselves to their husbands, and cherish and serve them, as the Church cherishes and serves Christ (Eph. 5:24); they should really be faithful in helping their husbands to achieve a pious and blessed life. Accordingly, they make an effort to marry their daughters to this kind of spouse, who will really love them and help them to be holy and devout, and who will show themselves to be truly salutary sources of direction, security, and stability for them such as does Christ the Lord for his body, the Church (Eph. 5:29).

For those who are joined in this kind of marriage in the Lord, our King, likewise, when he has blessed them with children, breathes forth his Spirit that they may start them off with utmost care, and form them in all piety, holiness, and righteousness, as those who recognize that they are teachers more than parents of their children, after they have consecrated them to the Lord in Baptism; for they know that those whom they have generated in the flesh unto death, Christ has regenerated in Baptism unto eternal life. They attend to it, therefore, that through their own efforts as well as those of schoolmasters (who also inculcate pious doctrine as a matter of primary importance in the Kingdom of Christ) and catechists of the Church, they be taught to acknowledge and hate the power of sin inherent in them and to seek from God the Father, through Christ, the one King and High Priest, forgiveness of sins and a spirit of righteousness, and this through a living faith and repentance, to which is always conjoined a zeal for mortifying the flesh and going forward in newness of life. This is that "discipline and instruction" [9] of God which the Holy Spirit commends so earnestly to parents in the letter to the Ephesians (ch. 6:4). By this discipline is fulfilled that which the Lord com-

---

[9] Bucer here used the Greek phrase of Eph. 6:4: *paideia esti kai nouthesia.*

manded concerning those who are baptized: "And teach them to observe whatever I have commanded you" (Matt. 28:20).

Unless the minds of children are formed to this norm and are made accustomed to the obedience of Christ as soon as they have the capacity for understanding, there grow from a root of evil origin briars and thorns of the kind of evils which drive away the seed of the word of God from their hearts so as to prevent it from being received, or choke and extinguish it once it has been received, so that later they can only be helped toward amendment by laws in the way that medicine helps a body wasted by disease, when that body would reject or even render the medicine harmful to itself.

Furthermore, just as our King orders and arranges each of his subjects most opportunely as members of his own body, so he also enables each gratefully to embrace and hold fast to his own place most energetically and faithfully, in whatever role he has been assigned, whether by the world's judgment it is humble, hidden, and full of hardships, or sublime, illustrious, and full of ease.

In this manner our King blesses and favors his citizens in their individual roles and in the functions and tasks allotted to them, so that they embrace each other, each and every one, as members in a body, with supreme love, and have a most attentive mutual concern for each other, as people who really have "one heart and one mind, and all things in common with each other" (Acts 4:32). This, however, in a kind of community which does not disturb any order of mankind established by God, and changes no condition of life designed by him, yet brings it about that each has his own honor and emolument and whatever else may contribute toward a devout and happy life.

Also the kings of the world ought, as I have said before, to establish and work out all these things for their subjects; but their full realization belongs properly to the rule of Christ which has the power to bring this about.[10]

Sixthly, the kingdoms of the world and of Christ have this in common, that they are perpetually at war both with evil men and evil spirits.

It is proper to the kingdoms of the world to use even carnal weapons against evil men. But the Kingdom of Christ fights only with spiritual weapons against its enemies, carnal as well as spiritual. These are the weapons described in the tenth chapter of the second letter to the Corinthians (vs. 3-6) and in the sixth chapter of Ephesians (vs. 14-17).

[10] *Hoc proprium est regni Christi et plane obtinentis.*

Seventhly, there is this similarity between the kingdoms of the world and the Kingdom of Christ, that just as the kingdoms of the world are subordinated to the Kingdom of Christ, so also is the Kingdom of Christ in its own way subordinated to the kingdoms of this world. For although Christ our King, now administering his Kingdom at the right hand of the Father, is subjected to no one and all things must be subjected to him in heaven and on earth, nevertheless, just as he himself, when he was in this world "was obedient even unto death" (Phil. 2:8), a most unjust death, under powers to which he himself had committed the sword, so he wills that his own also should obey from the heart not only the true kings and just princes of this world, but also very iniquitous lords and terrible tyrants to whom public power has been given (I Peter 2:13-17), not only to pay legitimate taxes, but to observe their edicts with a patient spirit, acquiesce to their unjust judgments, and studiously meet all personal obligations to the State.[11] This is what the Holy Spirit commanded in the thirteenth chapter of the letter to the Romans (1 ff.): "Let every soul be subject to the powers that are above them." For when he says "every soul," he teaches by this expression, as Saint Chrysostom rightly gathers,[12] "that this precept has been given not only to lay persons," as they are called, "but also to priests and monks, even if," indeed, "anyone is an apostle, evangelist, prophet, or whatever he is; nor," as the same Chrysostom piously says, "does this subjection overturn piety."

Further, as the Kingdom of Christ subjects itself to the kingdom and powers of the world, so in turn every true kingdom of the world (I say kingdom, not tyranny) subjects itself to the Kingdom of Christ, and the kings themselves are among the first to do this,

---

[11] Bucer's word *respublica* is here translated "state." Elsewhere we generally use "commonwealth." On the significance and meaning of the term *respublica,* cf. the highly instructive discussion by E.-W. Kohls, *Die Schule bei Martin Bucer in ihrem Verhältnis zu Kirche und Obrigkeit* (Heidelberg, 1963), pp. 121–129 (Exkurs II: "Zur Bedeutung und Geschichte des Begriffes 'gemeinnutz' ").

[12] John Chrysostom, *On the Epistle to the Romans,* Hom. XXIII, 1 (*MPG,* Vol. 60, col. 615). The many quotations from the Fathers and also from Canon Law (Gratian) and Roman Law (Justinian I) which are contained in *De Regno Christi* are cited by Bucer from a florilegium, or anthology, i.e., a notebook that he had filled, in accordance with the custom of medieval scholars, with excerpts from the writings of ancient authors (cf. François Wendel, "Un Document Inédit sur le Séjour de Bucer en Angleterre," *Revue d'Histoire et de Philosophie Religieuses,* Vol. 34 [1954], p. 224) which Bucer formulated for the benefit of two Cambridge students who lived with him and his family and attended him as his famuli and menservants.

for they are eager to develop piety not for themselves alone, but they also seek to lead their subjects to it.

In holy Baptism, all are incorporated into the Kingdom of Christ and pledge themselves to its obedience; they come together frequently in sacred assemblies in order there to hear more fully the doctrine of Christ and adapt themselves more surely to his discipline. And if they fall into sin, they do not spurn the bonds of penance, as is exemplified by the conduct of that most religious emperor Theodosius in the Milanese church (Theodoret in his *Church History,* Book V, Ch. 18). For he not only bore it with equanimity but also made it for himself a matter of salutary penitence when Saint Ambrose, meeting him outside the vestibule of the church held him back as he wished to enter as usual and berated him severely because he dared to obtain admittance to the holy assembly, when he had not yet done penance for the cruel slaughter he had barbarously engineered against the Thessalonians on account of the stoning and the outrageous treatment of his judges. For after the people had been called together to witness a spectacle, he had sent the military in against them, and they had killed seven thousand men. He not only willingly accepted that dressing down, but he patiently submitted to the penance imposed by Saint Ambrose, and abstained from sacred functions for eight months. He was finally absolved when he showed his repentance to be real in its fruits and humbly begged for pardon with tears.

So also Valentinian I, although he was more experienced with soldiers than religion, when the Milanese church was without a shepherd, summoned the bishops to elect a bishop for that church, and said piously enough: "You who have been nourished on divine letters cannot be ignorant of how fitting it is for the man to whom the pontifical dignity is to be committed to instruct his subjects not only with doctrine but also by his life and manners, and to be an example of utter blamelessness, so that his service is a witness to his doctrine. Establish, therefore, at this time, a man on the bishop's throne, to whom we who rule the empire can also bow our heads sincerely, and whose corrections (for we are human and must offend) we can willingly accept as a healing medicine." This is what he said (Theodoret, Book IV, Ch. 6).

For true kings, who are none other than Christians, know that they hear Christ when they hear his true ministers, and that they reject Christ when they despise them (Luke 10:16). For the Lord sends his ministers as the Father has sent him (John 20:21). Hence, though pious kings of the world sometimes establish and restore priests of the Lord on their own authority, especially when the priesthood is vitiated and the Church depraved (as we read that David, Solomon, Hezekiah, Josiah, and many other pious emperors and kings did in the light of the New Testament) ; nevertheless, when the ministers of the churches have been legitimately established and they rightly fulfill their office, all true kings and princes humbly hear the voice of Christ from the ministers and respect in them the majesty of the Son of God, as they administer not their own but only the words and mysteries of Christ, the words and mysteries of eternal life.

For this reason, such princes yield fully not only to the public ministers of Christ and the pastors of the churches, but also to the churches in their entirety,[13] and nourish and adorn them with ardent zeal, to fulfill Isa. 49:23: "Kings will be your foster fathers, and their wives, princely women, your foster mothers; with their faces on the ground they shall bow down to you, and they shall lick the dust of your feet, and you shall know that I am the Lord, and that they shall not be ashamed who wait for me." Likewise, that word of the psalm: "And all kings will fall down before him, and all nations shall serve him" (Ps. 72:11).

All true kings have exhibited very many illustrious examples of this holy zeal for the Kingdom of Christ: as David, Hezekiah, and Josiah among the people of the Old Testament, and in the New, Constantine, Jovian, Theodosius, and many others, as ecclesiastical and other histories abundantly testify.

Further, since few men permit the Son of God fully to rule over them, they deserve to receive from him very few true kings, namely, those who know and procure what pertains to their salvation and happiness. Hence it happens for the most part that the citizens of the Kingdom of Christ have generally no support or service from the kingdoms of the world but are harassed and disturbed by worldly tyrants and whatever wicked men these foster.

But however much the world hates and opposes the Kingdom of Christ through its tyrants, nevertheless, "God sends out the scepter of his strength and dominates in the midst of his enemies" (Ps. 110:2), and our King himself gathers, protects, and feeds his

---

[13] *Totis Ecclesiis.* This entire passage is representative of Bucer's concern for the realization of the rule of Christ (*regnum Christi*) in the Christian commonwealth (*respublica Christiana*). He thought of this in terms of a Christocracy, a social order which is dependent upon a church formed and organized according to the authority of the Bible. If necessary, political rulers must help to establish it. Once established, it can rightly demand the allegiance of all, including political rulers. (For the historical content of these ideas, see the references given by Wendel in *De Regno Christi* p. 16, n. 12).

flock in the midst of wolves (Isa. 40:11), as was wonderfully shown in the early Church when he so suddenly increased and multiplied his church at Jerusalem among the fiercest enemies, and adorned it with heavenly gifts, so that it was awesome even to his enemies, and no one dared join himself to it unless our King himself had given him the gift of true faith in himself (Acts 2:47 and 4:4). For he must reign among his elect until the end of the world (cf. Matt. 28:20).

He reigns, however, among these according to his Father's and his own counsel, secret indeed but always just: now among many in fullness in order to open up the infinite treasures of his goodness in vessels of mercy; now among few and more faintly so in order to demonstrate his just severity against the impiety and ingratitude of men who suppress with their lies the truth insofar as somehow they know it.

But if our King, Christ, receives any people into his grace and favor, as of old he made the people of Israel a priestly kingdom, he sets over them princes and kings who, after the example of Moses and Joshua and similar leaders and guardians of the people of God, are primarily concerned about instituting and promulgating religion and allow no one in the commonwealth to violate openly the covenant of the Lord, a covenant of faith and salvation, either by neglect of sacred ceremonies or fixed holidays, or by admitted wrongdoings and crimes, and still less by contradiction or distortion of the Word of God.

It is the duty of all good princes to take every precaution to prevent any one of their subjects from doing injury to another, to prevent children from repudiating the guidance of their parents, slaves from escaping their masters or despising their commands, or anyone from neglecting his duty to any other man. How much more, then, is it necessary to see to it that all governors of commonwealths, when they realize that all their power is from God alone and that he has appointed them shepherds of his people, govern and guard those subject to them according to his judgment, and take care lest any one of those entrusted to them by God, their Maker, Father, and Lord, should weaken in faith or abuse his laws or in any matter take away his honor from him. Hence it is with a truly merciful judgment that God sanctioned in his law the stoning by all the people of anyone who had spoken blasphemy against him (Lev. 24:16), of those who had violated the Sabbath (Ex. 31:14, and 35:2), of those who had embraced a false religion or attempted to introduce one to others, and had deliberately transgressed his laws (Deut. 13:1-10 and 17:2-5; Num. 15:30-36).

When pious kings are thus guarding against wrongs against God, the impiety of many is not indeed eliminated, but it is suppressed, lest it be an outrage before God or a stumbling block for the weak. God, the wise and good governor of mankind, has judged it good to have things this way, that the impious may be compelled to contain their impiety within themselves and to feign piety, which matter would be harmful only to themselves, rather than permitting them to pour out the virulence of their impiety upon others, and to draw away in this manner many who are weak among his people from a true fear and worship of him.

According to his infinite goodness and mercy, he also offers salvation to all and he obviates the excuse of ignorance for anyone. As once he commanded all the sons to be circumcised, whether freeborn or slave (Gen. 17:12) in order that they should observe all his religious laws,[14] so he wills now that all should be baptized (Matt. 28:19) and then be taught under the discipline of the Church whatever he has commanded. This has this advantage, that no one among his people is deprived of saving doctrine and instruction in piety.

When, therefore, we acknowledge that "whatever things have been written" in Holy Scripture "have been written for our learning" (Rom. 15:4; I Cor. 10:11) and that whatever the ancient saints have done by the will of God is proposed to us as an example, so it certainly is the duty of those who want to be true kings of the people of God that in the administration of their kingdoms they prefer no human authority or corrupt custom to God's precepts and the examples approved by God as they are set before us by the ancient leaders and guardians of the people of God.

They shall take care, therefore, first of all, that the religion of Christ be administered by suitable priests of utmost sincerity and ardent zeal; next that according to the Lord's precept, whoever are consecrated to Christ in Baptism be taught assiduously to observe whatever our King has commanded. Nor shall anyone of their subjects contrive openly to subtract himself from the doctrine and discipline of Christ or have the impious audacity to be opposed to him. If, meanwhile, the reprobate make hypocrites out of themselves, rejecting in their hearts the piety which they publicly profess, they will harm only themselves, not others, but they must not be permitted to introduce their impiety to them by word or by deed.

The Lord promised the people such kings through the prophets,

14 *Religiones suas omnes observare.*

on condition that they fully accept the Kingdom of his Son. But in order to show the secret and celestial power of his Son's Kingdom, from the first revelation of his Kingdom to the Gentiles until Saint Constantine, he gave no king to his people; but he tried and proved them with cruel tyrants, even though he granted some respite of peace to them even under impious tyrants.

All the holy martyrs and Fathers have always recognized this, that it is a supreme blessing of divine mercy for true kings and princes to be in charge of human affairs, that is, those who put the Kingdom of Christ first for themselves and take pains to spread it among their subjects day by day more fully. Therefore, the people of Christ, "a royal priesthood, a holy nation, the special people of God" (I Peter 2:9-10), ought to rely only on Christ its King and they should not be disturbed if the petty governments of the world are permitted to be in the hands even of savage tyrants. But they should pray continually to the Lord that he set true kings and princes over the commonwealths, who will administer all things according to his own heart (Jer. 3:15), so that "they may be permitted to lead a quiet and tranquil life in all piety and uprightness" (I Tim. 2:2). And those whom God uses to govern the nations ought, as I have said, to strive and labor for this above all, that they use their power according to the laws of God and according to the examples of pious princes commended by God.

If these examples are religiously considered and the texts alluded to in the Scriptures diligently pondered, it will easily be seen what the Kingdom of Christ has in common with the kingdoms of the world, and what is proper to the Kingdom of Christ, and how they are conjoined and how they should serve each other in mutual subordination. For a better understanding of the power and nature of the Kingdom of Christ, it seems appropirate to suggest some texts of Holy Scripture which explain them more clearly and with greater vividness [15] by painting a picture of it.

For today the knowledge of the Kingdom of Christ is too much effaced and oppressed. And this is sufficiently proved by the actions of those who want to be regarded as those who know the Kingdom of Christ thoroughly and work for its realization.

[15] Bucer writes: *deinōsei.*

CHAPTER III

SOME MORE EMINENT PASSAGES OF HOLY SCRIPTURE CONCERNING THE KINGDOM OF CHRIST, IN THE LIGHT OF WHICH WHAT WE HAVE PROPOSED CAN BE BETTER UNDERSTOOD

Isaiah, more an evangelist than a prophet of the Kingdom of Christ, has described the properties of the Kingdom of Christ in many places with wonderful clarity, completeness, and gravity. The other prophets have also contributed their share. We shall mention only a few of the more obvious testimonies. We read, therefore, first of all in Isa. 2:2, "In the last days it will come about that there will be a mountain of the house of the Lord, solidly established on top of the mountains, and it shall be elevated above the heights of the earth, and all nations shall flow to it."

Because the Church of Christ was first instituted at Jerusalem, in the Scriptures it is therefore frequently called Jerusalem, Mt. Zion, and the Mountain of the Lord. In this we ought to recognize and see the firmly enduring stability of the Kingdom of Christ. For the kingdoms of the world are susceptible to constant changes.

We learn further from the same text that *there was to be established a mountain of the house of the Lord on top of the mountains, and elevated above the heights of the earth,* that all nations and kingdoms must in the end be subject to the Church of Christ if they want to have a gracious God and desire to be partakers of eternal life. For as the same prophet later testifies (Isa. 60:12), speaking the word of the Lord: "All nations and kingdoms shall perish, and altogether be destroyed, which are unwilling to serve" the people of Christ. For forgiveness of sins is not granted, or eternal life received, except in the Church of Christ.

What is added next, "all nations are to flow together to the mountain of the house of the Lord," shows the eagerness for receiving the Kingdom of Christ with which the Gentiles were so remarkably inflamed as soon as it began to be preached to every creature.

There follows in the same prophecy: "And so many peoples will go and say: Come, let us ascend to the mountain of the Lord, and the house of the God of Jacob, and he will teach us his ways, and we shall walk in his paths. For a law shall go forth from Zion, and the word of the Lord from Jerusalem" (Isa. 2:3).

By this forthcoming event, in which he predicts that many peoples will invite each other to ascend the Mountain of the Lord, he teaches enthusiasm for true community in Christ and mutual concern for achieving salvation. For whoever really believes in Christ cannot but proclaim his Kingdom, and invite to it those whom he can. "I have believed," so it is sung in Ps. 116:10, "on account of which I have spoken." Now because the Lord wants his own to be closely connected with one another as members of a body, and support each other in the life of God, he wants sacred assemblies to be held with great devotion for this very cause, in places consecrated to this purpose, not only at Jerusalem or on Mt. Gerizim (John 4:21), but all over the world.

What comes next in the prophecy, "And he shall teach us his ways and we shall walk in his paths" (Isa. 2:3), shows mainly the need of a true Christian congregation to have good, solid doctrine and to live up to it. It must be observed that the Lord himself teaches his own, and he teaches them his ways. Although he uses his ministers for this purpose, it is he alone who makes the doctrine of his ministers efficacious (I Cor. 3:5), and who enables his ministers faithfully to indicate and recommend his ways from his Scriptures, as he commanded them when about to ascend to heaven (Matt. 28:18-20), and as the apostles set about doing on the Day of Pentecost. For this reason he adds, "A law shall go out from Zion, and the word of the Lord from Jerusalem" (Isa. 2:3). By this saying we are taught two things: that the doctrine of salvation is to be sought from Christ alone and only in his Church, and that it is that doctrine which the apostles first began to teach at Jerusalem.

There follows in the prophecy: "And he will judge among the nations, and he shall rebuke many peoples, and they shall beat their swords into plowshares and their spears into pruning hooks; nation shall not lift up sword against nation, neither shall they learn war any more. House of Jacob, come, let us walk in the light of the Lord" (Isa. 2:4-5).

Here it is taught that there ought to flourish in the churches a severity of judgment against sins, so that sins will be remitted for the penitent and believing through the preaching of repentance and forgiveness of sins, but the sins of those who despise the gospel of Christ will be retained. But then if anyone has already been received into the Church of Christ and is more gravely delinquent, the judgment of the Lord ought also to be exercised in regard to such persons that they may be moved to true repentance and urged to bring forth the true fruits of repentance. Those who will not hear the Church in these matters are to be held as Gentiles and publicans, separated from the fellowship of Christ (cf. Matt. 18: 15-18).

What comes next, that "his people will beat their swords into plowshares," etc., is said of those who have truly accepted the Kingdom of Christ, for they deny themselves and seek not their own but only what contributes to the salvation of their neighbor.

In the saying, "House of Jacob, come, and let us walk in the light of the Lord," it is shown that no one is to be reckoned of the house of Jacob, that is, of the true Church of Christ, who does not enthusiastically frequent sacred assemblies and invite those whom he can to the same, that they may thus more clearly perceive and more earnestly follow the light of the Lord, that is, the pure doctrine of the gospel.

A prophecy of the Kingdom of Christ from the eleventh chapter of Isaiah: "There shall come forth a shoot from the stump of Jesse, and a branch shall grow out from his root" (Isa. 11:1).

By these words we are taught that Christ the Lord, as a man born of the seed of David, is the King and Savior appointed to us by the Father. For "he has given his authority to execute judgment because he is the Son of Man" (John 5:27); and because for us "he humbled himself and was made obedient even unto death, even unto death on a cross," the Father "has exalted him above all things and given him a name which is above every name, so that to him every knee shall bow, and every tongue confess him Lord" (Phil. 2:8-11).

There follows in the prophecy: "And there shall rest upon him the Spirit of the Lord, the spirit of wisdom and understanding, the spirit of counsel and fortitude, the spirit of knowledge and fear of the Lord" (Isa. 11:2).

By these words we are taught that as Christ our King did and taught nothing of himself but all according to the will and Spirit of his Father, so also no doctrine, no ceremony, no discipline can be attributed to Christ the King and to his Kingdom, which is the Church, except what has been instituted and come forth from the Holy Spirit by whom are moved all the sons of God (Rom. 8:14). This Spirit, both through the Scriptures and through hidden inspirations, leads his own unto every truth and instructs them in every good work. For he is the Spirit of wisdom, i.e., the one who gives a firm cognition of God and of his works and judgments. He is the Spirit of understanding, imparting a true and salutary understanding of the works and judgments of God. He is the Spirit of counsel, directing our love and judgment in what we have to do.

He is the Spirit of fortitude, for he strengthens the hearts of his own against all the terrors of the world and of Satan and makes them seek always in all things the glory of God and the salvation of their neighbor. He is the Spirit of knowledge, enabling his own knowingly to will and prudently to accomplish the glory of God in all things. He is the Spirit of fear of the Lord, i.e., of true religion, by which the citizens of the Kingdom of Christ, as they worship God more and more ardently day by day, thus obtain from him these gifts of the Spirit more and more generously.

There follows in the prophecy: "And he shall cause him to worship in the fear of the Lord nor shall he judge according to the sight of his eyes, nor reprove according to the hearing of his ears" (Isa. 11:3).

And here we are taught that there ought to flourish in the Church the Lord's judgment, by which those who really believe in Christ may be distinguished from the hypocrites who are insolent toward him; this judgment must be made (if indeed there ought to be a judgment of Christ) not by the mere exercise of human intelligence, nor only on the basis of what is seen and heard, although any tree should be known by its fruits, but religiously, with fear of the Lord, so that it may be a judgment not so much of the Church as of Christ himself, who alone "knows what is in man" (John 2:25) and has received from the Father the power to see and detect good and evil hidden in the hearts of men.

The prophecy continues: "And he shall vindicate the poor with justice, and he shall judge with equity in favor of the afflicted of the land: he shall strike the land with the rod of his mouth, and with the spirit of his lips he shall kill the impious" (Isa. 11:4).

This explains the nature of the judgment of Christ: for those who are poor and afflicted in this world, who feel the burden of their sins and the unbearable anger of God on fire against them, these, endowed with repentance and forgiveness of sins, Christ our King lifts up from the power of Satan and joins to his Kingdom, as he said: "Of such is the Kingdom of Heaven" (Mark 10:14; Matt. 5:3); and he so preserves them that nothing can hurt them but everything must work together with them unto salvation (Rom. 8:28). The song of Ps. 72 (vs. 2-4) and many another prophetic announcement are concerned with this judgment, for the just consolation of all devout men.

What is added about the land being struck with the rod of the mouth of the Lord and the impious being killed through the Spirit of his lips expresses the property of the Kingdom of Christ by which its enemies are struck and killed not by external force of arms but by the word and Spirit of Christ, either for their correction through the gift of knowledge of the gospel and their ceasing to be godless enemies or for their removal from any association with the sons of God.

The prophecy continues: "And righteousness will be the girdle of his loins, and faith the cincture of his reins" (Isa. 11:5).

Here we are warned, if we are true members of Christ, that we ought to be girded with all righteousness and enclosed all about with the faith which the gospel makes known to us.

There follows: "The wolf shall dwell with the lamb, and the leopard shall lie down with the kid. The calf and the lion and fat cattle shall abide together, and a little child shall lead them. The calf and the bear shall feed; their young ones shall rest together; and the lion shall eat straw like the ox. And the nursing child shall play on the hole of the asp; and the weaned child shall put his hand into the basilisk's cavern. They shall not hurt nor harm in all my holy mountain, for the earth is filled with the knowledge of the Lord, like the all-covering waters of the sea" (Isa. 11:6-9).

These words teach us three things: first, that we are in desperate condition when we are born into this world, uncultured and uncivilized, so that we deserve to be compared with lions, bears, leopards, wolves, and the most harmful serpents; secondly, if we are reborn in Christ and have become true citizens of his Kingdom, we ought to burn with such charity and eagerness to deserve well of others that no one would tolerate the discomfiture of anyone else but every individual would try, each according to all his capacity, to contribute as much as possible to the salvation and well-being of his neighbor; finally, that this humanity and love of the citizens of the Kingdom of Christ spring from faith and only from the knowledge of God (Gal. 5:5-6). For faith shows its power through love, which always manages to benefit men, and to be injurious to no one (I Cor. 13:5).

One must note carefully how great a knowledge of God is here promised to the Church, to be spread to all, far and wide. Hence it must be realized that those who wish the Kingdom of Christ to be restored among us ought to make it a primary concern that there be in the individual churches apt and faithful teachers to communicate richly to every baptized person a true knowledge of the Lord, that is, a firm faith in Christ, the only thing by which we live and are saved. They should do this both by sermons and explanations of Holy Scripture, by instructions of the unlearned, and by private admonitions and testimonies.

There follows in the prophecy: "At that time, the root of Jesse shall stand as a sign for the peoples, and the nations shall seek it, and its repose will be glorious" (Isa. 11:10).

Here the prophet foretells that the gospel must be preached effectively to all nations so that as many people as possible from all nations will go to Christ as a saving sign and find in him a glorious rest for their souls, both in this and in the future life, according to his promise (Matt. 11:28-30).

And it must be noted that Christ the King should be made known to all men by the sincere proclamation of the gospel so that all the elect may earnestly seek him and eagerly receive and embrace him as their only Savior; just as the standard of the emperor is raised up high in the midst of his army for all the soldiers to see from far off, that they may readily rally round him if it be necessary. In vain, therefore, do they glory in being the Church of Christ, among whom the clear and constant preaching of the gospel to the people of Christ is not a matter of primary importance and energetic activity, just as we read that Christ himself and his apostles fulfilled this obligation among the multitudes and wherever they encountered those who would listen.

From the thirty-second chapter of Isaiah: "All things will be a wasteland to the people of God, until the Spirit is poured upon us from on high, and out of the desert will come a cultivated land, and a cultivated land will replace the forest" (Isa. 32:15).

From these words we learn that no one comes into the Kingdom of Christ and perseveres in it except by the inspiration and renewal of his Spirit. Before we are inspired and renewed, we are like some horrid desert, producing nothing but thorns and brambles, i.e., works that are burdensome to ourselves and to others. But when our King, after the sending of his gospel, also pours out upon us his Holy Spirit from heaven, we who were before like a sterile thing or a cactus of the desert, now like a cultivated, fertile field bring forth plentifully the fruits of all good works, with such an abundance that we resemble fruitful trees and crops of a field, so densely packed that this field might seem a forest.

There follows: "And judgment shall dwell in the wilderness, and righteousness shall take its seat in a fertile land" (Isa. 32:16).

That is, among a people who before, without the Spirit of the Lord, were like a wasteland now shall prevail the judgment of the Lord, so that men will acknowledge and correct their sins and give themselves over entirely to living according to the law of God. And so righteousness will confirm and establish its seat among them;

whence they shall be filled with every temporal and spiritual happiness, and they will truly be like an excellently cultivated field, pleasant and fruitful.

There follows: "And the work of righteousness will be peace, and the service of righteousness tranquillity and confidence forever" (Isa. 32:17).

Our righteousness is faith, by which we believe that we have a gracious God through Christ the Lord.[16] As we acknowledge that God has been appeased for us and considers us among his sons (Rom. 8:16), and stands by us against all adversities, we then also know from this faith that he alone "accomplishes all in all" (I Cor. 12:6); what then must we seem to fear from flesh and blood or even from spiritual and heavenly dangers (Rom. 8:31 ff.)? Or what is there, finally, which is not to be undergone, undertaken, or done with grateful hearts, whatever the Lord has commanded or imposed on us, however much it might seem burdensome to our flesh?

And so in this, our faith, i.e., our righteousness (cf. Rom. 9:30), as we enjoy peace with God, so also we are always concerned, in regard to doing our share, to cultivate and preserve peace with all men, even our most bitter enemies. Thus we spend a life of wonderful serenity of spirit and divinely inspired confidence and we sanctify the name of the Lord, i.e., we enjoy that peace which Christ alone gives to his own (John 14:27) and the world can neither give nor take away, nor even know, "and which is beyond all understanding" (Phil. 4:6-7).

There follows: "And my people shall sit in dwellings of peace and in tabernacles of confidence, and on serenely happy seats" (Isa. 32:18).

These habitations, tabernacles, and seats of the Church of Christ are the sacred assemblies of those who believe in Christ, in which peace with God is daily offered to us and confirmed among us, and thence peace with every creature, through the gospel of peace and the sacraments of Christ. Whence we lead a confident and happy life in supreme security and contentedness.

We sit, however, in these chosen habitations, tabernacles, and seats, the churches of Christ, when, renouncing every allegiance to the world and to its prince, Satan, we consecrate ourselves wholeheartedly to the fellowship of Christ with all the saints and

---

[16] *Iustitia nostra fides est, qua credimus nos propitium habere Deum per Christum Dominum.* This is a summary of the basic teaching of the Protestant Reformers. Bucer's writings contain many such succinct statements of the fundamental tenets held by Luther and his followers.

to obedience to the gospel, and when we persevere with constancy in this blessed fellowship of Christ and obedience to his gospel, with ever greater progress and profit.

And this must therefore be learned from the foregoing, first that before we are renewed in the Spirit of Christ, we can produce only evil and noxious works; secondly, that they have nothing in common with the Kingdom of Christ who are not renewed and driven by his Spirit to doing the works of righteousness, i.e., believing in the Son of God with a solid faith, and through that faith, by his will, beginning and completing all things. This righteousness alone engenders and sustains peace, serenity, and confidence of spirit in every life. Lastly, we cannot enjoy these great benefits unless we inhere in the Church of Christ and reverence with utmost zeal the communion of Christ, both in sacred assemblies and elsewhere.

From chapter forty: "Get you up to a high mountain, O Zion, herald of good tidings; lift up your voice with strength, O Jerusalem, herald of good tidings; lift up your voice, fear not; say to the cities of Judah: Behold your God" (Isa. 40:9).

Here that property of the Kingdom of Christ is commended to us by which every church of Christ ought so to be a bearer of the good news that in every congregation of the saints the word of the gospel will sound constantly, with very great confidence and ardent zeal. Churches, therefore, where that voice is silent, call themselves in vanity churches of Christ.

The most important point of the gospel [17] is also here expressed, which is for us to show forth and offer as present the Son of God, and to say: "Behold your God," in other words, the forgiver of sins and the giver of all good things and of eternal life. Any true church of Christ should preach and proclaim this indefatigably and as clearly as possible, not only to its own members but also to whatever peoples and manner of men that it can: "Behold your God."

There follows: "Behold the Lord God will come with might, and his arm will have dominion according to his good pleasure; and his reward will be with him, and his recompense will be with him" (Isa. 40:10).

By these words we are taught that Christ alone implants us in his Kingdom, once we have been rescued by his might from the captivity and servitude of Satan, and he alone accomplishes the work of our salvation. Men, even though they sometimes begin many good works, and work very strenuously to complete them,

[17] *Summa Evangelii.*

are, nevertheless, not rarely frustrated from reaping any fruit from their own labors, so that neither they nor others receive any reward or recompense which they seek from their labors. But our King and Lord always presents the completed work of our salvation and an eternity to be enjoyed. For "the Father has handed over all things into his hands, and has given to him all power over all flesh, to be the giver of eternal life," and to perfect in all things those whom the Father has given to him (John 13:3 and 17:2).

There follows: "As a shepherd will he feed his flock, and he shall gather up the young lambs in his arms, and carry them on his breast, and he shall gently watch over those that are with young." (Isa. 40:11).

That quality of the rule of Christ is here commended to us by which he administers it with utmost gentleness and mercy toward those in the Church who are somewhat weak in faith. We are, then, here taught that even though Christ uses his own personally chosen ministers in order to care for and feed his flocks, yet the actual administration of salvation is in every case properly the product of his own personal working. Finally, we are warned, if we are truly of Christ, that as sheep we ought to know and follow the voice of our shepherd (John 10:3-4, 27), and to have no confidence in ourselves or in any other creature.

For as a sheep of the fold among other sheep is stupid and helpless and cannot care for or find pasture for itself, so that unless it is taken care of and fed by a good shepherd it will die, we also cannot know or arrange for ourselves anything at all that pertains to our salvation, and we are the certain prey of ravenous wolves unless our King and Good Shepherd himself introduces us to his sheepfolds, the churches, and in these cares for and feeds us.

When he does this, then what is praiseworthy in sheep prevails among us—insofar as they are not at all quarrelsome, they contribute in every way to the utility of mankind, not only by giving their wool but also by patiently offering their lives, and, lastly, they are not only contented with more arid pastures but actually feed better on them than on more fertile ones: so that we never take revenge for ourselves, but do everything for the utility and salvation of our neighbor, ready to pour out our property and our very souls for this purpose, and we contribute toward the wellbeing of those who would parsimoniously render to us the things which are pleasing to the flesh; indeed, we advance that much the more in the new life, the life of God, the less we have of those things which are desirable to the flesh.

From the forty-second chapter of Isaiah: "Behold my servant, on whom I depend, my chosen one, who pleases my soul; I have put my Spirit upon him, he will bring forth justice to the nations. He will not cry out or lift up his voice; nor will he make his voice heard in the streets. The broken reed he will not break, and the smoking flax he will not extinguish; he will make justice a reality. He will not be cast down in spirit or broken until he has established justice on the earth, and the islands shall attend his law" (Isa. 42:1-4).

Here the prophet teaches, first, that only Christ our King is pleasing to and approved by the eternal Father in all things, as one who has committed no sin, and who has shown himself in all things an obedient servant to him, i.e., a most faithful executor of what he has commanded. That God is said to depend on him is analogous to the kings and great princes who, to a large extent, are accustomed to lean on the shoulders of those who are their special favorites. Secondly, that which is just and equitable, i.e., true justice, comes forth for all the nations from Christ alone through the proclamation of the gospel and by the power of the Holy Spirit. In this we are again taught that the proclamation of the gospel is the main task of Christ the King and all his citizens, and most especially of those who have received a particular calling for this in his Church. Thirdly, the prophet teaches the wonderful clemency, indulgence, and tolerance of our King in bearing with, caring for, and saving the weak. It is also necessary for his ministers to exhibit all these qualities; otherwise, Christ does not live and act in them, nor are they true ministers of Christ.

From the fifty-third chapter of the same prophecy: "Thus it pleased the Lord to bruise him and plunge him into infirmity, that when he offered his soul as a victim for sin, he might see a long-lived seed, and the good pleasure of the Lord would be revealed to prosper through him" (Isa. 53:10).

Here the prophet teaches, first, that Christ our King has by his own death won back for himself his people, whom he calls "a long-lived seed." For this our King regenerates us by his Word and Spirit, so that we are his seed, and he regenerates us unto eternal life. The perpetuity of the church is also foretold as a long-lived seed. It adds that "the good pleasure of the Lord is to be revealed to prosper through him." For the Father wills all the saving of the elect in the whole world to be dispensed through him, by his death and resurrection, with wonderful success among all peoples.

There follows: "Because he has undergone trouble and labor, his spirit shall see glad things, and be satisfied with all good things, and he my righteous servant shall justify many by a knowledge of himself, and he will bear and wipe away their iniquities" (Isa. 53:11).

The prophet here more fully explains the fruit of the death of Christ, for because he has undergone this in obedience to the Father, he has seen the tyranny of Satan destroyed, and he has seen him "falling like lightning from heaven" (Luke 10:18); he has seen that the gospel bears his fruit in the whole world; and thus, thirsting for human salvation, he has been abundantly satisfied. Next he teaches how our King reconciles to the Father and justifies those whom he has rescued from the tyranny of Satan, i.e., brings it about that the Father forgives their sins and remits their deserved condemnation.

Here the prophet introduces the Father, witnessing concerning his Son, the more to arouse and strengthen our faith. He makes the Father call his Son his "servant," because he is about not his own but his Father's business. He calls him "righteous," because he alone has fulfilled the law of God and has not committed any sin; hence he has been appointed mediator between God and us and made the author of our justification. He brings this about in us, as a gift to be tested by us, when he illumines us with knowledge of himself, i.e., the sure faith of the gospel, by which we truly acknowledge him as our Savior and Redeemer, who has taken our sins upon himself and expiated them by his blood lest the Father impute them to us.

Hence, therefore, let us note it is characteristic of our King that "when we were his enemies, he underwent death for us," to restore us to the grace of his Father and make us blessed partakers of his Kingdom (Rom. 5:8-10). Accordingly, let us also here find confirmation of that true doctrine of our justification, namely, that doctrine which consists for us only of faith in Christ.

Finally, let us observe that we are here also taught that no one belongs to the Kingdom of Christ and is a true member of the Church of Christ who is not made strong through faith in Christ, and that a justifying faith.

From the fifty-fourth chapter of Isaiah: "Be jubilant, O barren one, who did not bear; burst forth in a jubilant cry and raise up a voice of exultation, you who have not been in travail. For the sons of the desolate one will be more than of her that was married, says the Lord" (Isa. 54:1).

Here the prophet teaches that the citizens of Christ's Kingdom are procreated by a unique regeneration by their exalted King, and that this had been remarkably begun among the holy ones of the Jews when that people externally deprived of their King were like a barren widow. For by the ministry of a few Jews the world has been filled with Christians inasmuch as it was in Judea alone that once upon a time God was openly proclaimed and known, and the Lord did not manifest this blessing of eternal life to any other nation (Ps. 76:2; Deut. 4:7; Ps. 147:19-20).

Also, here it must be observed with what zeal we should burn to gain as many as possible for Christ. For this is so important for true Christians that when they see many converted to the Kingdom of Christ, with joy and exultation of spirit they burst forth in jubilation and a voice of exultation; and rightly so, in view of the fact that even the angels rejoice if only one sinner is converted to the Lord (Luke 15:10).

From the sixtieth chapter of Isaiah: "Arise, shine; for your light has come, and the glory of the Lord has risen upon you. For behold, darkness shall cover the earth, and mist the peoples; but the Lord will rise upon you, and his glory will be seen upon you. And nations shall come to your light, and kings to the splendor of your rising" (Isa. 60:1-3).

By these words the prophet teaches two things: that God, as he is more fully revealed in the Kingdom of Christ, i.e., in the churches of the New Testament, is more clearly proclaimed and more reverently worshiped than before; secondly, when the Lord makes this light of life, i.e., the proclamation of the gospel, shine forth so brightly among his own, all peoples who despise this light seem by comparison to be the more oppressed by the weight of the darkness of their impiety. Furthermore, all the glory and dignity of the people of Christ consists in this, that they truly acknowledge God in Christ their King and worship him with a firm faith (John 3:19-20; 9:39 and 12:48).

There follows: "Lift up your eyes round about and see; they all gather together, they come to you; your sons shall come from afar, and your daughters shall be carried in the arms and nourished. Then you shall see and be radiant, your heart shall thrill and rejoice. For to you shall come a multitude of those who live on the seacoast, and the enormous strength of the nations shall come to you. An abundance of camels shall cover you, the young camels of Midian and Ephah; all those from Sheba shall come, they shall offer gold and frankincense, and shall proclaim the praises of the Lord. All the flocks of Kedar shall be gathered to you, the rams of Nebaioth shall minister to you; they shall come up with acceptance on my altar, and I will adorn the house of my glory. Who are these that fly like a cloud, and like doves to their windows? For the islands shall attend me, and the ships of Tarshish shall bring your sons from afar, their silver and gold will be with them, to celebrate the name of the Lord your God, the Holy One of Israel, because he will adorn you. Alien sons shall build up your walls, and their kings shall serve you, because in my wrath I have struck you, and according to my benevolence I have had mercy upon you. Your gates shall be open continually, nor shall they be shut by day or by night, that the power of the nations might be brought to you, together with their kings. For the nation and kingdom that will not serve you shall perish, and nations of this kind shall be completely destroyed. The glory of Lebanon shall come to you, the cypress, the plane, and the pine, to beautify the place of my sanctuary; and I shall glory the place of my feet. But the sons of those who have afflicted you will come to you humbled, and prostrate themselves at the soles of your feet, they who have insulted you, and they shall call you the city of the Lord, the Zion of the Holy One of Israel" (Isa. 60:4-14).

The prophet here rather magnificently describes the supreme happiness and glory of the Church of Christ; first, by the multitude of the nations which were eager to flow from all parts of the world to the Church of Christ, beginning with the Jews of the Dispersion, rightly called the sons and daughters of the earliest Church, who had a will and way of life most ready for this service; secondly, by the eagerness of the nations to dedicate and consecrate themselves and all that they had to the Church. For by what he foretells about the camels of Midian and Ephah, the gold and frankincense of Sheba, the flocks of Kedar and Nebaioth, in this he signifies by synecdoche [18] that certain nations would be most eager to offer the Lord whatever was important and dear to them. Whence he afterward says: "Their silver and gold is with them." He amplifies his account of the ardor of this zeal with which the nations were on fire to come to the Church, when he compares the nations and the Jews they were to bring with them to skimming clouds and doves seeking the security of their own window perches. Lastly, the prophet magnifies the glory and happiness of the Kingdom of Christ when he foretells that aliens shall build its walls and kings shall serve it, and that the nations which will not serve the Church will perish. In the end even the enemies of the Church of Christ will humble themselves before it.

It must be observed, however, that in this passage it is foretold by the prophet that Christ, our Lord and King, will effect all these things for the glory of his own name, in order that he may have a kingdom and a holy city on earth, i.e., the Church, adorned with

---

[18] A figure of speech putting a part for the whole.

all piety and virtue. He calls it the place of the feet of the Lord because only in the Church does God manifest himself as truly present proportionately to the mode of our capacity in this life. Otherwise "heaven" is his "abode," where he fully reveals himself; but "earth" for the saints is "the footstool of his feet" (Isa. 66:1), by which he manifests himself to us in part, insofar as we here have the capacity of receiving this gift.

It must also be noted that the prophet attributes to the nations who will come to the Church the duty of announcing the praises of the Lord; for this is the proper and main task of every Christian man. And for this purpose sacred congregations have mainly been instituted, as the Lord says in this same prophet, above, in the forty-third chapter: "Everyone who is called by my name I have created for my glory" (Isa. 43:7). Likewise, a little later: "This people, which I have formed for myself, will announce my praise" (Isa. 43:21). It must, therefore, be seen from this that people among whom the praises of the Lord are not proclaimed with continuous and vigorous enthusiasm have no right to call themselves the people and churches of Christ.

From the sixty-first chapter: "The Spirit of the Lord God is upon me, for the Lord to anoint me; to evangelize the meek he has sent me, and to heal the brokenhearted, to announce liberty to captives and the opening of prison to those who are bound. To announce the year of the good pleasure of the Lord, and the day of the vengeance of our God, to console those who mourn. To propose consolation to the mourners of Zion, to give them a glory instead of ashes, an oil of gladness instead of mourning, to mantle them with praise instead of a grieving spirit, to call them trees of righteousness, the planting of the Lord for glory. They shall build up the places which have been waste for ages, and they shall raise up buildings which have been from their beginning desolate, and they shall restore cities which have been waste and desolate for many generations. And foreigners shall stand and feed your flocks, and aliens shall be your farmers and vinedressers. But you will be called the priests of the Lord; they shall say that you are the ministers of our God; you shall enjoy the wealth of nations, and in their esteem you shall be lifted up" (Isa. 61:1-6).

Here the prophet explains eight qualities of the Kingdom of Christ. First: like Christ our King, all suitable preachers of the gospel ought to be inspired to this duty and office by the Holy Spirit, and as athletes in the Kingdom of Christ anointed and strengthened for that combat with the holy anointing of this Spirit.

Second: it is the sum and substance of the gospel to proclaim the forgiveness of sins through Christ to the penitent, for those who do not yet have this in faith are captives of Satan, detained in the prison of eternal perdition.

Third: only those who have a contrite heart, i.e., regret their sins with true repentance, receive the gospel of salvation.

Fourth: when the gospel is clearly proclaimed, this is a time of the singular benevolence and mercy of God but only to those chosen for the Kingdom of Christ, but to the rest it is a time of wrath and vengeance. For when they reject the gospel of grace, they strike Christ as a rock of scandal and are broken (Matt. 21:44), so that they are deprived of all right reason and salutary counsel in their affairs; a little later this stone falls on them and demolishes them, i.e., destroys them completely. For our King "is set for the rising and fall of many in Israel," and in all other nations (Luke 2:34).

Fifth: whoever are true citizens of the Kingdom of Christ should plainly manifest that they are trees of righteousness and plantings of the Lord, planted to show forth his glory, so that all may see this clearly and proclaim accordingly. For the true Church of Christ cannot be hidden, wherever it is; for it is "a city set on a mountain" (Matt. 5:14); and "the Kingdom of God does not consist in talk but in power" (I Cor. 4:20). And so the light of faith should shine forth in every church of Christ from every Christian, so that all, "seeing their good works, may glorify the Father, who is in heaven" (Matt. 5:16). Therefore, later in the same chapter, the prophet gives this testimony about the people of Christ: "And their seed shall be noble among the nations, and their offspring in the midst of the peoples; all who see them shall acknowledge them, that they are the seed and offspring to whom the Lord has given a blessing" (Isa. 61:9).

Sixth: it is the proper duty of the citizens of the Kingdom of Christ that they restore all the old ruins that have lain waste for many ages, i.e., that they lead many peoples who for generations have been deprived of any knowledge and love of God to faith in Christ and the development of righteousness.

Seventh: this too is characteristic of the Kingdom of Christ, that those who are truly its citizens are all likewise true priests of of God, i.e., by the confession of their lips and of their whole life they announce "his virtues, who has called them from darkness into his marvelous light" (I Peter. 2:9). Likewise, that those who feel themselves too little disposed to or trained for the preaching of the praises of Christ ought to render service to these external ways. For in the Church of Christ, men ought to be so ordered and distributed that those who are better at spiritual things should not be much occupied with temporal things, and those who are less instructed in and inclined toward spiritual matters proper to the Kingdom of Christ should be of service to them in the provision of the necessities of life. Human reason teaches, as can be verified by a reading of the philosophers, that those who have stronger muscles than minds should by the law of nature serve those who have the better minds (Plato, *Republic* II; Aristotle, *Politics* I).[19] This applies also to what the Holy Spirit testifies about the Macedonian and Achaian brethren when they had decided to go beyond friendly communication and send alms to the needy saints at Jerusalem. They decided to go beyond this and yet they were their debtors, as the Holy Spirit there clearly testifies; to which statement he adds this explanation: "For if," he says, "the Gentiles have shared in the spiritual things of the Jews, they ought in turn to minister to them in regard to carnal things" (Rom. 15:26-27).

Eighth: all the riches and glory of the nations are to be dedicated to the Church of Christ; concerning this, the prophet speaks here eloquently and at sufficient length, and also above in chs. 45 and 49, and likewise below in ch. 66.

CHAPTER IV

The Various Periods of the Church

Here it must further be observed that this external glory and happiness are indeed due to the Church and are proper to it, but not at any particular time. For there is a time when our King, to declare his heavenly might in the infirmity of his subjects and to illustrate their faith in him, permits Satan to stir up the entire world against them, and to bring it about that they are hateful to all men for his name's sake (Matt. 10:21-22), and they are handed over to be killed with inhuman cruelty, even a brother by a brother, children by their parents, and parents by their children.

There is likewise a happy time when our King provides for his subjects a surface calm and procures the favor of men, even under the rule of tyrants, as he did in the early Church, as Luke describes in Acts, the second, fourth, and fifth chapters.

Besides this, there is a time in which our King magnificently fulfills the prophecies mentioned about the happiness and glory

[19] Plato, *Republic* II, 371 e; Aristotle, *Politics* I, 5, 1254.

of the Church as he did under Constantine and the pious emperors who followed him, who adjoined and consecrated both themselves and their wealth and peoples to the Church of Christ insofar as they could.[20]

With what ardor Blessed Constantine was aflame, Eusebius of Pamphilia, in his orations about the life of this prince, and Theodoret, in the first book of his *Church History,* relate. For Eusebius writes about him in his fourth oration, that he observed all Christian feasts and ceremonies with utmost reverence and was most devoted to saying his prayers; and he inflamed his armies and his court in every way to have the same sort of zeal. For he showed himself an assiduous teacher and preacher to them and always had religious services conducted in his presence even in camp. He bestowed great honors, too, on the priests of the Lord, who were really fit for their office rather than being secular and courtly; when the people of God were on the increase everywhere in the cities, he built temples for sacred assemblies; in all places he wiped out the profession and equipment of idolatry. He made magnificent donations to the churches of Christ, both in lands and in annual endowments of income from the state to support virgins, widows, and all needy men, children, orphans, and women. And he did this with such great liberality that a third of this liberality was later abundantly sufficient for the churches, the amount restored by the Emperor Jovinian, when the great need of the state compelled him to such a reduction of the generous provision of Constantine. For the man who preceded him, the wicked Julian, had robbed the Church of all the benefits of Constantine (Theodoret Book, I, Ch. 2).[21]

How much care this same Constantine took to drive away from the Church the quarrels and controversies which arose and to preserve the churches and their leaders in devout agreement with the pure doctrine of Christ and true religious worship, no one can sufficiently admire and praise after reading what *Church History* has to say about the religion of this pious prince. So also no one has ever adequately celebrated his politeness, humanity, and attentiveness in assembling three hundred and eighteen holy fathers at the Council of Nicaea; he personally welcomed and embraced them as they arrived in public vehicles and urged them to do their duty; he himself was present at the Council, but he was seated in a place more humble than those which he had prepared for the fathers, and he also entered their discussion about religious ques-

---

[20] Eusebius, *Life of Constantine* IV, 14:18-24; 28.
[21] Theodoret, *Church History* I, 2; IV, 4.

tions, professing that he too was a servant and bishop of the Lord, as the fathers in matters spiritual, so he in matters temporal.[22]

Similarly, the holy fathers and church histories mention very many fine things about the religion and piety of Theodosius, his zeal for the peace of the churches, as well as his kind treatment of them.[23]

Truly in these periods the churches of Christ experienced that abundant kindness of the Lord toward themselves which the prophets had predicted.

Yet it must also be noted that in these prophecies the prophets have so described a temporal glory and happiness for the Church that they have included the eternal, which the saints will enjoy after this life. But because the Church has rarely had the great happiness and glory which the prophets foretold, it must be remembered that these promises were made not to the nominal but to the real people of Christ; they never have become so numerous as to cease to be a little flock in comparison with the rest of mankind.

But if one considers how lost in iniquity all kinds of men are, so that always in every people many are called but few are chosen (Matt. 22:14), he will certainly find nothing wanting in the period of Constantine and the emperors who followed him, in regard to the happiness of the Church of Christ promised through the holy prophets, when churches were raised up all over the world and flourished in exceptional piety.

However, as even very holy men always sin and it pleases the Lord to test and try the faith of his own by various temptations, so the churches never lack his chastising and proving by heretics or false brethren or worldly men, nor will they ever, while they are here on pilgrimage and away from the Lord (cf. II Cor. 5:6).

But the most difficult time of the Church, through which it still passes in so many nations, was when it was oppressed for so many centuries in the service of Antichrists, as can be seen in so many kingdoms of Europe today. For since the Lord preserved in these churches some echo of his gospel and Holy Baptism with the invocation of his name, it cannot be doubted that he had and still has many citizens of his Kingdom among them, although these are involved in very many grave errors and labor under a weakness of faith. For the Antichrists, the pseudobishops and clergy, following their head, the supreme Roman Antichrist, first horribly corrupted the teaching of the gospel with numerous harmful comments about the merits of the saints and those proper to each,

[22] Theodoret, *Church History* I, 7.   [23] Theodoret, *Church History* V, 15 ff.

and about the saving power of their ceremonies, things which are obviously impious and which they also conduct impiously. Furthermore, they present all this to the people of Christ in an alien tongue, and forbid the reading of the Holy Scripture. Finally, they completely overturn the sacraments and the discipline of Christ and do everything in their power to prevent them from ever being restored. Concerning this wretched oppression of the churches under these Antichrists and their extreme wickedness and obstinate perversity, Saint Bernard complained in his time as follows:

"Woe to this generation from the leaven of the Pharisees, which is hypocrisy: if indeed it can be called hypocrisy, when it cannot lie hidden for its very abundance and does not seek to be, so impudent is it. A stinking pestilence today crawls through the whole body of the Church: the more widely, the more destructively; the more dangerously, the deeper it goes. For if a heretic arises as an open enemy, he is cast out and withers: if a violent enemy, the church might hide from him. But now whom shall it cast out or from whom shall it hide itself? All are friends and all enemies; all for and all against; all domesticated and none peaceful; all neighbors and all seeking their own. They are the ministers of Christ and they serve Antichrist; they partake with honor of the good things of the Lord and they do not honor the Lord. Hence what you see daily, harlot colors, stage dress, court apparel; hence gold on bridles, on saddles, and spurs; and more spurs glisten than altars. Hence tables splendid with both food and drink; hence revelings and drunkenness; hence the zither and lyre and drums; hence the rumbling winepresses and full larders, giving forth this and that. Hence colored chests, hence custom purses. For this they want to be and are heads of churches, deacons, archdeacons, bishops, archbishops. Nor do they come to this by merit but by a transaction which walks in darkness (Ps. 91:6). Once it was predicted and now the time of fulfillment has come: Behold, in peace my most bitter bitterness (Isa. 38:17). Bitter first in the slaughter of martyrs, more bitter later in the conflicts with heretics, most bitter now in the characters of the Church's servants. One cannot flee them or rout them: so strong they have become and multiplied above numbering. Intestinal and incurable is the plague of the Church, and therefore in peace its most bitter bitterness. But in what peace? It is both peace and not peace (Jer. 6:14). Peace from the pagans, and peace from the heretics; but not, surely, from the children. There is a voice of wailing at this time: I have nourished and reared children, but they have despised me (Isa. 1:2). They have despised and dirtied me by a shameful life, shameful gain, shameful commerce, a business walking in darkness. What is left but for the noonday devil to rise from the middle of things (cf. Ps. 91:6), to seduce, if they are any left in Christ, those who persist in their simplicity; if indeed he has absorbed the rivers of the wise and the torrents of the strong and trusts the Jordan to flow into his mouth (Job 40:23), that is, the simple and humble who are in the Church. For he is the Antichrist who lyingly calls himself not only day but midday, and is extolled above what is said or is worshiped as God; him the Lord Jesus will kill by the breath of his mouth and destroy by the brightness of his coming (II Thess. 2:8); as the true and eternal midday, the bridegroom and advocate of the Church, who is God above all, blessed forever. Amen." (Bernard, Thirty-third Sermon on the Canticles.) [24]

Saint Bernard complained of these and similar things nearly five hundred years ago. But these evils of the Church have greatly increased and accumulated in the meantime. Truly, therefore, the churches of Christ in Europe never were in worse condition than after the Roman Antichrist established over so many Christian peoples the tyranny in which he maintains himself today with the support of so many great monarchs and nations.

Finally, the present time of the Kingdom of Christ is as yet fluctuating and uncertain. For in some places those who exercise public power rage against no criminals more cruelly than against those who belong to the Kingdom of Christ. In other places, those who are in control make concessions to their citizens and permit them to aspire to the Kingdom of Christ. For they allow them the reading of the Holy Scriptures and the preaching of the gospel as long as they are not held responsible for this and as long as they experience no inconvenience.

During the last thirty years there have also been some, especially in Germany, who have seen to it that a right preaching of the gospel was received and who have let it be their primary concern that the religion of Christ be rightly established. On account of this they faced no small dangers. Yet there still can be found only a few who have become entirely subject to Christ's gospel and Kingdom, indeed who have allowed the Christian religion and the discipline of the churches to be restored throughout according to the laws of our King. But until now the ministers of these churches have not accomplished much, insofar as they should make it their business, first, firmly to demand a confession of faith and

[24] Bernard of Clairvaux, *Sermons on the Canticles* XXXIII, 15 (*MPL,* Vol. 183, cols. 958 f.).

of obedience to Christ from all who have been baptized as infants, once they have matured, and then to see to it that those who have charge of the churches do their full duty by all the baptized by teaching and admonishing them not only publicly but also at home and privately. This is so much a part of the office of pastors and ecclesiastical administrators that those who neglect it are responsible for all those entrusted to their care who perish.

Much less has it been permitted to trusted and proved ministers of the churches, nor have many ministers yet wanted it to be conceded to them, that those who have not acquiesced to private warnings and have been unwilling to withdraw from their open sins, should be called together by them together with the elders of the Church elected for this in the name of the whole Church. They should bind them over to penance, and with the consent of the Church, pronounce those who refuse this remedy of salvation to be regarded as heathens and publicans (Matt. 18:16-17). All know that this discipline of penance was most seriously sanctioned by Christ the Lord and is very greatly salutary if it is reverently administered.

It is so remote a possibility for most princes or magistrates to admit this efficacious remedy for sins that they do not even leave the public preaching of repentance to the ministers of Christ, namely, for the plain correction of all the sins of all orders of people. Many have even demanded that the ministers of the churches give the most holy sacrament of communion of Christ to anyone who asks, without any probing into his faith and life. Nor have there been lacking among the ministers those who have preferred to do this rather than undertake the burden of listening to and admonishing sinners and undergo the odium of this ministry. Thus, real care according to what the Lord has commanded in his law is never taken that the holy days are really sanctified to the Lord.[25]

And so for the most part they seem to have learned only these things from the gospel of Christ: first, to reject the tyranny of the

---

[25] This passage reflects Bucer's efforts and experiences as a reformer, particularly in Strassburg. In this city, he made repeated attempts to establish church discipline but he was never entirely successful, chiefly because the city council, though in favor of the Reformation, refused to accede to his demands for fear the evangelical preachers would become too powerful in their control of the people of the city. Cf. François Wendel, *L'Église de Strassbourg, sa constitution et son organisation* (Paris, 1942), pp. 118 ff., 152 ff., 179 ff.; Walther Köhler, *Zürcher Ehegericht und Genfer Konsistorium,* Vol. II (Leipzig, 1942), pp. 448 ff.

Roman Antichrist and the false bishops. Next, to throw off the yoke of any kind of discipline, penitence, and universal religion which was left in the papacy, and establish and do all things according to the desire and whim of their flesh. Thus it was not displeasing to them to hear that we are justified by faith in Christ and not by good works, in which they had no interest. They never seriously considered what was explained to them about the nature and power of true faith in Christ, and how necessary it is to be prolific in good works. A number of them accepted some preaching of the gospel only in order that they might confiscate the rich properties of the Church.

And so it has happened that in a great many places the entire doctrine of the Kingdom of Christ has been faithfully announced to the people, but I for one cannot say in what churches it has yet been firmly accepted and Christian discipline publicly constituted.

Therefore, insofar as they have refused to accept the Kingdom of Christ entire as it was offered to them, the Lord has with just judgment remitted them to the tyranny of the Roman Antichrist and the false bishops and subjected them to the trials of many other calamities.[26]

In Hungary, by the grace of the Lord, there are now quite a number of churches which accept a solid Christian discipline along with a pure Christian doctrine and observe it religiously. Christ our King has brought it about that many are following the example of these churches.

From these things it can now be seen how varied the ways are by which the Lord treats his churches in this world. Meanwhile, however, there are no churches, or even private individuals, who, if they give themselves over completely to the Kingdom of Christ, will not perceive all the happiness which the prophets foretold, even in this life, in its fashion of the moment, in such a way that they cannot thank God enough, in joy and gladness. For the Lord really repays us a hundredfold, even with persecutions, for whatever temporal thing or comfort we have sacrificed for his name or for whatever discomfort we have sustained (Mark 10:30).

From Jeremiah, the twenty-third chapter: "I shall gather the remnant of my flock from all the countries to which I have driven them, and I shall lead them back to their fold, and they shall fructify and be multiplied" (Jer. 23:3).

---

[26] This is a reference to the defeat of the German Protestants by Charles V in the Smalcaldic War (1547) and to the imposition upon them of the terms of the so-called "Interim Peace" according to which they were compelled to reestablish the Roman Catholic order.

The prophet here teaches that the Church of Christ must be gathered from all nations throughout the world, and that this is a work proper to our King himself. But since this is the proper and supreme work of Christ, as so many times the holy prophets tell us, it is necessary that whoever are his own should serve him in his purpose, every individual person doing his share.

There follows: "And I shall set shepherds over them to feed them, so that they may not fear or be confused, that not a single one of them may perish, says the Lord" (Jer. 23:4).

And here we are taught that after men have been gathered to the Church, it ought to be the first concern of everyone who seeks the Kingdom of Christ that each one should serve Christ our King in this according to his own portion, so that suitable shepherds may be placed in charge of individual churches, to feed them in good faith, i.e., with deep concern to preserve them in the faith and obedience to Christ the King, and to live up to all the functions and roles of the sacred ministry, namely, by a sincere dispensation of the doctrine and sacraments of Christ and by a faithful administration of his discipline. As a result, after faith in Christ has increased among them, all will act confidently in the Lord, free from any fear or disturbance of spirit from all enemies, both spiritual and temporal, and no one will abandon the grace of the Kingdom of Christ which he has received.

There follows in the prophecy: "Behold, the days are coming, says the Lord, when I will raise up for David a righteous branch, and he shall reign as king and administer his charge prudently and happily, and he shall execute justice and righteousness in the land" (Jer. 23:5).

The prophet testifies, first, that only Christ the Lord is truly righteous and justifies those who believe in him; secondly, that he alone is the only true King, and administers a true kingdom among his own subjects, and brings it about that among them all things are inaugurated and pursued prudently and happily and therefore rightly and in good order, i.e., righteously.

There follows: "In his days Judah will be saved and Israel will dwell confidently; and this is the name by which he will be called: The Lord is our righteousness" (Jer. 23:6).

Here the prophet testifies that a sure and saving way of life can be found only in the Kingdom of Christ. All those will certainly obtain it who can dare to call him by this glorious name: "The Lord is our righteousness," i.e., Christ our King, true God and true man (for here is applied as a title the sacred name Jehovah), has reconciled us, freed from sins, to the Father and has obtained the spirit of righteousness, and so, in order that our sins may not be imputed to us in the judgment of God, he reigns and governs us effectively unto eternal life.

From the thirty-fourth chapter of Ezekiel: the Lord says: "I shall preserve my flock, and my sheep will not henceforth be open to attack, and I shall judge between sheep and sheep" (Ezek. 34:20-22).

The prophet teaches that the Kingdom of God and of Christ are one and the same, a saving kingdom in which no one of those who have been truly received perishes. But this Kingdom also has its judgment between sheep and sheep, namely, that of the admonition and correction of sinners.

There follows: "And I shall set up one shepherd over them, to feed them, my servant David. He shall feed them and be to them a shepherd. And I, the Lord, shall be their God, and my servant David a prince in their midst. I, the Lord have spoken" (Ezek. 34:23-24).

Again the prophet testifies that the Kingdom of God and of Christ are the same, a kingdom not only of utmost gentleness but also of most exact and singularly salutary care, as good shepherds watch over the helpless flock of sheep and take care of them. And it must be noticed that he says: "I shall set one shepherd over them," namely, Christ, the Son of David, whom he calls by the name of his father David. Likewise, he says this next: "He shall feed them, and be to them a shepherd." By these words we are taught, as from the following statement, "And my servant David will be a prince in their midst," that the Church of Christ has only one head, Christ, the prince and chief shepherd, and that he himself is always in their midst, and has no need of vicars, although he uses ministers, as has been said above.

It must also be observed that God the Father shows himself to be our God, i.e., the giver of eternal life, when we follow our shepherd, Christ, in his sheepfold, i.e., then we remain in the true fellowship and discipline of the Church.

There follows: "And I shall make with them a covenant of peace, and banish harmful beasts from the land; and they shall dwell confidently in the wilderness and sleep in the forests. And I shall set them around my hill and make rain to fall in its season, and they will be showers of blessing. And the trees of the field will give their fruit, and the earth will give its harvest" (Ezek. 34:25-27).

In these words the prophet teaches that to those who seek first the Kingdom of Christ and consecrate themselves to it, nothing shall be harmful anymore, but everything salutary (cf. Matt. 6:33). God at all events gives this to his people, who accept the entire Kingdom of his Son, even though he wants certain private individuals to give testimony to his goodness and the certain promise of eternal happiness, at the cost of all things present, and even of blood. In these, however, he also instills that fortitude of spirit, and he gives them such a taste for heavenly blessings that with their whole heart they exult and glory in what they suffer for his name's sake.

It has seemed good to me here to call to attention and note a few things from the words of the prophets concerning the Kingdom of Christ. For, as I warned above, there are still only a few who seek out and know enough about all the characteristics of the Kingdom of Christ. I shall next mention a little from the testimony of the psalms, and then from the Gospels and apostolic writings; then, from the foregoing and the prophecies to be mentioned, and the words of the Lord and of the Holy Spirit, I shall offer a definition of the Kingdom of Christ and what must be required of those who wish to keep this Kingdom among them.

From the Second Psalm: "I have anointed my king, my holy one upon Mt. Zion. I shall relate a decree: the Lord has said to me: You are my son; today have I begotten you. Ask of me, and I shall give the nations to you for an inheritance and the ends of the earth for your possession" (Ps. 2:6-8).

First of all, the prophet teaches that Christ our King has been anointed by the Father and constituted King of his Church, i.e., holy Mt. Zion, so that the nations of the world and their kings and princes oppose his Kingdom not only in vain, but also to their own horrible destruction, as they try to *reject* his easy yoke and break the salutary bonds of his doctrine and discipline. Hence the prophet urges all kings and rulers to kiss this Son of God, i.e., acknowledge him their King, lest in his anger "they perish from the way" (Ps. 2:12), i.e., they be cast out of this present life into Gehenna.

Next he teaches that this Kingdom is a kingdom of a proclamation, namely, of this proclamation, that our Lord Jesus is the only Christ and Son of God, whom the Father brought forth for this Kingdom when he raised him from the dead, as Saint Paul has interpreted this text in the address which he gave in the synagogue at Pisidian Antioch (Acts 13:32 ff.). Certainly everything in the Gospels is written about the Lord, as John testifies, "that we might believe that this Jesus is the Christ and that believing we might have eternal life in his name" (John 20:31). Therefore we should note here that where this proclamation of our Lord is *absent*, neither he nor his Kingdom is present.

Lastly, the prophet testifies that the Kingdom of Christ pertains to all nations. On this account, they who make no effort to extend this Kingdom as far and widely as possible are not of Christ.

From the Twenty-second Psalm: "Sovereignty is the Lord's and he shall be dominant among the nations. All the prosperous of the earth shall bow down and adore; before him all shall bend the knee who go down to the dust and whom no one can keep alive. Posterity shall serve him and be accounted to the Lord for generations. Men shall come and announce his righteousness, which he has done to a people yet to be born" (Ps. 22:29-32).

The prophet here sings, first, that the Kingdom of Christ is a kingdom of all nations; also, of all men, both living and dead; and of the living, whether they have social standing and wealth or are in need and oppressed.

Next, that those who have entered the Kingdom of Christ are going to eat the bread of life, "which comes down from heaven," i.e., they will enjoy the holy communion of Christ (John 6:33). For he has sung above that they are to be satisfied, from which satisfaction it comes about that they adore Christ and in him the Father, in spirit and in truth, and subject themselves in all things to his will.

Finally, he gives testimony about the permanency of the Church and its supreme function, which is righteousness, i.e., to proclaim and pass on to those who come after us the eternal goodness of our King.

The Forty-fifth Psalm sings magnificently of the omnipotence, magnificence, and splendor of our King and his Kingdom, i.e., the Church.

The Forty-eighth Psalm sings very clearly how immense the joy is which the Kingdom of Christ brings, and how it stands unconquered against all the world's power, so that in it alone is God's graciousness set forth and justly celebrated, and finally, with what great ardor we must reverence this Kingdom.

That our King, acting with power in fulfillment of hope, vindicates his own who are oppressed in the world, gives them the peace which passes all understanding, (Phil. 4:7) and multiplies them, subjects all nations and kings of nations to himself and humbles them, and fulfills all things abundantly out of his kindness. All this the Seventy-second Psalm celebrates (likewise, Ps. 96, 97, 98, and 99); likewise, Ps. 122 and 145.

Psalm 110 sings, first, of the exaltation of our King at the right hand of the Father and that all his enemies are to be prostrated at his feet as footstools; secondly, that the scepter of this our King, i.e., the administration of his Kingdom, is to come forth most powerfully from Zion and will rule in the midst of his enemies. Thirdly, that the people of Christ will be willing and strong, like the heavenly dew of the morning multiplied in the splendor of holiness, i.e., will glorify God frequently in meetings of worship. Fourthly, that the Kingdom of Christ is established by the immutable oath of God, and it will therefore be an eternal kingdom. It adds that there will be a priesthood according to the order of Melchizedek, as this Melchizedek blesses Abraham and his people, i.e., all the faithful, and is honored by them by all manner of gifts, such as are thought to please him. Lastly, that God will always have this our King at his right hand, and will destroy his enemies completely, and with drink from a heavenly torrent, i.e., the consolation and strengthening of the Holy Spirit, he will wonderfully console and strengthen this King in his members in every hardship and affliction from the hands of the godless.

From the Gospel of Matthew, the first chapter: The angel to Joseph, the foster father of the Lord, concerning Mary, the virgin espoused to him: "What is conceived in her is of the Holy Spirit; for she shall bring forth a son, and you shall call his name Jesus; for he shall save his people from their sins" (Matt. 1:20-21).

Here we are taught in prophecy that our Lord Jesus Christ, inasmuch as he is of the Holy Spirit, and, therefore, without sin and was made man, has come for this very purpose, to establish a kingdom of the elect of God to free them from their sins. He does this especially in the administration of his Kingdom, through all administration of its doctrine and discipline, that men might acknowledge their sins, be freed from them by him, and live to righteousness.

From Luke, the first chapter: The angel Gabriel said to the Blessed Virgin, the Mother of the Lord: "Fear not, Mary, for you have found grace with God, and, behold, you will conceive in your womb and bring forth a son, and call his name Jesus. He shall be great, and will be called the Son of the Most High, and the Lord God will give to him the throne of David his father, and he shall reign over the house of Jacob forever, and of his Kingdom there shall be no end" (Luke 1:30-33).

Here we are taught that Christ will reign only in the elect of God, i.e., over the house of Jacob, and his Kingdom will be eternal, i.e., it will endure until the end of the world. And thus there will always be churches of Christ, wherever they may be.

From Matthew, chapters three, four, and ten; and from Mark, the first chapter; and Luke, the tenth: "Repent, for the Kingdom of Heaven is at hand" (Matt. 3:2; 4:17; 10:7; Mark 1:15; Luke 10:9).

Therefore, it is a quality of the Kingdom of Christ that in it the repentance of sinners must always be preached. Hence where the Kingdom of Christ has been truly received, there it is necessary that the sins of all be severely rebuked, that men may give themselves up completely to the Kingship of Christ in order to be cleansed from their sins and endowed with the spirit of righteousness.

There follows in the fifth chapter: "Blessed are the poor in Spirit, for theirs is the Kingdom of Heaven" (Matt. 5:3).

Thus no one will have a capacity for the Kingdom of Christ unless he truly acknowledges his sins and feels the wrath of God aflame against them, so that he is poor in spirit and in need of good things, i.e., he is of a humble and contrite heart.

There follows in the same book, in the seventh chapter: "Not everyone who says to me, Lord, Lord, will enter into the Kingdom of Heaven, but he who does the will of my father in heaven" (Matt. 7:21).

Thus it is a hollow mockery that those who do not make a wholehearted effort to do the things that are pleasing to the heavenly Father should declare themselves citizens and members of the Kingdom of Christ.

There follows in the sixteenth chapter of the same book: The Lord said to Peter: "To you I will give the keys of the Kingdom of Heaven, and if you bind anything on earth, it will be bound in heaven, and if you loose anything upon earth, it will be loosed in heaven" (Matt. 16:19).

Here the Lord clearly teaches that he wishes his Kingdom to be closed to some, opened to others: opened to those who, if they are adults, show to the Church their good faith concerning their repentance and belief by their own confession which is proved by the witness of their lives; but closed to all who refuse to make this kind of a confession of faith and profession of obedience to Christ or who are found to negate by their own wicked deeds what they confess with their lips.

The Lord teaches us here, furthermore, that inasmuch as his Kingdom is to be closed through the sacred ministry to those who are obstinate in sins, those who are quite seriously delinquent but still curable must be brought to do penance and show the Church adequate fruits of repentance, just as in civil affairs the citizens are occasionally remanded for a time to prisons and chains on account of their crimes. We must note how gravely Christ our King sanctions this discipline when he remarks that those who have been bound and loosed in the Church will be bound and loosed in heaven.

Nor should we overlook that in this text this power is handed over to the whole Church and not only to Peter or his successors, as the Lord testifies clearly below in chap. 18 (Matt. 18:15 ff.). For although this power is to be wielded by the ordinary ministers of the Church, nevertheless this ought to be done with the consent of the entire Church; just as the apostle Paul was unwilling to hand over the incestuous Corinthian to Satan on his own authority alone, but rather by the assembled Corinthians, he being with them in spirit (I Cor. 5:3-5). Since Peter too made his confession to the Lord not only in his own name but also in the name of all his colleagues and thus of the entire Church, it is certain, as Saint Augustine and the other holy fathers have well concluded, that the Lord wishes his response to Peter to apply to the whole Church of Christ.[27]

There follows in the twenty-first chapter of the same Evangelist: "For this reason I say to you that the Kingdom of Heaven is to be taken away from you and given to a nation bringing forth its fruits" (Matt. 21:43).

Hence let us learn that the Kingdom of God does not remain, or even exist, where its fruits, i.e., the works of all piety and righteousness, are not manifested. And when this sterility of good works publicly prevails in some nation, the Lord transfers his Kingdom, i.e., the administration of man's salvation through pure doctrine and his salutary discipline, to another one.

We must also consider reverently those parables by which the Lord has wished to explain the properties of his Kingdom, as when he compared his Kingdom to a sower of good seed, only a fourth of which fell on good ground and bore fruit (Matt. 13:4 ff.). Likewise, to a good field planted with wheat, in which an enemy planted weeds (vs. 24 ff.). Also, to a net holding good and bad fish (Matt. 13:47 ff.). Then to a royal wedding and a great banquet, to which those invited were unwilling to come, some injuring and even killing the servants of the Lord sent to call them to the wedding; but one entered without a wedding garment, and was cast out into the outer darkness (Matt. 22:2 ff.; Luke 14:16 ff.). Finally,

---

[27] Augustine, *On the Gospel of John* XI, 5 (*MPL*, Vol. 35, col. 1478); L, 2 (*ibid.*, col. 1762); Cyprian, *On the Unity of the Church*, IV (*MPL*, Vol. 4, cols. 512 ff.).

to ten virgins, of whom the foolish were not careful to have oil with them for their lamps (Matt. 25:1 ff.).

For by these parables the Lord teaches, first, that it is proper to his Kingdom for the word of life to be offered to all, even though very few genuinely accept it, and that those who yield to this word in any way, unless their pretense is obvious, are to be received into the Church, kept in it, and continually called to a living faith in Christ until by their wicked deeds they plainly deny the faith they profess with their lips.

Next, that the true servants of our King should not desist from offering his Kingdom to all men simply because all too many do not accept it in their hearts, and some even reproach them with all manner of insults and wrongs on account of this very great favor.

Lastly, although the hypocrites must be tolerated in the Church, as long as they are hidden, they will nevertheless finally be separated horribly from the saints and cast into hell as men born and bred by the devil; they are nothing but a scandal in the Kingdom of Christ (Matt. 13:41).

We must also conscientiously consider that parable of the householder who hired laborers for his vineyard at various times during the day and gave the same pay to those who had worked for only one hour as to those who had worked from morning to night (Matt. 20:1 ff.). For by that parable we are taught that where Christ truly reigns, there will always be some who are brought to his Kingdom, and all who are really his serve the Lord with ardent zeal toward this very end. That the same pay was given to all shows that whatever good the Lord returns to us is due to the grace of our King and not due to human merit, although we seem to have labored long and hard and to have suffered much for his glory.

From Matthew, the last chapter: The Lord, about to ascend into heaven, says to his disciples: "All power is given to me in heaven and on earth. Go, therefore, and make all nations my disciples, baptizing them in the name of the Father, and of the Son, and of the Holy Spirit, teaching them to observe all that I have commanded you. And behold, I am with you all days, even to the consummation of the world" (Matt. 28:18-20).

Here the Lord teaches, first, that he has received power from the Father over all, both men and spirits, and even over all creatures. Next, that his Kingdom ought to be offered to all nations. Further, that all the citizens of his Kingdom ought to be incorporated into himself in Holy Baptism and to be dedicated to the communion and discipline of his Church. In this regard, it is the function of the ministers of his Kingdom to teach all the baptized to observe whatever he has commanded, to teach them diligently, perseveringly, and in every way both to care about the precepts of Christ and wholly to consecrate themselves day by day to be more fully perfected in all things.

On this account, loyal ministers of Christ would also not fail (besides giving public explanations of the Scriptures and exhortations derived from them) assiduously to instruct ignorant Christians in the catechism, admonish individuals privately and at home concerning their duties, and correct delinquents, and, finally, by pious conversations, come to the aid of those who adhere to some doctrine other than that of Christ and who are weak. Thus those confirmed in the gospel faith will not allow themselves to be moved by any current of false doctrine (Eph. 4:14). Lastly, he teaches that he will always be present to his own, and he will make the organization and teaching of his Church effective.

From the third chapter of the Gospel of John: "Amen, amen, I say to you," the Lord said to Nicodemus, "whoever is not born again cannot see the Kingdom of God." And a little later: "Amen, amen, I say to you, unless a man is born of water and the spirit, he cannot enter into the Kingdom of God" (John 3:3-5).

Here we may see that it has been defined that one not only cannot be received into the Kingdom of Christ, but cannot even know it, if he has not been reborn, and this must be of water and the Spirit, i.e., by Holy Baptism (received at least in intention if not in actual fact) and renewal of heart by the Holy Spirit.

From the letter of Paul to the Romans, the fourteenth chapter: "The Kingdom of God is not food and drink, but righteousness and peace, and joy in the Holy Spirit" (Rom. 14:17).

We must learn from this that in the Kingdom of Christ we have complete external freedom, and we must seek to realize this one thing, that righteously, i.e., living by the faith of Christ, we may enjoy peace with God and men, and hence with every creature, and thus rejoice and exult continually in our Lord and King.

From the first letter to the Corinthians, the fourth chapter: "The Kingdom of God does not consist of talk but of power" (I Cor. 4:20).

It is indeed fitting for the word of the Kingdom of Christ, i.e., the gospel, to be preached with utmost care and reverence, and not to be squandered rashly and inconsiderately; but we do not gain the Kingdom of God through this, however accurate and careful is the word we speak or however eagerly we hear; there must be

present a heavenly power to crucify and abolish the old man and
to form and perfect the new (Rom. 6:6; Col. 3:9) .

From the sixth chapter of the same letter; likewise from the fifth
chapter of the letter to the Galatians and from the fifth chapter of
the letter to the Ephesians: "Make no mistake: the unrighteous,
fornicators, idolators, adulterers, lovers of ease, homosexuals,
thieves, the greedy" (who seek worldly things immoderately) ,
"drunkards, slanderers, these will not inherit the Kingdom of
God," nor do they have any part in it (I Cor. 6:9-10; Gal. 5:19-21;
Eph. 5:5) .

Since, therefore, those who persevere in manifest wickedness
have no part in the Kingdom of Christ, once they have been exposed, they ought also to be excluded from any association with it,
through the discipline of the Church.

From the first letter to the Corinthians, the fifteenth chapter:
"Afterward the end, when he has handed over the Kingdom to God
the Father, after destroying every rule and every authority and
power. For he must reign until he has put all his enemies under
his feet" (I Cor. 15:24-25) .

The Kingdom of Christ in this world is the ministry of salvation
of the elect of God, by which our King, as he daily cleanses from
sins those who have been given to him by the Father, ever more
delivers them from the power of Satan and makes them acceptable
to himself and guards them from all evils. This is why there will
be nothing left of sin in the saints after the resurrection, and
"God will be all in all" (I Cor. 15:28) , and then there will be no
more need in the Kingdom of Christ and in its administration
for the elect of God to be delivered from sins and from the devil.
Then, therefore, having properly discharged his duty, Christ
our King will turn over to the Father his sovereignty and power by
which he has redeemed his elect from all evil and led them to the
life of God, and with the Father he will live in them eternally and
be glorified by them.

Then he shall also abolish every other rule, whether of men or
of spirits, all power and might, with no distinction as to what
serves or opposes his Kingdom (Eph. 1:21) . For he will have his
holy ones with him in heaven, perfected in all righteousness, need-
ing no outside government or regulation. The wicked, however,
both spirits and men, he will plunge into hell (Matt. 13:42) , from
where they will have no power further to trouble the saints. But
until these things are accomplished, and while the elect are yet in
this world, and there are enemies of Christ our King left in the
world, he must reign, i.e., administer salvation for his own and

vindicate them from sin and from Satan until he has subjected all his enemies under his feet, either by their conversion from their impiety to his Kingdom or by their rejection to Gehenna.

But since the work and governance of the Kingdom of Christ will not be perfected except by the regeneration of the elect of God through a blessed resurrection, eternal life and that perfect righteousness in the saints are sometimes called in the Scriptures "the kingdom of God." As when the Lord, already facing his passion, said to his disciples: "And I appoint to you, as the Father has appointed to me, a Kingdom, that you may eat and drink at my table in my Kingdom" (Luke 22:29-30). What Paul wrote to the Corinthians pertains to the same thing: "This, in truth, I say, brethren, that flesh and blood cannot inherit the Kingdom of God, nor will corruption inherit incorruption" (I Cor. 15:50). He means that while we are yet burdened with this flesh and blood, we cannot perceive our accomplished salvation and our restoration, by which God is all things to us; and for this reason we must first be renewed by corporal death and a blessed resurrection, and become completely spiritual. The rest is properly said to be, and is, the Kingdom of Christ, which he administers in this world by vindicating his own through the gospel and his Spirit from the power of Satan, and sanctifying them, and leading them to the Father.

Whoever considers devoutly the texts which we have here proposed will readily understand the nature and makeup of the Kingdom of Christ as well as its properties, and will see what must be sought and forsaken by those who wish this Kingdom of Christ to be firmly restored among them.

From these texts, therefore, we shall propose an organized definition of the Kingdom of Christ and itemize its properties in an orderly way for the sake of greater clarity for the reader, and we shall indicate how necessary these things are for salvation, and how earnestly they should all be renewed and restored. Those who neglect this, which, sadly enough, is today the case for not a few, can glory about the Kingdom of Christ in their midst with only empty words, for they show that they are still completely destitute of the reality.

CHAPTER V

WHAT THE KINGDOM OF CHRIST IS, AND WHAT IS NECESSARY FOR ITS RESTORATION

The Kingdom of our Savior Jesus Christ is that administration and care of the eternal life of God's elect, by which this very Lord and King of Heaven by his doctrine and discipline, administered by suitable ministers chosen for this very purpose, gathers to himself his elect, those dispersed throughout the world who are his but whom he nonetheless wills to be subject to the powers of the world. He incorporates them into himself and his Church and so governs them in it that purged more fully day by day from sins, they live well and happily both here and in the time to come. But perhaps it would be helpful for this definition of the Kingdom of Christ to be elaborated on at a little greater length and more clearly, once it has been comprehended in these few words.

A More Elaborate Definition of the Kingdom

It is, therefore, the administration and care of the eternal life of the elect of God in this world, by which the only-begotten Son of God, after sending them his gospel through ministers chosen by him for this purpose and the breathing forth of his Spirit, gathers them to himself from the world (although he wishes them to be subject for good to the powers of the world, indeed, to all men in the world, to whom he himself has made them neighbors [I Peter 2:13]); those so gathered he incorporates into himself and his holy Church which is his body by most holy Baptism and the compact and sanction of the solemn divine covenant, that is, adoption into sonship. And thus he rules and governs those who have been incorporated into himself and his Church, purging them daily more and more from sins and establishing them in all piety and righteousness and hence eternal life. He also shapes and perfects them, using for this purpose the ministry of his word and sacraments through fitting ministers, in public, at home, and in private, and also by the vigilant administration of his discipline, not only of penance, but also of ceremonies and of the entire life.

From this definition, then, let us itemize and, if you please, propose for consideration what things are proper to the Kingdom of Christ and must be required and recovered by all those who really want the Kingdom of Christ to be restored among them.

The first of these is that whatever is done in the churches should pertain to the ministry and contribute to the gaining of men's salvation in such a way that, cleansed from sins and reconciled to God through Christ, they may worship and glorify God in Christ the Lord in all piety and righteousness.

Whatever does not contribute to this end, and nothing can do so which has not been ordained for this purpose by the Son of God and so commended to us, should be rejected and abolished by those who wish the Kingdom of Christ restored among them: such as, for example, all dogmas of religion not derived from Holy Scriptures. Likewise, that men so impure and profane should control the priesthood in the churches; that sacred rites should be performed for the people in a foreign language; a corrupt and perverse use of the sacraments of Christ; the addition of sacraments of human invention; invocation of the saints who have completed their pilgrimage; idolatry, and the like. Hence it is also a valid conclusion that those who do not subject themselves in all things to the Kingdom of Christ and devote all their labors for it to be restored among them will not be partakers of eternal life.

Another property of the Kingdom of Christ is that the elect are gathered from the world into this Kingdom through the preaching of the gospel, ministered by fit ministers chosen and sent for this very purpose by the Lord himself, with the simultaneous breathing forth of the Holy Spirit, the Spirit of faith, through whom it is given to men to have a real faith in the gospel. In this way, certainly, both the Lord Christ himself and his apostles restored the sovereignty of God in the world.

And so it is necessary that those who wish the Kingdom of God to be restored among them pray to God, as a matter of first importance, that he send true and faithful preachers of the gospel to his people and to the churches.

"For how shall they preach unless they are sent" (Rom. 10:15) by our High Priest and King himself, Jesus Christ? For it is his alone to give to the Church "some apostles, some prophets, some evangelists, some pastors and teachers" (Eph. 4:11-12) to choose and gather his elect in his body. For on this account our King Christ "descended to the lower parts of the earth" (Eph. 4:9), "dead for our sins" (I Cor. 15:3), and again ascended into heaven, to the right hand of the Father (Rom. 8:34), "for our justification" (Rom. 4:24-25).

The Lord himself declared this very thing when he said to his disciples, after his resurrection, "As the father has sent me, I send you, and when he had said this, he breathed on them and said,

Receive the Holy Spirit; whose sins you shall forgive, they are forgiven them, and whose sins you shall retain, they are retained" (John 20:21-23). It is, therefore, only for the Son of God to send suitable and effective preachers of his gospel, and to instruct them by his Holy Spirit to discharge their duty in a saving way.

Further, whoever pray sincerely to this Lord of the harvest "that he send laborers into his harvest" (Matt. 9:38) and give many evangelists once more to his wretchedly oppressed and divided churches, evangelists instructed in heavenly virtue, such persons cannot fail to work and struggle diligently to seek out those whom the Lord has designated for this task, of whatever age or condition of life, and having found them, to help them in every way, so that they may be most thoroughly prepared, proved, and sanctified to meet this most holy calling redemptively.

On this account, as it is a principal function of kings and of governors to search and explore what function of life has been designed by God for each citizen, and to take care that each one is initiated, prepared, and helped toward this end from childhood, so certainly the same persons ought to exercise utmost interest and a primary concern among their subjects, and, wherever possible, to seek and find those whom the Lord seems to have appointed to this supremely salutary work, necessary before all others, of preaching the gospel. So Paul glories that he had been "separated for this work from his mother's womb" (Gal. 1:15). They should take care that such of these as they can discover be initiated and trained from childhood for this most holy office, and that those who have been duly tested and proved be used in their good time for this function. This is certainly necessary before all things else, to be realized with utmost zeal by all kings and princes of the people of God who pray from their hearts, "Thy Kingdom come" (Matt. 6:10).

A third property of the Kingdom of Christ, which we have already mentioned, is that, although this Kingdom is heavenly and governed only by Christ the Lord and not by this world, nevertheless, all its citizens, and all their pastors and teachers, ought to be subject to the world's authorities to whom the Lord has entrusted the administration of the sword, and, according to their capacity, they ought to strive to be of benefit to all men. We shall speak later about the duties in the state from which it is fitting for true ministers of the churches to be exempted, when we explain by what manner and means the Kingdom of Christ is to be restored among us.

A fourth property of the Kingdom of Christ is that adults should not be received into the Kingdom of Christ, i.e., his Church, unless they are first sufficiently instructed in the gospel of Christ, acknowledge and deplore their sins, renounce Satan and the world, profess complete submission to the gospel, and do not manifest a way of life and manners repugnant to this profession. Then, after this, the Kingdom of Christ should be bestowed upon them, and as their sins are forgiven and washed away in the most holy sacrament of Baptism, the covenant of salvation, their adoption as sons of God, should be confirmed and sealed. In this way we read that John and the apostles conferred Baptism and received men into the Kingdom of Christ (Matt. 3:11 ff.; Mark 1:4-5; Luke 3:16-21; Acts 2:38-41, 16:15, and 19:4-5) ; the ancient churches religiously observed this way of doing things, so that, when the gospel had been preached to a group before all things else, individuals confessed their own belief in it, and the churches grounded them in the catechism of Christ and every doctrine of piety, and made them disciples of the Lord, and then finally came Baptism, when, having confessed their sins, they renounced the world and Satan and professed obedience to Christ.[28]

This is the precise procedure which the Lord commanded, when after his resurrection he sent his apostles to preach the gospel of his Kingdom and to gather the churches. For he said to them: Go therefore, and teach the nations [29] "baptizing them in the name of the Father, and of the Son, and of the Holy Spirit" (Matt. 28:19) , i.e., teach all nations, and make them disciples to me by teaching, and this no one can be unless he has been taught the doctrine of Christ and has professed it.

Saint Peter has a similar teaching, when he writes, "We are saved by baptism, not the putting away of the filth of the flesh, but the interrogation [30] of a good conscience toward God, through the resurrection of Jesus Christ" (I Peter 3:21). In these words he clearly admonishes that adults who are to be baptized ought to be interrogated about their faith and profess it openly in the church.

But since our infants also ought to be baptized according to the promise of the Lord, "I will be your God, and the God of your seed" (Gen. 17:7) , both the parents of the baptized infants and the ministers of the Church must take the responsibility that, as soon as they have matured, they will be diligently catechized and

---

[28] Cf. Tertullian, *On Baptism* 2, 7, 8, 18–20 (*MPL*, Vol. 1, cols. 1309, 1315 f., 1329 ff.) .

[29] Bucer cites the Greek phrase of Matt. 28:19.

[30] Bucer writes *eperōtēma*. In this entire passage, he gives forceful expression to his conviction that Christian life and discipline must be based on the teaching of Biblical doctrine and Biblical ethics.

instructed in the doctrine of Christ, so that they may make for themselves publicly in church the profession of their faith which they were unable to do when they were baptized, confessing their sins, and embracing with a most grateful heart the grace of Baptism conferred on them in infancy, renouncing the world and Satan, and pledging themselves to the obedience of Christ.[31] For although human beings, whatever they promise, are unable to manifest anything of piety which Christ the Lord does not effect in them and they necessarily manifest all things which he does effect in them, nevertheless this same Lord makes it his gift that it is a sharp spur to his elect if they have promised anything solemnly.

For this reason, it pleased the Lord that the people of the Old Testament should confirm the covenant of salvation so often by the public profession of their obedience, as we read in Ex. 24:7, Deut. 29:10 ff., and 31:10 ff., and the last chapter of Joshua (24:16 ff.). These texts should be diligently read and pondered by all who wish the Kingdom of Christ to prevail among them. And in the texts of Deut., chs. 29 and 31, it must be most especially observed that the Lord wished the covenant to be renewed with his people every seventh year, and in the presence of the women and children.

But God has also instilled it in the nature of man, that although we see very many men not keeping their promises, not even oaths, except for their own gain (which they reckon falsely), nevertheless no citizen is received into the commonwealth, nor into any legitimate partnership, unless he swears and promises with his own lips the things that pertain to a good citizen or partner.

Since, then, whatever matters with regard to arousing men to a true obedience of Christ is to be taken advantage of with utmost zeal by all who seek Christ's Kingdom, who would doubt that this applies particularly to the churches of Christ? They should require of individual Christians their personal profession of faith and Christian obedience: of adults, before they are baptized; and of those who are baptized as infants, when they have been catechized and instructed in the gospel of Christ; and if any do not permit themselves to be catechized and taught and refuse to follow all the precepts of Christ and to make a legitimate profession of faith and of the obedience to be rendered to Christ and his Church, they ought to be rejected from the company of the saints and the communion of the sacraments, because those who are of this kind

---

[31] Confirmation in this sense was first introduced into the church of Strassburg by Bucer. It came to be regularly observed first in Lutheranism and then also in other Protestant groups through the influence of his written pleas (like this one) upon certain readers, e.g., Jacob Spener, one of the "fathers" of German Pietism.

openly repudiate the grace of Baptism and altogether separate themselves from the Kingdom of Christ. For the precept of the Lord is manifest in the last chapter of Matthew: that the baptized must be taught to observe whatever he himself has commanded.

A fifth property of the Kingdom of Christ is that all its true citizens offer themselves to Christ the King to be ruled and governed throughout life, i.e., to be purged from sins unto all piety and righteousness, i.e., to be instructed, trained, and perfected unto eternal life, and this through the sacred ministry of the Church. Hence it is necessary for every church of Christ to have this ministry duly constituted, i.e., to have priests [32] and ministers who both can and will, with utmost zeal and perseverance, instruct and advance toward eternal salvation, each and every member of the congregation in their care, by the administration both of the doctrine and of the sacraments and discipline of Christ and make this attractive to them by holy examples of life, both on their own part and on the part of those of whom they have charge at home.

We know what the Holy Spirit requires concerning the qualifications and duties of the ministers of the Church,[33] as expressed and explained in the letters of Paul to Timothy and Titus, especially in the third chapter of the first letter to Timothy (vs. 1-13) and in the first chapter of the letter to Titus (vs. 5-9). This canon is obviously to be observed reverently, and realized. For where the words of the Lord "He who hears you hears me" (Luke 10:16) do not apply to those who are in charge of the churches, the administration of the Kingdom of Christ cannot be rightly preserved. And since no private person is to be put up with in the Church if he denies by his deeds what he professes with his lips, how much the less should anyone be tolerated in the care and governance of the churches if he is discovered not really to love Christ (I Cor. 16:22) and to be neither fit for nor interested in introducing men to Christ's Kingdom, and establishing those introduced in all righteousness (II Tim. 2:2).

How much effort must be expended in this, that suitable and faithful shepherds be put in charge of individual churches, the Holy Spirit clearly teaches by the examples of Paul and Barnabas, who ordained elders [34] with prayer and fasting for the individual

---

[32] *Presbyteros et curatores.*

[33] *Canon Spiritus sancti de conditione et munere ministrorum Ecclesiae.* Bucer believed that the offices of the Church were prescribed by Scripture.

[34] *Presbyteros.* It should be noted that in the passages which Bucer quotes, reference is made to the ordination of "elders."

churches which they had gained for Christ (Acts 14:23). For this same reason Paul also left Titus in Crete, to ordain elders for individual towns (Titus 1:5).

Here, however, it must be observed that it is not necessary for all elders to be trained in letters and languages, or even in the ability of public teaching. This office, although it is also that of elders, pertains especially to the one who holds the first place among the elders, to whom the name bishop is uniquely given. As proof that one is fit to preside [35] over a church it is sufficient that he fulfills the ministry of Christ acceptably and faithfully, even if in a mediocre way, that he can teach others, and that he have spiritual prudence and zeal for governing the church, and that he is on his guard lest anyone falls from the grace he has received.

Such persons are evidently able with their fellow ministers of the doctrine and sacraments of Christ to exercise discipline, to admonish brethren of their duty both privately and in their own homes, and when anyone has to be admonished in the name of the Church or corrected or bound over to penance or excommunicated, to be present, and to pronounce sentence wholesomely, and truly to manifest themselves to these as apt teachers [36] (I Tim. 3:2), i.e., fit and eager to teach and tenacious and faithful of expression in teaching, and strong in exhorting through sound doctrine, and also in reclaiming those who deny the truth (Titus 1:9). Saint Ambrose testifies that there was this kind of elder both in the synagogue and in the early Church, and that this office was abolished not without a vitiation of doctrine and disadvantage to the churches. Commenting on the first part of the fifth chapter of the first letter to Timothy he writes: [37] "Do not slander an elder. Hence both the synagogue and afterward the Church had elders, without whose counsel nothing was done in the Church. What negligence abolished this I do not know, unless perhaps the sloth of

---

[35] Bucer here refers to the presiding elder or bishop as "senior." The distinction that he makes between at least two ranks of elders is noteworthy. The ministry of the Church as he conceived it and as he hoped to establish it in Strassburg (and, according to his recommendations in this work, also in England) was to consist of the offices of preaching and teaching elders, trained for their tasks; untrained lay elders who, together with the older ministers, would be responsible for the administration of discipline; and deacons who would be in charge of poor relief and the administration of benevolences. Calvin's conception of the ministry was similar (cf. Calvin, *Institutes* IV. xi. 1 and 6; and IV. iv. 2).

[36] Bucer again cites the Greek term of the New Testament, *didaktikous*. It should be noted that I Tim. 3:2 defines the qualifications of a bishop.

[37] Ambrosiaster, *Commentary on the Epistle to Timothy* (MPL, Vol. 17, col. 502).

teachers, or more likely the pride, when they wanted only themselves to seem to be something."

For clearly nothing should be watched out for with greater care than that none of the sheep of Christ should perish, and if any of them have strayed from the fold, they should be sought and brought back as soon as possible. And if they have broken any precept, i.e., if they have fallen into any grave sin, although they remain in the association of the Church, they may be healed by being charged with the obligation and the care of salutary penance. And those who begin to grow weak in the faith should be strengthened in time. And the healthy sheep which remain in the fold with their good shepherd should feed willingly, i.e., advance in all piety (Ezek. 34:16).[38]

But what single individual would be able to fulfill for many such offices of the good shepherd? It has therefore pleased the Holy Spirit from the beginning of the Church to join to the ministers of the word and the sacraments, namely, the presiding elders and bishops,[39] other men also from the body of the Church, serious men endowed with a gift for governing, to assist them in exercising a concern for individuals and in keeping and strengthening the discipline of Christ (I Cor. 12:28).

It is intolerable that, whereas in civil administration, even in tiny hamlets, some counselors and assistants are attached to the prefects, the administration of eternal salvation is committed only to one or two men, and for the most part to the kind of men who enjoy very little favor and authority in the Lord among the people of Christ, inasmuch as it is a matter of experience that men do not easily take correction, except from those whom they believe to be their friends, surpassing them in wisdom and justice.

The duties of this sacred ministry include the teaching of Christ, the dispensation of his sacraments, and the administration of his discipline.

CHAPTER VI

THE DISPENSATION OF THE DOCTRINE OF CHRIST

All doctrine must be derived from Holy Scriptures. It is not permissible to add or subtract anything (Deut. 4:2 and 12:32). It

---

[38] Cf. Bucer's tract on the ministry *Von der waren Seelsorge* (Martin Bucer, *Schriften der Jahre 1538–1539*, ed. by Robert Stupperich [Vol. VII of *Deutsche Schriften*], pp. 67–245).
[39] *Primariis presbyteris et episcopis.*

must be manifested to the people in these ways: first, by the reading of Holy Scriptures; next, by their interpretation, but one which has specifically been derived from the Holy Scriptures themselves; then, by the sound teaching of religion, i.e., by a lucid explanation and a sure confirmation of the dogmas of our faith; then, by pious exhortations, admonitions, reproofs, and testimonials taken from the same Scriptures; after that, by the religious instruction of the ignorant, and by repetition of what has been heard from the doctrine of Christ; further, if certain persons have difficulty with certain texts of Christian doctrine, or even contradict them, by holy conversations and disputations by which the doctrine of Christ may be more fully explained to the weak and the more firmly asserted against dissidents; lastly, also by private teaching, exhortation, consolation, and correction.

We read that Christ, the prince of the churches, the shepherd and teacher, observed all these things religiously in the ministry of teaching the gospel. For in the synagogue at Nazareth, when The Book of Isaiah the prophet had been given to him, he read something from it, which he thereupon interpreted, and derived salutary doctrine and a lesson from it (Luke 4:16-17). All the Evangelists have testified abundantly how prompt he was in responding not only to those who asked something about the doctrine of salvation for the purpose of learning, but also to those who openly attacked him and his teaching and plotted to find an occasion for blaming him.

But with what religious spirit the apostles followed this example of the Lord, Luke has testified to in Acts when, in the synagogue at Pisidian Antioch, so he recalls, Paul and Barnabas had a chance to exhort the people; after the reading of Moses and the prophets, they delivered a sermon about Christ derived entirely from the Holy Scriptures (Acts 13:14-43). That Paul showed himself quick to discourse about the doctrine of the gospel and to prove it to all, even by religious disputes and conferences, is abundantly obvious from the fact that immediately following his conversion he embarrassed the Jews by disputing in the synagogues of Damascus, showing from the Scriptures that the Lord Jesus is the Christ (Acts 9:20-22). Nor did he hesitate to dispute with the Epicureans and Stoics at Athens about the doctrine of the gospel (Acts 17:18 ff.).

Certainly no doctrine must be handed down and confirmed so accurately by every available method of teaching as the doctrine of eternal life. Even now all faithful professors of the learned disciplines [40] are ready, in addition to interpreting their authors and teaching publicly what they mean, to explain and confirm that same doctrine more fully to the dull-minded in appropriate conferences and disputations, and also to defend and safeguard them more completely against adversaries.

In accordance with the same common diligence of true teachers, everyone must acknowledge how useful it is, and how necessary, for the more unlearned to be taught by the catechism, whether they are children in age or in the amount of sense they have, so that they may be individually instructed by appropriate questions and answers in the fundamentals [41] of our religion. For what faithful schoolteacher, or teacher of any discipline or art, thinks that it is enough to have recommended good authors to his students, or to have handed on the rules of disciplines and arts, and does not also examine his students on what he has explained or shared in an effort to get them to learn better, questioning them to see how each has understood the matter and giving them an opportunity to ask him about anything that has not been well enough understood.

For, as I just said, there is no doctrine which ought to be learned more diligently than the knowledge of eternal salvation. Therefore with burning zeal and diligent care we must produce teaching methods and catechisms in the churches which surpass those used elsewhere.

Both the synagogue and the early Church exhibited a singular concern for this kind of catechizing. Also, our Lord Jesus Christ took part in something of this sort when at twelve years of age he remained in Jerusalem without the knowledge of his parents. For so Luke writes of him: "They found him sitting in the Temple in the midst of the teachers, both listening to them and asking them questions, and all who heard him were astonished at his understanding and his responses" (Luke 2:46-47). Jesus, therefore, then listened. To whom? Undoubtedly to the teachers, who were catechizing him and the other boys. For in all things he always exhibited utmost moderation; he both asked them questions and an-

---

[40] Bucer writes *omnes fideles disciplinarum professores*. He has in mind the teachers of the universities, the representatives of the learned disciplines. Moreover, he gives a brief description of the teaching methods used in medieval universities: In addition to the lectures in which they presented the teaching of representative authors in their own fields, the professors held conferences for the instruction of smaller groups of students; they also presided at public disputations (discussions) where the students had to defend the truth of the teaching they had learned.

[41] *De primariis religionis nostrae capitibus*. Bucer himself was the author of several catechisms. Catechetical instruction was the chief means used by all Protestant Reformers to spread their teaching among the people.

swered them when they asked him questions, which is really the nature of catechizing. Thus the ancient churches always had certain ministers assigned to this duty of catechizing; they were called catechists. We read in the fifteenth chapter of the sixth book of the *Church History* that Origen was one of those in the church of Alexandria and also Heraclas.[42] In other churches, there were others. By these methods Christian teaching is publicly administered wherever Christ has firm sovereignty.

Those pastors and teachers of the churches who want to fulfill their office and keep themselves clean of the blood of those of their flocks who are perishing should not only publicly administer Christian doctrine, but also announce, teach, and entreat repentance toward God and faith in our Lord Jesus Christ, and whatever contributes toward piety, among all who do not reject this doctrine of salvation, even at home and with each one privately.[43] Concerning this, one should read and piously ponder the speech that Saint Paul made to the Ephesus elders whom he had summoned to Miletus when he was setting out for Jerusalem (Acts 20:17 ff.). For the faithful ministers of Christ should imitate this their master and chief shepherd of the churches, and seek most lovingly themselves whatever has been lost, including the hundredth sheep wandering from the fold, leaving behind the ninety-nine which remain in the Lord's fold (Matt. 18:12).

How promptly the Lord dispensed heavenly doctrine, even at home and individually,[44] the Evangelists testify abundantly. For he spared no pains to teach the catechism to that Samaritan woman even though she had not led a pure life; indeed, he was so eager in spirit to instruct that woman unto salvation that although he was tired and hungry, he nevertheless refused to take the food brought to him by his disciples, saying that he had other food to eat, namely, to procure the salvation of that miserable woman (John 4:10-34).

So also the Evangelists recall that he entered private homes not at all unwillingly, and not only of friends and true disciples, but also of sinners and Pharisees, who were in the habit of reviling all that he said and did, and he revealed the doctrine of eternal life in their company also, by denouncing the sins of the hosts as well as those of the guests and by explaining the mysteries of his Kingdom (Luke 10:38-42; Matt. 9:10-13; Luke 7:36-50; 14:1-24).

[42] Eusebius, *Church History* IV, 15.
[43] This is a description of the practices which Bucer had advocated in Strassburg.
[44] *Apud omnes privatos.*

From these things, therefore, it can be adequately seen how doctrine must be administered, and this is the first function of the sacred ministry.

CHAPTER VII

THE ADMINISTRATION OF THE SACRAMENTS

Another function of the sacred ministry is the administration of the sacraments. There are two sacraments explicitly instituted and commanded for us by Christ. Moreover, the apostles so religiously used the sacrament of the imposition of hands in ordaining the ministry of the churches, as we read in Acts 13:3, the First Letter to Timothy 4:14 and 5:22, and the Second Letter, 1:6, that it appears very likely that they did this at the command of the Lord. For Paul writes about the use of this sign to Timothy as if writing of a sacrament of permanent practice. For he warns him not to impose hands on anyone hastily. But we have no express command of Christ on this in Scripture, as we do for Baptism and the Eucharist.

We further read that the early churches used the sign of the laying on of hands in the reconciliation of penitents [45] as well as in the confirmation of the baptized in the faith of Christ.[46] This the bishops customarily did according to the example of the apostles, who by this sign conferred the Holy Spirit on the baptized (Acts 8:17 f.) . And so those who wish the Kingdom of Christ rightly to be established once more among them must take special pains to reestablish the legitimate administration of Baptism and the Eucharist.

But this entails the following procedures: First, that holy and blameless ministers administer each sacrament, and that they administer them only to those whom they know to be holy and blameless according to the Word of the Lord.

For by Baptism men must be washed from sins, regenerated and renewed for eternal life, incorporated in Christ the Lord, and clothed with him, and all of these things are reserved only to those chosen for eternal life (Acts 22:16; Titus 3:5; I Cor. 12:12-13; Gal. 3:27) . Concerning the baptizing of the infants of believers, the Word of the Lord is sufficient: "I will be your God, and of your seed" (Gen. 17:7) , and "Your children are holy" (I Cor. 7:14) . But adults, as has been said above, ought to be catechized before

[45] Cf. Cyprian, *Letters* XV, 1; LXXI, 2.
[46] Cf. Tertullian, *On Baptism* 8 (*MPL,* Vol. 1, col. 1206) .

they are baptized and diligently examined as to whether they believe in their hearts what they profess with their lips.

So it is also fitting that faithful ministers of Christ have evidence of true repentance for sins and a solid faith in Christ the Lord from the fruits of those to whom they offer the Eucharist. Devoutly considering this, Saint Chrysostom said and wrote: "He should lay down his life before he would give the Lord's body to the unworthy, and suffer the shedding of his own blood rather than offer the most sacred blood of the Lord to any other than those who are worthy" (Homily 83, *On Matthew*).[47]

Hence in the times of the holy fathers, deacons walking through the church carefully saw to it that no unworthy person approached the Table of the Lord, as the same Chrysostom testifies.[48] For how would it be permissible for the ministers of salvation of God's elect to offer these most holy mysteries of salvation to those whose faith and piety they did not know? Hence they rightly must fear that they administer to men's judgment and condemnation what the Lord instituted for their salvation (I Cor. 11:27).

Secondly, since by these sacraments remission of sins and the holy communion of Christ are imparted, and the covenant of eternal salvation is sealed and confirmed, it is necessary that these mysteries be explained to those about to receive such sacraments in the presence of the whole church and that they be celebrated as reverently as possible. Hence the ancient churches spent an entire octave in celebrating the mysteries of Baptism. To accomplish this more effectively, they administered Baptism only at Easter and Pentecost, unless someone was in danger of death. Concerning this, there exist canons and laws even from the time before Charlemagne and his sons.[49]

At the administration of each of these sacraments, appropriate lessons from Holy Scripture should be read and explained as reverently as possible, and then the people should be exhorted earnestly to a worthy reception of the sacraments. There ought also to be added most ardent prayers and thanksgivings to the Lord, and also pious offerings. For since by these sacraments men receive the supreme benefits of God, the forgiveness of sins and inheritance of eternal life, certainly they ought not to appear empty in the sight of God (Ex. 23:15).

Also, since the Lord instituted that usage of the Eucharist which

---

[47] Cf. John Chrysostom, *On the Gospel of Matthew*, Hom. LXXXII (*MPG*, Vol. 58, col. 746).
[48] *Ibid.*, cols. 744 f.
[49] Cf. Tertullian, *On Baptism* 19. (*MPL*, Vol. 1, col. 1331).

was observed also in the early churches with great reverence, so that in him they were one bread and one body, likewise all those present at the Holy Supper should share in that one bread and cup of eternal salvation, the body and blood of the Lord commended and offered to the faithful through these sacraments (I Cor. 10:16-17). Surely this use of the Holy Eucharist ought with fervent zeal to be recalled to the churches: "Take and eat," says the Lord, "for this is my body." Likewise: "Take and drink of this cup all of you; this is the blood of the new covenant" (Matt. 26:26-28). And how would those not commit themselves to a grave contempt of the Lord and his mysteries who refuse to take the food and drink of eternal life offered by him, when he has so lovingly and kindly invited them to partake?

Nor, certainly, are those to be listened to who dare to say that the Lord did not command the reception of the sacrament of the Eucharist, because the apostle recalls these words of the Lord about the cup: "Do this, as often as you drink it, in memory of me" (I Cor. 11:25). These wretched despisers of such a great benefit of Christ do not consider what the apostle prefaced to that entire narration: "For I received of the Lord what I also handed on to you." (I Cor. 11:23). But the Lord handed on nothing except what would be truly salutary for us and could not be neglected without despising him. But he did not only command that when we eat his bread and drink his cup, we do so in memory of him; he also commanded us to do this very thing which he instituted and handed down in his Holy Supper. "Do this," he says, "in memory of me." Those commands also pertain to us, "Take and eat," etc., and "Take and drink," etc.

But those who have a distaste for such benefits of Christ are considering only the external things in these mysteries, nor do they recognize that Christ the Savior is in the midst of his own, offering himself to them in these sacraments as the food and drink of eternal life, i.e., for the sustenance, strengthening, and increase of faith and of an entirely new and blessed life (cf. John 6:54-56). Nothing carnal or worldly is here to be thought, for it is not a matter of food and drink for the stomach but for the spirit; but through it the body more readily obeys the spirit and is sanctified for the future resurrection.

Where, therefore, the sovereignty of Christ is truly and fully received, there also what they have described should be restored, the administration of both sacraments according to the precepts of Christ and the example of the early apostolic Church. Hence for the more reverent and salutary presentation of these sacraments to the faithful, it is clearly fitting that they should not be presented except when the whole church or the greater part of it is gathered together and irreligious and unworthy persons removed, so that all present, as they know that through communion with Christ they live and have every hope of eternal life, receive with hearts as eager as possible this communion of Christ offered to them in the Holy Supper. For those who do not seek to live and dwell in Christ the Lord nor for him to live and dwell in them (cf. John 15:4) ought not even to gaze upon these sacred mysteries but should be altogether excluded from the sacred assembly.

All these things concerning the administration of Baptism and the Eucharist have been handed down and commanded by our King and High Priest himself, the Lord Jesus Christ, and were commended everywhere to the churches through the apostles; the churches of Christ have also faithfully observed them at every time in which they have been governed by true bishops. Therefore, those who do not wholeheartedly strive that all these things be recalled to the churches and religiously observed pray in vain to the heavenly Father, "Thy Kingdom come" (Matt. 6:10).

We have spoken above about the laying on of hands for those who are consecrated to the sacred ministry of the Church; although we have no express command of the Lord, we have nevertheless the examples of the apostles (Acts 6:6; 13:3) and also a precept to Timothy (I Tim. 4:14; 5:22), so that it is entirely likely that the apostles used that sign for the ordination of ministers of the Church at the command of the Lord. On this account, this ceremony was observed in the early churches quite religiously, and in the Reformed churches it has now been devoutly recalled into use.[50]

Further, what the apostle said on this matter, "Do not impose hands hastily" (I Tim. 5:22), must be most diligently observed. For those to whom these mysteries of eternal salvation are to be entrusted must be tested most critically. "Let them first be tested, and thus minister": the precept of the Holy Spirit is clear (I Tim. 3:10). And so, whether the churches choose ministers for themselves or they are sent to them by princes and bishops, before everything else they must be examined most exactingly, and this by the standard of the Holy Spirit expressed in the letters of Paul to

---

[50] On Luther's recommendation (in 1525), the ordination of ministers was administered in Wittenberg by the laying on of hands. Other Reformers adopted the same practice. Cf. Calvin, *Institutes* IV. iii. 16. About the influence of Bucer's view upon Anglican practices, cf. Francis F. Procter and W. H. Frere, *A New History of the Book of Common Prayer* rev. ed. (St. Martin's Press, Inc., 1901), pp. 662 ff.

Timothy and Titus, so that it may be plainly evident to the churches as much as anything can be evident about human beings, that they both can and want to perform the ministry for the churches of Christ, according to the mind of our chief Shepherd and the Bishop of our souls, Jesus Christ.

Then, too, the example of the apostles in their institution of the sacraments is to be reverently recalled; Saint Luke reminds us in Acts 13:3 and 14:23 that they should be celebrated in the presence of the whole church and with the observance of prayer and fasting. Accordingly, appropriate Scripture lessons should be read at this ceremony and diligently explained to the people so that they may be the more aflame to pour out prayers to the Lord.

CHAPTER VIII

THE MINISTRY OF THE DISCIPLINE OF LIFE AND MANNERS

Now we must treat of the third function of the sacred ministry, which is the discipline of the Church. This falls into three subdivisions: first, of life and manners; second, of penance, if anyone falls rather seriously; third, of sacred ceremonies.

The discipline of life and manners consists in this, that not only the public ministers of the churches (though these principally), but even individual Christians should exercise a care for their neighbors. By the authority and magisterium of our Lord Jesus Christ, each person should strengthen and advance his neighbors, wherever this is possible, and urge them to progress in the life of God, as his disciples, in his faith and knowledge. And if any fall into error of doctrine or some vice of life or manners, whoever can should with utmost zeal recall such persons from all false doctrine and depraved activity, both for the purity of Christian doctrine and the sedulous conformity of all life to the will of God.

For we have the clear precept of the Lord: "If your brother sins against you" (and a Christian man considers *only* an offense against God to be an offense against himself), "go and rebuke him between himself and you alone; if he hears you, you have gained your brother" (Matt. 18:15). Let us therefore consider in these words both the majesty of the one giving the command and the divine reward which we receive in obeying this command of the Lord. For the Lord said, "If your brother hears you, you have gained your brother," specifically for salvation and eternal life. Hence the Holy Spirit commands in the sixth chapter of Galatians: "Brethren, if a man has been involved in any trespass, you who are spiritual restore him and call him back, in a gentle spirit" (Gal. 6:1). And from the fifth chapter of First Thessalonians: "Therefore encourage one another and build one another up, just as you are doing." And a little after: We exhort you, brethren, correct and instruct those who live inordinately, console those who are pusillanimous, tolerate and support the weak (I Thess. 5:11 and 14).

For Christ, our master and governor, lives and acts in each Christian. In each, therefore, and through the ministry of each he seeks and saves the lost. On this account it is necessary that whoever are really of Christ should have a vigilant concern for their brethren on his authority and power and eagerly exhort whomever they can to their duty, and keep all from sins according to their ability or rescue those who have fallen into them.

Hence it is necessary that those who are warned and corrected by their brethren according to the Lord's precept should acknowledge and accept in them the authority and magisterium of Christ himself and gratefully and earnestly receive and follow this kind of admonition and correction as becomes good disciples of Christ. Nor should they doubt that they spurn Christ himself if they despise one who admonishes and corrects by the Word of the Lord, and that they hear Christ himself when they pay attention to those devoutly correcting and encouraging them.

Further, since private Christians are in no small way lacking in the practice of this discipline of Christ, it is within the competence of the ones in charge of the church and of the elders, whose number should on this account be increased in proportion to the size of the population, that they repair industriously in this matter what has been neglected by private persons. They should, therefore, see both personally and through the deacons of the churches that they are well acquainted with each person committed to their charge, and diligently observe how each progresses in the life of God, or how he is remiss, at which time they should by holy admonitions correct in their brethren whatever trespass they have discovered. In this matter, those who have charge of souls should exercise a greater diligence than any teachers of the humanities and the arts in forming the minds of their students insofar as the knowledge of eternal life is more important and necessary to salvation than any other arts and sciences.

Those whom the Lord has put in charge of his sheep should therefore ponder seriously the fact that from their hands will be required whatever sheep perish by their negligence. They should thoroughly think over what the Lord said to them and threatened them with, through the prophet Ezekiel: "Son of Man, I have made you a watchman over the house of Israel; whenever you hear a word from my mouth, you shall give them a warning from me. If I say to the wicked, You shall surely die, and you give him no warning, nor speak to warn the wicked from his wicked way in order to save his life, that man will die in his iniquity; but his blood I will require at your hand," etc. (Ezek. 3:17-18).

Let them carefully consider and ponder what the Lord through the same prophet complains about the shepherds who do not strengthen the weak sheep, or heal the sick, or bind the broken limbs, and do not lead back the ones separated from the flock, or seek those which have perished (Ezek. 34:4). Let that grave admonition of Paul to the elders of Ephesus sound in their hearts: "Take heed to yourselves and to all the flock over which the Holy Spirit has made you bishops, to feed the Church of the Lord, which he obtained with his own blood" (Acts 20:28). Likewise, that which he commanded Titus (Titus 2:15): "Speak these things, and by them exhort and correct, with all authority as over those subject to you."

With grateful hearts they ought to embrace this blessing of Christ as supremely necessary and salutary; to them applies what the Holy Spirit urges through Paul to the Thessalonians in these words: "We beseech you, brethren, to respect those who labor among you and are over you in the Lord and admonish you, and to esteem them very highly in love because of their work. Be at peace among yourselves and with them" (I Thess. 5:12-13). And The Letter to the Hebrews, ch. 13:17. "Submit to those who are over you and obey them, for they are keeping watch over your souls as men who will give an account, so that they may do so with joy, and not sadly." This is what the discipline of life and manners consists of.

CHAPTER IX

The Ministry of the Discipline of Penance

The discipline of penance properly pertains to those who have fallen into more serious sins. For as has been said above, the faithful ministers of Christ should not tolerate in the company of the Church, nor admit to the sacraments of Christ, those whom they cannot and should not acknowledge by their fruits, according to the precepts of the Lord, to be his true disciples and followers.

Those who fall into more serious sins, i.e., crimes and wickedness, these obviously reject and break the yoke of Christ and deny by their deeds the piety that they profess with their lips. For this reason, such insults against God and defiance of the Son of God cannot be pardoned, unless the perpetrators earnestly acknowledge the horror of their impiety and deplore it, grieving with a living, productive repentance.

And when true repentance flourishes after such a lapse, it cannot fail at once to bring forth its fruits, i.e., a bitter regret for sins, deep humiliation of the flesh, and its crucifixion with its sick desires. To this end one must use not only an abdication of all the pleasures of the flesh, but also righteous fasting and ardent prayers, as the Holy Spirit teaches by very serious precepts in the first and second chapters of Joel (1:13-14; 2:12-17).

For this reason, penitents ought to frequent assiduously the religious services of the congregation in order that through the Word of God not only their fall may be pointed up by repentance but also a zeal to pray for pardon may be set aflame, so that they may not only by their own assiduous, burning prayers arouse God to pardon but also seek mutual help from the Church and the individual brethren.

They must also expend themselves entirely in all kinds of good works and show themselves most temperate and holy in all their present conduct, in bearing adversities patiently and bravely, in helping their neighbor and deserving well of him, both with material things and by good deeds, in a kind and enthusiastic way. For loving God with one's whole heart makes one also grieve deeply at every offense against God. But the Holy Spirit, as in his other gifts and works, so also in penance, is faithful to himself and brings about the same things in all his acts.

Now, it is evident that those whose repentance is proposed for an example to us in Scripture abundantly brought forth the fruits of penance which I have enumerated—David, the Ninevites, Manasseh, Peter, Paul, and the like (II Sam. 12:13; John 3:5-10; II Chron. 33:12-13; Matt. 26:75; Acts 9:3-6; II Cor. 2:5-11, 7:8-11, and 12:21). These fruits proceed so necessarily from the hearts of all who are truly and savingly moved by a living repentance for sins (as men can be well enough known by their genuine regret for offenses) that it cannot be doubted that those who do not exhibit such worthy fruits of penance when they have offended the Divine Majesty by more serious sins do not yet recognize the enormity of their wickedness, and so are not moved by a living repentance for them. Hence they must be reckoned serpents and vipers, as Saint John calls them, rather than disciples of Christ and participants in his Kingdom (Matt: 3:7).

It is within the office of rectors and elders in the churches to urge not only a true repentance of spirit concerning sins but also the doing of penance and the showing of its fruits, and to bind by the authority of Christ; and they are not to dissolve that bond until these persons have shown good faith to the Church concerning their true repentance and conversion to the obedience of Christ through those worthy fruits of repentance. For to hold that it is sufficient for someone only verbally to profess repentance for sins and to say that he is sorry for his sins and wishes to amend his life without the necessary concomitant signs and works of repentance which we have mentioned is of the priests of Antichrist, not of Christ.

Concerning not so much the severity as the necessity and the wholesomeness of this discipline of penance, would that there might be read and pondered what Saint Cyprian Martyr wrote in very many of his letters (Epistle 3, Book 1; Epistles 14 and 16, Book 3), and especially in the "Sermon on the Lapsed,"[51] and what he demonstrated by the clear witness of Scripture.

Saint Cyprian further recalls in his "Sermon on the Lapsed"[52] that some people in his time confessed with unfeigned sorrow even the hidden sins of their spirit to the priests of God, made a confession of conscience, exposed the burden of their spirit, and sought a salutary remedy, namely, of practicing penance, by means of self-denial however small and modest. The holy martyr lauds these persons for their greater faith and deeper reverence.

By the example of such consciences, this secret confession of sins gradually was received in the churches, but afterward it was wickedly exacted by false bishops, even from those who were unwilling. For we have no command of the Lord concerning this, as we have concerning the manifest performance of penance by those who have fallen into more serious sins which are known to the churches.

Nor, indeed, would everyone make such a secret confession in a salutary way; it is a matter of individual consciences, and not without danger for any minister involved. This confession can be a salutary remedy only to those consciences which need either private instruction or consolation and furthermore request this of the ministers of Christ. This can happen in a salutary way only with those guardians of the churches who are so endowed with the spirit

---

[51] Cyprian, *On the Lapsed* (*MPL,* Vol. 4, cols. 477 ff.).
[52] *Ibid.,* Ch. XXVIII (*MPL,* Vol. 4, col. 503).

of Christ that they can on this occasion better catechize the more ignorant in faith, and help those who experience less contrition to a definite acknowledgment of their sins. They will arouse a righteous sorrow in them on account of sins, or raise up greatly dejected spirits to a hope of divine mercy, and discover and demonstrate efficacious means for avoiding sins.

We have already indicated how severely, in a manner approved by the better part of the people of Christ, those who have committed more serious sins and refuse the path of repentance which the Lord gave to us must be cut off from any association with the Church and considered heathens and publicans. Concerning this, what the Lord and Holy Spirit commanded should be read diligently and pondered religiously (Matt. 18:15-18; I Cor. 5:4-5, and II Cor. 2:5-11, and also II Thess. 3:6).

"If, however," our King and Savior said, "he will not hear the church, let him be to you as a heathen and publican" (Matt. 18:17). These individuals were then kept from any association with the people of God either in religion or the rest of life. Therefore, the Pharisees rebuked the Lord because he ate with publicans (John 4:9; Matt. 9:11; Luke 15:2; and 19:5-7).

This ought to make us solicitous to recall that discipline of penitence, because the Lord here added, using his customary formula of emphasis, "Amen I say to you, whatever you bind upon earth will be bound in heaven, and whatever you loose upon earth will be loosed in heaven" (Matt. 18:18). From these words of the Lord we learn that these are heavenly remedies against sins, to bind those who have fallen into more serious sins to the doing of penance, and to loose from that bond those who have shown repentance by its worthy fruits. How great a crime it is that those to whose trust and care our salvation has been committed should be plainly and seriously deficient in any remedy which our Savior handed on and commanded to be used! How great an impiety against both God and his people!

How gravely and sharply the Holy Spirit rebuked the Corinthians to arouse them to this discipline of penance, when, with an incestuous man masquerading among them, he caused to be written by the apostle Paul: "And are you puffed up, and do you not rather mourn, that he who did this might be removed from among you?" (I Cor. 5:2)! Let us observe and devoutly ponder these words of the Holy Spirit. The Corinthians are accused of being puffed up, i.e., they pleased themselves more than was righteous and did not acknowledge their wrongs, because the entire church did not begin to mourn, i.e., fast and pray to avert the divine wrath on account of this wickedness, and reject that incestuous man from their association, because the wrath of God was justly kindled against the whole body of the Church, when the vice and ruin of only one member went unheeded. Let the examples of Achan and the Benjamites be pondered (Josh. 7:10-26; Judg., ch. 20, *passim*).

Let us also observe in this text that the Holy Spirit wished the whole Church to be gathered, in the spirit of Paul, for that man not only to be excommunicated by the common judgment of all, but also by the ministry of the same apostle "to be handed over to Satan for the destruction of the flesh, that his spirit might be saved in the day of our Lord Jesus Christ" (I Cor. 5:4-5).

Evidently by the castigation and affliction of the flesh accomplished through this handing over to Satan, whatever that was, that incestuous man was driven to such repentance for his wickedness that there was a danger that he be overwhelmed in extreme sickness of spirit. Hence, Saint Paul in the Spirit of God urged the Corinthians no less gravely to receive him into the favor of the Lord and of the Church, once he had sufficiently demonstrated his repentance of spirit for his sin. They were to dissolve the bond of doing penance for the man whom they had ordered to be excluded from the communion of the Church (before his declaration of penitence). The rebuke by many, i.e., notice and infliction of this punishment, which was his rejection from the company of the saints, profited this man (II Cor. 2:6-8).

From these things, therefore, it is clearly evident that entire churches bind themselves over to the ruin of those for whom they do not make the effort to use this remedy of salvation with utmost gravity and severity when it is needed.

It must also be considered that the Holy Spirit, among other things, said: "Do you not know that a little leaven ferments the whole batter? Clean out, therefore, the old leaven, that you may be a fresh dough," etc. (I Cor. 5:6-7). For in these words the Holy Spirit teaches that whole churches are corrupted and perish by the contagion of a few evil persons, indeed, of one wicked man. For if only one little crack is open for Satan to creep into the Church with Christian discipline relaxed, in the just judgment of God a great many evils are permitted to ensue, as we perceive has happened for so many centuries and still occurs today. Therefore, the Holy Spirit here prescribes *not even to eat* with openly wicked persons and to remove the evil from among us (I Cor. 5:11 and 13). Let us then perceive the reasons for religiously restoring this discipline; let us permit what ought to prevail among us to do so both because the Holy Spirit strictly requires this and because he teaches that it is so salutary to all the people of Christ, for those who have sinned as well as for the churches themselves.

Let us put into practice, finally, what the Holy Spirit wrote through Saint Paul to the Thessalonians concerning the avoidance of brethren living lawlessly, i.e., not keeping their place in the body of the Lord, not following their vocation to contribute something to the common good; they behave in a lazy way and as busybodies. For the Holy Spirit orders such brethren to be avoided and shunned by all the others and affirms that this is of profit to lazy and noisy brethren so that they are shamed, and feeling shamed, recalled to their duty, especially when they are not completely rejected as enemies but are warned and corrected as brethren (II Thess. 3:6, 11-15).

From this text we realize both how much authority has been given to us in order to apply to sinful brethren this remedy of salutary abstention and avoidance and how much the Lord wishes this very thing to work in healing the wounds of brethren. For those who are not entirely hopeless it is an intolerable torment of mind to be excluded from the company of the brethren and of the whole Church, and to be avoided by all, like men profane and alien to Christ the Lord. When such pressure is used, sinning brethren are moved to repentance and brought back to their duty much more effectively than by any other punishments.

As their poets and historians testify, the pagan nations that had their governments organized rather tolerably realized this by the light of nature which remained. By this means the Lacedaemonians certainly aroused their citizens wonderfully to a concern for virtue and kept them concerned; no one would give scoundrels and wrongdoers the dignity of lodging, or physical exercise in common, or a part in games, or many another and more serious involvement in life, as Xenophon testifies of them in a book about their republic.[53] Hence let us think over how much we harm both the sinning brethren and the entire Church when we deprive those brethren who are involved in misdeeds of this medicine of holy severity.

So much about the discipline of penance; those who do not labor with utmost zeal for its total restoration according to the precepts of Christ which we have enumerated cannot say in truth that they seek the Kingdom of Christ. It is necessary that those who love the Lord Jesus and truly want his blessed sovereignty to prevail among them know from the Lord's very words what we have brought out about the supremely salutary discipline of penance and work energetically to recall its practice.

[53] Xenophon, *On the Republic of the Lacedaemonians* IX, 4-5.

CHAPTER X

REFORMING THE CHURCHES' CEREMONIES:
FIRST, THE HALLOWING OF CHURCH BUILDINGS

Now let us see how the discipline of ceremonies should be reformed in the churches. These, indeed, are the necessary and common ceremonies of all Christians: the blessing of places in which the Christian religion is publicly administered, the sanctifying of seasons, in which the people grow in the Lord and take time for religion; a certain regulation of the ministry of the word, the sacraments, discipline; sacred offerings, and their distribution to the poor.

It is first necessary for Christians to have places appointed for sacred gatherings and forms of worship delivered to them by Christ the Lord, which should be open to no other usages, unless extreme necessity compels this. The Lord taught us this with profound earnestness when he drove from the Temple those who had merely set up the selling of victims in it in order to provide a supply for all the sacrifices, and when he overturned the tables of the money changers, by whom pilgrims were likewise helped to make sacrifices and to offer gifts partly commanded, partly recommended in the law of God (Matt. 21:12-13). But "he did not allow any vessel to be carried through the temple" (Mark 11:16).

On this account the early churches were always kept closed when there was no public worship going on in them unless some necessity of the Christian people demanded otherwise.

They went so far as to establish a holy order of clergy, the porters, for this practice, of which the papists retain only the name and the impious mockery of an ordination. For it was their function when worship was publicly going on to be on guard that no unworthy person should mingle in the sacred gathering and that no one should do anything out of harmony with the Christian religion in the holy assembly. After the public presentation of the teaching of the gospel and before the service of the Lord's Supper began, these men led from the church those ordered by the deacon to depart, first the catechumens, then the penitents; and they kept the service closed while the mysteries were going on. We read such testimonials, partly in the exhortation of bishops to porters at their ordination, partly in Saint Chrysostom's eighteenth and twenty-fourth Homilies on Matthew,[54] his eighteenth on Second Corinthians,[55] and many other places.

Whoever, therefore, is responsible for having Christ's Kingdom and religion truly repaired and flourishing among them should ponder the fact that the buildings consecrated for church assemblies and Christian worship are called in the Scriptures "house of God" and "house of prayer" (Matt. 12:4; Luke 19:46) and hence they should acknowledge what horrible blasphemy they are guilty of against the Divine Majesty, when they treat the Lord's churches as walkways and places so profane that they can talk and chatter about all sorts of impure and profane things with others who are like them, sometimes even while services are going on in the churches.[56]

But what private person, not to speak of a prince or king, would tolerate anyone who wanted to wander around his own home whimsically and libidinously before his very eyes, especially if such a person were chatting and making small talk by saying things ungrateful and unworthy of the man of the house? This is certainly such a great contempt of the divine presence that it alone would merit for us complete extermination from the earth, and that by most cruel torments. This great insult to Christ has been permitted for many centuries, and not only do princes and magistrates and prelates of the churches overlook it, but by their example they for the most part even teach and strengthen this practice.

Hence those who wish to be of Christ and wish not to be numbered among those who renounce him ("We do not want this man to reign over us," Luke 19:14) must surely, each according to his vocation and ability, make the effort and also make it happen that with all such great insults against God far removed, churches should not be open to any secular business but only for religious services unless extreme human necessity demands otherwise, as I said before.

For whoever are of Christ, in them Christ lives, and he does not only say words, but really proves the saying, "The zeal of your house has eaten me up" (Ps. 69:9; John 2:17). With that zeal, therefore, and through his own (in a manner appropriate to the vocation of each), Christ drives from his churches whoever attempts to transact alien business there, and consecrates and dedi-

[54] John Chrysostom, *On the Gospel of Matthew,* Hom. XVIII, 6, and XXIII, 3 (*MPG*, Vol. 57, pp. 271 and 311).

[55] John Chrysostom, *On the Second Letter to the Corinthians,* Hom. XVIII (*MPG*, Vol. 61, col. 526 f.).

[56] This was a complaint which Bucer frequently voiced in Strassburg.

cates them solely to the ministry of his word and sacraments and to holy prayer.

CHAPTER XI

SETTING ASIDE CERTAIN TIMES FOR THE WORSHIP OF GOD

Another common Christian ceremony is to set aside definite times for Christian religious services, and not only places. "The Lord" is indeed "to be celebrated" and invoked by us "at every time," as also "in every place of his dominion" (Ps. 34:2 and 103:22) ; but since this is to be done with the congregation of the faithful assembled, and hence with deeper religious spirit, it has seemed good to the Lord for his faithful to have certain especially consecrated times for this, just as they have special places (Num. 28:2). Accordingly, besides the two services which he wished to be held daily for his people of old, in the morning and in the evening, to which only those who had the leisure might gather to hear his word and to pray, he consecrated for his whole people, wherever they were living, one day in every week when they might have time to worship him in a special way. As strictly as possible he commanded all who were of his people, or stayed among his people, to keep that day holy to himself. For he willed that on that day no external work at all should be done, neither by man nor by beast, but for all in any way associated with his people to be called together and congregated in the synagogues, there to hear his precepts and to pour forth prayers to him, and to give thanks to him for all his blessings, and thus to establish faith in his word and all piety (Ex. 20:8-11; Deut. 5:12-15; Mark 1:21; Luke 13:10; Acts 17:2; 18:4). But where the Ark of the Covenant was, there he commanded double sacrifices to be offered to him on that day (Num. 28:9-10).

He so sanctified this Sabbath worship that he ordered those who had violated it to be cut off from the people and stoned (Ex. 31:14-15; and 35:2). And this deservedly, for we live by faith in God (cf. Hab. 2:4). But this matter has need of much serious restoration because Satan and our flesh never cease to weaken it. Since now our God in his singular charity toward us sanctified only one of seven days for the grounding of our faith and hence of our eternal life, and blessed that day that religious services held on it might effectively work toward our salvation, whoever would not be eager to sanctify that day to glorify his Lord God and the attainment of his own salvation (especially since God has conceded six days for our business and labors in order to sustain our present life for his glory) would surely show himself a lost despiser of so admirable a blessing of God on us and entirely unworthy of living among the people of God.

These things surely "have been written for our learning" (Rom. 15:4). For although we have been released from all the pedagogy of Moses and we are not so bound by the religion of the Sabbath and other feasts which he commanded for the people of old that we must "observe" the same "days, months, and seasons" (Gal. 4:10; Col. 2:16) in the way in which the ancient people were obliged to, nevertheless, as persons to whom the Kingdom of Christ has been more fully revealed, we ought to establish and assume for ourselves whatever can contribute to increasing faith in Christ with a much more ardent zeal than did the people of the old dispensation, and it is certainly our duty to sanctify publicly one day in the week for religious services.[57]

For we see very few people at daily religious gatherings, as those first Christians were accustomed to gather in the Temple. For some are impeded by the necessity of seeking their daily bread, others by religious indifference. Who, therefore, would not see how salutary it is for the people of Christ that there be one day in the week so consecrated to religious services that it should not be allowable to do anything else on that day except assemble in the congregation of worship, and there hear the word of God, pour out our prayers to God, confess the faith and render thanks to God, make sacred offerings, receive the divine sacraments, and thus with singular zeal glorify God and grow in the faith? For these are the works of holy days.

On that account, the Lord's Day was consecrated for such things by the apostles themselves (I Cor. 16:2; Acts 20:7; Rev. 1:10). The early churches observed this institution most religiously. The emperor Constantine also sanctioned it with most weighty authority, as Eusebius of Caesarea has testified in the fourth oration on his life.[58] Other emperors also followed him in this, Theodosius, Valentinian, Archadius, Leo, and Anthemius. By these it was forbidden under most severe penalties to show spectacles on this day or to indulge in pleasures, as can be seen by their laws, which are contained in the Code (about Festival Days).[59]

---

[57] *Religionibus.*   [58] Eusebius, *Life of Constantine* IV, 18.

[59] *Codex Justinianus, Code* III, 12, 2, 6, and 9. The collection and edition of Roman Law which the Emperor Justinian (483–565) caused to be made (known as the *Corpus Iuris Civilis*) consists of the following four parts: *Codex constitutionum; Digesta,* or *Pandecta; Institutiones; Novellae (Constitutiones)*. There is an English translation by S. P. Scott, *The Civil Law,*

Two causes are suggested why the apostles and the early churches dedicated to religious activities the first day of the week rather than the seventh, which in the law God had commanded to be kept holy: One, that they wished to testify that Christians were not bound by the teachings of Moses; the other, that in this way they might celebrate the memory of Christ's resurrection, which occurred on the first day of the week.[60]

Certain other special occasions were afterward added to Sundays, as the feasts of Easter and Pentecost, the observation of Lent, Christmas, and Epiphany; indeed, special days for remembrance of the martyrs were frequently set aside in the churches; and the ancients also observed the Wednesdays and Fridays of every week with religious services and fasting. They did likewise whenever some particular disaster beset the Church, when the blessing of God was renewing her or when she was gripped by some undertaking of great moment. Either pious princes or bishops initiated such a solemnity.

Since, however, in appointing holy days this one thing has to be aimed at, that the people of Christ be better grounded in religion and more fully inflamed toward every devotion, and since it has to be diligently guarded against that no occasion be given to men for doing their own will on the Sabbaths of the Lord, it must be a matter of special concern for those who wish the Kingdom of Christ to be restored among them that Sunday religious observance be renewed and established (Isa. 58:13).

It is in accordance with our piety also to keep holy certain other days in memory of the principal acts of Christ: as the day of his Incarnation, Nativity, Epiphany, Passion, Resurrection, Ascension, and Pentecost.[61]

But it is not so much a matter for concern that many holy days be established, as that whatever ones have been established be truly kept holy to the Lord. For how much God detests it if on days consecrated to his name we do our own will and follow the desires of the flesh, Isaiah has testified in quite horrendous words, chs. 1 (vs. 13-15) and 58 (vs. 3, 13). Therefore whatever special days it has seemed good to observe in various churches, there must be a keen vigilance that they are totally kept holy to the Lord, i.e., not

---

17 vols. (1932). We refer in these notes to these parts under the titles of this translation, namely, *Institutes, Digest, Code,* and *Novellae.*

[60] Cf. Acts 20:7; I Cor. 16:2; Justin Martyr, *Apology* I, 67, 3 and 8 (*MPG*, Vol. 6, col. 428).

[61] Until 1536, Bucer regarded as superstitious the observance of any other day than Sunday. But in 1537 he reintroduced the observance of Christmas. From then on, all other main Christian holidays were restored.

only that useful corporal works be omitted on such days, but much more that the works of the flesh be avoided. For we see that in this the people who are signed with the name of Christ have fallen frequently, so that on no days is God offended so gravely as on those days which are particularly set aside for the worship of God. Therefore the princes, priests, and elders of churches, and indeed all Christians, each according to his own share and vocation, who are not on the watch that whatever holy days the churches have dedicated to religion be also surely kept holy to the Lord by all the people, such persons certainly make themselves liable for all those sins and offenses against God which are committed by the people on the days consecrated to him.

CHAPTER XII

LENT AND OTHER FASTS, AND THE TAKING OF FOOD

Some believe that the Lenten observance was introduced by the apostles and some are of the opinion that it was introduced later. It is evident in ancient writings, however, that not all the churches observed this practice uniformly, but some fasted only one day before Easter, others seven, some more, others less. But those churches which observed a complete Lent did not condemn the ones which did not, since the former did not even compel any of their own people to fast, but merely invited them to do so by pious exhortations. On one day of every week (some on the fifth, others the seventh), they observed fasting (Chrysostom, Homily 11, *On Genesis;* and Saint Augustine, Letter 86, to Casulanus) .[62]

On certain days, they ministered the word of God and the sacraments until the ninth hour of the day, i.e., toward evening; after these services, those who were fasting would take food for the first time. Meanwhile, however, the holy fathers also consoled and praised those who, on account of the weakness of their body, took food beforehand and came nevertheless to the sacred gathering and heard the word of God.[63]

And so it is anti-Christian to prescribe fasting for Christians as something per se necessary for salvation (Chrysostom, Homily 10, *On Genesis*) .[64] For the Lord and the apostles, although they condemned making a ceremony out of fasting, nevertheless left its ob-

[62] Cf. John Chrysostom, *On Genesis*, Hom. XI (*MPG,* Vol. 53, cols. 92 ff.) ; Augustine, Letter 36 (*MPL,* Vol. 33, cols. 145 ff.) .

[63] Cf. Tertullian, *On Fasting* X (*MPL,* Vol. 2, cols. 1017 f.) ; Eusebius, *Church History* V, 24, 12.

[64] *MPG,* Vol. 53, cols. 81 ff.

servance free for Christians; just as fasting cannot be piously accomplished unless it is undertaken with a willing spirit (Matt. 6:16-17, and 9:15; I Cor. 7:7; II Cor. 6:5).

However, since the Lord himself and his apostles so highly recommended fasting to the churches, certainly they who observe no fasting at all cannot glory in the spirit and sovereignty of Christ. It is necessary, therefore, for those who wish to see the Kingdom of Christ solidly restored to retrieve the discipline of fasting, at least on some days of the year; and especially if some calamity presses the Church, if any persons in the Church have fallen into more serious sins, or if the Church has an opportunity to undertake something magnificent for the glory of God, the people should be gathered in holy assembly and earnestly invited from Sacred Scriptures truly to repent for sins and pour forth prayers to God (Joel 1:14 and 2:12; I Cor. 7:5). On these days there should be abstinence not only from illicit pleasures of the flesh but even from permissible pleasures; the degree of abstinence from necessary food and drink, however, must be freely committed to individual consciences. In this also the nature and customs of the people must be duly considered so that the number of days are dedicated to fasting which it may be hoped will be devoutly observed.

For in these matters every precaution must always be taken lest ceremonies which are instituted for the worship of God be twisted into blasphemy against God; we see that this has happened under the Antichrist's shepherds; [65] although during Lent and other times of fasting, sermons for the most part and individual prayers are observed among them and fasting is proclaimed as necessary to salvation, it is very rarely found that anyone knows the true nature of fasting, so absent is its observance in their midst.

They have read that among the ancients those who were fasting took nothing to eat until after the evening worship had been accomplished; in order to appear to follow this practice and not to take food before evening prayers, they say these prayers at the third hour of the day, or at the latest, at the fourth or fifth hour. What else is this but to mock God? They do just this when they hold public worship for the people in a foreign language; not even the sermons instruct men to any real and living repentance for sins. These abominations must, therefore, be driven far away from the churches of Christ and no trace of them left behind.

On this account, it is highly desirable that those who think that the government should forbid the use of meat on certain days in order that there may be a greater supply of meat for other days, and

[65] *Sub Antichristis pastoribus.*

that fish might be conveniently distributed, would choose other seasons than Lent for this, and days other than those which were formerly consecrated to religious fasting, and which, on the impious pretext of fasting and abstinence from meat, were converted by the Antichrists into a mockery of God.

When the holy fathers of the early churches, instructed by Sacred Scriptures, wished to consecrate one day of the week singularly to religion, they did not choose the seventh day which the Jews observed, lest they might seem to be in accord with the Jews who were seeking to impose the Mosaic Sabbath on the Church of Christ. Thus the later fathers, although they approved of a pious rather than a superstious fast even on Sunday, nevertheless, lest they might seem to concede anything to the madness of the Manichaeans, forbade fasting on Sunday as an occasion for offense.[66] How much the more does it befit us to flee all appearance of accord with the Antichrists in the choice of foods and the composition of the calendar as well as in other matters.

Further, even though there is no prohibition of the eating of meat on certain days, the economic use of fish for the sake of variety can still be maintained, not merely under the pressure of the scarcity of meat, but by the variety of tastes of men. This takes place among the Turks, and has happened before among all nations from the beginning of the world; each person used whatever food he could, at any time when this was permitted. It would contribute very much to the conservation of the meat supply if there were a limitation on the luxury of the self-indulgent and a repression of the insatiable avarice of certain persons rather than the kind of prohibitions which oppress no one more than Christ's poor. But whatever happens to be one's judgment concerning these prohibitions, it is nevertheless unworthy so to mix public policies with the practices and observances of the Church and of the Kingdom of Christ that the old superstition of not a few is confirmed and many good people are caused great inconvenience.

CHAPTER XIII

THE REGULATION OF CEREMONIES

A third thing common in the ceremonies of Christians is the arrangement and regulation of forms of worship among the sacred congregations of Christ, such as the ministry of the word, the sacraments, the discipline of Christ, prayers and psalms so that these

[66] Augustine, *Letter* 36. 28 (*MPL*, Vol. 33, cols. 148 f.) .

may be ministered and communicated to everyone reverently, "decently and in an orderly manner" (I Cor. 14:40), for the true building up of the faith. In this matter, Christ's churches must have their freedom so that each may define the content and method of presentation of sacred readings, interpretations of Scriptures, catechizing, administration of the sacraments, prayers and psalms, and similarly the public correction of sinners, imposition of penance, and reconciliation for those who have satisfied the churches by doing penance, all in such a way as each church judges to be of greatest profit for its people, so that as a result of these activities they may be moved to a true and living repentance, and strengthened and advanced in the faith of Christ.

However, in any country or realm of the Church, where the characteristics of men do not vary very greatly, these things may very conveniently be observed with as much conformity as possible, not only for beauty's sake, but also in order to engender a good opinion for Christian forms of worship.

CHAPTER XIV

CARE FOR THE NEEDY

A fourth common observance of all the churches, and one proper to the Kingdom of Christ, is the care for the poor and needy. For the Lord expressly forbids his people to allow anyone among them to be in need (Deut. 15:4). The early Church of Christ at Jerusalem observed this so religiously that of the alms collected by the brethren as much was distributed to each as was necessary for him to live decently and devoutly, so that not one of them was found to be in need (Acts 2:44-45; and 4:34-35). That this care for the poor might be better accomplished, the apostles, with the prior approval of the entire Church and using prayers and the laying on of hands, put "seven approved men" in charge of this, men "of good repute" and "full of the Holy Spirit and of wisdom" (Acts 6:1-6).

Until the Antichrists undermined this practice, the churches observed it with a high degree of reverence. The ministers in this area, whom they inducted into this office even by a rite of ordination, they called deacons of the churches. Although these men were also obliged to be at the service of the elders [67] and to help in the preservation and exercise of the discipline of Christ and the administration of the sacraments, it was their principal duty to keep a list

[67] *Presbyteris.*

of all of Christ's needy in the churches, to be acquainted with the life and character of each, and to give to individuals from the common offerings of the faithful whatever would suffice for them to live properly and devoutly. For those who, when they are able to do so, refuse to seek the necessities of life by their own industry and labors should be excluded from the churches. "He who does not work, let him not eat," says the apostle (II Thess. 3:10).

Therefore, all who have a deep desire to embrace the Kingdom of Christ should restore this practice also among them with utmost care. For among those "who have the good things of the world and see their brothers in need, and close their hearts to them, the love of God" does not abide (I John 3:17) ; neither, therefore, does the Kingdom of Christ.

Now, those who hear Christ and the Holy Spirit are eager to undertake and perform all good deeds in that order and manner which they acknowledge to have been determined for them by the Lord and the Holy Spirit.

Since, then, it is manifest that God has gravely forbidden his people to allow anyone among them to beg, and has established that care for the poor should be exercised by certain approved men in the Church, that the alms of the faithful may be distributed to needy individuals in proportion to the need of each, all those undoubtedly pray thoughtlessly, "Thy kingdom come" (Matt. 6:10), who do not extend every effort for this method of caring for the poor to be restored which the Lord himself commanded and the Holy Spirit established in the early Church.

Care must also be taken lest petty liars first steal what is owed to the needy of Christ, and also that no ambition for human praise and favor compromise the office of almsgiving. That this evil must be avoided at all costs the Lord taught clearly enough when he gave the comand to give alms that "the left hand should not know what the right hand is doing" (Matt. 6:3). This obligation can be very conveniently discharged if each person on Sunday puts as much as he can of the blessings of God into the collection box for the use of the poor (I Cor. 16:2).

For when each person wishes to distribute his own alms for himself, there is violated, first of all, the institution of the Holy Spirit and the legitimate communion of the saints. Secondly, alms due to the least of Christ's brethren, and therefore to Christ himself, are more often given to the unworthy than to the worthy. Nor can every single individual know and investigate each of the poor who happen to encounter him; for those who are least worthy are much better instructed at begging, indeed, extorting, the alms which should be dispensed to the poor alone. Furthermore, when everyone gives alms by his own hand, it is with great difficulty that he will exclude from his heart a desire for the appreciation and praise of men; and when he receives this empty reward from men, a real and sure one is not to be expected from God. Finally, since it is obvious that those who voluntarily give themselves over to beggary are men prone to every crime, what else do those people who foster them do but sustain and support very harmful pests of society.[68]

Therefore, anyone who has ever written wisely about the state has been of the opinion that such persons are not to be tolerated in it.[69] There is also extant on this matter the Valentinian law in Justinian's *Code,* concerning real mendicants.[70]

And indeed we must be ashamed and grieve when the right care of the poor has already been restored in very many regions which still serve Antichrist, whereas the very ones who glory in the reception of the gospel and the Kingdom of Christ, although they are not unaware how necessary this practice is, and how much it is a part of the salutary religion of Christ, still fail to reestablish it.

These practices, therefore, which we have mentioned, are proper to the Kingdom of Christ, and all who do not earnestly desire to see them restored, as Christ commanded, openly witness concerning themselves, however they may glory in words about the Kingdom of Christ, that in reality they neither acknowledge it truly nor seek it sincerely.

Whoever considers reverently, therefore, what we have here set forth, including the testimony of Sacred Scriptures which we have cited, will readily understand what the Kingdom of Christ is and what things and observances are proper to it, and are therefore of necessity to be recalled by all those (by each according to the gifts of the Lord and his own vocation) who seek in truth for the Kingdom of Christ to be restored again among them. Now, there-

---

[68] Bucer here summarizes the main ideas that governed the introduction of organized poor relief during the time of the Reformation. Under the leadership of Luther, the Protestant Reformers became sharp critics of the old practices of begging and private almsgiving. Cf. Karl Holl, *Gesammelte Aufsätze zur Kirchengeschichte,* Vol. I, *Luther,* 2d ed. Tübingen, 1923), p. 515 ("Die Kulturbedeutung der Reformation"); English translation: *The Cultural Significance of the Reformation,* tr. by Karl Hertz et al. (Meridian Books, Inc., 1959), pp. 91 ff.; W. Pauck, *Das Reich Gottes,* pp. 82 ff.; Otto Winckelmann, *Das Fürsorgewesen der Stadt Strassburg* (Leipzig, 1922), pp. 94 ff.; E. M. Leonard, *The Early History of English Poor Relief* (Cambridge, 1900).

[69] Cf. Plato, *Laws* XII, 936 1.

[70] *Code* XI, 26.

fore, something will have to be said about how salutary it is for all mankind, how altogether necessary for salvation and happiness, both present and future, for each Christian to exert himself with utmost care and all the strength each has obtained from the Lord that Christ's Kingdom may be as fully received as we have shown that it ought to be. Even if his very life must be expended, this is the obligation of each Christian.

CHAPTER XV

How Salutary It Is for All Men to Have the Kingdom
of Christ Firmly Restored Among Them and How
Necessary It Is for Salvation that Every Christian,
According to His Place in the Body of Christ
and the Gifts He Has Received from Him,
Aim and Work Toward This with Deepest Concern

I may seem here to be embarking on a pointless task in proposing to show how salutary it is for the Kingdom of Christ fully to be embraced among us, and how necessary it is for the salvation of each individual that he should contribute toward this, with deepest concern and burning zeal, whatever through God he is still able to contribute. For no one of those who have been touched but a little by the gospel wishes to appear to be unacquainted with this or to have any doubt about it. For the Lord said: "By their fruits you shall know them" (Matt. 7:16). Therefore, since thus far not only has there been a delay in the firm reestablishment of the Kingdom of Christ but very many even of the learned and prominent professors of the gospel have been remiss in total zeal for its restoration, and because not a few in their carnal wisdom judge that it would be harmful for the state to do this, the reality itself certainly proves and cries out that there are still very few who realize that a solid restitution and reception of the Kingdom of Christ is truly salutary and necessary for all happiness.

Therefore, it is by no means an accomplished fact when we admonish each other that we plainly learn from the eternal and immutable Word of God how salutary it is to receive the full Kingdom of Christ, and how necessary it is for each individual firmly to exert for its restoration whatever strength he has received from the Lord.

For how many do we see even among those who wish to be considered especially learned and enthusiastic about the Kingdom of

God who are either ashamed or irked to preach the gospel of this Kingdom to every creature and especially to those who are yet quite uninstructed, even though they are singularly committed to the trust of those very ones whose temporal things they gather; indeed, how many do you find who, however open and horrible a sacrilege it is, take the income of a number of parishes and yet do not render the ministry even to a single person either through helpers or by themselves. If in these splendid and well-attended places they have one or two, or a few more, sermons in a year, they think that they have discharged their duty admirably; they spend all the rest of their time in leisure, luxury, and worldly pomp.

What, then, shall we say of the understanding of Christ's Kingdom on the part of bishops and nobles who still confer a plurality of priestly benefices on these despoilers of churches, and sometimes give parishes to secular persons in order to receive a profit from them and put men in charge of parishes who are most inept for this role and so let themselves be hired for it at a lesser salary?

What do those who are worldly-wise think now about the Kingdom of Christ, those who want the holy preaching of the gospel restricted to fewer evangelists, indeed want it entirely omitted, because by this preaching, as they falsely say, controversies and disturbances are stirred up among the people? For they prefer that the prince of this world who is strong and armed hold men bound to his pleasure in quiet and calm rather than that he should be troubled and confounded by any external disturbance, or even the danger of a disturbance through a sermon of Christ's Kingdom which would snatch away from him the spoils he has taken from the elect of God whom he holds bound in the chains of perdition.

We know that the first work of our salvation is the announcement of the gospel to every creature (Mark 16:15). Toward this, Christ the Lord himself, his apostles, and all true Christians have always dedicated themselves with greatest zeal. But those wise fellows judge not only that this is not salutary, but that it is even harmful to society. Do they not thus bear clear witness concerning themselves, that they are of the opinion that Christ is not a saving king and that his Kingdom is not useful to society?

But the Lord has sanctioned his discipline, both of all life and of doing penance, and also of sacred ceremonies with plain and very serious words! But how few do you find, even among those who are held to be most notable among Christians, who, I do not say desire it from their hearts, but at least think it useful to attempt this uniquely saving discipline! Our times are different, they say, from those when this discipline flourished in the early churches. Men are different now, and it must be feared that by the restitution of this discipline the churches will be more disturbed than edified, and more men will be frightened away from the gospel than will be attracted. Finally, it must be feared that this attempt may culminate in a new tyranny of the false clergy over the people of Christ, they say.

But do not these also by their words and counsel clearly prove their terrible ignorance of the usefulness of the Kingdom of Christ and its benefits? For they are unaware that the Kingdom of Christ is a kingdom of all times and of all men who have been elected for salvation. They are unaware that Jesus the King, i.e., the Savior of mankind and the most excellent Shepherd of his sheep, has instituted and commanded nothing at all which is not salutary to his own at every time and in every place if it is used as he instituted and commanded it.

When, therefore, we still see everywhere, even among those who apparently want to love and seek the Kingdom of Christ, a great ignorance of how salutary it is to accept Christ's Kingdom completely and also how necessary it is for all to work with all their strength that it should be fully restored among us, surely for us to warn about this matter is not vain, but it is rather a duty required of all who truly belong to Christ.

And so I pray the God and Father of our Lord Jesus Christ that he may grant to his elect an understanding of the truth that "the carnal man is not able to perceive those things" which are of the Kingdom of Christ (I Cor. 2:14) and that "these things are hidden from the wise" of the world (Matt. 11:25), but that they can be learned and certainly known only from the Holy Scriptures, through a sure faith in Christ (II Tim. 3:15). May the Lord deign so to increase this faith in his own that they may firmly believe that he has come into this world as the Savior of all the sons of God, at whatever periods of time they live and by whatever infirmities of the flesh they are oppressed, or by whatever wickedness of the world they are vexed, so that he has taught nothing at all, instituted and commanded nothing, which is not uniquely salutary for all those who in true faith receive and undertake what he has instituted and commanded; and so this must necessarily be required and renewed by all, so that those who neglect to do so clearly reject Christ himself and his Kingdom. Therefore, in accordance with the obligation laid upon us, let us consider and ponder what the eternal Father has testified about his Son and what the Son has testified concerning himself. Let us adhere to these testimonies with our total being, driving far from our hearts whatever the wisdom of the flesh suggests to the contrary, or de-praved custom puts in the way, or our corrupt desires entice us to.

The Father, therefore, testifies concerning the Son that "he has anointed him King over Zion" (Ps. 2:6), i.e., the people of his elect, a true king who would teach, institute, and command noth-ing which did not contribute toward the eternal salvation of his own. For this reason he has commanded that we hear him in all things (Matt. 17:5). Thus through his whole Scripture he testifies that through this his Christ alone, our King, the doctrine and foundation of present and future bliss are offered to us and that those who have not heard him in all things will perish entirely and for eternity, which is clearly evident from those few texts which we have cited earlier concerning the Kingdom of Christ.

What Saint John the Baptist said must also be soberly observed by us: "He who believes in the Son has eternal life; but whoever does not listen to the Son will not see life, and the wrath of God remains upon him" (John 3:36). But no one truly believes and listens to Christ unless he is convinced it is true that all things he taught and commanded are the precepts of eternal life. Likewise, he accepts what the Lord testifies concerning himself, that "he was not sent by the Father to condemn the world but to save it" and "that whosoever believes in him is not to be condemned; but whoever does not believe, he is already condemned, because he does not believe in the name of the only begotten Son of God" (John 3:17-18). It is certain, however, that he does not believe in Christ, as we have already said, who does not acknowledge that an institution or precept of his is altogether necessary, in belief and practice, for salvation and eternal life. If there are those who either themselves neglect the precepts of Christ or do not strive with all their might that these should all be received and observed among all, they can hardly be said to acknowledge that the precepts of Christ (which they ignore or pretend to ignore) are necessary to salvation and to a blessed life. Therefore, they do not believe in the Son of God, and "the wrath of God remains upon them," and "they are already condemned" to Gehenna (John 3:36 and 18).

Let us also ponder that saying of the Lord: "I am the light of the world; whoever follows me will not walk in darkness, but will have the light of life" (John 8:12). Thus whoever is not eager to follow him in all things and observe all his precepts certainly cleaves to the darkness of eternal death.

Let us also consider this reverently: "The thief does not come except to steal, kill, and destroy; I have come that my sheep may have life, and have it more abundantly" (John 10:10). Likewise this: "My sheep hear my voice, and I know them, and they follow me, and I give them eternal life, and they will not perish forever, nor will anyone snatch them from my hand" (John 10:27-28). What else follows from these things but that those who do not hear the voice of Christ in all things and follow this Good Shepherd in all their lives repudiate eternal life, and, beyond that, plunge into everlasting oblivion, and offer themselves as plunder to evil demons?

The following words of the Lord, furthermore, ring continually in our hearts: "He who loves me will keep my word, and my Father will love him, and we shall come to him, and make our home with him. Whoever does not love me will not keep my words" (John 14:23-24). But "whoever does not love the Lord God, let him be anathema," says the Holy Spirit (I Cor. 16:22). And it must be observed here that the Lord asks that we should keep all his precepts, not whatever seems good to do according to the wisdom of our flesh. For he commanded his apostles to teach the baptized to observe all that he had commanded (Matt. 28:19-20). Thus those who do not consecrate themselves with all their hearts to observing all the precepts of Christ show that they do not love Christ the Lord, and that they despise the love of the Father as well as the Son, and their making of a home with them.

For our King is that Prophet given to us after Moses, as Saint Peter testifies (Acts 3:22-23), "whom it is necessary to hear in all things" which he said to us. For the soul which detracts anything from this is to be exterminated from the people of God. And since it was against the will of God to add or detract anything of the precepts of the Lord given through Moses, or to worship God in any manner which seemed good to men but had not been prescribed by him (Deut. 4:2 and 12:32), what an evil, wicked thing it is for those who boast that they belong to Christ to permit themselves to add to or subtract from the words and precepts of his Son as they please, and fabricate a ministry of his religion other than what he delivered to us. Let us, therefore, think this over: if God pronounced a curse on him who did not remain faithful even to the words of the law given by Moses (Deut. 27:26), how much more ought they to be open to a curse who do not adhere to all the words of the Son of God? And if he who despised Moses or another prophet speaking on earth did not escape punishment, but "one convicted by two witnesses was killed without mercy, how much more will they receive unbearable punishments who" knowingly and willingly "oppose" him "who speaks to us from heaven and whose voice shakes the earth." These persons who have such con-

tempt for the Son of God are rightly said "to trample him under-
foot, and defile the blood of him through whom they have been
sanctified, and inflict outrage on the spirit of grace" (Heb. 10:28-
29, and 12:25).

Whatever, therefore, human wisdom suggests to us to the contrary, whatever our depraved desires persuade us to, whatever the
tyranny of evil custom demands, let us always respond: "To whom
shall we go," to whom shall we turn? This our Savior and King
"has the words of eternal life" (John 6:68). He cannot deceive us
nor impose anything on us by his laws, unless its observance is
necessary for our salvation. He has commanded us "to seek first
his Kingdom" (Matt. 6:33), i.e., that he should rule us in all
things by his word and Spirit, also adding to us whatever we can
desire for our own welfare. Unless, therefore, we put his Kingdom
before all things else and act with utmost zeal that it should be
fully restored among us, each according to his vocation and the
gifts he has received from the Lord, we shall be deprived of both
present and future goods, and furthermore, plunged into Gehenna.

For who would acknowledge Your Royal Majesty to be King of
England, if any city or town on this island embraced only those
of Your Majesty's laws which seemed good to it (something which
not a few today do concerning the laws of the eternal Son of God),
and did not strive to obey all his laws and edicts? Is the obedience
that the Church today gives to Christ the King so complete an
obedience? Who might fittingly rule over us more fully than the
Son of God, who created and recreated us, and who confers both
present and eternal salvation on his own by his rule?

Plato, in his first book of *Laws* and in his *Politics,* does not want
younger men, indeed, not any of the people, to be allowed to dispute about human laws when they have once been accepted by the
republic,[71] even though he acknowledges that legislation cannot
be so wisely devised that the laws will always be of profit to all men
in all things, and therefore that there is very much need of some
epieikeia [72] (he wishes that only the wisest princes and magistrates
be conceded the right to interpret and apply laws for the well-being
of the citizens) [73]; and so is it right for us wretched little men, on
our own part completely ignorant of what is good, to modify the
laws of the Son of God and to get around them according to our
own impulses when they command nothing that is not always and
in every way wholesome?

[71] Plato, *Laws* I, 634e.
[72] Interpretation on the basis of *equity.*
[73] Plato, *Politics* 294a ff.

Indeed, we must seek to understand soberly and with certainty what the laws, edicts, and institutions of Christ our King are. Then we must unhesitatingly acknowledge that he shows himself in all these things as our Jesus, i.e., eternal Savior. Finally, we must spend ourselves and all we have in observing these things and actively fulfilling them with all that is in us whatever the whole world with its prince and its God thinks or does to the contrary, and however burdensome this seems to our flesh. For what eternal truth said cannot but be true: "Take my yoke upon you and learn of me"; hear me, the master of all life, "for I am meek and humble of heart; thus you will find rest for your souls. For my yoke is good and useful, and my burden light" (Matt. 11:29-30) .

Whoever has faith in the word of God will easily understand from these and all the other testimonies of Holy Scripture about the Kingdom of Christ that anything at all which Christ the Lord commanded and established for us is certainly a matter of great importance for our salvation if it is observed as he commanded and established it, however men and times vary; and we cannot knowingly and prudently neglect or omit any of these things for any reason without despising and repudiating Christ himself and all his sovereignty.

Nor can this be unclear to anyone who has read the Holy Scriptures and believes them to be divine, that there is no greater duty assigned to all men, and so necessary to salvation, as that each (according to his place in the Church of God and whatever gifts and powers he has received from the Lord) even in external things, watch, work, struggle, and labor that all the precepts and teachings of our King and Savior Christ are conveyed to all men, so that they may be received eagerly and observed with utmost reverence.

Now we must pass over to the third part of this writing in order that, as the Lord grants, I may indicate how I believe Your Majesty can establish the Kingdom of Christ in his realm most conveniently, build it up, and bring it, if not to its hoped-for goal (for today an all too horrible if not universal aversion and hatred of the Kingdom of Christ prevails among men, just as does ignorance of it) at least to an acceptable one.

End of the first book concerning the Kingdom of Christ.

BOOK TWO

CHAPTER I

BY WHAT WAYS AND MEANS THE KINGDOM OF CHRIST CAN AND SHOULD BE REFORMED BY DEVOUT KINGS

To begin, Your Royal Highness, I have no doubt that Your Majesty himself sees that the reformation of the Kingdom of Christ which we require, rather, which the salvation of all of us requires, cannot really be expected from the bishops while there are so few among them who are fully aware of the power of this Kingdom and their own official responsibilities but so many who by all possible means which they dare employ either oppose, postpone, or delay this reformation. Your Majesty must remember that sovereign power in this realm was entrusted to him by the supreme King of Kings and Lord of Lords, and that every soul was made subject to his royal authority, including the souls of bishops and all the clergy (Rom. 13:1). That is why it is fitting for Your Majesty to be quite seriously concerned about the restoration of their duty and ministry and to act with a more burning energy toward this very goal, the more the renewal of this office contributes toward the salvation of all and the more its neglect endangers and its dissipation damages everyone's salvation.

Worthy of Your Majesty's consideration and conscientious imitation are the examples of men like David, Solomon, Asa, Hezekiah, Josiah, and Nehemiah, whom the Scriptures praise resoundingly for their piety and the sound administration of their kingdoms. When true religion had seriously fallen apart in their times and the priesthood was perniciously corrupted, these men personally undertook the task of the renewal of religion as a matter of royal right and duty. For this holy and difficult purpose, they gathered around them as advisers and assistants some priests, prophets, and other devout men, who, they thought, gave promise in their knowledge of God and in their zeal of accomplishing very much indeed. They then took care before all else that the law of God was very energetically declared and explained to the people. The next step was to persuade all, after they had professed obedience to the law, once more wholeheartedly to accept and truly to reverence the Lord's covenant. Then, finally, they reorganized and renewed the estate and ministry of priests and Levites and the entire administration of religion, according to the law of God; and they watched most vigilantly that no one should destroy what they had done.

In regard to the efforts and attempts of these devout princes to reestablish the Kingdom of God for their people, passages of divine Scripture quite appropriate for pious reading and reflection are the following: concerning David, II Sam., ch. 6, and I Chron., chs. 13, 14, 15, 16, 23, and the three following chapters; concerning Solomon, I Kings, ch. 8, and II Chron., chs. 5, 6, and 7; concerning Asa, II Chron., ch. 15; and concerning Hezekiah, II Kings, ch. 18:1-7, and II Chron., chs. 29 and 31; concerning Josiah, II Kings, chs. 22 and 23, II Chron., chs. 34 and 35; concerning Nehemiah, the entire book of that name.

In these examples and histories, Your Majesty will clearly see, first, that it is within his official capacity to undertake the renewal of the important priestly order and office, just as the care for other estates and offices is within his prerogative.

CHAPTER II

Who Are to Be Used as Advisers for the Reestablishment of Christ's Kingdom

Then also he will see that those men who profess themselves to be priests and theologians with grand titles, and who have waded into the lavish stipends of these most holy offices, are not to be relied on as advisers, but rather those whom he discovers by their fruits to be endowed and aflame beyond others with the knowledge and the love of the Kingdom of Christ, just as "David consulted" about the renewing of religion first "with the commanders of thousands and of hundreds, and with every leader" (I Chron. 13:1). For only one who has himself submitted totally to the yoke of Christ can with any degree of consistency contribute his advice and work toward the restoration of Christ's Kingdom. Such men, indeed, Christ our King regenerates and forms for himself from whatever estates of mankind he chooses, nor does he assign this blessing of his to any particular class of men, much less to hypocrites with empty titles.

The fewer men there are in all estates who have a sure insight into what the Kingdom of Christ means and truly desire its restoration, the more diligently they must be sought out and chosen from whatever kind and condition of men they are to be found, as counselors of the first rank for Your Majesty in the purposeful task of establishing the Kingdom of God securely and for the work of calling all of Christ's subjects back to him.

Whoever needs to have the health of his body restored certainly does not obtain his physicians on the basis of fine titles and great wealth which some have accumulated for themselves by a pretense of medical skill, but rather those whom he knows to have a solid knowledge of healing and a real interest in curing. In the same way, no one willingly entrusts himself to a ship whose master has only the name and income of a navigator, but who does not know how to navigate; but everyone prefers to sail with a man who, although his name is unknown and his talents modest, nevertheless has all the knowledge and experience necessary for sailing a ship.[1] With how much greater care and effort are men to be sought by Your Majesty to whom he will entrust not bodies but the very core of the religion of Christ to be preached anew in which is contained the eternal salvation of all.

May, therefore, Christ our King help Your Majesty to select for a supreme council for the reformation of religion those advisers who both well know the power of the Kingdom of Christ and desire to realize it with all their hearts, especially for themselves but for all others also; men who are here looking for no human gain or favor but are prepared to undergo the limit of physical inconvenience rather than miss an opportunity for planting and cultivating the Kingdom of Christ. For this purpose, may they also be gifted with spiritual prudence, in order to begin a matter of such great moment creatively and to bring it efficiently to completion. It would contribute very much toward this goal if men of this kind excelled also in prestige, authority, and favor among the people. But before all things else it is necessary that they have a solid knowledge of religion and are on fire with zeal for it, and also that they are equipped with the spiritual prudence necessary for the renewal and spread of the Kingdom.

CHAPTER III

The Kingdom of Christ Must Be Renewed Not Only by Edicts but Also by Devout Persuasion

Furthermore, Your Majesty will consider this also from the Scriptural examples proposed that those devout kings and princes did not so much compel their people by decrees to recover the Kingdom of Christ as they persuaded them by serious and devout in-

---

[1] Plato, *Republic* I, 341c ff., VIII, 551c ff.; *Politics* 298a ff.

structions. Wise princes and legislators of old did the same sort of thing among the nations for whose citizens they promulgated laws (Cicero, 2, *De legibus*).[2] For men do not accept law and observe it consistently, least of all divine law, unless they are first instructed and convinced that that law is salutary for them.

Your Majesty will, therefore, take care most diligently and conscientiously to persuade, both personally and through others whom he shall find to be gifted by God for this sort of thing, first, that the great council of the realm which they call Parliament, and then also all the people of the kingdom, accept the whole plan for the full and firm restoration of the religion of Christ in doctrine as well as in rites and discipline; this plan has been clearly constituted and carefully described in His Majesty's highest privy council of religion. Since it is not possible to have a great gathering in any one place, as David, Asa, Hezekiah, Josiah, and others did, Your Majesty will have to arrange for the people to gather in various places of the realm wherever it is possible for them to come together.

CHAPTER IV

APPROVED EVANGELISTS MUST BE SENT OUT TO ALL PARTS OF THE REALM

Furthermore, since such great ignorance of the Kingdom of Christ holds sway over all everywhere, so that its power and its salutary effect upon its men and the fact that apart from it everything is harmful and destructive can hardly be explained, taught, and presented convincingly in one or two sermons, no matter how careful and accurate they are, there must first be sent out to all the churches of the realm evangelists who are appropriately learned and motivated for the Kingdom of Christ. They must announce assiduously, zealously, and in a timely fashion to the people everywhere the good news of the Kingdom. And they should teach from the Gospel, with strength and energy, whatever pertains to the Kingdom of Christ and whatever it is necessary to believe and do for present and future happiness.[3]

In delegating these men, utmost care will have to be taken that none are sent out except those from whose whole life and manner of devotion it is obvious that they are not in any way considering or seeking their own interests in this office but only those things

[2] Cicero, *De legibus* II, 5, 11 ff.; Plato, *Laws* IV, 722b–723a.
[3] C. Hopf (*Martin Bucer and the English Reformation*) describes how these and the following recommendations were carried out in England.

which pertain to the glory of Christ and the repair of the churches. Therefore, it will not be sufficient at all to have heard from them only one or two worthy sermons, just as it will not be at all possible to judge someone suitable for this office from the fact that he seems skilled and acceptable at preaching. Their whole lives, their habits of behavior and special interests, must be inquired into and explored, to see how strong a talent and a will they have for restoring the Kingdom of Christ.

In this regard, the rule of the Holy Spirit expressed in the letters to Timothy and Titus concerning this very thing, namely, what sort of ministers are to be put in charge of churches, should be very religiously considered; and with this as a standard, everything should be demanded of them which was also demanded of those who were first sent out to lay the foundations of the churches (I Tim. 3:1-13; Titus 1:5-9). Strict and exacting care should be taken that those who have the duty of laying these foundations by preaching the gospel greatly excel in their knowledge and zeal for the Kingdom of Christ those whose task it is to build the superstructure once the foundations have been laid (I Cor. 3:10). Their examination ought to be committed to individuals outstanding for their holiness, both resolute for and knowledgeable in the mysteries of the Kingdom of Christ.

It will be useful to prescribe to these examiners a suitable scheme for a canonical examination which is derived from the precepts of the Holy Spirit, which those charged to examine individuals should follow so as not to inflict on the churches for this most holy office any whom they have discovered not to have sufficiently, as a gift from the Lord, a strong talent and will for the reestablishment of his Kingdom. Certainly no one has sufficiently explored such gifts of Christ if he has only once or twice heard someone giving good answers on Christian doctrine, and promising to do faithful work in the ministry. From their previous life, as I have said, and their real fruits of piety, concerning which there should be weighty testimony of pious men and of the churches where the individual has lived or even ministered for some time, it must be established how much of a faculty and what gifts the Lord has given to each for the restoration of his Kingdom, and also with how great a desire and zeal he has inflamed the individual for this very thing. For those who neglect this supreme diligence and severity in investigating and testing the preachers of the gospel, as the Holy Spirit has commanded in so many places and so scrupulously, these indeed make sport of Christ the King and impiously betray the salvation of his elect.

In order that the preaching of these evangelists may be rather uniform and harmonious and in order that the true foundations of religion may be laid out by them in a like manner, it would be quite helpful to prescribe for them, in clear and definite terms, an outline of the principal dogmas of Christ, of those especially which are debated at this time, and also of the method of reading and explaining the Sacred Scriptures in the churches, and about the catechism and private instructions; likewise, concerning the true use of the sacraments, and the universal communion of the Church, and the discipline both of life and manners, then also penance and the other practices, as we have already briefly delineated them.

CHAPTER V

The Kingdom of Christ Must Be Reformed by Devout Persuasion and an Accurate Preaching of the Gospel, Rather than by Decrees

I am concerned, Most Serene King, that preparation must be made for the restitution of Christ's Kingdom, which is not so much something simply useful as it is something necessary for the people whom the Most High has entrusted to your piety for feeding, and this must be done first through the preaching of the gospel which I have mentioned, then also through the persuasion of Your Royal Majesty and of those in his councils whom he will find most suitable for this task. For we see, first of all, that pious kings and princes, acting with the guidance of the Holy Spirit, once used this approach successfully in restoring the Kingdom of Christ among their subjects, just as it is evident that Christ our King used the same method and way. For before all things else he commanded his apostles to preach the gospel of his Kingdom to all nations (Matt. 24:14).

It is indeed within the province of pious kings and princes, now that the covenant of the Lord has been renewed and the laws of God accepted, to allow none of their subjects to violate this covenant openly or to transgress these laws; I have already mentioned something concerning this; nevertheless, since no one can be a true citizen of the Kingdom of Christ except willingly, and all Christians, even princes, should, to the degree that the Lord endows them, strive to bring willing citizens to the Kingdom of Christ rather than drive unwilling hypocrites to it, anyone can readily see how fitting it is for religious princes to work out the repair of the Kingdom of Christ among their subjects, first by the plain and industrious preaching of the gospel, and then by holy and accurate persuasions, both on their own part and through those who have the holiest and most weighty authority among the people of the realm.

But because pious princes must plant and propagate the Kingdom of Christ also by the power of the sword, as by all the powers which they have received from the Lord, it is also their duty not to tolerate anyone who openly opposes and undermines the sound doctrine of the gospel. For however oppressed both the doctrine and discipline of Christ frequently were heretofore and how exceedingly great the number of superstitions that dominated the hearts of men for so many centuries, nevertheless, when all have been baptized into the Kingdom of Christ, not of Antichrist, they must be taught to observe whatever Christ has commanded and not what his demented vicars impose. Those who refuse to be taught the things that are of Christ's Kingdom should not be tolerated in a Christian commonwealth, much less those who dare to rebel against and vitiate these things.[4]

Your Royal Majesty realizes well enough how many evils have been caused, when without sufficient previous indoctrination, by mere act and edict false cults were wiped out from among your people, instruments of impiety snatched away, and the ministry of true religion enjoined by command. Some have, on this account, moved in the direction of horrible sedition, others have aroused dangerous unrest in the provinces, and today, wherever they are strong, they either stir up trouble or maintain and increase strife already rampant. Others completely convert the prescribed form of worship into papistic abuse when they deliberately recite the service of the sacrifice of Christ, in the vernacular language, indeed, but indistinctly and with words run together, so that they cannot be understood, and the people altogether refuse to listen to them with an effort to understand. Not a few of the sacrificing priests present the Holy Communion of Christ as a papistic Mass, nor do the people attend with a mind other than this. Hence in very many places, as they celebrated Masses before, so now they celebrate the Communion three times a day, and they designate them by the names of saints and of the mother of the Lord, calling them the Mass of Saint Nicholas, of the Blessed Virgin, or of other

---

4 The foregoing passages represent a brief statement of Bucer's lifelong conviction concerning the responsibility of political rulers for the establishment and maintenance of true religion. Cf. Pauck, *Das Reich Gottes*, pp. 53–63, and the literature cited by F. Wendel on p. 16, n. 12, of his edition of *De Regno Christi*.

saints; and hardly anyone takes the sacrament of the Lord's Table, except the one sacrificing priest or the sacristan, and he unwillingly. By these horrible mockeries of Christ's religion God's wrath is most gravely provoked.[5]

Since, then, we are so clearly taught by the precept and example of our King and Savior Jesus Christ and by the examples of all the pious princes whose ministry the Lord ever used to offer his Kingdom to men or to restore it, it is necessary before all things else, as his Kingdom is being restored to set forth and explain the mysteries of this Kingdom as diligently as possible to the people and exhort them by holy persuasions to take on the yoke of Christ, Your Royal Majesty will acknowledge his obligation to exercise total concentration and concern in this; nor must those be listened to who wish Christ's religion to be imposed on men merely by edicts and laws and who say that it is sufficient if the worship services are recited for Christ's people in any way men please.

For it must be greatly feared that these people are agitated by an adverse spirit who strives to restore the administration of Christ's religion to men who are as little qualified for it as they let themselves to be used for it. Thus they make it possible for greedy men that they not only despoil ecclesiastical wealth and power but also gradually abolish the religion of Christ entirely. For that spirit hopes that when the leadership of the churches has been destroyed, there will no longer be men who would want to prepare and fit themselves sincerely and earnestly for the sacred ministry of the Church. For it knows and has the experience of so many centuries that Christ's religion entirely fails among the people when the Church's sacred ministry has been handed over to inept and unfaithful ministers.

CHAPTER VI

WHERE SUITABLE EVANGELISTS ARE TO BE SOUGHT, AND THE MATTER OF THE REFORMATION OF THE SCHOOLS OF HIGHER LEARNING

But some will plead that the kind of preachers of the gospel which we require cannot be found in sufficient number in order that the gospel of Christ can be rightly announced and explained

[5] These are references to the troubles which beset England in 1549, particularly the so-called Western Rebellion. Cf. Gustav Constant, *The Reformation in England*, Vol. I, pp. 116 ff.; Philip Hughes, *The Reformation in England*, Vol. II (London: Hollis & Carter, Publishers, Ltd., 1953), pp. 165 ff.

to all the people in this realm. To these the answer must be given that it is hardly astonishing that up to this time very few of this kind have been found, since no one has looked for them as he should. As much as I have been able to learn, although I am an immigrant to this country and have battled serious sickness most of the time that I have been here,[6] I have no doubt that if they are diligently looked for many more men can be found who are suitable for this work of evangelizing than is now generally believed.

But it must be confessed that there is not so great a number of these men as the vast multitude of Christian people in this realm requires, and the number that rightly ought to be available if you consider how favorably the Lord has treated this realm before all others in the rest of the Christian world; through pious kings and other princes, and royalty of either sex, he has favored with excellent advantages the preparation of fit preachers for the task of advancing the gospel from day to day. For no churches or universities in the rest of Europe have colleges so endowed and established with good laws as the two universities of the realm.[7] If in these colleges, as it has been dutifully determined, besides the two masters assigned to the art of medicine and the two to the science of civil law, all the rest would study sound theology [8] and also reckon it their duty to teach it in the churches, how great a swarm of approved evangelists would then come forth for the churches!

But the plague of Antichrist has invaded also these colleges most seriously, so that very many in these colleges, after the fashion of the wicked monks and false canons, lazily abuse the good things of these colleges, decaying and growing old there in impious ease and preempting the place and opportunity of younger men who wish to dedicate themselves to true theology and the ministries of the churches. Not content with this perversity, although it is supremely damaging to the churches, most of them attack the pure doctrine of Christ wherever they can and dare and not only estrange the hearts of younger men from it but even frighten them away.[9]

And so the smaller is the number of those to whom the work of evangelizing the Kingdom of Christ can be rightly entrusted, the

---

[6] Cf. Introduction, p. 158.

[7] I.e., Oxford and Cambridge.

[8] Bucer wrote to Calvin on May 25, 1550 (*Calvini Opera,* Vol. XIII, p. 575) that in every college two masters of arts were assigned to the study of law and two to that of medicine, whereas all others were expected to study theology. There is no confirmation of this in any extant official document.

[9] Cf. Hopf, *Martin Bucer and the English Reformation,* pp. 69 f., 82 ff., 122 ff.

more promptly and strictly will Your Royal Majesty institute and complete the reformation of both universities and of the colleges in these matters, so, that, first of all, no one will be allowed openly to oppose the pure doctrine of Christ. Secondly, those who have completed their period of learning and do not have every desire to adapt themselves to teaching the churches should leave the colleges as soon as possible in order to make the colleges free to provide room for younger men who are prepared faithfully to learn the things that pertain to the Kingdom of Christ and in due time to communicate these things to the churches with utmost zeal.

There are involved here certain unwisely merciful men who have too much sympathy for the enemies of the Church of God or certainly for such as should clearly be excluded from the association with any church and the participation in its revenues (II Thess. 3:7-10), when the opportunity of damaging and defrauding the churches is taken away from these men according to the Lord's precept. They have more feeling for them than for the churches which are being defrauded by the ministry of these impious men and therefore gravely undermined. They cry out that it is inhuman and unworthy of the colleges to eject men who have been there for such a long time; that some deference must be had for their age and that we should be mindful of the commandment that we ought to do to others what we wish should be done to us (Matt. 7:12).

By these objections they certainly demonstrate that they have not yet learned that all else must yield to the glory of Christ and the well-being of the churches, and that true charity and mercy are shown to one's neighbor when, according to God's precept and in order that he might not wrong God and the Church, he is removed by legitimate force commanded by God if he cannot be dissuaded in any other way. How is this? These men certainly do not think correctly as they often boast.[10] For what is the consequence? These men have now defrauded the Church of Christ for a long time, and far from rejoicing in having fit and needed ministers, they have blocked this for the sake of their own indulgence and bellies. Must, therefore, compassion be shown to them, and must they be permitted still longer to afflict the churches of God with such damage? What common sense do these men seem to have when they infer from what the Lord commanded that we should do unto others what we would have them do unto us, that Christians should show whatever forgiveness to others they wickedly and wrongly want to be granted or conceded as if the Lord wanted us

10 *Quid? nec certe, de qua non parum gloriantur, hi dialecticam veram tenent.*

to owe to our neighbors whatever they asked for, however wicked their motivation, and did not rather will that we should do and render only those things to our neighbors which we could wish to be done or rendered to us according to right reason deduced from his word.

If, however, anyone from the colleges is impeded by age or sickness from fulfilling his obligations to the churches, since the churches should not stand by and allow anyone to be in need, therefore this sort of person is to be taken care of so that he will lack nothing for living piously and happily. But those who are well and strong of body and have the means to live to the Lord, or can easily find them, either from positions in the priesthood or by other means, why should not the very law of God apply to them, "Those who do not work, let them not eat" (II Thess. 3:10)? Let those only have a place in the most sacred institutions of the colleges, who wish to gain there a knowledge of the good arts and of the Sacred Scriptures so that in due time they may be able to have a better and more salutary ministry in the churches.

Your Majesty's universities and their colleges must therefore be restored as soon as possible, and with thoroughgoing strictness, to their proper role as ordained by the Word of God. With respect to those who unworthily control them and thus seriously compromise the churches, the manner of procedure and the rendering of mercy must consist in this, that Your Majesty deny them every occasion of afflicting the churches of God with such great wrongs and bring it about that the interests of the churches will be taken care of by suitable ministers, so necessary for the eternal salvation of the faithful, rather than by the godless laziness and gluttony of those pretenders. Cicero, a pagan writer, stated this as the first law of the bond of friendship, "that we should seek from friends only what is decent," and "pursue" only "honest causes of friends," and "not ask anything shameful of friends nor do such things when asked" (in *Laelio*). [11] And the Socratics acknowledged that a salutary remedy and a great benefit are obtained by those who have sinned, if just punishments are assumed by them (in *Gorgias*).[12]

Let us be warned by those horrible punishments suffered by the priest Eli (I Sam. 2:27-36; 4:12-18), King Saul (I Sam., ch. 15), and the whole people of Israel because of an impious indulgence and unwise mercy toward those against whom, by the command of God, who alone is truly merciful and clement, they ought to have exercised severity lest we think that any indulgent concessions are

---

[11] Cicero, *On Friendship* XIII, 44; XII, 40.
[12] Plato, *Gorgias* 476a–477a; 480 b–d.

to be made to anyone against God's precept and against the well-being of the churches. Christian mildness and mercy must be exhibited to the sheep of Christ in order to protect them from the wolves, and not to the wolves that they may scatter and destroy the sheep.

These colleges are clearly magnificent blessings of Christ. May Your Royal Majesty therefore not bind himself to horrible ingratitude against God's kindness and to a very serious wrong to the churches of Christ entrusted to him, but rather let him make every effort as quickly as he can and with all the strength and power at his command, to appropriate them both for Christ the Lord and his churches and restore them to their proper purpose.

CHAPTER VII

The Source and Support of the Evangelists and Pastors of the Churches

But it will be said that even if today the reformation of all the colleges of both universities were accomplished as fully as possible, nevertheless those who rightly should be sent out to preach Christ's gospel could not go forth from them so quickly. Those, therefore, who are already instructed by the Lord for this function must be sought for throughout the whole realm all the more diligently. It will undoubtedly be found that this will amount to no small number if they are sought in good faith. It will also be fitting that those who are now doing good parish work and have their parishes well established be released for the work of evangelizing for a time, during which period they might be replaced by those who have recently consecrated themselves to the Lord for the sacred ministry.

But another difficulty will be brought up here: Who will pay the expenses for these evangelists? But who else should very obviously have this obligation but those who receive the incomes of parishes where the evangelists will go to preach Christ's gospel in their stead? And if what is obtained from them for such necessary work is not enough, the remainder will most justly be requested of the bishops, whose proper task it is to send out and support not only evangelists for the churches committed to their charge but also permanent teachers and shepherds. It is also a duty, not a burden, for them to support those who will announce Christ's gospel in each diocese, and this will be required with even more right because by their negligence it has come about that the churches of

Christ have been so long without legitimate ministers and suitable heralds of the gospel and all of Christ's religion has been so far obliterated among the people as to approximate utter extinction. They also know that they ought to leave all secular business for others to do and not burden themselves with profane ministers, but devote all their resources to this one thing, with all the people they have at their service, that the ministry of Christ be rightly provided to the churches commended to the charge of each of them. Therefore, they should have about them as ministers only those who have dedicated themselves to the ministry and to clerical discipline.

But after a fair multitude of Christ's people have assembled on individual feast days in opportune places throughout the realm (which all must do by Your Royal Majesty's authority), and the gospel of Christ has been as clearly as possible proclaimed and as widely as possible explained, and everything necessary for the full undertaking of Christ's Kingdom lucidly manifested and very gravely urged (and for this matter a reasonable amount of time must be taken, at a minimum seven or eight feast days, on every one of which two sermons should be delivered), then finally there will have to be trust in the goodness of God that he will give Your Royal Highness a reformation of the churches complete and perfect in all its numbers and parts, as a persuasive argument not only to the Great Council but to all his people, that they both receive it with prompt hearts, and retain it with an abundant fruit of piety.

But meanwhile, attention must be given that whatever well-instructed persons the Lord has offered to minister to the parishes be at once placed in charge of those parishes which are without pastoral care, with a mandate to renew the whole doctrine and discipline of Christ in those parishes to which they are sent, according to the manifest precepts of the Lord and the rule based thereon as outlined by Your Majesty and his Supreme Council for religious causes about which I have previously made mention.[13]

That the necessities of life may be supplied for these true pastors of churches in order that they may discharge their sure ministry for the churches of Christ, this will have to be required of those who have parishes incorporated, or appropriated, as they say, or in any other way so controlled that they themselves receive the income. For it is hardly credible that the income of the convents and parishes which Your Royal Majesty's father awarded to certain individuals should not be sufficiently abundant so that fair stipends could not very easily be given from them to pastors, without any

[13] Cf. Book Two, Ch. IV.

burden on those who now have those incomes. But such stipends will have to be established and regulated through very dedicated and conscientious men whom Your Majesty will have authorized for this very thing.

And if certain parishes cannot be taken care of by this sort of income, then bishops and other wealthier prelates will have to be called upon so that from their abundance they aid the parishes in need. They have left over whatever they have not spent for the sacred ministry of the churches and for the poor. They are not ignorant of the fact that this has been so decreed by both divine and canon law. Let the bishops therefore finally acknowledge their very serious guilt, that they have for so long a time and so horribly not so much neglected as devastated the churches. For they have not done their episcopal duty to them in teaching and in providing them with suitable ministers but have rather given them most unworthy men, and often more than once. Let them strive to make reparations for the great damage they have done to the churches, restoring them by means of their own ministry as well as that of other good men.

CHAPTER VIII

How the Full Restitution of Religion Must Be Advocated and Enacted [14]

When, therefore, the Lord has granted that after sufficient preaching of the gospel throughout the realm consent has been given also by the Great Council of the realm for the full reception of Christ's Kingdom, then men will have to be chosen and sent to individual assemblies, men whose zeal for Christ's Kingdom is apparent from their fruits and who have very much favor and prestige in the realm, in order that they advocate and commend earnestly in Your Royal Majesty's name the reformation of the churches.

When this has been done, since then the Lord's covenant will have been once more received and established by the supreme authority of the realm, it will be the duty of Your Royal Majesty to sanction this covenant with holy laws and just provisions against its violators, and to preserve this most vigilantly and constantly. He will then zealously sanction, indeed, restore among his subjects,

---

[14] On the problem here discussed, see A. G. Dickens, *The English Reformation* (London: B. T. Batsford, Ltd., 1964), pp. 205 ff.; P. Hughes, *The Reformation in England,* Vol. II, pp. 150 ff.

the laws that Almighty God established concerning the care and preservation of Christ's religion (Num. 15:40; Deut. 13:4-18; and 17:2-3).

CHAPTER IX

The First Law: Children Must Be Catechized and Educated for God

And first, just as all by most holy Baptism have been made members of Christ's Kingdom and then received the covenant of eternal salvation, so Your Royal Majesty will make a law that orders parents to educate and establish their children in Christ's faith and obedience with great care, with a just penalty appointed for those who themselves infect their children with either false doctrine or bad morals or permit them to be infected by others. Next, it must provide that they diligently make the Church's catechism known to them when they are old enough to understand it. For unless the foundation of the Church is firmly laid in early childhood through the catechism of Christ, its upbuilding will proceed very poorly from then on. For those who do not labor with utmost zeal to instruct and train those whom they have consecrated to Christ the Lord in Baptism expose themselves to dire retribution. For those who neglect this when it is in their control snatch back the children whom they have consecrated to the Lord and hand them over to the dominion of Satan.

CHAPTER X

The Second Law: The Sanctification of Holy Days

Further, the law of God regarding the true sanctification of religious days singularly consecrated to God will have to be restored (Ex. 31:12-17; 35:2-3; Num. 15:32-36) that no one do unnecessary corporal works with impunity on such days, even if they are per se useful, much less be absent from the sacred gatherings and do works of the flesh, such as making shameful gains, disturbing the religious spirit of brethren by demanding repayment of debts, and forcing the pursuit of secular business; likewise, the surrender of oneself to dissolute games, intemperate dining, and other vicious pleasures. Decent recreation must indeed be conceded to the people at the proper times, but since God has so severely prohibited useful corporal works on days sanctified to his name, how much the more gravely is he offended when those days are profaned by sporting and works for the most part harmful?

Six days shalt thou labor, he says, namely, do what is helpful for conserving and even gratifying this present life; "the seventh is the rest of the Lord, on that day thou shalt do no work at all" (Ex. 20:9-10), clearly nothing which the Lord himself has not prescribed to be done on that day; but the things which he has commanded are all the highest acts of religion on holy days. The Lord has prescribed that his people assemble in his name on these days in order to hear his word, pour forth prayers to him, give thanks for benefits received, share in his sacraments, make holy offerings, and so establish all piety (Isa. 58:13; 66:23; Jer. 17:21; Acts 13:14-15).

Your Majesty will therefore give it some thought that no legislator can equal God in wisdom or goodness with respect to laws; nor can anyone have greater clemency toward delinquents, which is indeed a true and salutary clemency. But God has so sanctified the religion of holy days that he has ordered anyone who has violated his Sabbaths to be stoned by the whole people, that the people as a whole might exculpate themselves of such a crime and individually vindicate such an insult to God (Num. 15:32-36). For since we have received all that we are and have, indeed, the gift of life from the gratuitous goodness of God and receive all this every day, is it not also right and fitting for us to assemble daily to thank him and establish religion among us, both by worship of him through the word and sacraments which he has instituted for us and by holy prayers which he assiduously requires of us? How shocking, therefore, is that impiety and contempt of the Divine Majesty, not even to give oneself over on one day of the week to these acts of our salvation.

We all have such a weak and fluctuating faith that its assiduous confirmation and restoration are completely necessary for us. Who can sufficiently explain in words what a great wickedness it is, what a great crime, to spend so many days at our own work, namely, the affairs of this life, and this with the help and favor of the Lord, and to be unwilling to sanctify totally to him for the accomplishment of our own salvation such a few days that are dedicated to his name for the purpose of fostering and increasing piety among us, and furthermore, as almost everyone commonly does, to anger and offend God's majesty on these days much more seriously than on other days.

It is, therefore, altogether pertinent to Your Majesty, over against this great offense against God and such unbridled profanation of holy days, to restore the authority of divine law and also to follow the example of pious princes whose laws we know concerning this very matter, as I have previously advised.[15] These allowed neither *theatrical plays* on these days, nor *races*, nor *tragic spectacles of wild animals*, and they thought remission to military service and proscription of inheritance a fit punishment for those who attended *spectacles on a feast day* or contaminated themselves with *obscene pleasures*.

For unless men are influenced by daily teaching of the word of God and holy exhortations as well as by royal authority, so that they again become accustomed to sanctify periods of time wholly consecrated to religious services and the worship of God by these very actions (and this with greater care and solicitude than they give to any days appointed for public or private interests and the satisfactions of men inasmuch as God is greater than any man), the Kingdom of Christ can never be truly restored among men of this kind.

We see, however, how much concern the average man has and how much careful preparation he expends for the fullest observance of feast days appointed only for the pleasure of the people by princes, governments, or groups, and how securely he avoids all other affairs, however useful and urgent, on these days. Indeed, as to family weddings, other feasts with friends, and gatherings for recreation, how diligently do men then prepare for their own purpose and pleasure as they invite others to their weddings, feasts, and gatherings, banishing all other cares and concerns from their minds.

How great a contempt of God is committed by men in this, when they neglect the correct observance of days set aside by our God for the establishment and accomplishment of our eternal salvation. It is the business, therefore, of those whom God has put in charge of his people as shepherds with supreme authority, kings and princes, with all their might to confront this evil with holy laws and just provisions against the transgressors of these laws.[16]

---

[15] *Corpus Iuris Civilis, Code* III, 12, 9; cf. Book One, Ch. XI, n. 59.

[16] Throughout his career, Bucer was greatly concerned (and much more so than other major leaders of the Reformation) that holidays, and particularly Sundays, be kept holy (cf. his *Commentary on the Gospels* [*Enarrationes in Evangelia*], 3d ed. [1536], pp. 300 f.). In this respect, he surely must be regarded as a precursor of English Puritanism and especially of its Sabbatarianism. Cf. A. Lang, *Puritanismus und Pietismus*, p. 254. See also the interesting and informative discussion of the history of Sunday observance in England by Max Levy, *Der Sabbat in England. Wesen und Entwicklung des englischen Sonntags* (Leipzig, 1933). Unfortunately, Levy does not discuss Bucer.

CHAPTER XI

THE THIRD LAW: THE SANCTIFICATION OF CHURCHES

We have shown previously to some extent (Book One, Ch. X) with what holy respect places consescrated to the worship of God must be made accessible to just this one thing and kept sacrosanct.

But the horrible profanation of these places has been commonly prevalent: Not heeding the reverence due the divine presence, people walk around in them according to their fancy, as if they were in any common field or street that would have no religious association, and they chat about all kinds of impure affairs and about matters displeasing to God. So it is necessary to remove this scandalous offense against the Divine Majesty, not only by the teaching of the word of God and pious exhortations but also by severe laws of pious kings and princes, and by the prompt and consistent enforcement of these laws. Thus it may be brought about that the holy churches of God are open for no other activities except those for which they were sanctified to the Lord and that no one can with impunity fail to adapt himself to the atmosphere of religious worship there.

The salvation of your people, therefore, demands of Your Majesty that he establish a law which will forbid the use of churches consecrated to the Most High for any other activities except those for which they were consecrated by the Lord, namely, only for the reading and explanation of the Sacred Scriptures, the administration of the sacraments, prayers and thanksgivings, and the exercise of ecclesiastical discipline. This law should also guard against anyone's doing any other actions than these in church. Thus Your Royal Majesty will cause the words of the psalm to be fulfilled, "In his Temple all will declare his majesty" (Ps. 29:9) ; likewise, "We meditate upon and await your goodness, O God, in the midst of your Temple" (Ps. 48:10) ; and this: "But I, depending on your great kindness, shall enter your Temple; I shall adore at your holy Temple in fear of you" (Ps. 5:7) .

CHAPTER XII

THE FOURTH LAW: THE RESTORATION OF THE MINISTRIES OF THE CHURCH

Further, since it has pleased the Lord that his religion be planted and kept watered by suitable ministers (I Cor. 3:5-8) , and that he therefore give to the churches in which he deigns fully to restore his Kingdom, "besides apostles and evangelists, also pastors and teachers" (Eph. 4:11) in order to dispense all the mysteries of God in the Church by a permanent ministry, about which we have already said something,[17] it will have to be incumbent on Your Majesty with all his might that in the churches throughout his realm the sacred ministries be securely restored according to the institution of the Holy Spirit, as soon as this is possible.

This task will be of utmost difficulty, as there has frequently been, sad to say, an almost infinite perversity in every rank and order of the clergy, and as Antichrist strenuously protects his fortress and his plunder, closing off every approach to the Kingdom of Christ as soon as he can. But because the restitution of these ministries is not difficult to the same degree as it is necessary for the salvation of the elect of God, Your Majesty must take thought that just as all things are possible to Almighty God they are also possible to one who has faith (Mark 9:23; Matt. 17:20); indeed, all things are easy, if a pious and consistent effort is made, with assiduous work.

Now, we learn from a review of the churches since the time of the apostles that it has also seemed good to the Holy Spirit that among the elders to whom ecclesiastical administration is chiefly committed, *one* exercises singular care for the churches and the sacred ministries and in that care and solicitude presides over all the others (Acts. 20:28). For this reason, the name of bishop has been especially attributed to these chief administrators of the churches, even though these should decide nothing without the consultation of the other presbyters, who are also called bishops in the Scriptures because of this common ministry (Phil. 1:1; Titus 1:7). Thus Your Majesty will have to undertake first of all the reformation of the order of bishops.

As these precede all the rest of the orders of the sacred ministry in dignity and have a primary mandate of concern for the churches, they ought also to burn with a will and a zeal before all others for rightly ministering to the churches and they should excel in every opportunity to build them up. One who is but a little acquainted with the Holy Scriptures, the writings of the ancient churchmen, and the laws of pious emperors knows that this has been amply sanctioned and handed down and is also strictly required by divine laws, the holy canons of the early churches, the writings of all the holy fathers, and finally also by many sanctions of pious princes.

[17] Cf. Book One, Ch. V.

It is therefore necessary that bishops before all other ministers and caretakers of the churches, putting away from themselves all the matters and affairs of the world, devote themselves totally to the reading and teaching of the Holy Scriptures, pouring forth private and public prayers to God; and to all kinds of ministry both of the doctrine and the discipline of Christ, adorning these with an exemplary life so as to render themselves more commendable to the people of God; and also to the care of schools and the poor.

It is also their duty to watch and see to it that individual churches have their approved pastors and ministers who do their pastoral work so faithfully and so carefully that not only the rest of the clergy give blameless and holy service to the churches, whatever their special ministerial responsibility may be, but also that individual persons among the people are preserved from any fall into sin, as much as this is possible, and if they have fallen, that they are raised up again through salutary penance and make steady progress in piety.

For this reason, each bishop ought to visit his diocesan churches annually if he is in any way able to do so in view of his health and the more serious affairs of the Church. Whatever faults he may find to have crept into the doctrine or discipline of Christ he ought to correct with pious severity, and offer corrective preaching and stabilize the entire administration of religion according to Christ's precepts.

One should read and weigh diligently what the Holy Spirit has prescribed concerning the office of bishops in the twentieth chapter of Acts (vs. 28 ff.) , in the letters to Timothy (I Tim. 3:1-7) and Titus (ch. 1:5-9) , in the fifth chapter of First Peter (vs. 1-4) ; likewise, the canons of the early councils may be read, indeed also what Gratian has compiled from the various councils and rescripts of the holy fathers, from the twenty-third to the ninety-sixth distinction.[18] He has indeed intermingled much hearsay and superstition, especially about the celibacy of those ministering to the churches, about the boundless tyranny of the Roman pontiff, and about some matters alien to Christ's pure religion; meanwhile, however, he offers a great number of things very worthy of reading and necessary for the restoration of the churches. These things the holy fathers derived from the very canon of the Holy Spirit concerning sacred ministries and they amply explained them. One should further read what pious emperors have decreed concerning the office of the priests of Christ (Code concerning Bishops and Clerics) ,[19]

[18] *Corpus Iuris Canonici: Decretum Gratiani* I, dist. 23–96.   [19] *Code* I, 3.

and in Authentica VI, "How Bishops Should Act," and in the hundred and twenty-third, "Various Ecclesiastical Chapters." [20] Although some things foreign to the canon of the Holy Spirit have been interjected here, as those concerning the celibacy and monasticism of the ministers of the Church, all the rest are evidently dependent on the same canon of the Holy Spirit. One should also read the third book of Chrysostom, "On the Dignity of the Priesthood," [21] "The Apologist" of Saint Gregory Nazianzen,[22] Saint Jerome, "To Nepotianus," [23] and also the writings which other holy fathers have left concerning this office.

Since, therefore, we know not only from Holy Scripture and the writings of the holy fathers, but also from the regrettable experience of too many centuries (with bishops being lax in their office, not to mention their completely overturning it, as they have been doing for such a long time), that Christ's religion is waning terribly both among the other leaders of the churches and also among the people; and since we know that massive impiety and impurity of life take hold of everything in demanding ways, it certainly will be Your Royal Majesty's duty to establish and to carry through with greater resources a complete reformation of the episcopal order and office, i.e., a restoration to that form which the Holy Spirit in his Scriptures has left clearly described for us, a summary of which I have just presented.

Today, however, some nominal bishops are allowed to hold episcopal sees in Your Majesty's realm who all too openly demonstrate by their way of life and all their actions that they are in no way qualified to assume true responsibility for the care and the edification of the churches, so that the churches will be harmed by them day by day in both spiritual and temporal affairs if the highest government of the churches is entrusted to them.

But it would be inhumane, many say, to deprive someone of the dignity and income which he has received and owned according to the custom of so many centuries. For, as I have complained before, certain people are moved by much greater mercy for those who have once seized the income of the churches even by most manifest sacrilege, when they are kept from plundering the churches, than for Christ's churches themselves which they so wretchedly despoil not only externally but also of the very religion of Christ.

---

[20] *Novellae* 6 and 123.
[21] John Chrysostom, *On the Priesthood* III (*MPG,* Vol. 48, cols. 640 ff.).
[22] Gregory Nazianzen, *Apologetic Oration* II (*MPG,* Vol. 35, cols. 407 ff.).
[23] Jerome, *Letter* LII (*MPL,* Vol. 22, cols. 527 ff.)

Whatever Your Majesty decides, for the sake of public peace and humaneness, toward those who cannot or will not remove or disengage themselves from such a long-established heap of errors, namely, to leave the bishops [24] some part of the ecclesiastical spoils, this will have to be regulated in such a way that the churches lack nothing necessary for the fulfillment of the episcopal office.

Cephas, Paul, and Apollo, and the whole world belong to the churches of Christ; the churches, however, belong to no one but our one King and Lord Jesus Christ, just as he belongs to God (I Cor. 3:22-23). Their well-being, therefore, must be placed ahead not only of the deplorable greed of the false bishops but also of all apparent advantages of the world. The churches are the brides of Christ the Son of God, whom he has acquired for himself by his own blood; for this reason, they commit the crime of lese majesty who for any cause that can be feigned detract anything from the rights of the churches or do not stand in the way of detractors when they can and should.

The ancient churches had the custom, if a bishop ever became useless for his ministry, through age or sickness, of supplying someone as a coadjutor for him, to discharge the episcopal duty for the people of Christ in the interim; [25] how much more, therefore, must those suitable for the episcopal office be substituted today for those who, in sickness of spirit and poor health of mind, prevent the churches from having true bishops, so much so that they are not only useless to the churches but even harmful.

For what greater harm could they do to the churches than that, since they hold the places of bishops, they not only do not themselves administer the doctrine and discipline of Christ for the people but do not make ministration available through others; indeed, they confer priesthoods, and sometimes more than one, on those who, besides depriving the churches of any pastoral care, even confuse them with false teaching and by an impure life draw them completely from the obedience of Christ as far as possible. They take no interest in establishing schools or caring for the poor, but they squander the episcopal income mostly on profane persons and the secular pomp in which they parade themselves like satraps.

Whoever, therefore, will be found among the bishops both rightly animated and properly instructed for doing their duty, to these it will be convenient for Your Majesty to have proposed that

[24] *Episcopis aposkopois.* Bishops who were appointed by Henry VIII and who refused to join in the reformation of the church were given a pension when they were deposed from office. Cf. A. F. Pollard, *England Under Protector Somerset* (London, 1900), p. 124.   [25] *Corpus Iuris Canonici* c. 7, q. 1.

general summary of the doctrine and discipline of Christ, of which I have made mention,[26] after using them as chief counselors in the cause of religion, and also as general examiners, as I have also mentioned; it should be required of them that they swear according to this formula or statement that they will administer their episcopal office in good faith. This oath will not only have the advantage that these bishops will be held to their promise, but also that those who complain that they are too severe when they advance the reformation enjoined, can be told that this zeal is necessary on account of this oath. Thus the work of pious reformation already begun can be carried on and completed with less offensiveness and resentment of curable men.

But because it is the duty of the bishops to administer the churches not by their own arbitrary judgment alone, but with the counsel of presbyters and the ministry of deacons, it will be necessary, inasmuch as the ministries of the churches are now all dissipated and disordered, to join to each of the bishops, even if he is much approved, a certain council of presbyters and the ministry of deacons.[27] These presbyters and deacons will also have to be earnestly examined and tested to see whether they have received it of the Lord that they can and desire to be of assistance to their bishop in the administration and care of the churches, the presbyters as helpful counselors and the deacons as obedient ministers.

In this examination and probation, the bishop to whom these presbyters and deacons are to be adjoined should be especially listened to as if he were a kind of consul to whom they are attached as senators and subordinates so that as he himself acknowledges them to be worthy of the position and on this account receives them with stronger love, he will use them, their advice, and ministry for the edification of the churches both more willingly and more graciously.

And for this reason an oath should be required also of these men with the promise that they will faithfully fulfill their office and serve the bishop in good faith and utmost reverence, in the care of the churches. And when these presbyters and deacons, who are the special helpers and assistants of the bishops in the administration of the churches, have been chosen by those general examiners and assigned to bishops, by Your Majesty's order, this will both free the bishops from resentment of this choice and provide even greater authority to such presbyters and deacons in the churches.

[26] Cf. Book Two, Ch. IV.
[27] *Corpus Iuris Canonici* I, dist. 95, c. 5; dist. 93, c. 14.

The most important and highly urgent consideration in all these things here is that Your Majesty must leave nothing untried and so establishes all things that the churches may have the prospect of true and suitable ministers, and that these enjoy in the churches the highest influence and authority.

Now, since it is necessary for bishops to be unburdened of every concern for external affairs so that they may concentrate entirely on obtaining the salvation of souls, it seemed good to the fathers of old that bishops, even those unwilling, be given managers elected from the clergy and the people of Christ in order that they would regulate the revenue of every bishopric. It will therefore be within Your Majesty's prerogative to summon bishops for this purpose from external affairs to the fulfilment of their special duty.[28] In this matter, Your Royal Highness should attribute much more importance to the decree of the Holy Spirit given through Saint Peter when, with the suffrage of the Church, he established seven deacons to care for widows and the poor than to the wisdom or greed of any mortals. "It is not," says the apostle, "pleasing," namely, to God and all who judge with the Spirit of God, "for us to wait at tables and leave the ministry of the word of God. Therefore, brethren, pick out from among you seven men of good repute, full of the Spirit and of wisdom, whom we may appoint to this duty. But we will devote ourselves to prayer and the ministry of the word" (Acts 6:2-4).

It is required, indeed, that the managers,[29] deacons, and sub-deacons administer the affairs of the Church, according to the law of the Lord, with the knowledge and approval of the bishop and his board of presbyters, about which we have spoken. To them they should give an accounting at stipulated times. But the actual administration of ecclesiastical business should be carried on, not through the bishops, but through the managers, deacons, and sub-deacons so that the bishop may be able to have time for a freer and more efficient administration of religion. This matter certainly demands vigilance of spirit and concentration which would allow no concern at all for other things.

There are already now those among the bishops whose help Your Majesty uses in the administration of the realm who make Your Majesty's sailing more tolerable at this time, in this veritable storm of the churches, because they can act for Your Majesty both in a more timely fashion and with greater success for the cause of Christ's religion, which patently requires agents in this position who are keen and vigilant. The less they are able to take an in-

---

[28] *Ibid.,* dist. 89, c. 2–5.   [29] *Oeconomi.*

terest in their churches, not only because of absence but also because of preoccupation with the affairs of the realm, the more it is necessary that both the presbytery and the ministry we have suggested be assigned to them; but in order that everything concerning the administration of the churches which are entrusted to such bishops may be done more harmoniously and in an orderly way, it will be necessary that individual bishops in this category have some vicar appointed for them from among the presbyters who will faithfully exercise all the episcopal functions while bishops involved in the affairs of the realm are absent from the churches. And it will be appropriate for these vicars to be approved in religion and inducted in the same manner as those presbyters and deacons are conjoined to the bishops in the care of the churches.

For since nothing in this sphere of the care of men has been recommended by the Most High which ought to be carried on and cared for more solicitously and conscientiously than concern for religion, that is, the eternal salvation of God's elect, it would be a supreme outrage to put any other affairs ahead of that concern or to place any obstacle in the path of the Church's complete fulfillment of her ministries. Moses was richly gifted with the Spirit of God, and he excelled in incredible wisdom, and he also burned with a most ardent zeal for the planting and preservation of true religion; but when he had to govern the entire commonwealth of Israel, by God's command he put his brother Aaron, with his sons, in charge of religion, so that they could concentrate entirely on this. For this reason, the ministry also of the Levites was dedicated to them, and there were many thousands of them (Ex. 29:1-35; Num. 3:39; 8:5-26; 26:57-62).

The Maccabees indeed conjoined civil and ecclesiastical administration; but history testifies with what success (I Macc. 14:47). On this account, it is to be wished that the bishops, according to the law of God, will concentrate on taking care of religion only and leave all other matters, however helpful to mankind, to those who totally dedicate themselves to them and have been divinely prepared to specialize in them. The early churches religiously observed this way of procedure and it was highly useful to the churches. They started horribly to collapse and disintegrate as soon as the Franks and other kings began to use bishops in civil affairs.

This holy work certainly cannot be entrusted in good conscience to those bishops who, up to this time, have had the position of bishops but have clearly neglected the episcopal office and have even opposed the pure doctrine and the real discipline of Christ.

For the law of God, to which heaven and earth should yield, demands that no one should be admitted to this function unless he has been thoroughly investigated and sufficiently tested that he is equipped with singular knowledge of the Kingdom of Christ and burns with very great zeal for it (Rom. 12:7-8; I Tim. 3:10; 5:22; Titus 1:7-9). Whatever humaneness therefore, as we have just said, it seems good to Your Majesty to show to these men, it should certainly be so tempered that meanwhile the churches, which they have occupied and laid waste up to this time, may not be lacking either true ministers or coadjutors for the episcopal office.

Nor should Your Majesty listen to those who say that bishops of this kind (who are not really bishops) are now prepared to receive and follow Your Majesty's decrees concerning religion and should therefore be left in the administration of their episcopal office. However, the fact that they do not assent to the royal decrees wholeheartedly but rather for the sake of keeping their episcopal dignity and wealth is sufficiently obvious from their perpetual neglect, indeed, perversion, of the episcopal office up to this time, from the papistic superstitions they still retain as much as they have dared to retain them in their fear of coming to royal notice, and from the fact that not even today they accept anything of the established Reformation, nor promote it, except what they have been compelled to do by Your Royal Majesty's authority.[30]

Whatever they now pretend, either verbally or in public sermons, or whatever they otherwise profess, the rule of the Holy Spirit which forbids that neophytes, i.e., recent converts to the faith of Christ, be admitted to this order should prevail against these *aposkopous* [31] (I Tim. 3:6). Nor do these men demonstrate anything similar to the knowledge and zeal for building up the churches of Christ such as shines forth in Saint Paul, Ambrose, and some others, according to which this chapter of the sacred canon was devised. If the Holy Spirit forbids recent converts to Christ to assume the order of priests or bishops, even though they have sufficiently demonstrated their conversion to the churches of God by worthy fruits of faith, unless the power of the Holy Spirit is so outstanding in them that it is clearly apparent that they are summoned to the sacred ministry of the Church by the Holy Spirit, is

[30] The Act of Uniformity was passed by Parliament on January 21, and received royal assent on March 14, 1549. Cf. G. Constant, *The Reformation in England,* Vol. II, pp. 88 f.

[31] Professor Satre, who helped to revise this translation, suggests that the word *aposkopoi* which Bucer uses from time to time in an obvious play on words (in relation to *episkopoi*) means probably "false bishops," i.e., those who "look away" from their flock.

it then not clear how much this prohibition of the Spirit must be applied to those who so far have shown themselves enemies of Christ's Kingdom and until now have not manifested any change of mind by any fruits that would prove this? For it is not enough for someone in order that he take on this responsibility that he can preach well; what must be required, as I have already advised, is a solid knowledge of the whole pastoral function and a permanently solicitous concern for the building up of the churches, and each of these must be thoroughly investigated and approved for the churches on the basis of the candidate's past life.

Just as it is the duty of bishops to work vigilantly and efficiently (cf. II Tim. 4:5) that in the individual churches commended to the episcopal charge of each, approved and faithful pastors serve the interests of religion in a conscientious way (and there is, sad to say, all too small a number of these today, with men in possession of parishes who either cannot or will not discharge their pastoral duty), an accurate and strict visitation must be undertaken in the beginning by each bishop who has parishes in his trust. In this matter they will have to have the help of Your Majesty's authority and power, insofar as among those laying waste the churches in the office of pastors there has obtained and prevailed an imprudent audacity as intolerable as their numbers and the patronage prepared for them by many people. The reality itself therefore demands that Your Majesty enjoin the bishops, on the occasion of that first visitation of the churches, to drive out the wolves, thieves, and hirelings from the fold of Christ, with the help of men endowed with great influence and authority in his realm, and properly equipped with Your Majesty's mandates adequate for this purpose.[32] For here again a strong attempt will be made to cause trouble by that preposterous and impious recommendation of mercy toward the wolves, thieves, and robbers of the sheep of Christ (John 10:8 and 12), if they are to be kept from scattering and losing the sheep of Christ and from despoiling the churches through manifest sacrileges. What good does it do to count them as Christians when they doubt that the glory of Christ and the eternal salvation of his sheep are to be put ahead of the seeming advantages of the whole world, not to mention the wicked greed of the enemies of Christ.

If, however, any of these men injuriously occupying parishes

---

[32] Cf. J. Gairdner, *The English Church in the Sixteenth Century* (London, 1904), pp. 247 ff., and, concerning the visitations undertaken by John Hooper, bishop of Gloucester, A. G. Dickens, *The English Reformation* (London: B. T. Batsford, Ltd., 1964), pp. 242 f.

truly mend their ways, and, having rejected their impiety, are converted to the Lord, the churches must make sure that they have the
necessities of life, so that nothing is wanting for them to live well
and piously, as we have testified previously.

But when they continue to show themselves enemies of the Kingdom of Christ, what humaneness or charity would it be, I ask you,
to nourish and foster them in such very bad crime? To be sure,
we must feed even our enemies if they are hungry and give them
drink if they thirst (Rom. 12:20), but in such a way that they will
not find an opportunity in this kindness for making trouble for
the churches of God, or for despoiling them of all spiritual and
material advantages.

Here we must think and really do what the Lord said to the
crowds who were following him: "If anyone comes to me, and does
not hate his father, and his mother, and wife and children, and
brothers and sisters, and even his own soul, he cannot be my disciple" (Luke 14:26). And Moses said in praise of the Levitic tribe:
"Who said of his father and mother, I regard them not, and dis-
owned his sons, and did not acknowledge his brothers, these observe your word, and keep your covenant" (Deut. 33:9).

But here, too, it will be objected that there is such a small number available of those who are fitted for this office of properly
administering the churches. To this objection I make the same answer as before: First, if they are really sought earnestly, many more
will be found than are now judged to be available. Secondly, inasmuch as very few men of this quality can be found, it is better
for the churches to have no pastors than those who are actually
wolves, thieves, robbers, or at least hirelings. For whoever seeks
his own and not the things that are Christ's can only be harmful
to the churches. Furthermore, the parishes which cannot yet be
given pastors ought in the interim to be helped by neighboring
pastors. Finally, if the proper reformation of the universities is
accomplished, as previously indicated,[33] the Lord will daily furnish
men who can usefully serve the churches. And whatever difficulty
exists in this matter on account of our negligence and crooked
desires, nevertheless the word of God can yield to no creature.
Since he saves eternally those who obey him and condemns forever
those who repudiate him, let us not doubt that this must be put
before the wisdom and the will of all men. For we know that it
has been ordered that every *bishop* and priest *ought* to be not
only *irreprehensible,* but also singularly adorned with all manner
of virtues (I Tim. 3:2-7), and tenacious in faithful speech for

[33] Cf. Book Two, Ch. VI.

teaching the people of Christ, "that he may be able to give instruction in sound doctrine, and also to confute those who contradict it" (Titus 1:7-9). Likewise, the ministries of Christ are "to be entrusted only to men who are faithful and suitable to teach others" (II Tim. 2:2). And again, they must first be tested and thus admitted to these ministries (I Tim. 3:10; 5:22).

Further, as men easily relapse into worse things, this must also be enjoined on the bishops that each must inspect his churches not only every year, in the company of some persons selected from the primary presbytery and the diaconate adjoined to him for the administration of the churches, but as often as he understands that there is some wrong being done in the churches against either the doctrine or the discipline of Christ.

But in order that the bishops may know about it in time if any such thing is the case, the old division of dioceses must be restored so that out of every twenty or so parishes one of their administrators who seems suited for this function before the others should be put in charge as auxiliary bishop [34] who will be especially on guard on behalf of these churches against the snares and insults of Satan, and if there is anything which he cannot himself correct either among his colleagues or among the people commended to his care, he should refer it to the bishop as soon as possible.

And so that nothing may go without correction or punishment this officer should frequently, at specified times, call his colleagues together and by means of explanations of the Holy Scriptures and exhortations derived from them, and also by pious conversations among all of them, strengthen the faith and knowledge of Christ both for himself and for his colleagues and kindle more and more their desire and zeal for the Kingdom of Christ. These suffragan bishops should also visit the people of each area [35] commended to them, when the concerns of their own parishes permit, and administer to them the word of eternal life, especially to those parishes which have pastors less learned or fervent for the Kingdom of Christ.

Furthermore, it will be the duty of the bishops of each province to hold two synods annually, as it has been provided for in so many canons and laws of pious emperors.[36] At these synods there should be gathered and heard not only the bishops of the cities, but also

[34] Bucer uses the term *chorepiscopus,* a title now equivalent to that of a suffragan bishop.   [35] *Cura.*
[36] *Novellae* 123, 10. Throughout his career, Bucer was an advocate of synods, having first observed their usefulness in connection with the introduction of the Reformation in Switzerland, especially Bern. Cf. Wendel, ed., *De Regno Christi,* p. 129, n. 35.

the rural bishops and other priests and deacons who have been gifted with fuller knowledge of and zeal for the Kingdom of Christ, in order that the evils which have crept into the churches may be corrected more effectively, and the piety of all renewed.

It will be very useful to these synods if Your Majesty appoints men zealous for Christ's religion and endowed with the highest authority to preside with the metropolitan in the synods, in Your Majesty's name, and keep decent order, as pious emperors and kings of old were accustomed to do for the highest good of the churches. Indeed, they sometimes themselves presided at the synods and took part in the disputations, as did Constantine, in a praiseworthy way, at the celebrated Nicene Council, and some other emperors and kings in other councils, as one can read in the acts of the ancient councils.[37] For since all souls are subject to the rule of kings (Rom. 13:1), it is their duty to be concerned above all else that the Christian religion [38] and the priestly office in which is contained the eternal salvation of all souls be administered in a holy and salutary manner and preserved from every failing.

Thus the churches await from Your Majesty this fourth law by which the entire order of the clergy may be restored and really led back to the discipline of the Holy Spirit as here outlined.

CHAPTER XIII

The Fifth Law: Claiming Ecclesiastical Goods for Christ the Lord, and Their Pious Use

There can be no doubt that the ministries of bishops and of other priests and clergy, or proper inspections of the churches, or synods cannot be restored in the churches unless Your Majesty would first remove, along with every appearance of simony, those execrable sacrileges and such monstrous despoliations of the churches which have been allowed, so that stipends of sacred ministries have been conferred for favor and a price to these most unworthy men, and very often two, three, four, five, or more to one individual who has no desire to satisfy even one. This state of affairs gains entrance if the priesthood is conferred on anyone for a reason and purpose other than that the churches may be built up in the faith of Christ through faithful and fit ministers, or if any temporal consideration, a price or a service or a favor, is involved in the bestowal.

---

[37] Cf. Eusebius, *Life of Constantine* III, 10 and 13; Theodoret, *Church History* I, 12 f.; II, 29; II, 31.   [38] *Christi religio.*

Another obvious sacrilege in the looting of the churches is that which the Roman Antichrist exacts from bishops and other priests, "the fruits and tenths of the first year," as they are called.[39] In view of this Your Majesty understands well enough how alien it would be to his piety for him to imitate Christ's adversary in this matter. It is indeed the duty of the churches and of all ministers of religion to help Your Majesty to meet the needs of the realm with ready hearts as much as they can. For as to every soul it has been divinely commanded that it "should be subject to powers" bearing the sword, so also it is required of every soul, both of priests and of the rest of mankind, to give "tribute" to him "to whom tribute is owed, tax to whom tax is due, to render honor to him who is worthy of it, reverence to whom reverence is appropriate" (Rom. 13:1; 6-7).

Thus, on the basis of this right, devout emperors required fiscal payments and canonical conveyance of estates which either the churches or the clergy possessed.[40] And this so strictly that if at some time churches were not able to meet fiscal debts in any other way, they conceded the transfer of ecclesiastical real estate in order to pay these debts, which was otherwise most sacredly forbidden.[41] The churches also contributed to the constructions of roads and bridges and also to the costs of sudden emergencies arising from unexpected needs [42]; nor were the churches and clergy kept exempt, except from the obligation of sewage disposal and from extraordinary giving of evidence, and from the burden of giving hospitality to the court retinue or the militia.[43]

Meanwhile, however, just as these emperors paid salaries to the clergy, so they also supported the poor from the public income of the empire. As we previously mentioned, this had been instituted by Constantine the Great. A third part of this liberality, which Julian had completely taken away from the churches, Jovian restored to them, influenced by public demand to satisfy the churches both in regard to the stipends of clerics and poor relief. But this pious prince Jovian promised the churches that he would restore what Constantine had established as soon as a famine which then was raging had abated.[44]

Those pious emperors held ecclesiastical possessions to be so sacrosanct, however they had come to the churches, that they in no way allowed them to be alienated nor even to be exchanged for imperial property, unless for possessions equally good, or even

---

[39] The so-called annates.
[41] *Novellae* 46, 1.
[43] *Ibid.*, I, 3, 1.
[40] *Code* I, 2, 5; I, 3, 3.
[42] *Code* I, 2, 5, and 7.
[44] Theodoret, *Church History* I, 11; IV, 4.

better. In this regard, the sanction of Justinian may be quoted here, since it contains much that is pertinent to our consideration.

"If there is any common advantage and cause respecting the welfare of the commonwealth and there is demanded possession of such real estate as we have proposed, it is allowed to receive it from the holy churches and other venerable houses and colleges, always observing an indemnity to the sacred houses, compensating them for that which has been received with something of either an equal or a greater value. For what else should the emperor do but give better things, to whom God has granted abundance and power, so that he can readily give, and especially to the holy churches in which magnificence in giving is an excellent rule. Hence, if any such a thing happens and takes place in a business-like way, with the requirement that the empire receives some part thereof, and a better, or richer, or more useful thing has been given in compensation, let the exchange be permanent; and let those who are in charge of the houses to which what is alienated belonged and who have the responsibility of administration be entirely without complaint and without fear of the penalties threatened by Leo of pious memory and confirmed by us; it is so agreed, since the priesthood and the empire do not differ much from each other and sacred things from common and public property, seeing that an abundant state of all things should always be made available to the holy churches out of the munificence of the empire. No charge will be leveled against anyone for decent compensations. But we permanently declare invalid any other sale or contract of transfer [45] made either to the empire or to any person whosoever." [46]

Pious princes have followed this one policy in giving goods to the churches and conserving them, really and reverently providing fair salaries for the church ministry and the means whereby the necessities of life might not be wanting to any of the poor. On this account they most gravely prohibited the distribution of any ecclesiastical goods either to those who were not legitimately ministering in the churches or to those who were not really needy. And perhaps it will not be useless to quote some of the words of laws of this kind.

The *Codex De sacrosanctis ecclesiis* contains the Valentinian and Marcian law sanctioned in these words: "The privileges which by general constitutions princes have heretofore bestowed on all the holy churches of orthodox religion, we decree shall be preserved firm and intact in perpetuity. All the pragmatic sanctions,

[45] *Emphyteusis.*   [46] *Novellae* 7, 2.

which have been produced for the sake of favor or gain with references to the ecclesiastical canons, we command to be held void in their force and strength. And since we owe it to our humaneness to benefit and help the needy, so that sustenance will not be lacking to the poor, the allowances which have been administered until now to the holy churches for various kinds of public assistance, we order now to be bestowed undiminished and intact, and to this most forthright liberality we give permanent force." [47]

Likewise, the third Authentica, toward the end: "Inasmuch as we have delineated the provisions pertinent to it, it is appropriate that the holy patriarch and reverend clergy should see to it that the remainder of what is received from church revenues should not be used for other purposes than causes that are pious and pleasing to God, for the good of those who are really in need and have no other source of sustenance of life (for these are the things which are generally propitious to the Lord God). Nor should what is supplied for ecclesiastical use be distributed to the well-to-do for patronage or human pursuits, so as to defraud the needy of the necessities of life. Let the administrators in their great love of God know, both those who are so now and those who will be, that if they are in any way delinquent in these matters, they will not only be liable to heavenly penalties but will also of their own substance render an indemnity to the holy Church." [48]

And the fifty-eighth Authentica states: "Many of the clergy on the occasion of the filling of vacancies in certain oratories, or perhaps even as replacements for some of them, as soon as they have received the solemn compensation too often have nothing at all to do with the sacred mysteries (for what motive, they themselves know too well), or on any given occasion withdraw completely from the holy Church in which they have a place. We therefore decree, lest this impediment be inflicted on the sacred ministry, that the bishops who have a responsibility for these churches, in their great love of God, when they perceive such things, should replace them with others. For we do not wish to concede to any that they should convert to their own gain the compensation now derived from the churches. Nor do we wish that there be any pretext or occasion for some to profit by defrauding others, but rather that whatever remuneration has been available from the beginning should continue without any limitation of time, nor should the sacred ministry be corrupted and decay in this matter; and those who withdraw from the churches will have no license, after others have replaced them, appointed by the holy patriarch or the pro-

[47] Code I, 2, 12.   [48] Novellae 3, 3.

vincial bishops, to derive anything from the replacements if they wish to return. Nor may they compel those who support this payment to undertake double compensation, both to the replacements and to themselves who wish to return; but (as we may say most simply) if they do return, they may not be accepted; to those, however, who have need after a prior retirement, an annual pension should be provided, with no gain derived from those who are accustomed to supply for them, so that those who would attempt to make a profit on such things will, in regard to the pension benefits and other benefits received from the replacements as a hereditary adjunct to succession, have knowledge that if they are detected in fraud, certain property of their patrimony will be confiscated for our private religious fund, for payments to be made to them from it.[49]

From this Your Majesty will easily understand how the Church must reverently preserve its goods and redeem them for their rightful purposes, namely, to provide the necessities of life for those who minister well to the churches or who are really indigent.

So Your Majesty should impose on estates and persons fiscal and canonical obligations and collections for urgent necessities or public works in such a way that there is no appearance of simony, such as the exaction of the fruits of the first year. Nor should he be harder on the true ministries of Christ, needed schools, and the poor, than on the other citizens of his realm, and thus make the preservation and spread of the Kingdom of Christ a matter of lesser importance than his ancestors did. For they showed themselves to be so very munificent even toward depraved and false ministries of the Church, when they thought that they were right and true, and toward schools and projects for the poor, yet they kept a magnificent court and successfully waged difficult wars.

But Your Majesty will not be seen only by men but will be judged by God himself if he does not try to do his duty to God and the churches with all the strength and power which he has received from the Lord: first, that no one should receive the established compensations for the holy ministries of the churches who does not reverently fulfill those ministries in the churches. On this account, Your Majesty must prevent as a most grave sacrilege any priests or prelates from deriving pensions which they pass on to men who neither minister in the churches nor are truly needy. For the pensions should be derived from richer benefices, to be transmitted to faithful ministers of the churches for whom there is no other source of help and to other persons in need.

[49] *Ibid.,* 11, pr. and c. 1.

For no reason should anyone be allowed to make an exchange of goods with the churches or their ministers, unless someone wishes to give property to the churches which is better than what he receives, or at least of equal value. For it is said that some very valuable possessions were formerly taken from some colleges and churches under the appearance of an exchange and that nothing but the goods of plundered parishes were transferred to the colleges and churches in place of the preempted possessions.[50]

Secondly, that Your Majesty should not impose a greater tax to be paid to the state on the possessions of the churches and their ministers than he is accustomed to impose on the private possessions of men. For who could be excused from manifest impiety if he burdened with more taxes and held in lower esteem the true ministers of Christ's religion, i.e., of eternal life, and his little ones (on whom we bestow whatever we have of humanity and kindness) than other men who perform services to the state and the churches which are neither so necessary or salutary nor so commended to us by the Lord for every good work.

The kings of Egypt, as we read in the story of Joseph, made only the lands of priests exempt (Gen. 47:22), but the true churches of Christ do not agitate for this exemption; they do not resent at all the payment of the usual tax, provided that they are not held in a more unfavorable position than other groups of men or private persons. And the ministers should be left immune at least from those obligations which they cannot meet without a serious impairment of the service they owe the churches for the eternal salvation of men.

Lastly, it will have to be arranged by Your Majesty that whoever has the endowments or possessions of parishes should, from the income of these parishes, if there is any surplus, establish funds to pay those who are rendering faithful ministries to the parishes of Christ. If, however, there is not enough of a surplus from the parishes to make it possible for faithful ministers to be taken care of, then certainly, as we have said before,[51] the means of providing for such despoiled parishes must be sought from the bishops and wealthier priests. Here the communion of saints must be exercised that the churches which have an abundance should help those which are in need. For it is said that there are not a few parishes where there is no more left from the lavish incomes that they used to have than four or five pounds, or a little more.

[50] Cf. A. F. Pollard, *England Under Protector Somerset*, pp. 122 f., 269; A. G. Dickens, *The English Reformation*, p. 205 ff.; G. Constant, *The Reformation in England*, Vol. II, pp. 156 ff.   [51] Cf. Book Two, Ch. VII.

And so let the law of the Lord apply: "The laborer is worthy of his food and pay" (Matt. 10:10; Luke 10:7). Likewise: "Let the elders who rule well be considered worthy of double honor, especially those who labor in preaching and teaching" (I Tim. 5:17). But these ought also to teach other Christians by their example, as when they are given "the means of nourishment and being clothed, with these they are content" (I Tim. 6:8). Let that law of the Holy Spirit also apply: "Your abundance should supply their want, so that their abundance may supply your want, so that there will be equality among you, as it is written: He who gathered much had nothing left over, and he who gathered little had no lack" (II Cor. 8:14-15; Ex. 16:18).

Your Majesty will therefore give a fifth law to the churches, by which the goods and assets of the churches, according to the aforementioned plan handed down by the Holy Spirit, may be claimed for and restored to their legitimate uses.

I hear that Your Majesty's treasury has been somewhat debilitated by long wars.[52] Also, the churches, therefore, should help that it is restored as fully as possible to every usefulness to the commonwealth, to which the churches themselves belong as well as their ministers, their schools, and their poor. But this can be done by means which are common in all well-constituted kingdoms, so that there is no need to imitate the sacrilegious inventions of the Roman Antichrist. Precautions must also be taken lest those who assume responsibilities for restoring the treasury of the realm act in their own interest rather than that of Your Majesty and the commonwealth.

Something which must not in any way be admitted is the entreaty of those who are accustomed to say: "Your Majesty's father enriched so many ministers from the goods of monasteries and churches; why should not the son follow his father's liberality in regard to his own ministers?" [53]

For to these, Cicero, a pagan, gives this answer: "Kindness should be no greater than one's assets, nor is the fountain of kindness to be exhausted by kindness." [54] Where are the possessions of the monasteries today, so that Your Majesty would be able to be-

---

[52] Henry VIII was at war with Scotland (1542; 1544; 1545–1546) and with France (1543–1546). During the protectorate of the Duke of Somerset, the English were at war with Scotland (1547–1548) and with France (1549–1550).

[53] Cf. H. A. L. Fisher, *The History of England from the Accession of Henry VII to the Death of Henry VIII* (London, 1906), pp. 499 ff.; S. B. Liljegren, *The Fall of the Monasteries and the Social Changes in England* (Lund, 1924), pp. 32–118.   [54] Cicero, *De officiis* I, 14; II, 15.

stow them on his ministers? But if he should attack the goods of bishops and of other rich prelates, where will the means be found to restore the ministry necessary for eternal salvation to the despoiled parishes, to repair the schools, to foster the studious, to care for the poor? [55]

But they say: for what need of the churches, schools, or poor do the bishops and wealthy prelates apply today the wealth of the churches? They feed a lazy, inert, and profane household, enjoy themselves, and indulge themselves in all manner of luxury and mundane pomp. And if they are liberal to some, they are liberal to those joined to them in the flesh; they will adorn wives and children so as not to be outclassed by the nobles.

But what do the churches reply, indeed, what does the Lord Christ, the bridegroom of the churches, reply to these things? Because the false bishops and deceitful prefects of my churches have thus until now ripped apart and ruined my patrimony, which is not rashly called the patrimony of the crucified, is it becoming to you who glory in my gospel to waste and destroy what their sacrilegious rapacity has left over for me? Do you think it is for you so to complain about those drones which take the honey of my bees that you may join them as new drones and eat all the honey of my bees which they still have left over? Do you acknowledge that it is your duty to drive those drones away from the hives of my bees, and to keep their honey safe from all drones? Have you made up your minds or not that you want me to reign over you in the kingdom of religion and of eternal life? Then see, if you want my Kingdom to be restored among you, whether it is necessary for this purpose to educate, establish, and nourish men selected by me for the ministries of my Kingdom, and therefore to repair the schools everywhere, and to foster and help those whom I have granted outstanding talents, when this cannot otherwise be accomplished? Then, since my Kingdom requires that love for all men and that sharing of the goods of daily life among those who believe in me which provides that no one will lack the necessary means to live piously and well, judge for yourselves whether or not my Kingdom should have its own treasury, and a rich one, to provide for my poor those things without which they cannot live a life that is pious and useful to the commonwealth. Say, finally, whether or not that liberality toward the needy is worthy of my

---

[55] On the confiscation of episcopal properties, especially by order of the Duke of Warwick (Lord Protector after 1550), see G. Constant, *The Reformation in England,* Vol. I, pp. 161 ff. P. Hughes, *The Reformation in England,* Vol. II, pp. 150 ff.

Kingdom, when the pagans judged it to be the duty of every man who is well off, specifically that he should redeem captives from robbers by means of his own possessions, borrow money to undertake the cause of friends, help in the espousals of daughters, and assist good and honest citizens in things that have to be sought and done.[56]

Certainly, it was for the purpose of such generosity that the holy fathers of old judged that the sacred vessels and ornaments of the churches were to be broken up and sold; on this point one may read what Saint Ambrose wrote in his book, *De officiis* II, Ch. 28.[57] One may easily suppose what elaborate expenditures these would demand of the treasury.

But the Lord, rich toward all and bestowing all largesse so munificently on all, says to the unworthy and the ungrateful: "To you, O wretched mortals, who have deserved nothing but hell from me, I bestow generously all things on all, and I ask of you in behalf of my ministers, and those who are being prepared for my ministries through which I administer your eternal salvation, and for my little ones, indeed, for myself: for these I ask not pleasures or some pomp or luxury into which you have ruinously converted my goods, but only food for the hungry, drink for the thirsty, shelter for the freezing, clothing for the naked, care for the sick, and consolation for the prisoner [cf. Matt. 25:35-36]. And far from spending my assets and gifts on these needs which are not so much pious as salutary for you, you even snatch and pour out and consume to your damnation what your ancestors have consecrated to me for these purposes."

Indeed, was there ever a commonwealth so barbarous, so impious, which with the exception of public and private matters subject to human jurisdiction, did not hold sacred things consecrated to religion? [58] And these things were to those heathen men a matter of divine law, and so sacred were all these goods that if on the occasion of a compelling necessity of the commonwealth some of these goods were taken as a loan for the use of the commonwealth, they were bound and eager to restore it at once to sacred usages as soon as the government had been freed from such a difficulty. For among them there prevailed the belief that it was part of natural law and the law of nations that mortals be able to use nothing at all taken from the immortal gods.[59]

In this religion, it was judged to be a sacrilege if anyone took

---

[56] Cicero, *De officiis* II, 16; Demosthenes, *De corona* 268.
[57] Ambrose, *On the Duties of Ministers* II, 28, 136–143 (*MPL*, Vol. 16, cols. 148 ff.).   [58] *Digest* I, 8, 1.   [59] Cicero. *De haruspicum responso* 14.

anything sacred, and this crime was considered much more serious than the misdemeanor of appropriating public funds.[60]

Provided they are consecrated to his service, the Lord indeed allows and praises the expenditure of things even for private, not to mention public, necessities. In order to purchase peace for the people of God from an Assyrian tyrant, Hezekiah the King gave to him "whatever he found of silver in the house of God," and removed the silver from the doors and posts of the Temple, after he had covered them with it, and the Lord did not disapprove of the deed; for an advantage of his people had been sought (II Kings 18:14-16). When, therefore, this refers to the salvation of God's people, it pleases the Lord if these external things, his own earthly gifts, are expanded freely for the public advantage of his people, no less readily than he gave his own blood. For he wishes heaven and earth, and all that is contained therein, to be of service to the salvation of his people. He wills, however, that his churches have private property, things consecrated to his name, in order to preserve among his own the ministry of his Kingdom, i.e., of religion, and for the sustenance and support of his poor and not to reward the hirelings, thieves, and robbers who so criminally usurp the name and place and income of caretakers and shepherds of his flock, but to provide food, just and necessary wages, for "those who labor in the word and doctrine" (I Tim. 5:17-18), whence a means of subsistence may be available to the schools, i.e., teachers of pious and good arts, and for studious adolescents and young men fit for the ministries of the churches, whence widows, orphans, those broken by age or disease, and other needy persons may be helped and enabled to live. He wills whatever is left over from these uses of our salvation, either from what has previously been consecrated to his name or from what is newly consecrated to him, to be held sacred, and not to be converted to other uses (Lev. 27:28-29), so that whoever deals with them in any other way should be held guilty of sacrilege, under penalty of anathema. He wills that we should acknowledge that there is no other obligation to be fostered and met by us on a par with religion, i.e., the administration of our salvation, and we should hold no citizens of the commonwealth more useful than those who meet this obligation in good faith; and we should not doubt that whatever we spend on his needy ones produces dividends for us, with immense interest, namely, of all good things both present and future. For these needy ones of the Lord "will receive" us "into everlasting tabernacles" (Luke 16:9).

[60] *Digest* XLVIII, 13, 4 and 11.

But some object to this as follows: the goods of the churches have to a large extent been assembled and accumulated by means of impious deceits and impostures by men who were wrongly persuaded that liberation from purgatory and heavenly thrones could be bought and purchased with the donations with which the colleges and chapels were endowed, that very much, therefore, was taken in sacrilegious fraud from communities and distinguished families, so that it is just that some of these ill-gotten gains of the churches be restored to the communities and the noble houses; for "God does not tolerate rapine in sacrifice" (Isa. 61:8), nor, therefore, fraud.[61]

It is clear enough what must be replied to this objection. First, these goods cannot be preserved more certainly for the utility of the commonwealth than under the sanction of divine law, nor expended more usefully than for the conservation and spread of Christ's religion and for nourishing and fostering our Lord Jesus Christ among his little ones. Second, as far as those families are concerned from whom the false clergy took away very many ecclesiastical properties by their godless persuasions and promises, how many, I ask, of these families are left? If they are left and are in need, they should be helped before others by the generosity of the churches. As for the rest, men of jurisprudence are of the opinion that donations made to communities hold force, even when given for profane use, so that if anyone bequeathes a legacy on any city for some impure spectacle, which that city is then unwilling to exhibit to its citizens because of Christ's religion, that legatee is not on this account obliged to yield it to the gain of the heir, but it remains in the public control of the city to which it was given: "The principals of the city are to ignore the claims of the heirs, in regard to the way in which they should use the matter entrusted to them, where the memorial of the testator is celebrated in a manner other than licit, ff." [62] How much more, therefore, should the things donated to the churches of Christ be left in their control but converted to pious uses, even though the things donated have by the false clergy been destined for impious Masses and other false cults by error of the donors.

But would that those who make such objections may themselves

[61] This was the argument advanced by those who favored the complete secularization of ecclesiastical property. Like all major Reformers, Bucer recommended that these properties be used for the benefit of churches and schools and for poor relief. In this vein, he had written and spoken from the beginning of his career as a reformer.

[62] *Digest* XXXIII, 2, 16.

abstain with horror from every fraud and spoliation not only of private persons, but also very much more of the churches of Christ, and may they not betray the churches to their defrauders and despoilers. For we see that there are many who prefer to confer sacerdotal riches, as an insult to Christ and an injury to the churches, to those who already occupy several benefices sacrilegiously rather than to leave one uncircumscribed and unmutilated to faithful ministers of the gospel.

Since, therefore, Your Majesty's realm in relation to the religion and Kingdom of Christ is very gravely endangered by the indicated pillage and dispersion of church property, Your Majesty must quickly and conscientiously take care and bring it about that, just as the government has its treasury, its property, so our eternal King Jesus Christ, as he has his Kingdom in Your Majesty's realm, should also have his treasury and property. This should be held so sacred that Your Majesty himself should not exercise his generosity from it or allow any of his subjects to share in it, except the true and faithful ministers of pure religion, who really do their work faithfully, and those who are being instructed and educated for this ministry, and their teachers and educators, and finally those who are really needy.

The Lord will undoubtedly give and will give most abundantly all other things to Your Majesty as he thus seeks first his Kingdom and righteousness (Matt. 6:33), that he may be able to show himself an abundantly liberal and munificent king to all his faithful ministers and to all men worthy of his kindness. For as the pagan teachers rightly prescribe, these precautions must be observed in generosity and good works: First, "generosity should not injure either those who will obviously receive it or others." Secondly, "kindness should not exceed one's assets, and should be rendered according to the worthiness of each individual.[63] For as the illustrious Ennius said: Misplaced do-gooding I judge to be evildoing." [64]

CHAPTER XIV

THE SIXTH LAW: POOR RELIEF

When the things long consecrated to his name and worship have been thus preserved and sanctified to Christ the Lord, as much as possible and to the degree that we trust him and love him as our Savior and the giver of all good things, and when equitable assets have been set aside and by ample patrimony constituted by the lay-

[63] Cicero, *De officiis* I, 14.   [64] *Ibid.*, II, 18.

ing down of law VI for the churches of Christ in his Kingdom, Your Majesty will restore that holy provision for the poor and needy which the Holy Spirit has prescribed and commended to us (Acts 2:45; 4:32-34; 5:1-11; and 6:1-6). Without it there can be no true communion of saints, and Your Majesty will see to it that each church has its deacons in charge of providing for the poor, concerning which I have before advised,[65] "men of excellent repute" and "full of the Holy Spirit and of wisdom." Each church will have as many of these as is necessary to care for the needy, in proportion to its population and the numbers of the poor.[66]

Their duty and office is contained under these headings: First, they should investigate how many really indigent persons live in each church for whom it is equitable for the church to provide the necessities of life. For the churches of Christ must exclude from their communion those who, when they can sustain themselves by their own powers, neglect this and live inordinately, accepting borrowed food (II Thess. 3:6); it certainly is not the duty of the church to foster such people in their godless idleness. Against these, therefore, the saying should prevail: "Whoever does not work, let him not eat" (v. 10).

What the Holy Spirit commanded concerning widows should also be understood and observed in regard to all the needy: "If any one of the faithful has widows, let him take care of them, and let the church not be burdened that it may take care of those who are really widows" (I Tim. 5:16). Thus if any needy persons belong to anyone's circle, either by blood or marriage or by any other special relationship or particular custom, it is certainly their duty, if they have the means of the Lord, to provide for their own the necessities of life and spare the churches in order that they may have more to nourish and assist those who have no home or family who would want to or could help them.

This horrifying pronouncement of the Holy Spirit should resound in the hearts of all: "If anyone does not look after his own, and especially his own household, he has denied the faith and is worse than an infidel" (I Tim. 5:8). For those whom the Lord has given to us in special close relationships fall particularly under the second great commandment, in which the whole law is contained and fulfilled: "Thou shalt love thy neighbor as thyself" (Matt. 22:39). For the Lord gives to each as neighbors in a special sense

[65] Cf. Book One, Ch. XIV.
[66] On Bucer's proposals for poor relief, see the discussion in W. Pauck, *Das Reich Gottes*, pp. 92 ff.; C. Hopf, *Martin Bucer and the English Reformation*, pp. 116 ff.

those whom he associates and unites to him by blood, marriage, domestic service, or other particular custom.

The first requirement of deacons in charge of the giving of alms is to inquire as diligently as possible who are really in need and cannot themselves alleviate their own need, and who are the ones who either feign need or invite it by laziness and soft living, and who have or do not have neighbors who can or may undertake their care and provide for them. The deacons should keep a special written record of the names, kind of need, and behavior of those whom they have discovered to be unable to obtain the necessities of life for themselves and who have no one close to them to provide for them. At certain times they should visit them or summon them in order to learn more precisely how they are enjoying the alms of the faithful, and what things they may be in need of at any given time.[67] For just as the wicked are never satisfied, and beggary knows neither moderation nor limit, so also reputable and prudent men dissimulate and conceal their need and judge whatever is provided for them by the churches to be too much. But the Holy Spirit has prescribed both how and to what extent to distribute the assets of the churches, so that absolutely no one may be in need, and that to each may be given what he has need of in order to live piously and well (Acts 2:45, and 4:35). And who would not see from this alone how necessary it is for the churches to select deacons of this sort for the responsibility of almsgiving, to investigate and obtain information not casually but accurately concerning those who seek the help of the church, whether one is in need and what he needs, and how much must be contributed to each by the churches toward a decent and pious life. Then also if they have members of their households who are natural sources of assistance given by the Lord to help them in time of need, they should accept this. For such should be compelled by the churches to take care of their own; toward this end the deacons ought to be at hand and of service to the bishop and the elders, as for the entire discipline of Christ.

Another function of the office of the deacons is that they should keep an account of whatever comes to the churches for the use of the poor, either from the proceeds of property or the offerings of the faithful, and from this give to each of the poor whatever shall be found to be necessary for them to live to the Lord. And they must keep a faithful record of this in a book of expenses; for they

[67] Bucer's recommendatons agree largely with the practices followed in the city of Strassburg. Cf. O. Winckelmann, *Das Fürsorgewesen der Stadt Strassburg.*

should render an account of all receipts and expenditures to the bishop and presbytery, "aiming at what is honorable," after the example of the apostle, "not only in the Lord's sight, but also in the sight of men" (II Cor. 8:21). On this account the Holy Spirit requires also of deacons that they be men approved, with a good reputation among the people of Christ (Acts 6:3). For as men work because of a desire for money, so with the least reason they burden with unjust suspicion those who administer public funds. Strongly suspicious and complaining in these matters are the poor who have not learned from Christ's Spirit "both to abound and to suffer want" (Phil. 4:12).

And for this reason, in order that the deacons may have fuller authority with the whole flock of Christ and be more surely recommended to its trust, the early churches assigned them a rank near to that of the presbyterial dignity and admitted them to a part in the sacred ministry of both teaching and the sacraments. The Antichrists have plainly voided the office of these men, as also all others of the sacred ministry, and reduced them to an empty display, so that today there are very few who think that deacons have any other function than to minister at the Masses of bishops and priests and there do the reading of the Gospels. This was originally a minor responsibility of this order, as I have said, so that their ministry among the people of God in caring for the poor and asserting the discipline of Christ obtained greater authority as well as greater credit.

Care for the properties of the churches and the collection of income therefrom and of other proceeds designated for the use of the poor of the churches pertain to the office of subdeacons and administrators, so that the deacons may spend themselves completely: first, in the correct distribution of the assets of the churches already collected, namely, to give to each only what he truly needs in order to live to the Lord; secondly, to maintain the discipline of Christ among those who are fed by the churches, so that those who receive food from the churches for this very purpose will strive to live to the Lord; finally, to advance this discipline among the rest of the Christians, whose life and habits they are able better to know and investigate from their care for the poor. This distribution of the duties of deacons and subdeacons was still observed in the time of the Roman bishop Saint Gregory, as may be read in many of his letters.[68]

However approved and wise the deacons are to whom the

[68] Cf. Gregory I, *Letters* I, 2 (*MPL*, Vol. 77, col. 445); II, 32 (*MPL*, Vol. 77, cols. 566 ff.).

churches assign poor relief, the poor will be little helped unless
there is some source of supply of things to be distributed to them,
and this must be provided by Your Majesty, so that the churches
may supply whatever the cause of the needy demands.

In former times, a fourth part of all the assets of the churches
which came from the property or the gifts and offerings of the
faithful was set aside for the poor.[69]

Furthermore, pious princes and men of wealth established
homes and hospitals, some to nourish and care for the needy who
were in good health, some for infants, others for orphans, still
others for the aged infirm, others for those laboring under various
forms of sickness, and some for pilgrims and displaced persons.[70]

There is no doubt that in this realm many things have been
donated and provided by Your Majesty's ancestors and other reverent nobles and men for the use of the needy, and in the course of
time false cenobites [71] and clergy charged with the supervision of
these provisions for the poor have converted them to the use of
their own pleasure and pomp, after they were supposed to have
surrendered such things, having rejected all concern not only for
the bodies of the needy brothers but also for the souls of themselves and the whole people of Christ and all religion, under the
pretext of zeal for spreading the worship of God, i.e., cumulating
their cursed Masses and other abominable ceremonies. For they
had removed all power and authority of kings and legitimate
magistrates from themselves and persuaded the common people
that it was far better if these goods were expended on their godless
cults for the benefit of the living and the dead than if Christ the
Lord by this means fed the hungry, gave the thirsty to drink, offered hospitality to pilgrims and the homeless, clothed the naked,
and visited the sick and prisoners (Matt. 25:35-36).

If, therefore, in the visitations of the churches any remains are
found of funds given for the use of the poor, Your Majesty certainly ought to claim them for the cause of the needy of Christ and
restore them to the use for which they were originally consecrated
to the Lord.

Then it will also be suitable for certain payments to be imposed
on the more well-to-do priestly benefices, as I have said a little before this,[72] to feed the poor, to the extent of a fourth part of all the
revenues of the churches, as it is assigned to them in so many
canons.

Then, in order that unworthy persons may not appropriate the

[69] *Corpus Iuris Canonici* II, c. XII, 9.   [70] *Code* I, 22.
[71] *Pseudocoenobitae.*   [72] Cf. Book Two, Ch. XIII.

alms of the churches and of the faithful from those who are truly deserving and really in need, Your Majesty must renew the law of God and of the emperor Valentinian that no one should be permitted to beg, but that those who are able to sustain themselves by their labors should be compelled to work and not be taken care of by the churches. Each should live by his own resources without begging, so that our brethren and members may be nourished (Deut. 15:4; II Thess. 3:6, 10-12).[73]

In order that this may come about more conveniently and equitably, Your Majesty must also decree that each person should provide nourishment for the members of his household and the poor specially related to him if his means make it possible for him to do so; and that each city, town, and village should support their poor who cannot be taken care of by their own households, and not send them away to others.

But since it can happen that some town or village may have more slender means than are sufficient to provide the necessities of life for all its needy, the cost of taking care of these efficiently will be met by Your Majesty's order in such a way that in each district some holy men gifted with spiritual prudence will be put in charge of this undertaking, in order to transfer to richer churches, on Your Majesty's authority, those who cannot be taken care of by their own churches. For all of us Christians are members of one another (Eph. 4:25), under which title the Gentile churches, at the time and by the inspiration of the apostle Paul, helped churches struck by famine in Judea, and acknowledged it to be their duty to do so (Rom. 15:26-27).

Finally, since from our nature, depraved and always rebellious against God, we continually compromise the instructions and precepts of God, and according to our desires and misdirected judgments, are always eager to follow paths and ways other than what God has prescribed, however holy the care of the poor is, there will be some who will refuse to put their alms for the poor into a common fund, and say that they prefer to provide for the poor by their personal generosity if it seems good to them to do so. Their arrogance will have to be countered both by Your Majesty's law and through the discipline of the Church; by a law which imposes a double offering to the Lord's fund, if anyone is caught giving anything privately to the needy; by the discipline of the Church, so

---

[73] *Code* XI, 26. Among the Protestant Reformers, Bucer was the most insistent in forbidding begging. Henry VIII issued a law prohibiting begging in 1536 (27 Henry VIII, c. 25; *Statutes of the Realm,* Vol. III, p. 558) which was renewed in 1550.

that if anyone puts nothing into the Lord's fund, he should be admonished of his duty from the Word of God by the ministers of the churches, and if he should resolutely despise this admonition, he should be held a heathen and a publican. For although it must be left to the judgment of every individual how much he wishes to offer to Christ the Lord for the use of his little ones, nevertheless no one in the Church can be allowed, against the express precept of God, to come empty-handed into the sight of the Lord (Deut. 15:7; 16:16), for he would completely spurn the instruction of the Holy Spirit concerning the care for the poor (Acts 6:2-4); indeed, rather, through his private almsgiving he would overturn it.

But here human wisdom, which always puts itself before the divine, will object that it is inhuman that the hands of the faithful are closed so that they cannot do good according to their own judgment to those whom they have found to be really in need; for there are to be found excellent men among the poor, who are ashamed to seek the Church's alms, however much they may be in need. To this it must be replied, first, that no man's hand is closed by this law, to interfere with his opening it to whatever poor persons he can and will provide for; but according to God's precept and the instruction of the Holy Spirit, care must be taken that the sons of God do not give, what they really ought to be giving to the needy little ones of Christ, to the enemies of Christ, or to those who are not needy, or to those who evidently exaggerate their indigence. For a private person cannot, as I said before, investigate the poor as certainly as those who, as they are given this duty by the churches, daily meet it with utmost effort. And the Lord does not fail to give his gifts and an increase of the Holy Spirit to those whom he has chosen for himself and called to this office through his Spirit (I Cor. 12:7-11).

Secondly, even if someone is well acquainted with his needy neighbors and knows their ways, nevertheless, in order that others may not also wish by his example themselves to dispense their alms and very often to those who are little known or investigated (in view of the fact that those who are least worthy of alms are accustomed to beg them all the more imprudently and deviously), it is far better for everyone to send those whom he encounters in need of help, however well he knows them to be good and virtuous, to the deacons of the Church, so that they may obtain from these what they need. We must be very much on guard that we open not even a crack to our innate arrogance of being wise against God and deflecting our aim from his precepts and instructions either to the right or to the left.

And if shame embarrasses some so that they would rather not go to the whole diaconate, let them present their need to one of the deacons, or if this too is difficult for them, then those who are thoroughly acquainted with their need and honesty may bring them to the attention of the deacons and obtain the necessary alms for them.

No Christian, even though he has fallen into poverty (and regardless of the high social standing which he once enjoyed) should be ashamed of the cross of Christ and the salutary remedy administered by the Lord through need. It is even less proper for Christians to find it distasteful to accept alleviation of their need through the ministry of his Church as from the very hand of the Lord, by whose most righteous, and to them no less salutary, judgment they have been plunged into poverty and humility of life.

This, however, is also within the competence of the deacons, that they take into consideration not only the need of various persons but also their faintness of heart, and that with prudence and liberality they offer assistance in such a way that in no case they add the affliction of shame to the affliction of poverty, and that they do not reduce those whom the Lord previously blessed with ease and comfort to an unbearable harshness of diet and dress, even though this may be satisfactory to other men who have been accustomed to this according to their living conditions. Here we must consider the precept of the Holy Spirit, that we distribute to each whatever he needs to live well and blessedly (Acts 2:45; 4:35). But it is apparent that, as all do not have equal health of body, nor are all geared to the same manner of life, so some have need of more, others of less; some need softer, others rougher, diet, dress, and various other things. In appreciation of this, when noble men and women were despoiled by the Lombards, Saint Gregory appointed especially liberal pensions for them from church property.[74]

Accordingly, may Your Majesty offer this sixth law to Christ the Lord and his Church. In its first chapter he should decree that no one should be permitted to beg, but that each person should provide for the members of his household and his relatives by blood and marriage if he has the means to do so; the ordinary magistrate of every place ought to be the judge in this matter. The city, town, or village should sustain those who do not have any family assistance. If any city, town, or village through scarcity is unable to provide for its needy, judgment should reside with the superior

---

[74] Gregory I, *Letters* I, 39 (*MPL,* Vol. 77, col. 493).

magistrates of each district, and the poor ought to be transferred to some wealthier church in that district.

In a second chapter he should prescribe that in the first visitation of each church there should be selected by the visitors both deacons approved among the people and caretakers of the poor, such as we have already described,[75] and dutifully enjoin them, according to the norm we have noted, that they should thoroughly investigate what various persons need and faithfully give them these things as far as they are able, and render an account of the receipts and expenses to the bishop and presbytery at appointed times.

In the third chapter, he should forbid private almsgiving and urge his people to entrust their offerings, according to God's precept and the instruction of the Holy Spirit (Acts 4:34), to the Church and its ministers appointed for this, rather than personally dispense them according to an innate arrogance and against the word of God and the instruction of the Holy Spirit.

In the fourth chapter, he should lay claim for the needs of the poor of any gifts of our ancestors offered to Christ for this purpose which are discovered still to be available. And to whatever degree the remains of these donations are found to be less, he should impose more liberal payments for the sustenance of the poor on wealthier priests to the extent of a fourth share of all the income of the churches, which is due from them according to so many canons.

In the fifth chapter, he should prescribe grave penalties for those who dare to blaspheme this most holy instruction of the Holy Spirit or to dissuade anyone from it; he should command that if it seems to anyone that something must be corrected among the deacons and in all the care of the poor, he should especially admonish the deacons of this. And if they do not act according to that proper admonition, he should defer the matter to the bishop and presbytery so that in all things the authority of the Word of God may prevail and the wicked pride of men, which approves of nothing established by God, may everywhere be countered in time. Then the prayer of the people of Christ may be answered that the least of Christ's brethren are so graciously provided for that eventually we may happily hear: "Come, you blessed of my Father, and receive the Kingdom which was prepared for you from the beginning of the world; for I was hungry and you gave me to eat," etc. (Matt. 25:34-36).

[75] Cf. Book One, Ch. XIV, and the first paragraph of this chapter (Book Two, Ch. XIV).

Nor is it sufficient for the kindness of Christians to give food, shelter, and clothing to those in extreme need; they should give so liberally of the gifts of God which they have received that they may even be able, as has been said previously,[76] to endow and help marriageable girls who are honest and devout, who, because they are without dowry, are kept from marriage longer than is fair, so that they can be married in due time and joined to suitable husbands; they should help boys of outstanding ability who have no patrons to be educated toward studying for the sacred ministry of the Church; finally, they should help, both by gifts and loans, faithful men who are unemployed, that they can make a living by their trade and feed their children and educate them in the Lord and show themselves more profitable citizens of the commonwealth.

For it hardly suffices for the churches of Christ that their people should merely be alive but it must also be provided for them that they live to the Lord for a certain and mutual usefulness among each other and within the State and the Church.[77] Hence the churches must provide that all persons baptized into Christ should from childhood be properly educated and learn decent skills so that each one according to his portion may be able to contribute something to the common good and prove himself as a true and useful member of Christ. Concerning this characteristic of the members of Christ we have already commented above.[78] This concludes our comments on poor relief.

CHAPTER XV

THE SEVENTH LAW: THE SANCTIFICATION AND REGULATION OF MARRIAGE

Besides these things, Christ our King and his Church ask of Your Majesty that he also assume proper responsibility for the ordering of marriage.[79] For one cannot say how very many good consciences are here entangled, afflicted, and endangered since there are no just laws, and no effective plan has been designed according to the Word of God for this very sacred relationship, the

[76] Cf. Book Two, Ch. XIII.
[77] *Ad certam et mutuam inter se atque totius reipublicae et Ecclesiae utilitatem.*
[78] Cf. Book One, Chs. II and III.
[79] The development of Bucer's conception of marriage and divorce is described by François Wendel, *Le mariage à Strasbourg à l'époque de la Réforme* (Strasbourg, 1928), and by Walther Köhler, *Zürcher Ehegericht und Genfer Konsistorium*, Vol. II (Leipzig, 1942), pp. 427 ff.

font of the human race. For since marriage is a *res politica,* in order that men may rightly contract and enter marriage, observe it reverently, and not dissolve it unless compelled by extreme necessity, they must be oriented and influenced not only by the doctrine and discipline of the Church, but encouraged, helped, and compelled toward this by the laws and judgments of the state also. Pious emperors, acknowledging this and here accommodating themselves to the law of nations, made laws concerning the legitimate contracting and celebration of marriage and a proper respect for it, and also, where unhappy necessity should require it, for rescinding it. This can be seen in Justinian's *Code,* from the beginning of the fifth book through the twenty-fourth title,[80] as well as in the twenty-second Authentica of Justinian,[81] and some other places.

But in order to transfer the power of the emperors to themselves, the Roman Antichrists, first by fraudulent persuasion, afterward even by force, assumed all power of making judgments and decrees concerning matrimony just as they did in most other matters. Thus for some time kings and governments have not been entrusted with the concern and administration of this matter as an area within their competence. But, meanwhile, where the gospel of Christ is being received the laws of the Roman Antichrist are being repudiated as the religion of Christ requires. Once these laws and judgments have been rightfully repudiated, if kings and governors do not assume this responsibility so that both by the authority of laws and strictness of judgments they ensure that marriages be piously contracted and entered into, reverently preserved, and, if the case should demand it, be legitimately dissolved, it is plain to see what confusion and trouble will be brought upon this most sacred relationship and what great torture prepared for very many excellent consciences, while they have no sure laws to follow, and no precedents to cite if something intolerable should occur.

How important it is for the decency and well-being of the commonwealth that matrimony be contracted and reverenced according to the will of Christ and not dissolved without a just cause! Who would not understand this? For unless that first and most sacred union of man and woman is established in a holy way, so that household discipline flourishes among the spouses according to God's precept, how can we expect a race of good men? [82]

---

[80] *Code* V, 1–24.   [81] *Novellae* 22, 74, 4.
[82] This is John Milton's translation of the phrase *quis probatorum civium proventus possit expectari (Complete Prose Works of John Milton,* Vol. II, ed. by Ernest Sirluck [Yale University Press, 1959]) , p. 442. In *The Judg-*

Let Your Majesty, therefore, acknowledge that this also is his duty, and certainly one of first importance, to assume to himself the proper concern for and the administration of marriage, and both by holy laws and by judgments to sanction and safeguard the religious quality of this first and divine institution among men. All wise lawgivers obviously did this in the past with singular zeal, and the founders of governments and pious emperors of Christian states acted in the same way.

CHAPTER XVI

What Must Be Established Concerning the Contracting and Entering of Holy Marriage

In the first place, therefore, Your Majesty will propose laws to his subjects concerning the correct contracting and holy entering into marriage so that no one will be associated wtih another in matrimony unless it is according to God's will for one person to be joined with another in this agreement and the contract concerning this union is entered into gravely, deliberately, and religiously, as befits those who have professed piety.

CHAPTER XVII

Which Persons It Is Proper to Join in Matrimony

It will first of all have to be established by Your Majesty which persons he wishes to be joined in marriage. The law of God and of the emperors forbids marriage only to those who are related in the ascendant and descendant line, and collaterally to paternal and maternal aunt, to sister, sister's daughter and granddaughter, to brother's daughter, likewise by affinity to stepdaughter, step-

---

ment of Martin Bucer concerning Divorce (London, 1644), John Milton translated large parts of Chs. XV–XLVII of the second book of *De Regno Christi*. This is now readily accessible in the Yale edition of Milton's prose works (Vol. II, pp. 416–479), with a preface and notes by Arnold Williams and a discussion by the editor, Ernest Sirluck, of Milton's purpose in publishing the translation (pp. 137–158). A. Williams also provides "Notes on Milton's Method of Translation in 'The Judgment,' etc." (pp. 808–818). He is of the opinion that Milton "must have found the style of Bucer often prolix, loose, and graceless, no matter how useful his arguments" (p. 808). C. Hopf (*Martin Bucer and the English Reformation,* pp. 107–115) relates Bucer's views to those prevailing in Tudor England, and especially to those expressed in Cranmer's *Reformatio legum Ecclesiasticarum* which was formulated in the years 1551–1553.

mother, daughter-in-law, mother-in-law,[83] brother's wife, father's wife, to wife's daughter and granddaughter (Lev. 18:7-18) ; [84] certain laws of emperors add brother's and sister's grandchildren.[85] They also forbid marriage to those who are too disparate in condition of life, so that a plebeian may not marry the daughter of a senator, or a senator a plebeian, nor a free person a slave.[86] They also forbid marriages to adopted daughters [87] and godchildren,[88] of a tutor to his pupil,[89] or that a provincial governor or his son takes a wife from among his subjects.[90] The law of both God and the emperors permits marriage to cousins, whether they are so related through two sisters, or brother and sister, i.e., whether they have this relationship on the father's brother's or sister's side, or are cousins properly so called. For although at the time of Augustine, as he recalls in the sixteenth chapter of the fifteenth book of *The City of God*,[91] marriages of cousins were forbidden by law, nevertheless that law was at once revoked, as is clear in the law of Arcadius and Honorius,[92] and in the *Institutes* of Justinian.[93]

Certain Roman pontiffs forbade the marriage of relatives to the seventh generation.[94] Afterward they reduced this prohibition to the fourth generation.[95] But Gregory I allowed the Angles to marry in the fourth degree of kindred and forbade them in the second, i.e., with cousins, but he gives a rather shallow reason for his prohibition. For he writes that he has learned from experience that offspring cannot come from such a marriage.[96]

Saint Augustine in the passage just cited gives two reasons why it is suitable for Christians not to take spouses from among their own relatives: first, that by affinity with outsiders, charity among men and interdependence are the more expanded; secondly, that "there is something natural and laudable in human modesty which keeps one from a union with a woman to whom respect is due because of consanguinity; the union may be for propagation, but is nevertheless lustful, one which we see even conjugal modesty blushing over." [97]

---

[83] *Code* V, 4, 17.   [84] *Code* V, 5, 5; *Digest* XXIII, 2, 13, 3.

[85] *Code* V, 5, 9.   [86] *Digest* XXIII, 2, 23, 27, 44; *Code* V, 7 and 3.

[87] *Institutes* I, 10, 1.   [88] *Code* V, 26, 2.

[89] *Digest* XXIII, 2, 59 and 60. [90] *Digest* XXIII, 2, 38, 57, 63, 65.

[91] Augustine, *The City of God* XV, 16, 2 (*MPL*, Vol. 41, col. 459) .

[92] *Code* V, 4, 19.   [93] *Institutes* I, 10, 4.

[94] *Decret.* II, c. XXXV, q. 2 and 3, c. 17 and 21.

[95] *Corpus Iuris Canonici* X, IV, 14, 8.

[96] *Decret.* II, c. XXXV, q. 2 and 3, c. 20.

[97] Augustine, *The City of God,* as cited in n. 91 above.

Further, we read that the ancient holy fathers, Abraham, Isaac, and others, preferred to unite their children with relatives of whose character and pious education they had more knowledge (Gen. 20:12; 24:40; 29:10-28). And this, certainly, must be looked for in arranging a marriage that those involved be in proper accord in regard to religion and ways of life, which can be determined more easily among friends and relatives than among strangers.

Moreover, unless the love of Christ, which disregards blood relationship, arouses and preserves the love between relatives, we observe that relationships between one's relatives and outsiders very often cause contention, hatred, and sometimes even wars, rather than that they prove to be the means of a broader goodwill and love. For whatever property is transferred by matrimony to relatives by marriage, blood relatives who are not moved by the Spirit of Christ think that it has been wrongfully snatched from their own grasp.

On this account, I myself am of the opinion that it is fitting for pious princes and governors of states, in defining the degrees of consanguinity and affinity pertinent to the association of marriage, to follow the laws of God and the examples of the holy patriarchs praised in Holy Scriptures, rather than what men have later invented and observed in this matter, especially since pious emperors also preferred in their laws to follow the divine arrangement rather than human judgment.

I confess that we being free in Christ are not bound by the civil laws of Moses any more than by the ceremonial laws given to ancient Israel, insofar as they pertain to external circumstances and elements of the world; nevertheless, since there can be no laws more honorable, righteous, and wholesome than those which God himself, who is eternal wisdom and goodness, enacted, if only they are applied under God's judgment to our own affairs and activities, I do not see why Christians, in matters which pertain also to their own doings, should not follow the laws of God more than those of any men. We have no need to observe circumcision, sacrifices, multiple purifications of the body and of outward practices which the Lord especially commanded to the Jews through Moses; but from the things which the Lord commanded concerning such matters, we rightly and devoutly learn with what reverence we ought to administer holy Baptism and the Eucharist, and to receive them as well, and what great purity and chastity we ought to observe in the use of all things corporal. How much more, therefore, must we diligently observe what the Lord commanded and taught by the examples he gave concerning holy marriage. We use it no less than the ancients by God's institution.

This is what I have to say about persons who may fittingly be joined in matrimony.

CHAPTER XVIII

Marriages Should Not Be Held Valid Which Are Contracted Without the Consent of Those Who Have Power Over the Ones Who Make the Contract, or Without Suitable Advisers

Since in contracting holy matrimony people today act more superficially and unheedingly so that the marriage relationship has become a matter of considerable concern, and if it is not entered into responsibly, they may be in danger, clearly Your Majesty ought also here to come to the aid of the human weakness of his subjects.

For against the laws of God and the Church, which they have tried to dissolve in every respect, the Roman Antichrists have introduced that supremely godless dogma that the compact of matrimony made verbally by the contracting parties, as they say, binds at once, if only those who contract are of the age of puberty, and that such a pact is not invalidated if it is made without the knowledge or consent of the parents, out of blind love and the desire of the flesh, and for the most part out of the deviousness of seducers and the wantonness of the seduced.[98]

But it is obvious that it is repugnant, not only to the laws of pious emperors, but also to the law of God and of nature and to every law of nations, that children who are in the power of their parents do or attempt anything of great moment outside the knowledge and will of the parents, much less emancipate themselves completely from the power of their parents and withdraw themselves from their control, as occurs in matrimony. "For on account of this, says the Lord, a man will leave father and mother and cleave to his wife" (Gen. 2:24). After God, certainly the greatest honor and reverence is due from children to their parents. But what greater contempt can be inflicted by children upon their parents, and what greater insult rendered to them than when they spurn their counsel in a matter of such great moment and such great peril, and when they disregard the parents whose dearest

[98] *Corpus Iuris Canonici, Decret.* II, c. XXXI, q. 3 and c. XXXII, q. 2, c. 14. Cf. Peter Lombard, *Sent.* IV, dist. 28.

tokens of love they are and withdraw themselves from their embrace, use, and power in which God has so sacredly commanded them to be?

Therefore, the laws of the early Church and of pious emperors define it as rape if anyone joins a woman to himself in matrimony without the knowledge and consent of parents, even if the woman consents.[99] Since the laws provide such a severe punishment if anyone against the will of another takes just a little money, or some beast, or some other thing that in no way can be compared with children, how much more severe a punishment ought to be inflicted on those who take from parents their own children, than whom they hold nothing in the world more dear or more precious.

For when parents themselves find husbands for their daughters and accept wives for their sons, if indeed they do this in the Lord, they provide for themselves sons-in-law and daughters-in-law who will be like sons and daughters to them. Thus when they give their children in matrimony, they do not so much alienate them from themselves or lose their services as they receive a filial son-in-law when they give a daughter, and when they receive a wife for their son, they get a daughter in their daughter-in-law along with their son, and they double for themselves the services of sons and daughters. And this is far different from what happens if they get married without the consent of their parents.

God did not want to hold valid the vow of a daughter if it displeased her father (Num. 30:4-6). Should the promise of a girl made to a man against her father's will then be valid?

From these things Your Majesty easily understands how necessary it is for the well-being of his people to restore and sanction for them the law of God and nature not so much against a rash as a godless compact of matrimony, which is made without the counsel and consent of the parents, or, in their absence, without the counsel of those whom everyone justly ought to have in the place of parents, such as tutors, guardians, relatives, patrons and special friends, singularly outstanding in piety and prudence.

In the absence of these, a person nevertheless acts impiously if he enters the marriage contract, that lasting and highest union of human nature, without the counsel of important and pious men through whom he may be able to know the mind and will of God with more certainty. In less serious matters involving money and other things, the investment of which is often more profitable than the keeping of it, men who do not trust their own judgment use as counselors those whom they judge to have a bit more knowledge

[99] *Decret.* II, c. XXXVI, q. 1, c. 3; q. 2, c. 2, 6, 8, 10; *Novellae* 150, 1.

than they themselves in such matters; who does not see, therefore, that it is a mark of impious temerity and pernicious lust for a boy on his own responsibility to enter into an indissoluble covenant with a woman who, according to God's will, is to be his body and helper for life, or for a girl to be linked in a similar bond to a man who must prove himself as her head and savior as Christ presents himself to his church (Eph. 5:22-30)?

Formerly among the Romans divorce was not valid "except before seven mature Roman citizens, besides the freedman of him who was making the divorce." [100] Who, then, would doubt that a legitimate contract of matrimony likewise demands as much, if not more, counsel, evidence, and seriousness?

Testaments, which make settlements almost exclusively with regard to external endowments, are not considered binding except if they are witnessed to by seven men who are free, prudent, reputable, and honest.[101] Should a contract then be held valid without an adviser, without a counselor, without a witness, a contract not only of body and of goods but also of the soul, such as certainly occurs in the marriage contract, since marriage is a "sharing of all life," and "a communication of divine and human right"? [102] This godless temerity and immeasurable levity has to this day brought forth perjuries in matrimonial trials, with most individuals falsely abjuring the matrimonial pact which they had made secretly and without witnesses.

According to the norm, therefore, which the very law of God ordains and the law of nations and of nature teaches, and which we see all pious and honest men follow as established custom, written laws to the contrary permitting, it will have to be established that no matrimonial agreement is valid which is not accomplished with the consent of those who have power over those who contract; and if some have neither parents nor relatives nor other special patrons whose meritorious counsel and approval they may use, the counsel, assent, and testimony of at least three or four pious and honest men should be required. Most religious men use for this contract also some priest of the church in order that everything may take place more gravely and religiously, and that by the Word of God and prayer this contract may be sanctified with greater zeal.

Clearly, "whatever things are true, whatever honorable, whatever just, whatever pure, whatever lovely and gracious, whatever of good report, if there is any excellence, if there is any praise, these

---

[100] *Code* V, 4, 18, 20, 25. [101] *Code* VI, 23, 21.
[102] *Digest* XXIII, 2, 1.

things are to be thought about," these things are to be sought and done by us and by every person according to his place and role in the body of Christ (Phil. 4:8) . God has prescribed this law for us. Now no one doubts that it is honorable and just and holy for children to do or attempt nothing at all without the approving consent of their parents, much less free themselves entirely from their power through matrimony and to undertake a matter of such moment and peril without their counsel and authority.

Thus no one can be ambiguous about it that it is holy, just, and honorable that whoever embarks on the marriage contract should do so not clandestinely, not according to the rash passion of the flesh, but with very serious and religious men called in for deliberation and agreement in such a great matter. And clearly every Christian should influence and motivate in this direction all he possibly can.

But here it is objected that children are sometimes impeded by embarrassment at exposing to parents either the desire for marriage or the identity of the ones they wish to marry. Some parents also either restrain their children from marriage longer than is equitable or force on them unwanted marriages. But what is alleged concerning embarrassment is nothing. It is hardly fitting for children to be ashamed to ask a chaste and holy marriage of their parents. For that petition is honorable and not to be ashamed of. But it ought to be a shame and reproach to them so to despise their parents and so to violate both human and divine right according to their fancy as to pledge themselves to marriage without the counsel and consent of parents and those who properly take the place of parents. For this audacity, supremely injurious, is also really shameful and disgraceful. And it is surely a fine reason for embarrassment not to dare to ask holy and honorable nuptials of parents and presently in open disregard for parents, against human and divine right, to cohabit with those to whom they have joined themselves not so much unadvisedly as with impious rashness and cupidity.

Further, if parents should be unwilling to allow the honorable vows of their children and proceed to abuse their power over them, they must be admonished and persuaded by a warning, prayers, and the urging first of relatives and friends, and secondly of the presbyters of the church. But if harsh parents should ignore all these, then the magistrates must interpose their authority, lest anyone by the wickedness of his parents be either kept from marriage longer than is fair or driven to a less acceptable marriage, provided that those who have such inhuman parents are not seeking to be joined with corrupt men of little honor and piety. There was a provision concerning such things even in Roman laws.[103]

From this Your Majesty can sufficiently recognize how much it is his duty to provide safeguards by laws and judicial processes that no one contracts a marriage without the advice and consent of those in whose authority and power God has willed him to be, and that no marriage whatsoever shall have force when it is contracted without the grave counsel and testimony of religious men, but that those who in a matter so holy and so greatly requiring reverent deliberation boldly have the impious temerity to put their base desires before divine and human rights should be subject to the punishment they deserve.

CHAPTER XIX

Whether It May Be Permitted that the Promise of Marriage May Be Rescinded Before It Is Fulfilled

Another question here arises about engagements, i.e., matrimonial agreements, when they ought to be held entirely valid and unchangeable. For religious emperors were not of the opinion that an agreement of matrimony would have to be held indissoluble until the bride was brought home and the solemnities had been celebrated. For they judged it a thing unworthy of natural and divine equity, and of the just reflection needed by human infirmity for deliberating and coming to a decision, when a space of time was given to renounce other contracts of much less moment which were not yet confirmed before the magistrates, and to deny this to the matrimonial contract, the holiest of all, which required most accurate circumspection and deliberation. However, lest pacts of this kind should be rescinded without just cause and to the injury of one to whom marriage had been promised, they decreed this penalty that he who rescinded the pledged matrimony against the will of the one to whom he had pledged it and without judicial approval of the cause of this revocation should pay to the one to whom he had pledged it the double amount of earnest money rather than what he had paid for the confirmation of the conjugal agreement,[104] or as much as the judge should pronounce to have been involved either for the fiancé in taking the one espoused to

---

[103] *Digest* XXIII, 2, 19, 21, 22; *Code* V, 4, 12.
[104] *Code* V, 1, 5.

him as a wife, or for the bride in marrying the one to whom she had been espoused by his parents.[105]

Since it is already abundantly obvious that there are very often second thoughts about an agreement of matrimony and there are discovered just and honorable causes for withdrawing from this agreement, it certainly cannot be alien to the office of pious princes that they make possible for persons in such situations the same arrangement for withdrawing from a promised marriage as did pious emperors of old, especially when only a promise of matrimony and no carnal intercourse has been involved. As there is no true marriage without a true assent of hearts between those who make the agreement, it is appropriate for pious princes to take very special pains that no marriages take place among their subjects without this assent and love. For when the wedding feast has been celebrated and plenty of carnal intercourse thus enjoyed, it is the right time for the nuptial agreement to have its full confirmation.

I confess that Your Majesty is in no way bound by the laws of the Roman Empire and may administer his realm free from obligation to any alien laws; but it is the duty of a Christian prince to embrace and follow whatever he has learned has anywhere been established and observed concerning pious, holy, just, and equitable causes and what is in itself for himself and for his own people true, honorable, just, and gracious (Phil. 4:8).

But in view of the fact that in the divine laws and the examples of the holy fathers we read nothing about this, it is not astonishing that the opportunity was given to ancient Israel, indeed, the precept given, that one whose wife was entirely displeasing, and who was unwilling to turn his heart to a true love of her, should dismiss her from him, after giving a bill of repudiation, even after carnal relationship and also long cohabitation (Deut. 24:1; Mal. 2:16, Vulg.). This is enough to authorize any pious prince to grant the favor of changing the kind of conjugal pact about which I have spoken, both because it is certain that the Antichrists have invented the indissolubility of the marriage promise made verbally for the present,[106] and because it is the duty of every pious prince to take care, as much as he can, that marriages take place as the Lord has appointed. Everyone must receive his spouse with the affection and love with which as we read Adam received Eve as

---

[105] Aulus Gellius, *Noctes Atticae* IV, 4. Milton abbreviates this passage and writes "or as much as the Judge should pronounce might satisfie the dammage or the hindrance of either partie" (*Complete Prose Works*, Vol. II, p. 445.) [106] *Corpus Iuris Canonici* X, IV, 4, 3 and 5.

his own so that we may hope that those who are joined in matrimony will become one flesh and one also in God, etc. (Gen. 2:24) .

CHAPTER XX

THE CELEBRATION OF NUPTIALS

In order that Your Majesty's subjects may enter into marriages earnestly agreed upon and mutually approved up to the time of the marriage feast and may do so with reverence, a proper order has been prescribed in the Book of Common Prayer [107] of this realm. But in regard of those parts of the marriage ceremony which they ought to recite, admonish, and pray, very many priests recite, admonish, and pray so coldly, confusedly, and irreligiously, and also for the most part in a voice so subdued, as in the case of other services of worship, that very few of those present, indeed, very often not even the bride and groom, are able to derive any fruit of piety from this. Meanwhile, some of the people wander around in the church and some openly gossip and amuse themselves.

Since such doings involve a serious dishonor to the Divine Majesty, Your Majesty acknowledges that here also his authority and law are required in order to bring it about that his subjects so come and are present at the consecration of their nuptials, and give their attention to everything said to them by the priest, as becomes those who come into the presence and stand in the sight of God Almighty and Christ the Savior, and hear or invoke him through his minister; and the priests, as befits true ministers of Christ and faithful stewards of the mysteries of God, should read, exhort, and pray all these things with utmost dedication.[108]

For how often God is offended and how greatly his anger is provoked when in his sight and in his assembly men appear without supreme reverence and fear of him and do not share in his service with an alive penitence and an upright faith, much less if they there misbehave impiously and make sport of his majesty, this can be learned from Isa. 1:11-15 and 58:13; Jer. 7:10-11, 21-23; Ps. 50:14-23; and many other texts of the prophets and apostolic writings.

This concludes the subject of the pious contracting of holy matrimony, and the just ratification and holy initiation and consecration of it.

[107] Bucer refers here to the first edition of The Book of Common Prayer (1547) which he had read shortly after his arrival in England.
[108] *Summa religione.*

CHAPTER XXI

THE PRESERVATION OF HOLY MARRIAGE

Since marriages legitimately agreed upon and reverently entered into should be preserved with no less care than that with which they are piously and deliberately contracted, it will be worth the effort to appoint to every church singularly important and godly men whose task it will be properly to be on watch and investigate whether husbands are showing themselves wholesome guides and guardians of their wives, really love their spouses, and faithfully keep, cherish, and help them, especially in all piety, and also provide for them the conveniences of this life; and if wives are truly subject to their husbands and eager to offer themselves to help them, especially in all piety, and also in the rest of the activities of life (Eph. 5:22-33; Col. 3:18-19). And if these guardians of matrimony discover that anything different prevails among spouses, either that they do not eagerly render the duties of matrimony to each other or one is absent from the other for a long time without a just and urgent reason or give suspicion of an irresponsible and impure life or fall into manifest wickedness, they should seriously and in a timely manner admonish those whom they have noticed to be delinquent in their duty and in every way exhort them to do their duty.

But if any should despise their authority, these guardians of matrimony [109] should defer their names to the ordinary magistrates so that by the inflicting of punishments they may compel this kind of violators of matrimony to fulfill their matrimonial pledge and restrain and guard themselves from wickedness and probable suspicions of wickedness. And if any have admitted suspicious consorting with others, the magistrates ought to enjoin them from such associations, and if any do not avoid them, punish them as adulterers, according to the law of Justinian.[110] For unless this fountain and nursery of good citizenship, holy marriage, is most vigilantly preserved from every failing and disturbance, what, as I have said before, can be hoped for the coming generations of good citizens and the desired ordering and sanctification of the

[109] *Custodes matrimoniorum.* These "guardians of marriage" were undoubtedly lay elders. It is characteristic of Bucer's conception of a Christian commonwealth and, in connection therewith, of his views about the relationship between Church and state that he here suggests that these guardians report any irregularities to the civil magistrate. Cf. Pauck, *Das Reich Gottes*, p. 33.   [110] *Novellae* 117, 9, 5.

state? [111] We certainly know that it is not enough for Christians to abstain from wicked affairs and deeds but that they also must avoid as earnestly as possible every appearance of evil (I Thess. 5:22).

CHAPTER XXII

WHAT THE ANCIENT CHURCHES THOUGHT ABOUT LEGITIMATE DIVORCE [112]

CHAPTER XXIII

THE ANCIENT FATHERS ALLOWED MARRIAGE EVEN AFTER THE VOW OF CELIBACY

CHAPTER XXIV

WHO OF THE ANCIENT FATHERS ALLOWED MARRIAGE AFTER DIVORCE

CHAPTER XXV

A DISCUSSION OF THE SAYINGS OF OUR LORD AND OF THE HOLY SPIRIT THROUGH THE APOSTLE PAUL CONCERNING DIVORCE

[111] *Quid queat . . . de bonorum civium proventu . . . sperari?*
[112] Here follow the headings of the next twenty-five chapters. A full translation of these chapters is here not offered, because the argument contained in them must be considered as a digression from the discussion of the laws which, in Bucer's opinion, ought to be promulgated and made to prevail in a Christian commonwealth.

Moreover, this is that part of *On the Kingdom of Christ* which John Milton chose to translate into English in his *Judgment of Martin Bucer concerning Divorce,* to which we have already referred and which is readily available in any edition of Milton's prose works.

Bucer's verbose and repetitious defense of divorce and the right of remarriage is noteworthy for the following reasons: (1) He insists that the control of marriage is properly the function of the political power and not of the church; (2) he argues that there are many reasons besides adultery why divorce should be granted to married persons, e.g., incurable disease (leprosy) or impotence, etc.; (3) he defends the right of legitimately divorced persons to remarry; (4) he employs very strained reasoning in order to demonstrate that in all these opinions he has the support not only of Scripture but also of many of the fathers of the Church. In particular, he tries to show that the sayings of Jesus as recorded in Matt. 5:31-32 and 19:3-11 must not be understood as forbidding divorce, except in the case of adultery.

CHAPTER XXVI

GOD IN HIS LAW DID NOT ONLY GRANT BUT ALSO COMMAND DIVORCE TO CERTAIN MEN

CHAPTER XXVII

WHAT THE LORD PERMITTED AND COMMANDED TO HIS ANCIENT PEOPLE CONCERNING DIVORCE APPLIES ALSO TO CHRISTIANS

CHAPTER XXVIII

OUR LORD CHRIST INTENDED NOT TO MAKE NEW LAWS OF MARRIAGE AND DIVORCE OR OF ANY CIVIL MATTERS

CHAPTER XXIX

IT IS WICKED TO STRAIN THE WORDS OF CHRIST BEYOND THEIR INTENT

CHAPTER XXX

ALL NARRATIONS OF THE GOSPELS MUST BE CONNECTED WITH ONE ANOTHER

CHAPTER XXXI

WHETHER THE LORD IN HIS WORDS WHICH THE EVANGELISTS MATTHEW, MARK, AND LUKE RECORD ALLOWED FINAL DIVORCE BECAUSE OF FORNICATION

CHAPTER XXXII

A MANIFEST ADULTERESS OUGHT TO BE DIVORCED AND CANNOT BE RETAINED IN MARRIAGE BY ANY TRUE CHRISTIAN

CHAPTER XXXIII

ADULTERY MUST BE PUNISHED BY DEATH

CHAPTER XXXIV

WHETHER IT IS PERMISSIBLE FOR WIVES TO LEAVE
THEIR ADULTEROUS HUSBANDS AND TO MARRY SOMEONE ELSE

CHAPTER XXXV

AN EXPOSITION OF THE WORDS OF THE HOLY SPIRIT
CONCERNING DIVORCE GIVEN TO US IN WRITING
THROUGH THE APOSTLE PAUL

CHAPTER XXXVI

ALTHOUGH IN THE GOSPELS OUR LORD APPEARS TO ALLOW
DIVORCE ONLY IN CASE OF ADULTERY, HE NEVERTHELESS
ALLOWED DIVORCE ALSO FOR OTHER CAUSES

CHAPTER XXXVII

TO WHICH MEN AND WOMEN DIVORCE IS GRANTED
IN THE CODE OF CIVIL LAW

CHAPTER XXXVIII

AN EXPOSITION OF THOSE PASSAGES OF HOLY SCRIPTURE
WHEREIN GOD EXPLAINS TO US THE NATURE OF HOLY WEDLOCK

CHAPTER XXXIX

A DEFINITION OF THE CHARACTERISTICS OF HOLY WEDLOCK

CHAPTER XL

WHETHER THE CRIMES LISTED IN CIVIL LAW (cf. Chapter XXXVII) DISSOLVE MATRIMONY IN THE SIGHT OF GOD

CHAPTER XLI

WHETHER A DESERTED HUSBAND OR WIFE MAY MARRY SOMEONE ELSE

CHAPTER XLII

INCURABLE INABILITY TO PERFORM THE DUTIES OF MARRIAGE IS A JUST GROUND FOR DIVORCE

CHAPTER XLIII

TO GRANT DIVORCE FOR ALL THE CAUSES WHICH HAVE SO FAR BEEN LISTED AGREES WITH THE WORDS CHRIST HAS SPOKEN AGAINST DIVORCE

CHAPTER XLIV

TO THOSE WHO ARE LEGALLY DIVORCED A SECOND MARRIAGE OUGHT TO BE PERMITTED

CHAPTER XLV

THERE ARE SOME MEN SO DESTINED FOR MARRIAGE BY THE LORD THAT IT IS REPUGNANT TO GOD'S DECREE THAT ANYONE SHOULD FORBID THEM MARRIAGE FOR ANY REASON

CHAPTER XLVI

AN EXPOSITION OF THE WORDS OF THE HOLY SPIRIT (I Cor., ch. 7) IN PRAISE OF CELIBACY

CHAPTER XLVII

CONCLUSION OF THE ENTIRE TRACT ON MARRIAGE

It has seemed good, Most Serene King, to cite these things, both in order to explain for what causes, according to the Word of God, Christian princes and governors of states can grant that unhappy but sometimes very necessary aid of divorce and admission to remarriage, and also in order to demonstrate how the words of the Lord are related to each other in regard to this concession. The things which I have cited are indeed many and have been treated rather elaborately, with frequent quotation of the oracles of God and of first principles in this treatise (especially when it seemed required in order to make the opinions that I propose more easily understandable). These oracles and principles ought always to be held fixed in the mind of him who on this subject would know with certainty and be sure what must be done and allowed according to the judgment of the Lord. But if we consider to what an extent Antichrist has obscured this subject, and how strongly a great number of people still persist in this pernicious contempt of holy marriage and in this admiration of celibacy, even those who have by no means been called to it by God, I fear that all that has been said may not be enough to persuade many so that they would cease to make themselves wiser and holier than God himself in showing themselves so severe in allowing lawful marriages but so easy in conniving not only for all the wickedness of fornication (although among God's people no fornicator or fornication should be tolerated [Deut. 23:17] but also of rape and adultery.

Our Lord Jesus Christ, who came to us to destroy all the works of Satan (I John 3:8), wants to give his Spirit to all Christians, and especially to Christian rulers, both in the administration of the Church and of the state (and, certainly, about Your Majesty's judgment I have no doubt, since he so assiduously, religiously, and with such judgment reads the Holy Scriptures); Christ wants them to acknowledge how much it provokes the wrath of God against us that in such a wicked and pernicious way every kind of unchastity is not only tolerated but also fostered. Thus frequent and abominable ravishings and adulteries are winked at, but, by the mere persuasion of Antichrist, holy and honorable marriage is forbidden to men who without this remedy cannot save themselves from eternal death.

For no one who has even a speck of honesty will deny that it must be a primary concern of pious princes and governors of states to bring it about that genuine purity and decency obtain and prevail among all men, and that if this is neglected, plainly all righteousness will also fail, all fear of God will be struck down, and true religion will become entirely obsolete.

Who would deny that chastity and sanctity of life cannot be publicly restored or retained unless they first find their place and prevail in individual homes whence citizens must be born and come forth. But to accomplish this, no one who is wise and a lover of an honorable life has ever doubted that it is completely necessary for princes and governors of states, first, by utmost severity and just penalties to cut off and strike down not only seductions and adulteries but also all wandering lusts, all illegitimate unions of males and females. Then they must exercise as vigilant a care as possible in this matter, that marriages be first contracted responsibly and in the Lord and then preserved in good faith. When unhappiness demands it, let them be dissolved, but only legitimately, and allow remarriage, as the law of God and of nature as well as the sanctions of pious princes have decreed, as I have demonstrated from the evident authority of Scriptures and other testimonies and memorials of the holy fathers. May the Lord grant that we may have the will to prefer his eternal Word, always righteous and wholesome for us, to those inventions of Antichrist (too deeply rooted in many) and his false and blasphemous interpretation of the words of the Lord. Amen.

This is what I have to say about the purification and the conserving in purity of holy matrimony, the seedbed of the human race and font of good citizens. Now let us see about the fruitful civil education of youth.

CHAPTER XLVIII

THE EIGHTH LAW: THE CIVIL EDUCATION OF YOUTH AND THE SUPPRESSION OF IDLENESS

Although the Lord promises that he will deal kindly "to a thousand generations with those who love him and keep his commandments" (Deut. 7:9), i.e., give them a very long succession of children, grandchildren, and great-grandchildren whom he destines for virtue and piety, and that "to those who seek first his kingdom and righteousness he will add all other things" as liberally as possible (Matt. 6:33), he nevertheless demands that not only every private person but also every state and commonwealth should educate, form, and train its children for him with utmost care, and adapt each of them to those skills and activites for which the Lord himself has created each to be most suited; thus each person, as a sound and useful member in the body of the commonwealth, may contribute his share also to the good of the entire commonwealth, and no idle person may feed as a drone on the labors of others. For the divine law decrees: "Whoever does not work, let him not eat" (II Thess. 3:10-11).

Just as the churches, therefore, ought to exclude from their communion whoever lead idle lives, neither should a Christian state [1] tolerate anyone who does not dedicate himself to some honest work or labor which is useful to the commonwealth. For men obviously cannot do nothing. And so, when they are engaged in no proper activities and salutary concerns, Satan implicates them in evil and harmful pursuits and deeds. For when men of this kind foully and shamefully reject the nature and image of God (for which they have been made and created by him), who always acts to provide good things for his creatures, they despise and neglect the means by which they may prove themselves industrious citizens, fruitful to their neighbors and to the entire community, and they surrender to Satan as captives to his whim, so that he may use them as instruments to inflict all manner of harm on men.

They are the ones who commit treacheries and shameful acts and think up pernicious pleasures. They introduce an intolerable luxury of food, drink, clothing, and other things pertinent to the use or adornment of the body; they undermine laws and overthrow public moral discipline. They subvert reverence and obedience due to princes, magistrates, and men outstanding in prudence and authority; they cause the increase of thefts, bloodsheds, and robberies and stimulate insurrections.

And I hear from a great many good and religious men that all too many in this realm perish because of idleness; [2] for not only the nobles but even certain bishops and prelates feed an exces-

---

[1] *Respublica Christiana.*

[2] In his concern for the alleviation of the evils connected with idleness and unemployment Bucer was of one mind with several English moral and social reformers. This passage indicates that he had obtained his concrete knowledge of English social and economic affairs from personal contact with some of these advocates of social reform. Cf. Wendel's discussion in the Introduction to his edition of *De Regno Christi* (pp. LII f.) and his notes on Book II, Chs. XLVIII–L, and the literature there cited. One should consult also Helen C. White, *Social Criticism in Popular Religious Literature of the Sixteenth Century* (The Macmillan Company, 1944), and W. Pauck, *Das Reich Gottes*, pp. 70–92.

sively large crowd of idle men, and others imitate the idleness of these as much as they can. The consequence is that those who are assigned to the ministries of churches and schools are so sluggish and slow to teach that there are so few workers and among them not many who are skilled; agriculture is quite neglected, and the cost of work and workers is increased and is growing daily. And when so many lower-class men give themselves up to idleness, it also follows that many abstain from holy marriage and procreation of children so that there is a reduction in the number of citizens. And while they are engaged in no honest business and lead an unmarried life, not for the sake of the Kingdom of Heaven but because of their laziness, they create a very grave danger to chastity as I have said, and bring on the very plague. Furthermore, this is the wickedness on account of which the wrath of God also comes upon nations alienated from the knowledge of Christ. How much less, therefore, would God leave such things unpunished among a people glorying in his Kingdom? And so the salvation of so many people entrusted to Your Majesty clamors for a wholesome law against this pest of the community, this slothful and pernicious idleness; it calls for the strict observance of this law in order to cut the roots of these great evils and to provide a holy industry useful to the state, and to orient everyone from childhood toward a zeal for productive work.

The first heading of such a law ought to establish this, that in every village, town, and city there should be appointed a certain number of men, in proportion to the population. They should be men of outstanding piety, wisdom, and prudence whose task it would be to be in charge of education from childhood through young manhood in every jurisdiction and to arrange that every citizen should give his children over to the learning of certain skills, and each one to the particular skills to which it seems that the Lord has made him best suited in the opinion of these youth directors. For everyone brings forth children more for Christ the Lord, the Church, and the commonwealth than for himself; which Plato also recognizes (Laws XI).[3]

And since we acknowledge that all our people, in however humble a station and condition of poverty they have been born, have been made in the image of God and redeemed by the blood of the Son of God for their restoration to this image, faithful pastors of the people of God certainly must see to it, as much as the Lord wishes to use their ministry in this matter, that each person committed to their governance should be restored and led back to this

---

[3] Plato, Laws I, 643 b–d; VII, 804d; XI, 923a.

very image of God, both by pious learning in the knowledge of salvation and by faithful exercise toward every virtue.

And since the assiduous reading of Holy Scripture (which as Saint Gregory [4] piously wrote, "is a letter of God to all" his "creation") most contributes toward the restoration of this image of God, another heading of the law which will restore holy industry by putting an end to godless idleness should decree that the children of all Christians, girls and boys, should learn to read and write as diligently as possible. This is why the ancient holy fathers wished to have a school at every church, in which all the children consecrated to Christ the Lord through Holy Baptism should be taught the writings and the catechism of our religion.[5]

It is necessary, as has already been said, that many such schools be established among us if we want Christ fully to reign among us. Hence, it must be arranged that the children of all be sent to these schools in order there to learn the writings and the catechism of our faith. This should occur as soon as they are old enough and able to do so. The children of citizens of the lower classes should learn the art of reading and writing and the fundamentals of our religion at a tender age, when they cannot yet be used for other tasks. Moreover, pious citizens whose means are not sufficient for the instruction of their children in reading and writing and in various other special skills ought to be helped by the churches when such children have an aptitude for learning.

But when the boys have learned the writings and the catechism of our religion, those *paidonomoi,* directors of youth education,[6] must find out which of the boys have talents for acquiring greater learning and arrange that boys of this kind are instructed more liberally in literature, languages, and the fine arts and thus better prepared for a fuller service to Church and State. They may be left in the schools in which they are or sent to others where better teaching is available, at the expense of their parents if the Lord has given them abundance, otherwise at the expense of the Church.

For why should Church and State find it a burden to prepare for themselves ministers of life eternal, and of such great advantages of the present life? Nor can the parents rightly refuse to per-

---

[4] Gregory I, *Letters* IV, 31 (*MPL,* Vol. 77, col. 706) .
[5] This plea for education is characteristic of all major Reformers. However, it may be said of Bucer that his concern for the education of all was particularly pronounced. Cf. A. F. Leach, *English Schools at the Reformation,* (Westminster, 1896) , pp. 114 ff.; G. M. Trevelyan, *Illustrated English Social History* (London: Longmans, Green & Co., Ltd., 1954) , Vol. I, pp. 108 ff.; A. G. Dickens, *The English Reformation,* pp. 211 f.
[6] *Paidonomoi, praefecti educationi iuventutis.*

mit the churches to have their children for this kind of instruction, or to support and foster their studies at their personal expense. For, as has been said, they have given birth to their children for Christ the Lord and his Church and the State and pledged and consecrated them thus in the new birth of Baptism.

Therefore, for whatever offices of his Church and the State the Lord has signified that they ought to be prepared and trained, who would find it a burden to hand over his children and advance them toward those offices most eagerly, unless he wants to reject Christ the Lord and all his benefits at the same time? Nor could anyone choose a more honest and blessed condition of life than the one for which Christ our Maker and Savior has destined each individual.

Further, if some of the boys who have already learned reading, writing, and the catechism of our faith, or who even have applied themselves for some time to the learning of liberal arts, appear not to be gifted by the Lord for the reception of further academic instruction, let these be directed to other pursuits, each to that for which each seems more naturally endowed and gifted.

CHAPTER XLIX

The Restoration of Various Crafts and Honest Pursuits of Profit

In his singular kindness the Lord has given to this realm a very abundant supply of excellent wool. How many the crafts and how various the fine techniques of wool-making are is demonstrated by the techniques which have been imported into this realm from Spain, France, Belgium, and even from the Turks. All these techniques can be used by the English, and thus those very great amounts which are now expended in exporting wool and importing wool products and in the manufacture of these products can be gained for this realm. For it is certain that the English have enough ability and more so that they can learn any skills they put their minds to.[7]

In the same way, the wicked and perniciously widespread profiteering of idle and noxious merchants may be diminished for the state. Here too, therefore, an effort will have to be made to develop all possible wool-making techniques in this realm, through hiring technicians from wherever this is permitted and entrusting to them the adolescents and young men who are found to be gifted by the Lord for these skills. Nor should it be doubted that since the

[7] Cf. Trevelyan, *op. cit.*, pp. 129 f.; Pauck, *Das Reich Gottes*, pp. 87 ff.

Lord has given the English such an abundance of wool-making material, he also demands of them singular diligence that they themselves should prepare this material for human use, and not hasten to send it all away to be worked by others. For even if the English manufacture their wool to the utmost of their ability and need, there will still be an abundant surplus for exportation to other peoples.

Now, it is apparent that this island has been adorned by the Lord with such good soil and climate that it should be able to produce far richer farm products than it now does, if the fields would be cultivated with a right diligence and if all land were cultivated which used to be and should be cultivated on its own merits and for the good of the commonwealth, at the expense (at least partial if not entire) of the profit in wool. Insofar as this profit provides only harmful pomp and luxury, it should be turned over to the purpose of giving sustenance to human beings who are the sons of God. They say that this trade in wool has now so increased that in most places one man uses as much land for the pasture of his sheep as was used a short time ago to support the life of more than a thousand men.[8] But what person not completely destitute of the mind of Christ can fail to acknowledge that Christian princes must make it a major project that there should be as good men as possible everywhere who live for the glory of God; therefore, such princes must in every way be on guard lest a few evil and harmful men, such as they all are who try to advance their own interests more than those of the commonwealth, excited by the infinite stimulus of greed,[9] should displace men from the lands, and rob the state of its greatest riches and ornaments, namely, good citizens, and deprive the Church and heaven of worshipers praising God. The saying of Prov. 14:28 must be pondered: It is to the greater glory of the king if his people increase and multiply; it is a measure of diminishing majesty if his people diminish and decrease in number.

And so also this part must be included in a law which would suppress godless idleness in order that an industrious concern for agriculture and all farm work may be aroused.

For this it will be necessary: first, to designate for the pasture of sheep that portion of land which the Lord himself seems in his

---

[8] On the problem of "enclosures," see the literature quoted by Wendel in his edition of *De Regno Christi* and particularly Richard H. Tawney, *The Agrarian Problem in the Sixteenth Century* (London, 1912), pp. 147 ff.; 185 ff.; 219 ff.; 351 ff.; 362 ff.

[9] *Infinito tēs pleonexias oestro concitati.* Cf. Hopf, *Martin Bucer and the English Reformation*, pp. 19, 122 ff.

generosity especially to have provided for this work and which ancestral followers of God adapted to this use; secondly, that lands fit for planting should be rented for cultivation at a fair price. For this price really began to increase enormouly after the lands of the monks had come into the power of those men whose insatiable avarice for everything necessary for the sustaining of present life increases daily; lastly, that some men singularly endowed with a knowledge of agriculture and with zeal and industry, discovered by scouting wherever they are distributed through rural areas, should attack the laziness and correct the inertia of other farmers. In this way, many prudent men in many places have within a few years marvelously restored among their tenants an agriculture that had become almost extinct and they put an end to the extreme helplessness and need into which the neglect of farming had driven them.

In this way an interest will be aroused also for gardening so that not only the pleasures of the eyes and nostrils will be served, as is now the case, but also many salutary forms of nourishment supplied, as well as ready remedies for various diseases.

To these things must be added spinning so as to dispel the idleness which plagues the female sex not less than the male, as the outcry of so much wickedness indicates; this artful labor is now almost as much despised as its luxury is abused. Certainly, English soil rightly prepared therefor will not refuse to bear flax, nor are English women wanting in the ability to prepare it for various uses of their own and those of their husbands if they will only apply their own industry to this purpose.[10]

And so when this agricultural skill and diligence have been restored, not only the pernicious idleness of soul and body in either sex will be exchanged for employment and workmanship, and citizens made ready for the commonwealth with bodies strengthened and hearts aroused and instructed toward every virtue (which are clearly very great advantages for the state), but the annual crop will always be more easily produced and there will be a greater supply of livestock from grazing.

To these labors, which are no less pleasant to those who rightly regard God and nature than they are useful in many varied ways to the workers themselves and to the commonwealth, the Lord adds this blessing: as work and labor wonderfully harden and

[10] A similar proposal was made by Thomas More in his *Utopia* (pp. 68 ff.). Several of Bucer's suggestions in connection with the proposed Eighth Law against idleness bear a close resemblance to More's ideas of a justly ordered commonwealth.

strengthen their bodies for military service, their spirits are also singularly uplifted and endowed with strength and courage, so that in time of war they show themselves as fully as strong and ready defenders of their country as they are diligent and energetic farmers in time of peace.[11]

And so the commonwealth will obtain in this one operation the means of feeding itself, and, when necessary, of defending itself, nor will there be need of external or domestic military service, which, lost in luxury and idleness, is as harmful in peace as it is useless in war. Clearly the Roman republic was never defended more honorably or more successfully than when generals and dictators were summoned from the plow and, in the conscription for military service, the country people were preferred to the city people.[12]

When farming has been restored in this manner, in the raising of cattle as well as in the cultivation of fields and gardens, there will also be a great increase in leather from which one can make various useful as well as fine finished goods as other nations show to whom such a great quantity of leather is exported from this realm. And so if these skills of making various leather goods are made appealing to this people, so that the leather work is done here rather than that the leather is exported to other nations, a great many advantages would accrue to the realm. But all such things and their concomitant utility can be had in no other way than through a holy and honest occupation of the mind and exercise of the body in reputable and useful work.

Experts in these matters furthermore affirm that very many places on this island are not lacking in various kinds of metals, in the mining and preparation of which for human use a great multitude of men could be honestly and usefully employed! [13] And this offers the occasion also for the establishment of penalties for crimes for which the death penalty is normally not inflicted; such punishments would be far more effective (than those which are now in force) for correcting those who have fallen and for deterring the rest from crimes, and they would, moreover, produce some work product for the commonwealth. In this way, the ancient Romans and other nations used to condemn such dangerous people either

[11] Plato, *Laws* V, 737e.   [12] Columella, *De re rustica*, Preface.
[13] Bucer appears here to be dependent upon the pamphlets of Thomas Starkey, *A Dialogue between Cardinal Pole and Thomas Lupset,* ed. by J. M. Cowper and S. Herrtage (Early English Text Society, Extra Series, Vols. XII and XXXII; London, 1871–1878), p. 173, and John Hales, *A Discourse of the Common Weal of this Realm of England,* ed. by E. Lamond (Cambridge, 1893), pp. 92, 126 ff.

to the mining of metals or to quarries and other harder and more sordid tasks, which were nevertheless useful to human life and very often necessary.[14] How much better is this method of punishing criminals than the one which now prevails, when men are long detained in the idleness of chains and prisons and for the most part rendered useless for the future by the length of time they spend in prisons or in chains or in harmful exile among foreign peoples.

Then also a great amount of cloth becomes worn out in this realm from which an enormous supply of rags could be collected to make paper, rags which now are exported to foreign lands and reimported as paper that is expensive and not of a very good quality. If, therefore, mills and factories for making paper were built, as could be cheaply done, also this skill, the uses of which are so widely extended, would be encouraged in this realm and many men would benefit from this work, by providing both them and their families with an honest living and the commonwealth with a fruitful industry.[15]

So, then, if from childhood every individual citizen were assigned to the pursuit of some special skill, either in philosophy or in manual industry, and if those not really suited for government service or that of religion, or for letters and philosophy, or for governing or defending the state, were shunted aside to manual or base labor, that fertile root of all vices, godless idleness, cut off at the source, would easily be driven out from all the common people and an immense advantage to the commonwealth would be gained with a most desirable establishment of morals and conformity to every virtue.

This would be the case especially if the nobility were a shining example to the common people, as it should be. For this is the purpose for which the nobles have received from the Lord such wealth and dignified name and rank that, as they excel the rest of the people in these matters, and much more in wisdom and broad knowledge of philosophy and also in every form of virtue, they might seek to the utmost of their ability the interests and advantage of the whole commonwealth and its individual citizens, in times of peace as well as in times of war.

Everyone knows that the chief responsibilities of the nobility are the following: in peace, to assist Your Majesty energetically in the just and generous governance of God's people entrusted to him; in war, to be brave and advantageous defenders. If those who belong to this class wish to prepare themselves for these duties,

[14] *Digest* XLVIII, 19, 8, 4–10; *Code* IX, 47, 11. Cf. More, *Utopia,* p. 69.
[15] More, *Utopia,* pp. 157 f.

they will obviously have to be quite busy and overcome their laziness. While they are preparing their strength and faculties for both kinds of responsibility, those necessary for peace and war, they must acquire the following for the salutary governance of the people of God: a precise wisdom and a comprehensive knowledge of government; familiarity with laws; justice and sanctity, which are closely connected with the trustworthiness and authority that rulers always need; for necessary and successful defense: military knowledge, a brave contempt of dangers, an enormous love of virtue and country and of all mankind, and finally, an uncommon strength and agility of body.

But if anyone of this class of men happens to be, as is often the case, prevented by physical or mental handicaps, or both, from performing a service to the state by advising, judging, ruling, or fighting, he should consecrate himself to farming, gardening, and cattle-raising. For most of the nobles have lands and cattle, and the practice of these skills is very fitting for nobles, unless it was unworthy work for very noble and outstanding men like Abraham, Isaac, Jacob, Job, David, and almost innumerable other patriarchs highly praised in Holy Scriptures. In the same class was that great king of the Persians, Cyrus the Younger, whom Xenophon so greatly praises for his interest in and love for agriculture.[16] And among the Romans there were: M. Curius, who triumphed over the Samnites, the Sabines, and Pyrrhus; L. Quintius Cincinnatus, who was summoned from the plow to the dictatorship, and this was a most happy augur for Roman affairs; M. Valerius Corvinus, who extended a life of farming to his hundredth year; Cato the Censor, and very many others.[17]

If, then, the order of nobles should turn to such industry (and there is nothing more fitting for them and more useful for the maintenance and growth of the nobility), it will be easy to cut off every occasion for that godless idleness which is made possible by the profit-seeking of noxious hucksters and retailers.

CHAPTER L

THE REFORM OF MARKETING

Marketing is a business which is honest and necessary for the commonwealth if it confines itself to the export and import of things that are advantageous to the commonwealth for living well

---

[16] Xenophon, *Oeconomia* IV, 20–24.
[17] Cicero, *De senectute* 59, 55, 56, 60, 51.

and in a holy way, but not those which encourage and foster impious pomp and luxury. In order to benefit men's piety, this purpose ought never to be absent from the thoughts and deeds of Christians but should always be considered and weighed as scrupulously as possible.

Therefore, inasmuch as merchants pretty commonly reject this purpose, they burst forth with wickedness and greed,[18] so that next to the false clergy there is no type of men more pestiferous to the commonwealth. For, in the first place, for the sweet odor of gain, of which they accumulate an immense amount with little work through their nefarious skills, and for the splendor of pomp and luxury, of which they recognize no measure or limit, they attract the more outstanding talents, which if they were dedicated to philosophy, could be of very great use both to the State and the Church. In the second place, just as Plutus is not unrealistically depicted as blind and fearful,[19] they blind and emasculate the hearts of well-born adolescents and youth. For they cover their minds with the darkness of perverse judgment, so that they judge nothing to be important but to excel in the accumulation of wealth, through good and evil means, and in the expenditure of what has been accumulated in all kinds of worthless ways of life.[20]

This matter is a grave occasion for envy, and occurs not without danger and harm to many, indeed to the entire commonwealth, as these harpies push themselves to the fore and then bend and soften up all disciples they can find with an extreme adulation for all who they suspect have the ability to resist their destructive activities, making them at the same time the recipients of their largess. And since they must often live immoderately, they perpetrate frauds in business, multiply profits wherever they can, increase monopolies in order to make a gain not only for their limitless luxury but also for the constant increase in the interest they are taking.[21] It also happens frequently that they influence the councils and impede the law courts of the princes for their own ends, so as to remove the obstacles to their artful trickery. They imitate Verres, who said that he stole not only enough for his own luxury, however extreme, but also in order to have enough to give to his

---

[18] *Pleonexias* ("greed").

[19] Aristophanes, *Ploutos*, v. 86 ff.

[20] Bucer looked upon all business and trade carried on for the sake of profit with great suspicion and even hostility because he believed them to be irreconcilable with Christian morality. Cf. also, Plato, *Republic* VIII, 544b–555a; *Laws* XI, 916d–917e; Aristotle, *Politics* I, 9, 14, 1257b.

[21] Cf. C. Hopf, *Martin Bucer and the English Reformation*, pp. 122 ff.

patrons, defenders, and the judges themselves so that he might escape the penalties for his thefts.[22]

Furthermore, they daily invent astonishing enticements for the purchase of their trifling wares, which are designed and prepared only for impious luxury and pomp, and they seduce nobles and other wealthy men of little thrift into buying them. And when they do not have enough money for these trifles which are esteemed as the ornaments of the nobility and its social status) , there is at hand the money of the merchants, but at interest, and such a poisonous interest that within a very brief time whole families are destroyed and overthrown.[23]

To this point of ruin these leeches of the commonwealth bring a great number of people by their ostentatious luxury, while men of more honorable origin and station judge it disgraceful to yield to the merchants who have but recently emerged from an obscure and sordid station through their nefarious skills. And so while these emulate the excessive luxury of the merchants in the splendor and magnificence of their buildings, in the ornateness of their clothing and other adornments, in the pomp and lavishness of banquets and other displays of luxury, they bring their own patrimony to ruin and so fail in their resources that their better belongings are transferred to those very merchants themselves. Thus the commonwealth is daily drained of men of finer and more generous spirit, as can be seen by the ruin of so many outstanding noble families which has been accomplished within the space of a few years, and by the irresponsibility and sloth in regard to all the pursuits useful to the commonwealth on the part of those who succeed the old families in power and dignity.

Since in so many ways this crooked kind of merchants and tradesmen [24] is harmful and pernicious for the people of God, there must also be a chapter for the reform of merchandising in the law under which, for the suppression of godless idleness, a wholesome industry is to be restored.

And in this it must be ordered, first, that nobody should be allowed to enter merchandising whom officials have not judged suitable for this sort of thing, having found him to be pious, a lover of the commonwealth rather than of private interest, eager for sobriety and temperance, vigilant and industrious. Secondly, that these should not import or export merchandise other than what

---

[22] Cicero, *In Verrem actio prima* XIV, 40.
[23] A law of 1545 (37 Henry VIII, c. 9, *Statutes of the Realm,* Vol. III, p. 996) limited interest to 10 percent but actually it was frequently much higher.
[24] Chrēmatistōn.

Your Majesty has decreed. And he shall decree that only those things are to be exported of which the people of the realm really have an abundance so that their export may be of no less benefit to the people of this realm, to whom these things are surplus, than to those who take them to foreign countries and make a profit on them. So also he should permit no merchandise to be imported except what he judges good for the pious, sober, and salutary use of the commonwealth. Finally, that a definite and fair price should be established for individual items of merchandise, which can easily be arranged and is very necessary (so fiery is human avarice) for conserving justice and decency among the citizens.

The same statutes must apply to peddlars and retailers, to which task, as it is lowly and sordid, no one should be admitted unless he is lacking in ability or has a physical incapacity so as to render him unsuitable for more liberal skills, as was the opinion of Plato also.[25]

CHAPTER LI

THE CARE OF PUBLIC INNS

Public decency furthermore demands that public inns and hospices be entrusted to the particular care only of men who have been recognized to be endowed with piety, chastity, and decency, so that they may take an interest not only in the physical well-being of the guests but also in the holiness and integrity of life and morals. Lazy men, who are wasters of their inheritance, whether they are on a journey or are local people, should be excluded from these places.

CHAPTER LII

THOSE WHO HAVE NO APTITUDE FOR HONORABLE SKILLS SHOULD BE REDUCED TO MANUAL LABOR AND HUMBLE TASKS

People who are found not to be endowed with any particular skill should be designated to humble and harder work, whether they do work by the day in proportion to their need or commit themselves to service for a certain period of time. It will be the duty of a supervisor to determine their trustworthiness and indus-

[25] Plato, *Republic* II, 371 c–d.

try in performing their work and to pay for their labors in an equitable way.[26]

CHAPTER LIII

Prefects Must Be Appointed for Skills and Labor

For this procedure of assigning citizens to definite virtuous and whole lives, whether philosophical or mechanical, and for their assignment to work useful to the commonwealth, it will be necessary to appoint guardians and overseers in charge of individual crafts and classes of skilled and unskilled laborers in order to make sure that everyone applies himself seriously to the skill or work for which he has been designated, either in order to learn it or to practice it. And in case any persons are found to have been negligent in their duty, if they were enrolled in the more liberal disciplines, either in the service of religion or that of the state, they should be reassigned to baser skills and tasks. Drones should not be tolerated in any class of citizens, least of all in the rank of clerics and of men of letters, who should outshine the other citizens also as examples of industry.[27]

CHAPTER LIV

Honest Games

Further, since human nature has that weakness by which it cannot always concentrate on grave and serious matters but demands other rest besides sleep, there must also be provision made for certain relaxations from work and useful studies and a certain recreation of the strength both of the spirit and of the body in play and games, especially when grave and serious obligations have been satisfied, and by all means in proper moderation and prudence, so that the kind of games is prescribed and presented for adults and youth in which there need not be feared any relaxation of morals or delight in wicked idleness and from which there may also be gained a certain strengthening of health as well as some improvement in the cultivation of the mind. As a pagan philosopher wrote, "We have not been so fashioned by nature that we seem to have been made for sport and games but rather for hardship and for certain more serious and more important pursuits.[28]

---

[26] Plato, *Republic* II, 371e; *Laws* XI, 921 a–b.
[27] Plato, *Republic* III, 415 b–c.   [28] Cicero, *De officiis* I, 29.

These games must be derived from musical and gymnastic art.[29] From music one will take poems and songs that present and proclaim nothing futile, nothing inappropriate to the Christian profession and nothing obscene and wicked, but rather the praises of God and the Savior derived from all his works and judgments as these are expressed in Holy Scripture; the praise of virtues and of men excelling in virtue; laws and precepts of a pious life, and well-known and helpful historical narratives.

To these may be added dances (but the dances of pious girls must be separate from the dances of young boys) which may be danced to pure and holy songs,[30] with chaste and modest motion befitting those who profess piety, as Miriam, the sister of Moses, danced and the matrons of Israel when they had crossed the Red Sea and sang the praises of God for such a wonderful delivery of their nation from the slavery of Egypt (Ex. 15:20-21). Such was the dance of holy girls who celebrated David and Saul in a song of victory when they returned from the slaughter of the Philistines (I Sam. 18:6), the kind of dance the Holy Spirit requires in Ps. 149:3 and 150:4 when he says, "Praise the Lord with timbrel and dance."

For what do we remember and sing about in this world which more properly fills us with joy and arouses exultant gladness in us than those innumerable blessings and benefits of the divine love toward us? God has manifested this love to us in our creation and the creation of all other things for our sake, and he continually manifests it in very wisely governing and so munificently preserving us and the whole world because of us. He exhibits his love also in imparting his law and religion, divine and saving wisdom, in giving his Son, our eternal advocate, and with him all things, the Holy Spirit, a new and heavenly life, the blessed fellowship of his Church, and so many external advantages and gifts, both public and private.

In pious singing, therefore, we are reminded of these gifts from such an immense goodness of God. And should the spirit not rightly leap with joy and gladness and excite the body to bear witness to this joy and impel it to express this gladness, by action, however, becoming to every age and nation? Certainly a deeper recollection of divine blessings strongly moved David, although he was a king, when he was bringing in the Ark of the Lord, so that he danced before it (II Sam. 6:12-15). He was a Palestinian, I admit, of a nation far more emotional and uninhibited than our

---

[29] Plato, *Republic* II, 376e.
[30] Plato, *Laws* II, 654 ff.

European people. But since our young people delight in dancing, why are such dances not introduced among us too, who have become citizens of heaven [31] through the blood of Christ, so that they spring forth from a pious and holy exultation of the mind over the goodness of God and strengthen and increase that exultation and inflame the spirit with a desire for all piety?

Certainly if we belong to Christ, if he is our life, if eternal salvation is from him and about him, every cause of joy and gladness ought to be ours; and complete exultation both of spirit and of body should be aroused, something which anyone will acknowledge who has experienced but a little of what it is "to love God with your whole heart, your whole mind, and with all your strength" (Luke 10:27), indeed, who has ever known any of the power of human love and exultant gladness.

This is clearly true for all believers in Christ: "Exult in the Lord, O you righteous! Praise becomes the righteous. Celebrate the Lord with the lyre, make melody to him with the harp of ten strings. Sing to him a new song, make a fine melody with jubilation" (Ps. 33:1-3). Likewise: "I shall bless the Lord at all times, his praise will be always in my mouth. My soul will glory in the Lord; the meek will hear and be glad" (Ps. 34:2-3). And again: "My heart is prepared, O God, my heart is prepared, I shall sing and make melody; awake, O my glory, awake harp and lyre; I shall awaken early, I shall celebrate you among the peoples, O Lord, and I shall sing to you among the nations, because your great kindness extends to the heavens, and to the clouds your truth" (Ps. 57:8-11). And in another place: "My soul will be satisfied with abundance and fullness, and my mouth will speak praise with exultant lips" (Ps. 63:5). And again: "Bless the Lord, O my soul, and whatever is within me bless his holy name; bless the Lord, O my soul" (Ps. 103:1-2). "I shall praise God as long as I live, and I shall sing melody to my God as long as I exist" (Ps. 146:2). "My soul magnifies the Lord, and my spirit exults in God my Savior" (Luke 1:46-47).

Thrice miserable and lost are people whom nothing can delight except what is, if not obscene and dirty, yet inane, profitless, ridiculous, and unworthy of man. Also, Plato was of the opinion that it should not be allowed privately, much less publicly, that any songs be sung or dances danced except ones which are chaste, holy, and suited to foster and promote piety.[32] For this reason, no singing nor any kind of dancing should be allowed, either privately or pub-

---

[31] *Quibus coelestis contigit per sanguinem Christi municipatus.*
[32] Plato, *Laws* II, 660a; VII, 801 c–d; 802 a–c.

licly, which has not been approved by wise and religious men to whom this responsibility will be referred by Your Majesty.

Youth could also perform comedies and tragedies, and by such means a useful form of entertainment, honorable and contributing toward an increase of piety, may be staged for the people; but it will be necessary that devout and wise men experienced in the Kingdom of Christ compose these comedies and tragedies, in which there may be presented on the stage the plans, actions, and events of mankind, whether common and ordinary as it occurs in comedies or unique and eliciting admiration as it is characteristic of tragedies. All this will contribute toward a correction of morals and a pious orientation to life.[33]

If a comedy is presented, take, for example, the quarrel of the shepherds of Abraham and Lot and their separation from each other (Gen. 13:5-12). For although Abraham and Lot are heroic figures appropriate to tragedy, yet the quarrels that arose among their shepherds because they had too many sheep were common and ordinary. It was also common and ordinary that these holy householders were somewhat disturbed with each other by the quarrels of their servants, so much so that Abraham rightly decided that they should separate from one another. In a comedy of this kind, the following themes might be treated and presented for useful entertainment and pious instruction:

First, how very kindly God treats all who have left something for his sake, as Abraham and Lot had left their native soil and many of their dear kindred at the call of the Lord.

Second, that men, by the suggestion of Satan and the corruption of their own nature, are often wont to call down upon themselves many disadvantages in the face of the more liberal blessings of God in their external affairs, as the shepherds of Abraham and Lot took the occasion of the great number of their sheep to quarrel among each other and disturb their masters.

Third, there could be depicted that disease of servants and domestics by which they are accustomed to commit their masters to false and untimely accusations of each other because of their own iniquitous wranglings.

Fourth, the weakness of human nature for preserving mutual benevolence and tranquillity could be explained.

Fifth, how much better it is for friends and relatives to dwell apart and to get together more rarely and thus to keep their feelings toward each other more friendly and peaceful than to stay together or to get together more frequently with offended feelings

[33] Aristotle, *Poetics* II, 1448a.

and disturbances or at least with the danger of some offense and disturbance.

Sixth, the example of Abraham can be praised as a role of real humanity and pious humility, by which he as the older one and an uncle yielded and gave the option of choosing a place to the younger man, his nephew, and also the result of this humility, the very ample kindness and munificence of God toward Abraham.

In the same manner, pious comedy will be supplied with material rich and very suitable for the building of piety from the story of Isaac's seeking, finding, and marrying his bride, Rebekah (Gen. 24:2-67). From this story there can be described the pious solicitude of parents in seeking religious marriages for their children; the good faith and efficiency of reputable servants; the power of holy prayer; the desired outcome of events as an answer to pious prayer; the character of the girl, a really modest person and also humane and hospitable; likewise, the readiness of the parents to marry their daughters piously; also their humanity in not joining them with those with whom they do not wish to be united; likewise, the wonderful power of God in uniting people in marriage, which appears in the case of Rebekah, when she so readily consents to set out with a man whom she has not yet seen, and this with the abandonment of parents, brothers, everything at home, and her fatherland. Here there comes up for praise the ingenuity of modesty, as Rebekah was not ashamed to confess her willingness to marry a pious man, and again the force of honest decency and modesty, that at the sight of Isaac she got down from the camel and covered her face. Here may also be preached the piety of Isaac while he was yet a youth, observing the evening hour of prayer so religiously; likewise, his singular love for his wife. It will also be appropriate to commend a holy marriage which is contracted by those who are known and joined to each other by religion.

A not dissimilar plot could be derived also from the story of Jacob, in the part in which it is described that in fear of his brother, leaving his parents, he went to his uncle Laban and there was enriched with two wives, children, and great wealth, by the goodness of God, because of the faithful service he performed for his uncle. Likewise, how on his return he was restored to the favor of his brother (Gen. 28:10 to 33:20). There is also a tragic aspect to this story in the apparition of the Lord on the way and the struggle with the angel. But these consolations of God are not foreign to any real Christians, although they are not set forth to all in visions and signs of this sort as they were to Jacob. For it is clearly a mark of all Christians that they live in God and before

God and have the Father and the Son abiding in them and angels ministering to them.[34]

Although the Scriptures contain very many stories from which holy comedies befitting Christians can be portrayed, apt and pious poets can nevertheless produce many such things from other stories and from occurrences in daily life.

The Scriptures everywhere offer an abundant supply of material for tragedies, in almost all the stories of the holy patriarchs, kings, prophets, and apostles, from the time of Adam, the first parent of mankind. For these stories are filled with divine and heroic personages, emotions, customs, actions, and also events which turned out contrary to what was expected, which Aristotle calls a reversal.[35] Since all such things have so wonderful a power of confirming faith in God and enkindling a desire and love for God and likewise an admiration of piety and righteousness, and of engendering and increasing the horror of impiety and all perversity, how much more does it befit Christians to derive their poems from these things, in which they can represent the great and illustrious plans, efforts, characters, emotions, and events of mankind, rather than from the godless fables and stories of the pagans.

It must be observed, however, that when in both kinds of poetic material, comic and tragic, the activities and sins of men are described and actively presented to be seen with the eyes, it should be done in such a way that although the crimes of reprobate men are related, yet a certain terror of divine judgment and horror of sin should appear in these things, and a shameless daring and an exultant delight in crimes should not be expressed. It is better here to take something away from poetic fitness rather than from the concern for edifying the piety of the spectators, which demands that in every representation of sin there be felt the condemnation of one's conscience and the horrible fear of God's judgment.

But when pious and good actions are shown, they should express as clearly as possible a happy, secure, and confident sense of the divine mercy, but moderate and diffident as regards the self, and a joyful trust in God and his promises, with holy and spiritual pleasure in doing good. This is the way by which one can present most skillfully the saints' character, way of life, and emotion for the establishment of all piety and virtue among the people.

In order that the people of Christ may receive this enjoyment

[34] For a discussion of dramatic literature produced at the time of the Reformation, cf. Hugo Holstein, *Die Reformation im Spiegelbilde der dramatischen Litteratur des sechzehnten Jahrhunderts* (Halle, 1866), and particularly, Günter Sknopnik, *Das Strassburger Schultheater* (Frankfurt, 1935).

[35] Aristotle, *Poetics* XI, 1452a.

from holy comedies and tragedies, men must be put in charge also of this matter who have a singular understanding of poetry as well as a known and constant zeal for the Kingdom of Christ so that no comedy or tragedy is enacted which these persons have not seen and decreed fit for performance. These will also take care that nothing shallow, or histrionic is admitted in the acting, but that everything is shown by means of a holy and grave, though agreeable action, for the saints alone, in which there are represented not so much the actualities and activities of men and their feelings and troubles, but rather their morals and character; these should be presented in such a way that what has been piously planned and rightly done arouses the spectators to an eager imitation, but what has been wrongly designed and done, strengthens them in their detestation of it and stimulates them to a vigilant avoidance of it.

When these precautions are observed, much material for the diversion of youth can certainly be presented which is indeed useful for nourishing and promoting virtue, especially when a desire and an interest have been aroused for this sort of comedies and tragedies, both in the vernacular language and in Latin and Greek. There are now available some of these comedies and tragedies with which one cannot be displeased. Although in the comedies of our time the scholars miss that acumen and wit and pleasantness of speech which people admire in Aristophanes, Terence, and the tales of Plautus, and in the tragedies the gravity, cleverness, and elegance of dialogue of Sophocles, Euripides, and Seneca, yet those who want to know the Kingdom of Christ and who desire to learn the wisdom of living unto God do not miss, in this poetry of our people, heavenly doctrine, emotions, behavior, speech, and adventures worthy of the sons of God. It is desirable, however, that those to whom God has given more of a talent for this sort of thing will prefer to use it for his glory rather than to retard the pious enthusiasms of others by their untimely criticisms, seeing that it is more satisfactory to stage comedies and tragedies in which, even if they lack poetic art, the knowledge of eternal life is excellently exhibited, rather than those in which for the sake of some contribution to the cultivation of genius and language, spirit and behavior are dirtied by filthy and scurrilous imitation.

Now, from gymnastic art those sports will have to be proposed to youth which, besides what they contribute to the health and preservation of the body and the production of graceful movements, also render men fit and ready for military service and the advantageous use of arms. Young men should therefore exercise themselves in running, jumping, wrestling, horseback riding, the handling of all arms and weapons which are used for open and hand-to-hand combat, the arrangement of battle formations, the positioning of camp, and mock battle.[36] To these, nobles may add the exercise of hunting.[37]

These exercises which pertain to military science ought to be so constituted and conducted in such a serious manner that they approximate as much as possible the actual operations of war, as Plato has said.[38] If young people are able to learn military science and the practices of war at home and in their own country, under good laws and pious magistrates, there will be no need to send them to military service in foreign lands, which (on the assumption that wars waged in these times are just) is so replete with wickedness and lacking in every discipline that is indeed required by Christian soldiers, that they who hope for successful warfare and victory from the Lord cannot put their own sons into that army, according to the words of the psalm: "It is God who girds me with strength for war and prepares my path" (Ps. 18:32).

In charge of these sports, as of the kind previously mentioned, there should always be men singularly experienced in the field involved, men of universal wisdom most zealous for all piety and virtue, who are admired and therefore have the authority and power to relate and to adapt all youthful sport to a zeal for and practice of the virtues, which is the one goal of all sports among Christians; for we have been created for the praise of God and the glory of his name and we have been redeemed by the blood of the Son of God in order to obtain the salvation of our neighbors and not in order to be destroyed in pernicious buffoonery and empty vanity.

Therefore, for the pious and wholesome regulation of sports, singing, and dancing, there should be issued this seventh chapter of the law by which pious industry will come to be repaired among the citizens. For as by these methods each citizen is applied from childhood to good skills and practices salutary to the commonwealth, the use of diversions such as we have described will be ordered, and godless and pernicious idleness, that perennial and overflowing spring of vices and of every wickedness, will be removed from the citizens; there will be procured for them a pious and holy industry, an inexhaustible vein abounding with every advantage and convenience, by which the commonwealth will be spiritually and physically adorned and wonderfully helped. For we

[36] Plato, *Laws* VII, 803c, 813 d–e.   [37] Plato, *Laws* VII, 824 a–c.
[38] Plato, *Laws* VII, 813 d–e.

must very much deplore and be ashamed of the fact that so many ancient nations, although ignorant of God, drove out idleness and laziness so severely and educated and compelled their citizens to serious activities useful to the state (one reads that Draco the Athenian was of the opinion that laziness deserved the death penalty [39]), and that we who regard ourselves as the sons of God so greatly neglect the responsibility for this holy and salutary matter that the Turks ridicule and detest us particularly for this reputation.[40] For neither at home nor in military service do they tolerate idle men, with the result that they abound both in men and power and that they have achieved and continue to achieve remarkable victories.

So much for the civil education of youth, the suppression of idleness, and the introduction and increase of honest crafts and business affairs.

CHAPTER LV

THE NINTH LAW: CONTROLLING LUXURY AND HARMFUL EXPENSES

Since pleasure and luxury are the greatest pitfall for healthy industry, Your Majesty should also arrange for his people a sumptuary law against these pests of human life in order to prohibit, as unworthy of those who profess piety, all luxury, pomp, and excess in housing, clothing, ornamentation of the body, food and drink, and all things contributing more to the delight of the flesh than to the virtue of spirit and the true utility of the commonwealth.[41]

Your Majesty will readily establish a standard for all these things in conformity with our religion once he has considered that to Christian men, whatever they do, "whether they eat, or drink, or whatever else they do in word or in work, everything is to be done in the name of the Lord Jesus for the glory of God," so that in these things too and in all our actions "we may give thanks to God and the Father through him," and be on our guard "not to put

[39] Plutarch, *Vita Solonis* XVII, 1–2.
[40] Because of the fact that during the first half of the sixteenth century (i.e., during the period of the Reformation), the Turks under Suleiman II threatened to invade the Holy Roman Empire from the Balkan peninsula, they were viewed not only with apprehension and fear but also with great interest, especially so because they were infidels. However, their political and social discipline was greatly admired by many, particularly by the critics of the feudalistic *corpus Christianum* and, among these, also by the Protestant Reformers.
[41] Cf. More, *Utopia*, pp. 27, 75.

any stumbling block in anyone's path, neither for Jews nor Greeks nor the Church of God"; but we should work "to please everyone in all things and not seek our own interests" either in property or in pleasure, "but that which is of interest to the many, that they may be saved" (I Cor. 10:31-33; Col. 3:17; Rom. 15:2). These words of the Holy Spirit expressed to us in I Cor., ch. 10, and Col., ch. 3, should be religiously pondered, for he has here prescribed for us a certain rule for the use and regulation of all things by which the life of the body is maintained, fostered, and adorned.

Let the words which the same Holy Spirit specifically commanded through his apostles, Saint Peter and Saint Paul, concerning the dress and adornment of women be added: "Similarly," he says, "I wish women to adorn themselves modestly and sensibly in seemly apparel, not with braided hair or gold or pearls or costly attire but by good deeds, as befits women who profess the worship of God" (I Tim. 2:9-10).

And through Saint Peter: "Of these women let not the adorning be in the curling of hair and ornamentation of gold and the wearing of garments, but let their adornment be the hidden person of the heart, with the imperishable jewel of a gentle and quiet spirit, which spirit is a precious thing before God. So once the holy women who hoped in God used to adorn themselves" (I Peter 3:3-5).

Let us ponder these precepts of the Holy Spirit as they have been directed to women, to whom, however, as to the weaker sex, God has always indulged a little adornment and concern for the body, so much so that among his singular blessings on his people he has numbered the adornment of daughters as compared with the sculptured and ornamented corners of the Temple or of any exceptionally well-built palace (Ps. 144:12); how much more, therefore, do these precepts refer to men whom it befits to express the image of God more perfectly and to excel the women in the full development of sanctity as their heads (cf. I Cor. 11:7)!

Let us observe, therefore, that all the decoration and adornment of Christians (of women and much more of men) are found in the interior man, in reverence, moderation, gentleness, a tranquil spirit disturbed and corrupted by no depraved affections, in good works, i.e., the benefits that we render to others by feeding them, giving them drink, by receiving them under our roof, by clothing, caring for and consoling whoever need these ministrations (Matt. 25:35-40). Whoever have been really intent on such things will surely have small concern for worldly dress and adornment: indeed, whatever time or money they spend in the adornment of their own body, they will deem lost for that true and salutary adornment of everyone by which they strive to gain the approval of God and his angels and the Church of God.

And the Holy Spirit, judging that these precepts about the internal and proper garb and adornment of Christian men would not be sufficient to repress the foolish and childish affectation of external dress, added: Christians ought not to be adorned with the curling of hair, gold, silver, gems, and costly clothing, not because these are not gifts of God given for the use of men, especially the saints, but in order to show that although his sons can and should also use these gifts which he has supplied for the observance of public decorum according to the vocation and function of each person, yet he does not wish his sons to put their concern in these matters, lest they surrender to these adornments and be captivated by them and attach more importance to them than their callings and their civic offices demand for the preservation of orderly discipline and the protocol of the state.

In the consideration and regulation of these things, lest anyone deceive himself, the Holy Spirit has set a certain norm which must always be respected when he concluded his precepts concerning the dress and adornment of the body with these words: "This is becoming to women who profess piety and a worship of God through good works" (I Tim. 2:10). Likewise: "So the holy women who hoped in God used to adorn themselves" (I Peter 3:5). For those who wish to live up to the profession of piety and the worship of God and who put all their hope in the living God clearly ought to manifest a pleasing worship of God, glorify the holy name of God, propagate and adorn his Kingdom, even in dress, even in housing, even in food, drink, care of the body, in all corporal matters and activities, and in such a way as to declare themselves in these matters also "crucified to the world, and the world to them," and to be abhorrent of all glory which does not consist "in the cross of our Lord Jesus Christ" (Gal. 6:14); inasmuch as they are in Christ, all Christians should show themselves to be, in all dress and adornment of the body, a new creature, whose whole concern it is day by day more fully "to put off the old man with his erratic and damnable desires and put on our Lord Jesus Christ, taking no care for the flesh and for its desires" (Rom. 13:14; Eph. 4:22), and on this account to escape in every way from conformity to this age, i.e., to the lost men of this world (Rom. 12:2).

Cicero, a heathen writer, recommended that the norm to be observed in clothing and other care of the body should be found in this, "that we be approved by those with whom and among whom we live," [42] but we are not of this world, "our city is in heaven" (Phil. 3:20) ; we must live everywhere and always in the sight of God the Father, Son, and Holy Spirit, and of all the angels and holy men of God in heaven and on earth. In these things, therefore, it is necessary for us to take the trouble and work to be approved and to approve ourselves in all dress and adornment of the body before God, our heavenly Creator and Father; his Son, crucified for our sake, our only Redeemer; the Holy Spirit, our teacher and perfector; and all his angels and saints (Matt. 16:27) .

A person mindful and always considerate of these things will never fail to observe a practical and decent modesty in all external appearance, which is pleasing to God and useful to the Church of God, and he will not detract, diminish, or impede the duty of love for anyone by excessive expenditure, but so as not to confound, neglect, or dishonor the distinctive adornments of persons which should properly be observed in these matters, such as those of princes, nobles, aristocrats, and magistrates. And so according to this regulation, Your Majesty will give to his people vestiary and sumptuary laws; he will control all luxury in housing, dining, dress, and adornment in such a way that, as he will happily arouse, promote, and strengthen a necessary modesty in Christians and frugality among his people, so he will also remove great public and private damage from his realm which results in these days from those extravagant luxuries in trifles that are devised both in foreign lands and at home.

CHAPTER LVI

The Tenth Law: On the Revision and Elaboration of Civil Laws

When Your Majesty has supported and strengthened wholesome industry for his people in the manner indicated, so that from childhood everyone will be educated and assigned to a definite task and function in life useful to the commonwealth, and everyone will be urged to do his duty perseveringly, efficiently, and energetically; and when he has also driven out and suppressed all intemperance, wickedness, and luxury, the next thing to do will be to clarify and strengthen those laws by which communication of obligations and exchange of goods are regulated among men.

For everywhere I hear good men complain that the laws of this realm concerning property and its exchange, inheritances, and

[42] Cicero, *De officiis* I, 35 f.

other kinds of civil commerce and contracts are very obscure and complicated, and so written in a certain obsolete language that they can be understood by no one who has not both learned that language and very studiously pursued an understanding of these laws; and hence it comes about that very many of those who in some way have come to know these laws and are counselors of law rather than of justice abuse these very laws as traps for men and nets for money. Since this disadvantage to the realm could not be tolerated, they say that that most excellent prince, Your Majesty's father, was once so moved as to delegate certain men to correct and explain these laws.[43]

But since these designated reformers [44] of laws, either terrified by the scope of the task or hindered and distracted by other affairs, have as yet brought forth no remedy for this evil, and it is said that the abuse and perversion of laws are daily becoming stronger, it will certainly be the duty of Your Majesty to elaborate quickly and firmly the means by which these laws may be clarified as correctly and plainly as possible and so defined in language as well as in method that, inasmuch as they ought to be observed by all the citizens, they can also be read and understood by all. Then all occasion for bewildering good and simple men and taking advantage of them will be taken away from disreputable lawyers and shysters.[45] All men of wisdom agree on this, that no government can stand without laws [46] which the citizens should accept and follow as the dictates and prescriptions of God. But what difference does it make whether no laws exist or those which do exist are unknown to the citizens?

Therefore, for the restitution of the Kingdom of Christ among his subjects and for the procurement and the preservation of justice, peace, and the well-being of his subjects, Your Majesty will give his attention to the selection of most excellent men from the entire realm, men of piety toward God and country, who also have a knowledge of and desire for what is good and equitable; to these he will assign the task with all possible speed to define and explain all the laws which affect, influence, or oblige Your Majesty's subjects, as regards the individual's duties of justice to God, country, and neighbor and this with perspicuity, brevity, and orderliness so

---

[43] Bucer here refers to the Common Law which was written in Old French. Thomas More (*Utopia*, p. 114) and Thomas Starkey (*Dialogue*, pp. 122, 136, and 192 ff.) made similar complaints. There is no record of a project initiated by Henry VIII, as Bucer suggests, to codify civil law.

[44] *Instauratores legum.*

[45] Cf. the similar complaint of Thomas Starkey, *Dialogue*, p. 191.

[46] Cicero, *De legibus* II, 5; III, 1.

that they may not only be understood by all but also easily remembered and observed.

In order that this may be brought about more conveniently, they should also be redacted, after the manner of the ancients, into certain brief epitomes and chants which may quickly be learned by growing children in their childhood instruction and chanted by all the people.[47] For should not the diligence and zeal which the wise men of the pagans are known to have observed in order to improve citizenship, also be applied by Christian princes? [48]

Inasmuch as no sanction or constitution made for the regulation of men's life and behavior can sustain the name of law unless it is derived from the principal law of God and received according to the mind of the provident ruler of all things, so also all the law of God and the entire teaching of the prophets depend on these two headings as our Savior Jesus Christ has affirmed: "Thou shalt love God Jehovah with thy whole heart, thy whole soul, and all thy strength, and thy neighbor as thyself" (Luke 10:27), certainly all laws, whether divinely handed down or issued by men, must be referred to these two headings. In all things whatsoever, therefore, which are known, commanded, or forbidden, all who give, revise, and institute laws must first of all see to it that only that is prescribed to men which is accommodated to a pure and sincere worship of God and a firm and dutiful love and beneficence toward one's neighbor, and that whatever is contrary to these things is prohibited.

Therefore, whatever Your Majesty will order concerning the teaching, strengthening, promotion, and protection of Christ's true religion, about which we have previously advised,[49] what is contained in the first table of the divine law will hold first place in the laws of his realm and will embrace all duties of piety as they are enjoined in the following four commandments (Ex. 20:2-10): the one true God, as he has revealed himself in the Scriptures, must be heard and worshiped; all strange gods and cults not commended in the Holy Scriptures must be avoided and condemned; perjury and all abuse of the divine name must be abhorred, and therefore there must also be a most holy confession and celebration of that same name and the majesty of God the Father, Son, and Holy Spirit; the Sabbath must be kept holy, i.e., at every time, place, and service by which God wants the knowledge and worship of him to be observed by men and to be spread by the preaching

---

[47] Plato, *Laws* II, 665c; Plutarch, *Vita Solonis* III, 4.
[48] Plato, *Laws* I, 630e–631d; Cicero, *De legibus* I, 22.
[49] Cf. Book Two, Ch. IV.

and admonition of the gospel, the use of the sacraments, and the entire Christian discipline, with prayers, praise of God, and thanksgivings.

There follow next the decrees and sanctions which are contained in the Fifth Commandment of the Decalogue, the commandment of obeying and honoring one's parents and all who take the place of parents in the offices of teaching, admonishing, ruling, correcting, nourishing, safeguarding, and helping both in civil and ecclesiastical education and in the application of each person to his own task, about which we have spoken a little before.[50] In this there is principally contained the essence of so-called distributive justice or what Plato calls political justice, according to which there is attributed to everyone the task, honor, and emolument which is due to him for the utility of the entire commonwealth in proportion to his nature, ability, virtue, and industry.[51] For it is an iniquity to give equal preferment, dignity, and occupation to those who are disparate in ability and in the effort they make for the advantage of the commonwealth.

Then in the third place there may follow laws to regulate the exchanges of goods and services of this life and voluntary and involuntary contracts. Here the highest rule is that everyone do to others as he would have them do to him (cf. Matt. 7:12), and this out of a sincere love. In the formulation, emendation, and elucidation of laws of this kind, one must take the greatest care to exclude from the commerce of the citizens all greed [52] (i.e., excessive cupidity in seeking for oneself things, honors, or pleasures) and also all fraud and deceit. If such creeps in, it should receive the strictest attention and be gotten rid of. The citizens must be made to realize that that person ought not be tolerated, neither in the Church of Christ nor in any Christian commonwealth, who is found to prefer private to public advantage or to seek his own interests to the disadvantage of others, and who is not disposed to cultivate among his neighbors mutual benevolence and beneficence, trust, honesty, and appreciation.[53]

For whatever man has the will and desire to deceive, defraud, and harm his neighbors, although he may have the name and shape of a man, he is in nature and desire a savage beast,[54] to whom nothing is lacking but the occasion for overthrowing not only private citizens but also the commonwealth itself. He will readily

---

[50] Cf. Book Two, Chs. IX, XLVIII, XLIX, L, LIV.
[51] Plato, *Laws* VI, 757 b–c; *Republic* I. The term *iustitia distributiva* occurs in the Latin translation of Aristotle's *Nicomachean Ethics* V, 5, 2, 1132b.
[52] *Pleonexia.*   [53] Cicero, *De officiis* III, 5.   [54] *Ibid.,* I, 30; III, 6, 20.

seize every opportunity to do so for he is a captive of Satan and subject to his deceitful lust which is in every way so ruinous for mankind. The Holy Spirit has borne witness to this when he affirmed that "he who hates his brother" (and he who knowingly and willingly harms someone hates him) "is a murderer" (I John 3:15). Therefore, in every condemnation of the godless, Scripture always takes special note of fraud, malice, and lying, and execrates them.

And so in all laws it must first of all be required that all self-love and all greed [55] be suppressed and that everyone embrace and help his neighbors and transact all things with them in the same good faith that everyone wishes others to have in entering into and making contracts with himself. These things, therefore, should be considered and regarded by the correctors of all laws which are promulgated for the observance of so-called commutative justice, by which men are made to acknowledge that they have been born not for themselves but for God, Church, country, and neighbor, and that they wickedly injure God and the commonwealth and deserve to be rejected from the human community if they should be discovered to have preferred in any matter their own good to the good of the commonwealth and their neighbor. This is part of the law of nature, not only of the gospel, which indeed all profess in Your Majesty's realm.[56]

CHAPTER LVII

THE ELEVENTH LAW: THE APPOINTMENT OF MAGISTRATES

Further, since it is evident that however wisely laws are enacted and however fully they are explained, they are of no use to the well-being of the commonwealth unless they are strenuously defended by ordinary magistrates and unless the obedience of all is very strictly exacted; good magistrates are called "living laws." [57] And so Your Majesty will most earnestly take care that there will never be lacking to his subjects pious, holy, and prudent magistrates who love the commonwealth. For such is the propensity of human weakness for all vices that there is no one who does not need a watchman, monitor, and overseer of piety and virtue.

Our God, who knows what is in man (John 2:25) and what remedies his salvation requires against the innate diseases of impiety, wickedness, and iniquity, has sufficiently declared this when

[55] *Pleonexia.* [56] Cicero, *De officiis* III, 5–6.
[57] *Novellae* 105, 2, 4. Cf. Cicero, *De legibus* III, 1–2.

he established an order of magistrates for his people so that every ten householders should have their own guardian, curator, and moderator, a leader of ten [58]; and again one captain of fifty was put in charge of every five leaders of ten; one centurion for two captains of fifty; ten centurions were under one leader of a thousand; all the leaders of thousands together with all the other magistrates obeyed the supreme tribune of each whole tribe as a moderator; and over all these presided one supreme judge and governor of all the people (cf. Ex. 18:21, 25; Deut. 1:15; Judg. 2:16).

From this division of the magistrates the commonwealth will obtain this advantage, that more exact accounts of the lives of individual citizens could be had, that the vices of all could be observed and corrected in time, and that virtues could be aroused, defended, and promoted; if the lower magistrates were deficient, the higher ones could readily amend and repair their negligence rather quickly and salutarily.

In order to accomplish this conscientiously and consistently, the Lord willed these magistrates of his people to be selected with utmost care, by an accurate investigation of his gifts to individuals, so that they might be specifically 'an^eshē ḥayil, i.e., "men endowed with heroic virtue, fearing God, loving virtue and hating dirty lucre and gain" (Ex. 18:21).

No man will preserve laws and justice against wrongdoers, (whose number is everywhere and always quite great) and remove all respect of persons far from himself, something completely necessary for the duties of the magistrate, unless he is of a noble spirit and unheeding of the perils which befall those who serve the commonwealth and which they must undergo out of a love of justice.

But because no righteousness can thrive among men who are unjust and impious against God, the first concern of every Christian magistrate ought to be directed to this: that the citizens be faithfully taught and eagerly learn pure religion. Therefore, it is necessary for the magistrates themselves to excel others in both knowledge of and zeal for the Christian religion. This is why God has commanded that magistrates of the law should be approved and praiseworthy in the fear and true worship of his name.

As, however, every corrupt factor of human life, after the neglect of the fear of God, comes from this, that men, as they are by nature born fraudulent and lying, do and contract nothing among each other with complete sincerity and candor and without deceit and cleverness or some pretense and dissimulation, it is necessary that

[58] *Decanus.*

the magistrates, who have been put in charge of the correction of the character and behavior of men, should with singular enmity prosecute all fraud and deceit, all treacherous hypocrisy, and continually burn with an ardent zeal for truth, simplicity, and integrity. Therefore, on this account, God specifically requires of the magistrates of his people that they be men of truth, i.e., singular lovers and supporters of and fighters for truth and sincerity (Ex. 18:21).

It is also evident that one of the principal causes of civil distress and the disturbance of the commonwealth is greed,[59] that disease by which everyone tries to surpass others in riches and the conveniences of this life or obtain more than his share of honors and pleasures. Secondly, it is a matter of experience that in governing the commonwealth with equity and a good conscience and in rendering to each man his rights, wealthy men are very much ensnared by their possessions. Finally, all know that singular liberality and generosity are required in magistrates. Accordingly, for these reasons God demands of magistrates that they hate all base gain and wicked lucre, so that they will abstain from all unrighteous greed for possessions and be able to see more clearly and safeguard more constantly what is just and fair. Then they will protect the comonwealth from this plague of human society, the desire for having more than is fair (and the stricter they are, the more successful they will be in this) and they will arouse, foster, and champion humaneness, kindness, and generosity.

Now, men who are outstanding in these virtues, namely, in heroic fortitude of spirit, sincere religion and piety toward God, honesty, liberality, and kindness, and who excel in other virtues, these are suitable to be put over other men in order to rule them, and they will execute rightly and happily this divine office of pious and salutary governance, whence they are called gods in the Scriptures (Ps. 82:6).

And so such men are to be sought with utmost diligence from among the entire people. Whenever men of this kind are recommended by others, they must be investigated and examined most strictly in order to determine whether they are such; here care must be taken not to impose moderators on the people of God other than those who truly desire to show themselves faithful and salutary ministers of God, both for the deterrence and suppression of all impiety, wickedness, and injustice, and for the conservation, promotion, and stimulation of every desire for piety, frugality, and justice.

[59] *Pleonexia.*

In this examination, it must be diligently investigated how each has lived from childhood, and whether he has approved himself before all good men through his entire life in his desire for and pursuit of those virtues which I have mentioned from the law of God. Plato thinks that also knowledge of the virtue and holiness of the parents is required.[60] For although God calls very many to himself at the ninth and the eleventh hour (cf. Matt. 21:5-6, and sometimes those whom he has brought late to his Kingdom adorn themselves with more virtue than many whom he has brought early), nevertheless it suits men in every choice of magistrates to follow the rule of the Holy Spirit, and to designate and promote to the divine office of governing the commonwealth those especially who are not guilty of any crimes and are commended for all piety and justice by the constant and frequent testimony of good men, so as not to invite for the commonwealth the danger of imposing rulers on it who only seem to be good and wise men. Those who really are good and approved will enjoy more trust and authority among the people.

From these things one can readily see how far there must be driven from the comonwealth that stain of infamy and deadly corruption which has invaded some monarchies, namely, that prefectures and other governmental offices are assigned for carnal favor and a price, and sometimes a number of them to one person.

Some, once they have been appointed to these duties, are even allowed to obtain whatever substitutes they wish for the administration of their responsibilites, not people who are more suitable for the duties delegated to them, but persons who are relatives of theirs or who pay more to be such substitutes or who return to them the greater part of the salary appointed for these offices. For by this license of greed [61] and invitation to avarice it comes about that, because the magistracies are held for a profit, they are most corruptly administered. Indeed, everyone is anxious to get back what he has spent on the magistracies, with interest.

Aware of this, the emperor Justinian decided to require an oath of those entering magistracies in which they would swear that they had spent nothing for the magistracy and had promised nothing to anyone for any patronage or franchise, and that they had not given and would not give anything for a recommendation made to the ruler and that they had promised and contracted nothing, and that they had received the magistracy gratis,[62] so they would administer it purely, gratuitously, and in good faith toward their

---

[60] Plato, *Republic* III, 412e, 413c; *Laws* VI, 751c.
[61] *Licentia tēs pleonexias.*   [62] *Amisthon.*

subjects, content with the ordinary stipend from public funds. The law of the emperors Theodosius and Valentinian may also be considered, which is found in the *Cod. Ad legem Iuliam repetundarum*, with this formula for the oath, which has been placed in the ninth section among the Authenticae of the emperor Justinian. What must be noted here is that those who undertook the magistracy had to swear "that they had kept and would keep the communion of the most holy, catholic, and apostolic Church of God, and that they would not in any way at any time oppose it, or permit anyone to do so, insofar as they were able." [63]

And so Your Majesty will also be on guard, in accordance with the law of God and the examples of all pious and wise princes: first, not to give any public office to anyone or let it be conferred to him by a subordinate, unless his piety, prudence and virtue, and political knowledge have been investigated and ascertained so that there is no doubt that he can and will do his duty to the commonwealth in a wholesome way, i.e., for the honor of the glory of God and for the increase of the people's welfare. For those who do not seek first the Kingdom of God and his righteousness are slaves of Satan, and they will only show themselves to be pests who are the more harmful to the republic the more ample the power is they obtain in it. And those who are not equipped by God with a gift and ability for governing, although they can show themselves good and reputable private citizens, cannot assume the task of being good rulers over others.

Next, Your Majesty will take care that just as he confers all offices of public government gratuitously and for the favor and consideration of nothing else than furthering the glory of God through the good administration of these offices for the well-being of God's people, so also should all his princes and superior prefects observe the same sanctity, integrity, and responsibility in selecting and appointing magistrates, deferring in no way at all to carnal favor or the intercession of powerful people, and least of all for a price or a personal favor.

For these offices are not the gifts of men which can rightly be donated to private persons according to the will and desire of the giver, but they are divinely assigned responsibilities which should be given only to those who can be expected to fulfill them for the sanctifying of God's name and the obtaining of the salvation and happiness of God's people. The cost of this constant observance of sanctity in the selection and acceptance of magistrates will be the establishment of very heavy penalties for those who have been ap-

[63] *Code* IX, 27.

prehended paying something to anyone for the sake of a magistracy or who in receiving it have given or promised to give anything or who have received or contracted to receive anything from anyone.

Nor are two magistracies to be conferred on anyone however well-prepared he is for governing the commonwealth, since each magistracy requires so much care and work that it is most rare for any one single person to be able to satisfy all its demands. Much less is it to be conceded to anyone that he should obtain a replacement for any public office and, least of all, that anyone should receive a part of the salary of any magistracy who has not personally administered and fulfilled that magistracy in good faith. For any of these indulgences cause the magistracy to be carried out less reverently, less faithfully, and less wholesomely for the commonwealth.

There will also have to be an end put to those useless and harmful abuses of expenditures which in most places those entering the public office are compelled to make and which must be made at some other times while they are administering the office. For by this abuse, men who are very well fitted for this office are often kept from magistracies because they are not able to bear expenses of this kind on account of the modesty of their estates; then, too, God is gravely offended and he denies his blessing to the exercise of government when such divine responsibilities as these are not undertaken and performed with a responsible invocation of his name and with the exclusion of all luxury and pomp unworthy of Christians.

Then Your Majesty will also take measures to see that as each has received his magistracy entirely gratis, so he will also administer it gratuitously, sincerely, and in very good faith, and consider it criminal (and Your Majesty will provide very severe penalties for this crime) to accept any gift from anyone subject to him. For although the giving and receiving of gifts are a function of charity if they are given for a truly holy charitable purpose, nevertheless, since the weakness of human nature is such that even wise and outstandingly just men are easily corrupted by gifts and led away from truth and justice, it has seemed good to God, who alone is wise and truly loves men, that every single taking of bribes [64] and acceptance of gifts should be utterly forbidden to those who exercise government and preside at trials.

For this is the command of Ex. 23:8 and Deut. 16:19: "Do not accept a bribe; for a bribe blinds the eyes of the wise, and perverts just verdicts." Behold God, who alone knows what is in man (John

[64] *Dōrodoxia.*

2:25), pronounces that bribes blind even wise men, men of good vision, men who are attentive and perspicacious in detecting and clearly seeing the good, the true, and the just; they pervert the speech and the verdicts of men who otherwise love and pursue justice. Therefore, Your Majesty will take the precaution of strictest law that no one of those whom Your Majesty entrusts with the administration of judgment and justice for his people should invite such great danger of blindness and iniquity to himself through the reception of gifts which immediately brings with it partiality and subverts all responsibility of legitimate and healthy government.

Furthermore, as "all the imagination and feeling of the human heart is prone to evil from his youth" (Gen. 8:21), for impiety, wickedness, and iniquity, on account of an innate ignorance of God and an unlimited desire [65] for power and honor and pleasures, by which men violate not only the rights of men but also the laws of God, desiring and attempting to get everything for themselves, so individual men, of whatever age they are, not to mention individual states, have constant need of very close watchfulness and very vigilant direction, no less than a ship which is perpetually tossed about in the middle of a stormy sea, as Plato has written.[66] Therefore, no village or town should be left without its approved governors and overseers who discharge the responsibility of pious government assiduously and studiously. They must be very careful to watch that the ship of state receives no damage from the waves of luxury, impiety, and injustice, which Satan never ceases to stir up with the hidden power of his suggestions, nor from the winds and storms of the monstrous devices and madness by which he never fails to enforce his horrible slavery on men for the disturbance of all law, human and divine.

So that there may always be a remedy available for these evils, it has seemed good to our God, first, as has been said above, that every ten men should have their own magistrate; and five groups of ten one chief of fifty; two companies of fifty one centurion; ten divisions of one hundred one leader of a thousand; individual thousands a supreme chief and leader of every tribe; and all these a supreme judge and governor of all the people (cf. Deut. 1:15; Judg. 2:16). Then also, that individual cities and towns should have their judges and prefects: "You shall constitute," he says, "judges and prefects for yourself in all your portions which the Lord your God has given you, according to your tribes, to judge," i.e., govern, "the people" and to rule "with just judgment and governance" (Deut. 16:18).

[65] *Pleonexia.*   [66] Plato, *Laws* VI, 758a.

In order to observe this law as he should, David appointed the prefects for the people of God and the judges of the six thousand only from among the Levites, because they were learned in divine law (cf. I Chron. 23:4). In this example it must be carefully observed that David appointed as many Levites governors and judges as he found to be learned and prudent above others in divine law. For this divine duty in particular is to be entrusted to wise and prudent men (Deut. 4:6).

And so the fourth chapter of the law for the regulation of government should be that no community at all, however small, should be without its overseer and moderator for a pious, frugal, and righteous life, and that in more densely populated areas there should be in charge of these inferior magistrates other moderators and overseers who, inasmuch as they exercise greater power and authority, should also be of more ample wisdom, sanctity, and equity; and for these there should be again others, so that there may be nothing unsupervised,[67] not only among the people but also among the prefects and governors of the people, but so that everyone, a private person as well as one appointed to public service has his watchman, inspector, and observer who will urge him to do his duty if he should fail it in some manner or if he should sin in any way.

In order that this can be effected conveniently and realized successfully for usefulness to the commonwealth, Your Majesty himself will also visit the provinces of his realm at opportune times, after the example of pious and wise kings. He will investigate how they are being ruled and honor those who he learns have faithfully done their duty to the commonwealth; and he shall give attention to those whom he discovers to have conducted themselves otherwise, in order to engender a supreme concern for their duty in all his prefects and administrators of public affairs, that inasmuch as this work is most holy, it is carried on in good faith and in a holy way, as the office [68] and government of God.

And since Your Majesty cannot personally make this inspection of the provinces too often, he will make sure that it is done through men fit for this task every year or at the most biannually. For Your Majesty can hardly be unaware that Christian government has fallen horribly in its responsibility.[69]

But the Holy Spirit provides us with an illustrious example of

---

[67] *Ibid.*, 760a.
[68] *Iudicium* = judicial office.
[69] *Nam, ut horrende collapsa sit religio Christianae gubernationis, Serenissima Maiestas Tua haudquaquam ignorat.*

this royal office in King Jehoshaphat, in regard of what Your Majesty can do personally for the inspection of the provinces as well as what he can do through delegates. In both respects he will exercise utmost care to bring it about that his subjects everywhere are taught the rights and law of God in very good faith, and that according to the same law they are zealously governed and judged by magistrates and judges who are pious, prudent, strong, and holy, as the law of God requires. Your Majesty should want to consider this example seriously and imitate it sedulously. And so, concerning the visitation of the kingdom which Your Majesty may do personally, we read in the story of King Jehoshaphat as follows:

"Jehoshaphat dwelt at Jerusalem; and he went out again among the people, from Beersheba to the hill country of Ephraim and brought them back to the Lord, the God of their fathers. He appointed judges in the land in all the fortified cities of Judah, city by city, and said to the judges, Consider what you do, for you judge not for man but for the Lord; he is with you in giving judgment. Now, then, let the fear of the Lord be upon you; take heed what you do, for there is no perversion of justice with the Lord our God, or partiality, or taking bribes. Moreover, in Jerusalem Jehoshaphat appointed certain Levites and priests and heads of families in Israel, to give judgment for the Lord and decide disputed cases. They had their seat at Jerusalem. And he charged them: Thus you shall do in the fear of the Lord, in faithfulness, and with your whole heart: whenever a case comes to you from your brethren who live in the cities, concerning bloodshed, law or commandment, statutes or ordinances, then you shall instruct them that they may not incur guilt before the Lord and wrath may not come upon you and your brethren. Thus shall you do, and you will not incur guilt. And behold, Amariah the chief priest is over you in all matters of the Lord; and Zebadiah the son of Ishmael, the governor of the house of Judah, in all the king's matters; and the Levites will serve you as officers. Deal courageously, and may the Lord be with the upright" (II Chron. 19:4-11).

In this illustrious and truly regal example Your Majesty will observe these things: First, that it is written that King Jehoshaphat *again* set out to visit the people of his realm. Hence one must understand that he had previously granted to his subjects this benefit of inspection, and had judged it to be required as necessary of a pious king. Secondly, that this pious king visited all the people of his kingdom from Beersheba, at one end of his realm, to Mount Ephraim at the other end. Further, that in this inspection of his subjects he was primarily concerned about the restoration of religion, for he led them back to the Lord their God. This inspection, therefore, was not idle and useless, but a pious king brought it about that the true worship of God was received by all both publicly and privately, with no one now daring to contravene it in word or in deed. And so if anyone did not do this with a sincere heart but as a pretense, he was harmful to himself only and not also others. This king realized that he could never relax in his earnest efforts for the salvation of men and the renewal of religion.

It must further be considered that this king appointed throughout all the cities of his realm judges, i.e., governors, not only in order to punish crimes but also in order to prevent them. And individual cities had a certain number of villages connected with them, which also had their justices, according to the law of the Lord of Ex. 18:26 and Deut. 16:18. Further, he earnestly admonished the judges appointed by him to be mindful that they were rendering judgment for the Lord, not for men, and that the Lord was with them in every judgment, according to the words of the Ps. 82:1: "God stands in the assembly of the gods, and acts as a judge among the gods." From this admonition of King Jehoshaphat, one can readily understand that he set up as judges and governors for his people the kind of men about whose piety and reverence and fear of God there was no doubt.

It must also be observed that he furthermore constituted a supreme tribunal at Jerusalem, both from among the priests and the Levites, on account of their knowledge of divine law and concern for religion, in which it befitted them to excel the others, and also from among the fathers of the entire people, men outstanding in wisdom, justice, sanctity, and authority, in order that this supreme tribunal would be administered with a more ample and definite responsibility, and with authority and power more agreeable to all the people and deserving their reverence.

Nor should one fail to ponder most reverently what this king said to his prefects and judges: "Instruct them not to incur guilt before the Lord, that wrath may not come upon you and your brethren" (II Chron. 19:10). For the entire people is responsible for sins which are of public connivance; God has shown this sufficiently when he struck down the whole people because of the theft of Achan alone, (cf. Josh. 7:1) and also because of the preposterous indulgence of the priest Eli toward his sons, who were committing such horrible crimes (cf. I Sam. 4:4, 11-18).

Finally, it must be considered that he put a high priest in charge of the religious affairs, and a powerful prince in charge of the royal concerns of the realm; for these affairs require different knowledge and care, and hence also different ministers. And each responsibility demands more than the whole man.

Now, let us examine an example of an inspection which this king made through suitable delegates. We read about this in the same book, in the seventeenth chapter:

"In the third year of his reign he sent his princes, Ben-hail, Obadiah, Zechariah, Nethanel, and Micaiah, to teach in the cities of Judah; and with them the Levites, Shemaiah, Nethaniah, Zebadiah, Asahel, Shemiramoth, Jehonathan, Adonijah, Tobijah and Tobadonijah; and with these Levites, the priests Elishama and Jehoram. And they taught in Judah, having the book of the law of the Lord with them; they went about through all the cities of Judah and taught among the people. And the fear of the Lord fell upon all the kingdoms of the lands that were round about Judah, and they made no war against Jehosaphat. Some of the Philistines brought Jehoshaphat presents and silver for tribute; and the Arabs also brought him flocks of sheep, seven thousand seven hundred rams and seven thousand seven hundred he-goats. And Jehoshaphat grew steadily greater in power," etc. (II Chron. 17:7-12).

In this story it must be noticed, in the first place, how promptly King Jehoshaphat, in the third year of his reign, put his mind to restoring a pure and holy administration of religion and government for his people, and what great success this effort had for himself and his entire kingdom.

Next, it must be observed what an illustrious delegation of princes, Levites, and priests this king sent out for the first inspection of his realm. Then, because he did not wish to effect the reformation either of religion or of public government by edicts alone and by the removal of the implements of impiety, he first provided a careful indoctrination derived from the book of the Law, which he took care to have administered to his people as faithfully as possible through his delegates who were outstanding men of every estate of the realm, and this not only throughout all the provinces and districts of his kingdom but also in each of the cities; and in order to emphasize the certainty and purity of this teaching, he ordered the delegates to carry the book of the Law around with them.

From all this Your Majesty will now easily see how it is a truly royal task, singularly wholesome both to himself and to his realm, to provide for his people everywhere as their magistrates, overseers, and governors men who are pious, prudent, just, of heroic spirit, and utterly alien to all avarice and depravity. He will also arrange to visit and inspect them both personally and through delegates suited for this, men gifted with piety, wisdom, and justice, and a salutary constancy and gravity of spirit who on account of this possess authority, so that he is constantly kept informed how his people are being ruled and governed, and that each magistrate is doing his duty and seeks to correct whatever vice has crept in, whether in regard to religion or another department of the state. And he will take special measures against those officials who are caught in having failed to do their duty either by laxity of law enforcement or by conspiring in crimes, or by striking and despoiling their subjects, or by contaminating the administration of their high office by any base gain.

In order to become informed about such evils in time and in order to punish them with the severity they deserve, it will be very useful to Your Majesty to pass a law for his magistrates such as many ancient states had most wisely instituted for themselves, Athens and others, namely, that all those who have served in a public office should render a public account of their services and actions at stipulated times, whether they are discharged from their office or whether they are still performing it; they must make themselves available and let themselves be accused by all who think they have anything against them, with the herald crying: "Does anyone want to bring a charge?"

If Your Majesty decrees, observes, and enforces these things about the appointment, approbation, visitation, correction, investigation, and (in case anyone is discovered to have failed in his duty) punishment of his magistrates, the Lord will add an increase of his Spirit and efficacy, so that Your Majesty will always find such officials to appoint, through whom he may obtain and preserve for his subjects all those things which are necessary for a pious government and salutary custody. Then his people and citizens will be instructed from childhood through a prudent and faithful education, through excellent laws, and through a constant teaching and strict enforcement of the laws. They will become accustomed to and be impelled toward the true worship of God, a purity of life in every way, toward all charity, toward humaneness and kindness to fellow citizens as well as foreigners, toward application to honorable skills and a salutary industry. Then, in view of the fact that idleness will have been outlawed, everyone will learn these skills in time and carry them out and faithfully and steadily fulfill the duties of life, whatever the skill and lifework may be for which every individual has been made by God and to which he has been assigned by the rulers of the commonwealth. Then every person will not only conduct himself and his household honestly, without any aggrievance of the Church, the state, or even private persons, but he will also be able to help and greatly enrich the commonwealth both personally and through his household, by raising up for it good and wholesome citizens, and by contributing to the public good; whence public expenses can be generously sustained, and it will be possible to provide for the needy, not only among the citizens but also among foreigners, what they need in order to live uprightly and in a manner that is useful to the commonwealth.

For everyone would readily acknowledge that unless these foundations necessary for a good and virtuous Christian life are laid, fixed, and made very solid in the hearts of citizens from childhood on through careful, persistent, and holy education and instruction, a future downfall cannot be avoided, whatever good morals you may afterward try to build up through good laws and strictness of the courts; nor are there effective remedies against deeply ingrained vices that stem from protractedly corrupt morals, however strict the watch and sedulous the correction, any more than physicians can heal bodies weakened through long intemperance,[70] however much salutary medicine they administer to them with utmost care.

Therefore, Your Majesty must with great care, persistence, and solicitude make provision that once the laws and all pious human life have been diligently purged and ordered, he appoints by these very laws men gifted with piety, wisdom, and every virtue, and aflame with every zeal and love for the commonwealth, in order that they may rule in all his villages, towns, cities, and counties as teachers, counselors, overseers, inspectors, and protectors; and with utmost vigilance and severity Your Majesty will safeguard and preserve the diligence and responsibility of these men in the performance of their duty through timely inspections and corrections and by demanding at the proper time from each an account of services rendered.

The actions of these officials, with a blessing on their work by our God and heavenly Father, will implant in Your Majesty's citizens from childhood on a feeling of shame and horror toward all impiety, wickedness, injustice, and detestable idleness, and such

---

[70] *Nec . . . profici remediis . . . quam medici proficiunt in sanandis corporibus iam per diuturnam intemperantiam kakochymikois kai kachektikois.* The French translation renders this passage as follows: *Il n'y a non plus de remede qu'il y a aux medecins, de guarir ceux qui par leur intemperance et vie desreiglee sont devenus de tout cacochymes, c'est a dire qui ont des humeurs naturelles du tout corrompues et hectiques, quelque medecine qu'ils leur puissent appliquer* (Bucer, *Opera Latina*, Vol. XV *bis*, p. 271).

an ardent zeal for all piety, frugality, justice, and salutary industry that the judges, whose role it is to correct by punishment whatever offends against the laws and good behavior, will have little work to do.

And since the Lord cannot fail to add all the true advantages of this life to those who seek first his Kingdom and its righteousness (Matt. 6:33), there will undoubtedly be a superabundance of all the things that one can desire in this life. For God will also grant that the actions of good officials will preserve for them most equitably all his blessings, providing to them all things required for the use of this present life as they are exchanged and shared, and none will be permitted to seek his own gain at the disadvantage of others. Finally, this realm will be terrible to all enemies, when the Lord himself presides and reigns in it through such a holy administration of the commonwealth.

CHAPTER LVIII

The Twelfth Law: The Establishment and Correction of Tribunals and Judges

Upon this restoration and repair of written and living laws, i.e., of magistracies, there ought to follow next the reform of courts, by which suitable remedies may be provided to the commonwealth against law violation. For in regard of these things many dreadful complaints are publicly circulated by men of unquestionable piety.[71]

First, they complain that trials throughout the realm take place under men who are hostile to or plainly negligent of pure religion, who are openly avaricious and ready to take bribes and given to other vices so that the judgments rendered by them are in many ways vicious and corrupt. And it is said, and the truth of this is only too clearly evident to all, that when wicked judges do not dare to gratify themselves for their own favor or gain by a judgment adverse to either the defendants or the plaintiffs, they allow amazingly fraudulent amplifications of the procedures, so that if they wish some defendant exempted beyond the right of prosecution of a just plaintiff, they transfer him to a far distant prison without the knowledge of the plaintiff; and so when the trial is held in that place, a place unknown to the plaintiff, a defendant who by rights

---

[71] Thomas Starkey, *Dialogue*, pp. 117 f.; Henry Brinkelow, *The Complaynt of Roderick Mors*, ed. by J. M. Cowper (Early English Text Society, Extra Series, Vol. XXII; London, 1874), p. 20.

ought to be condemned is absolved from a very serious crime because no plaintiff is present.

On the contrary, if men of influence and power wish an innocent defendant, falsely accused of crimes, to be detained for some time in prison and chains, while there is despair of obtaining his release or his conviction, they are suborned. And when the defendant comes to be absolved, after the first plaintiff has proved nothing, they intercede and ask that he be kept in custody as an accused, for they claim to have something of Your Majesty's business to bring against him in another trial. And so, for several more months, that wretch is compelled, contrary to everything right and holy, with no calumniator's complaint outstanding against him, to risk both his health, because of the squalid condition of the prison, and the order of his household, because they lack his care and control, and at the same time he must undergo no small loss of his assets, since in the meantime he is neither able to do any work himself nor can he set his servants to work.

Frequent complaint is furthermore heard about various fraudulent aspects of other trial procedures and also about frustrating delays, which are extremely irritating to those who go to law but lucrative to the judges, attorneys, procurators, and godless litigants, partly on account of the obscurity and complexity of the laws, about which I have warned above,[72] partly on account of the insatiable avarice of these men and their unlimited extravagance, the parent of this avarice.

And so Your Majesty, mindful that "all judgments are made not for men but for God, and that God is present in the administration of all law" (II Chron. 19:6), will work with most watchful and efficient care to restore to his people the purity and holiness of the courts, and will bring it about, first, that the office of a judge is not entrusted to anyone unless, according to the testimony of all good men, he is a man of observed and proved sanctity, tried and celebrated piety, legal ability and virtue, who is not afraid to offend evil men and professes and practices perpetual and implacable [73] enmity against all vices and evildoing.

Also, Your Majesty will see to it that the number of judges is so increased and these so distributed to convenient places that the remedy of a responsible judgment is available always and everywhere to those who have suffered wrong and that punishments are ready for those who violate the laws and offend against the commonwealth and good morals. For God demands that administrators of justice should avenge as soon as possible those who have been

[72] Cf. Book Two, Ch. LVI.   [73] Cf. II Tim. 3:3.

wronged (Luke 18:2 ff.) as everyone with right reason wishes to have done in his own case; and there is no other responsibility which pious judges can rightly put before this one, provided that the state is at peace and that there is domestic tranquillity. For this is their proper office and concern by which they should worship God and give help in human affairs. Realizing this, the emperor Constantine decreed that "in whatever case a man is accused," whether there is a private plaintiff or a matter of public concern which has brought him before the court, a judicial inquiry must at once be made: he must either be punished as an offender or released as an innocent man." [74]

Furthermore, the same inviolability is to be required of judges that is required of magistrates in the performance of their duty, so that they undertake the function committed to them gratuitously and mindful of the commonwealth, and also discharge it gratuitously, rejecting the snares of bribery and everything sordid (cf. II Chron. 19:7) .

Finally, this must also be required of judges, that they judge sincerely according to the laws, i.e., according to the meaning germane to the laws, and not permit themselves to relax any part of the laws in any case. For if some case demands an amendment of the laws or if in another case a dispensation is required, this is to be sought from superiors and the magistrates appointed for this very purpose, and even from Your Majesty himself. For as there is need of as many judges as possible, so it is the duty of only a few to write good laws and also to amend them or to decide what their exceptions ought to be.[75] Therefore, Aristotle rightly counseled that, wherever possible, whatever might happen in any case should be explained and defined by the laws, so that as little as possible should be left to the judges to decide or modify besides the one point: whether the deed brought into court was done or not, whether it was rightly done or otherwise, whether there was much offense or little.[76] For what profit is it to make excellent laws if it is conceded to the judges that they may depart from them according to their good pleasure in making judgments, or even that they interpret laws fraudulently? And so judges should take an oath that they will judge according to the laws, and this must be demanded of them with utmost severity, and those who have manifestly not acted in very good faith should be most severely punished.

[74] *Code* IX, 4, 1 pr.
[75] Thomas Aquinas, *Summa theol.* Ia IIae, q. 97, a. 1–4; IIa IIae, q. 67, a. 4.
[76] Aristotle, *Rhetoric,* I, 1, 1354 a–b.

In order, however, that these men may not be caused by the laws to make frustrating postponements and conclusions and adjournments, Your Majesty will take care that certain well-explained methods are prescribed for making inquiries and judging cases by which any litigation can take place as soon as possible and be justly heard and judged, and by which the proper procedures can be effectively observed by all in as serious a manner as possible.

CHAPTER LIX

THE THIRTEENTH LAW: THE CUSTODY OF ACCUSED PERSONS

This realm is guilty of a grave sin against God by its rather harsh and unjust imprisonment of accused persons. Men plainly innocent are sometimes cast into prison on slight suspicion and detained there for some months before their case is heard. Who would not acknowledge that this is unjust and cruel? [77] For this is the decree of the divine law and the law of nature as given concerning prisoners by Gratian, Valentinian, and Theodosius: [78] "Concerning those who are imprisoned, we order definitely either that a convicted person must undergo his penalty quickly or that a person who is to be set free is not to suffer from lengthy incarceration." It is certainly unfair and cruel to cause the torment of an innocent man even for one hour. And what should judges deem more useful and necessary for them to do than to render judgment and justice and deliver the innocent from all wrong?

And so Your Majesty will take care that a suitable remedy is applied also to this disease of the commonwealth; and on this account, he will decree, first, "that no one be cast into prison before he is convicted" [79] or before he is arrested under the very grave and serious suspicion of having committed a felony, as they say; and that the accuser is to be subject to the *lex talionis* ("an eye for an eye") and must be kept bound to it if he is discovered to have been a calumniator, according to the law of God (Deut. 19:17-21).

Your Majesty will also take care that the case of those imprisoned is taken up for a hearing as soon as there is a way of doing so, so that, as the law of pious emperors has it, a guilty man "may

---

[77] In the oration which W. Haddon delivered at Bucer's funeral, he mentions that during his stay in Cambridge, Bucer took a personal interest in the fate of prisoners (*Scripta Anglicana,* p. 891).

[78] *Code* IX, 4, 5 pr.

[79] *Code* IX, 3, 2 pr.

undergo a quick punishment" or an innocent man be restored to his activity as a free person.

And although imprisonment belongs to that kind of punishment by which coercion is applied to wicked citizens, it would nevertheless be better to devise another kind of punishment for them, such as the condemnation to some labor; this penalty, since it more effectively deters from crimes, would also be of profit to himself and his family, since those kept in prison are subject to less disgrace and are not only useless to themselves and others, but also in more than one way harmful.[80]

CHAPTER LX

THE FOURTEENTH LAW: THE MODIFICATION OF PENALTIES

Lastly, the well-being of his people also demands of Your Majesty a serious and thorough modification of penalties, by which wrongdoing and crimes are kept in check in the commonwealth. But since no one can describe an approach more equitable and wholesome to the commonwealth than that which God describes in his law, it is certainly the duty of all kings and princes who recognize that God has put them over his people that they follow most studiously his own method of punishing evildoers. For inasmuch as we have been freed from the teaching of Moses through Christ the Lord, so that it is no longer necessary for us to observe the civil decrees of the law of Moses, namely, in terms of the way and the circumstances in which they are described, nevertheless, insofar as the substance and proper end of these commandments are concerned, and especially those which enjoin the discipline that is necessary for the whole commonwealth, whoever does not reckon that such commandments are to be conscientiously observed is certainly not attributing to God either supreme wisdom or a righteous care for our salvation.

Accordingly, in every state sanctified to God capital punishment must be ordered for all who have dared to injure religion, either by introducing a false and impious doctrine about the worship of God or by calling people away from the true worship of God (Deut. 13:6-10 and 17:2-5); for all who blaspheme the name of God and his solemn services (Lev. 24:15-16); who violate the Sabbath (Ex. 31:14-15, and 35:2; Num. 15:32-36); who rebelliously despise the authority of parents and live their own life wickedly (Deut. 21:18-21); who are unwilling to submit to the

[80] Cf. Book Two, Ch. XLIX.

sentence of a supreme tribunal (Deut. 17:8-12) ; who have committed bloodshed (Ex. 21:12; Lev. 24:17; Deut. 19:11-13) , adultery (Lev. 20:10) , rape (Deut. 22:20-25) , kidnapping (Deut. 24:7) ; who have given false testimony in a capital case (Deut. 19:16-21) .

No one knows better or provides more diligently what is for man's salvation than God. In these sanctions of God, we see that he judges that the death penalty should eliminate from his people whoever has openly defected from him or held him in contempt or persuades others to do the same, to the betrayal and vitiation of true religion; those who have done injury to his name and who have obstinately detracted from the authority of God as it is administered through his ordinary agents, fathers of families or of country; or finally, those who have attempted to take the life of a neighbor or of his wife or children. For those who are involved in such enormous crimes cannot but inflict great ruin on mankind. By the responsible cooperation of all good men, these pests are therefore to be exterminated from human society no less than fierce wolves, lions, tigers, dragons, and crocodiles which occasionally attack men in order to tear them to pieces and devour them.

For in God alone "we live and move and have our being" (Acts 17:28) , and by his unique kindness we receive all things we can desire; those, therefore, who reject God and make themselves enemies of God rob themselves and others of all good. This is manifestly true of those who do not acknowledge, hear, invoke, and worship God as their God, and who do not constantly seek to increase in themselves that worship which consists of trust in his words.

For these persons rob God of his divinity, as far as they can, and openly deny him to be God, so that they prefer themselves and other creatures before him. What evil, therefore, is not to be expected of those who go to such lengths of impiety that they obstinately refuse to hear the Word of God, and therefore God himself, and to acknowledge that he is their God, as is demanded of us by the First Commandment of the Decalogue: "I am the Lord your God," etc. (Ex. 20:2) . What, then, if they also dare, as is the necessary consequence of that impiety, either to adore instead of the true God images made by themselves, or attempt to worship as the true God the imaginations of their hearts and the works of their hands? God has forbidden this in the Second Commandment of the Decalogue, by which he forbids the worship of strange gods and idols (Ex. 20:3-5) . Or what if they ridicule and blaspheme the Divine Majesty in their rashness, using his holy name for mat-

13:14) . He sings thus in Ps. 101:8: "Early in the morning I shall strike all the wicked on the earth, and I shall cut off from the city of God all doers of iniquity."

For thieves and robbers (except in case one is caught breaking into a home, in which case God has given the one catching him the power of killing him [Ex. 22:2]) God has decreed only the penalty of restitution, either five times, four times, double, or simple repayment. Nor do the Roman laws avenge simple theft with capital punishment,[83] but most of the Gentiles, since they were not able adequately to repress rash thievery by lesser penalties, sentenced thieves to death and strenuously observed this severity.[84]

But what shall we say is the reason that theft is dealt with so fiercely, whereas all too many wink at rape and adultery, at offenses against divine worship, at the distortion of the heavenly doctrine in which both the present and eternal salvation of men is contained, and at blasphemy of the Divine Majesty? Why, unless it is because money and external wealth are so much more dear to men than God himself, their eternal salvation, and decency and honesty?

And when the worldly-wise are today so severe against so-called common thieves, how is it that they not only cooperate but even give great honors to much more harmful thieves, namely, those who exact most wicked and pernicious usury, monopolies, and a thousand other frauds by which they mislead and rob their brethren? Certainly one can imagine no other cause for this than the fact that in these great thefts which are so harmful to the commonwealth rather rich and powerful men are involved, who either themselves preside over the administration of government and justice or have those who regulate such things obligated to them; but those more common thefts are committed by unimportant men who rely neither on wealth of their own nor on powerful patrons. As the common German proverb goes which circulates among us: "Big thieves, who have accumulated immense lucre by stealing and defrauding, are hung with golden necklaces; little thieves, with hemp nooses."

For if it seemed good to drive injustice, fraud, and injury of one's neighbors from the commonwealth, as it is fitting and as God requires and urges in his law and prophets, clearly those thefts, robberies, and plunderings should first be punished, and as severely

[83] *Institutes* IV, 1, 5.
[84] Thievery was generally punished by the death penalty (hanging) in England. Cf. Pauck, *Das Reich Gottes*, p. 73. Many protested against this severity. Cf. Thomas More, *Utopia*, pp. 20 and 29 ff.

as possible, which damage and harm men most; for example, cruel usuries, monopolies, portentous frauds in merchandise, counterfitting and fraudulent exchange of money, wicked pricing of goods, embezzlements and devaluations, wickedly increased prices for produce and all the goods that the present life cannot do without.[85]

Your Majesty should decree such penalties for these frauds and wrongs as will drive away and stamp out from his people every attempt to harm one's neighbor either publicly or privately, and bring it about that everyone truly favors and seeks the advantage of others, so as to buy and sell, lend and repay, and conduct all business of this present life in such a way as to make it manifest that he desires and seeks with his whole heart not only the public but also the private advantage of every neighbor and puts it ahead of his own interests. Moreover, in view of the fact that luxury, feasting, and pomp generate such ruinously harmful avarice, and arouse and encourage boldness for robbing both the commonwealth and private persons, these pests of human life will also have to be excluded and driven from the common life by means of very grave penalties.

In this institution, modification, and enforcement of penalties Your Majesty will prove his trust and zeal for governing the commonwealth in a holy way for Christ the Lord, our heavenly King, if for every single crime, misdeed, or offense he establishes and imposes those penalties which the Lord himself has sanctioned. By means of these, in addition to changing and arousing to true repentance those who have sinned, he will strike the others with fear and dread of sinning; thus he will seek to burn away, i.e., deeply excise and exterminate, not only all licentiousness and boldness in wrongdoing, but also all yearning and desire for it. This is the purpose of penalties and punishments which God proposes in his law.

For the nature of all men is so corrupt from birth and has such a propensity for crimes and wickedness that it has to be called away and deterred from vices, and invited and forced to virtues, not only by teaching and exhortation, admonition and reprimand, which are accomplished by words, but also by the learning and correction that accompany force and authority and the imposition of punishments. Remedies of this kind are so efficacious and salu-

[85] All these were common complaints during the Tudor period. Cf. C. W. C. Oman, *The Tudors and the Currency* (Transactions of the Royal Historical Society, New Series, Vol. IX [London, 1895]), pp. 167 ff.; A. G. Dickens, *The English Reformation*, pp. 160 ff.; also, Wendel's edition of *De Regno Christi*, p. 292, n. 11.

tary for mankind against its inborn ills that Plato rightly judged it the proper role of the art of true rhetoric to require the accusation before a magistrate even of oneself if one had committed some offense, and also of close friends and relatives if they had been in any way delinquent, and to seek punishments prescribed by law as a necessary medicine of primary importance.[86]

FINAL CHAPTER

CONCLUSION OF THE WORK

It seems good to conclude here this undertaking which I should describe as a suggestion and counsel rather than a full explanation of the ways and means by which, as we are taught by the eternal and only salutary Word of God, Your Majesty, Christian kings and princes, and all governors both can and should firmly restore for their peoples the blessed Kingdom of the Son of God, our only Redeemer, i.e., renew, institute, and establish the administration not only of religion but also of all other parts of the common life according to the purpose of Christ our Savior and supreme King.

My words are many; but if you consider that many vices of considerable harmfulness have invaded the administration of both the Church and the State, and that there are only a few who recognize the ills and deadly diseases of the people of God and understand and are ready to use the true and proper remedies against them, I know that Your Majesty, who reads and meditates on the Sacred Scriptures daily with piety and diligence, will judge that these my suggestions and admonitions, whatever their quality, are very narrowly restricted.

I am not unaware, likewise, that there will be at least a few educated men who profess the gospel of the Crucified, who, if they read these commentaries of mine, will find much to criticize in them: they will criticize some things as commonly known and noted and considered not only by Your Majesty but also by those who have but slightly dipped into the literature and are imbued with the religion of Christ in a mediocre way, other things, however, as being too paradoxical,[87] and impossible to institute and realize because they are strange to and out of accord with the ways and views of our age and our people.

Those, however, who are offended by these suggestions and admonitions of mine about the restitution of the Kingdom of Christ among us because they are common and trite should please ponder

[86] Plato, Gorgias 480 b–d.   [87] Paradoxa ("contrary to opinion").

what a man no less holy than that delightful orator Isocrates wrote to Nicocles: "What one writes concerning the instruction of life and morals should not be new and unheard of" (as God has always provided from the beginning of the world men to pass on salutary precepts concerning these things), "but must be selected from whatever things are the best." Christians, for whom it is unholy to add to or detract from or in any way change the Word of God handed down from the beginning (cf. Deut. 4:2), should take singular precautions not to inject anything new and recently invented into any doctrine and teaching of life. But since I am unable to do what Isocrates added, "Express these things as elegantly as possible," [88] I have tried to explain them simply and honestly.

Further, those who think that what I have presented is too different from present ways of doing things and the thinking of modern men, a matter of wishful thinking rather than practicality, and that I want to design some so-called Platonic republic, I earnestly ask, for the sake of the Kingdom and coming of our Lord Jesus Christ and the salvation all of us have in common, that they would judge and estimate what I have proffered and suggested not on the basis of the judgment of men of this or an earlier age, but by the eternal and immutable Word of God. Those who make an earnest effort to do this will undoubtedly see and acknowledge that all these things are not remote and different from the aims and practices of modern men who glory in the rule of Christ, but rather that they are easy to receive and observe for all who have not decided to renounce Christ as Lord ("We do not want this man to reign over us" [19:14]) and that they are necessary for the salvation of mankind both now and forever.

For how can one acknowledge and adore Christ, God and Man, our only Savior, also as one's own Christ, Redeemer, King, and God, and not accept all his words and try to follow them wholeheartedly, just as they are, the words of eternal life? And is it not necessary for those to whom this has been given, that they receive and embrace the salvation which Christ the Lord offers in his gospel as well as in the sacraments and in all the precepts of his discipline, with as much more ardent a desire and greater a gratitude of spirit as the Creator excels every creature, as God excels men, and as the sure eternal life and happiness excel a false, empty opinion and an imagined semblance of the good?

And, indeed, these will hear nothing more eagerly, beyond any comparison, and follow nothing with a firmer faith than the words and precepts of Christ—all of them; they will receive nothing with

[88] Isocrates, *In Nicoclem* 41

more devotion and greater spiritual pleasure than his sacraments; and finally they will observe and care for nothing more diligently and solicitously than that his discipline flourishes among them. And so they will establish all ministries of the Lord among them and they will take care to carry them out most reverently, and everyone will submit to them in a most willing spirit.

Thus they will not wink at the sins of anyone in the churches, if he is delinquent; but they will use on him the remedies of salutary censure as they are divinely revealed, and will turn those who have sinned toward a pious and effective repentance; and they will never cease to invite, influence, and compel every single person to all the duties of piety, by pious teaching and exhortation, both public and private, on the part of individual brethren acting as members of Christ as well as on the part of the regular leaders and shepherds of the churches.

With the Son of God thus reigning among people of this kind, how could true sanctity and dutiful charity not prevail? They would impel a person always to learn and do some good work so that everyone would contribute his share for the use of the churches; thus the Church would so thrive in each and every member of Christ that no one would be in want, not only of necessary food, shelter, and clothing, but also of any other means of commodity for living well and happily in the Lord, our King Jesus Christ, and in his universal Church.

If, therefore, the one dispenser of kingdoms and powers and the preserver of all, Christ the King, gives to this his people also external sovereignty and a free administration of the commonwealth, because they love and worship this their King "with their whole heart, and soul, and strength" (Luke 16:27), he will give them also all political power and all external strength, so that his Kingdom and his pure and genuine religion may grow and flourish among them and prevail everywhere as fully as possible.

Accordingly, whoever holds the external and political power among these people of Christ will not only not tolerate any manifest neglect of pure religion among his subjects who are consecrated by Baptism to Christ the Lord, much less any vice or attempted opposition to him in word or deed; but he will also see to it, first and foremost, that the churches enjoy suitable ministers of probity and trustworthiness; and, lest these ever be wanting, they will also make every effort to make sure that there are many schools of learning and piety, and that all who have been destined for this by God are instructed and trained in them for these ministries of the churches, whether they have been born of rich or poor parents. They will likewise see to it that none of the common people lack anything by which he and his family can show themselves productively useful to the saints of Christ and his churches.

Just as, therefore, these will take care that every private person and corporation and the commonwealth itself have and keep their own resources, and will very severely punish all those, whoever they are, who take private and public wealth and resources by theft or embezzlement, so, in accordance with the high concern and solicitude which we should devote to the churches of Christ, to which God has pledged the whole world and the angels themselves (I Cor. 3:22), they will also do all they can in order to maintain for the churches their property, indeed the patrimony of their Head and Spouse, the Crucified One, and to keep it sacrosanct, while they will inflict very severe punishment upon those who have dared to attack or to ruin it by fraud or sacrilegious force.

Therefore, they will in no way allow that any person unworthy of and useless to the churches, even if he should be their father or son, has on any pretext or excuse a share in those goods which have been consecrated to Christ the Lord for the use of religion, the schools, or the poor; or that to anyone more should be distributed or granted from these than he deserves according to the Word of God for his saving ministry as it is performed in good faith for the churches, or for the true and continuous work of preparation and instruction for the ministry, or for an evident need which a person is not able to deal with.

With equal care they will be on watch that no enticements to and occasions for sin creep in. By the award of public and private honors, ranks and compensations, they will strive to arouse and impel men to a desire for virtues, and by threatening very severe penalties they will deter and keep them from sins and crimes. Reprobates will not be admitted to honors in the state, or to honorable offices, or to privileges. And finally they will not tolerate any idlers, but they will compel all their citizens to pious and fruitful industry for the commonwealth.

This, in summary, is what I advise and affirm should be restored and undertaken with all zeal by those who wish the Son of God to reign among them. But who is there who ever reads his Gospel with an attentive spirit who would not acknowledge all these things which I have just mentioned to have been most clearly revealed and sacredly commanded by Christ the Lord himself in countless places in his Scriptures?

Those who truly belong to Christ know and feel that all the words and commandments of Christ their Savior are "words" and commandments "of life" and "eternal" salvation (John 6:68) ; how can they then fail to sense that they are not only "not burdensome" (I John 5:3) , much less impossible but that they must be very much sought after and pursued with a most ardent zeal? For they have tasted and experienced "how good and pleasant the Lord is" in all his commandments and words (Ps. 34:8) ; they know that "the Lord's yoke is" so "easy and his burden so light" (Matt. 11:30) that no men can achieve true rest and tranquillity for their souls who have not submitted to this yoke and labor with their whole heart. These, therefore, will find that there is nothing new in all that I have here suggested and advised, nothing unusual for true sons of God, nothing which must not at all times be sought after and practiced wholeheartedly by all men who have been given to Christ the Lord by the Father.

Moreover, when I began to write about the full restoration and renewal of the Kingdom of Christ, I had necessarily in mind only those men "whom" God, as he "selected them for himself from the world" (John 15:19) , and "chose, foreknew and predetermined them before the foundation of the world" (Eph. 1:4) , also "calls, justifies, and glorifies" in his own time (Rom. 8:29-30) . For those who are of the world are wise about worldly things (Rom. 8:5) , not the things of Jesus Christ; they hate and kill him and all his members (John 15:18-19) , so far are they from accepting his words; and so they remain in evil, and the wrath of God broods over them, for the Son does not pray for them (John 17:9) . It was therefore not fitting for me, as I dealt with the Kingdom of Christ, to dwell on what the accused enemies of this Kingdom approve or disapprove or what they support or do not accept.

But it will be said by those who wish the Kingdom of Christ to be restored only to the extent that their partnership and communication with the passing world will not be disturbed, that the world is crammed full with worldly men. For the Lord himself has said, "Many are called but few are chosen" (Matt. 22:14) ; and so there is some reason for taking account of these persons in the restoration of the Kingdom of Christ, at least for the purpose of keeping external peace in the nation.

But to these the apostle responds when he writes to the Corinthians: "What partnership have righteousness and iniquity? Or what fellowship has light with darkness? What accord has Christ with Belial? Or what has a believer in common with an unbeliever?" (II Cor. 6:14-15) . Likewise in Romans: "Do not be conformed to this world" (Rom. 12:2) . And to the Galatians: "I am crucified to the world, and the world to me" (Gal. 6:14) .

Moreover, it is obvious that pious men should pray to our one Savior and King to whom the Father has given all power in heaven and on earth (Matt. 28:18) for the favor of external peace; and this peace is promised only to those who subject themselves to his sovereignty, not to those who are opposed to it or do not fully accept it and who prefer to his grace and glory the grace and benevolence of lost men. As this depends upon us, external peace must be sought and kept as far as possible with all men, but by yielding and deferring to them in the things that belong to us and not those which belong to the Son of God, our Lord Jesus Christ, or to his Church (Matt. 5:9 and 10:13; Rom. 12:18). We must work to please all, but "for good" and "for the edification" of the salvation of men (Roman. 15:2); those who wish to please men in another way cannot be the servants of Jesus Christ (Gal. 1:10).

There were a great number of men hostile to Christ and there were few truly zealous for his Kingdom also in the times of David, Hezekiah, and Josiah. David complains about his times in so many psalms, as do the Lord's prophets Isaiah and Jeremiah concerning the times of Hezekiah and Josiah; however, because these kings knew that to a believer in God nothing is impossible at least of those things which God requires of us; they restored all things that God had commanded his people, despite the fact that evil demons and men were unwilling and strove against them, and they had all vices and wickedness in religion and the rest of life eliminated; and God was present with them, so that what they had begun to do in his name with a constant faith they were also able successfully to accomplish.

And despite the fact that under Hezekiah and Josiah there were many who kept the impiety of heart which they were compelled externally to reject, nevertheless so pleasing to God were the efforts of these pious kings for his Kingdom that in their times he granted immense blessings to the whole people and forgave them the punishments they deserved.

Therefore, mindful that "heaven and earth will pass away, but not one jot or tittle of the word and law of God will ever be removed" (Matt. 5:18); "and that God brings the counsel of the nations to nought and frustrates the plans of the peoples, but that his counsel stands forever, and his thoughts extend from generation to generation" (Ps. 33:10-11), Your Majesty will let the false and pernicious decisions of men be what they are, but he will follow and abide with a strong heart in the words and judgments of God, which are always true and always salutary, whatever the whole world with its god produces and brings forth to the contrary.

And from these words and judgments of God he will learn what things belong to the Kingdom of Christ and the best method of restoring it in this country as fully as possible; and he will arrange that this method is very exactly and explicitly outlined, joining to himself for this purpose a distinguished council of men whom he will know to be both solidly instructed in and excellently motivated for the Kingdom of Christ; and by their service and labors he will in all counties seek for and send out to the people approved evangelists, who will preach to them with supreme faith and pious skill the whole gospel of Christ and every means of restoring his Kingdom among us.

When this procedure will have been approved by the nobles and the Parliament of the realm, he will recommend it to the people for adoption through men fitted for such a task, and ratify it definitely by laws; at the same time he will appoint to all bishoprics and parishes men suitable for such offices as soon as he shall have found them, men who will do all their pastoral duty for the churches with utmost zeal as the chief Shepherd and Bishop of our souls, the Son of God, our Lord Jesus Christ, has ordained and commanded it to be done.

In order to obtain suitable ministers for these positions, he will not only restore the universities as soon and as fully as possible to their original constitution for the true use of the churches, but he will also make sure that many other schools are opened in which as many suitable persons as possible will be educated and trained for the ministries of the churches.

In order also to supply to these and all needy Christians, indeed, to Christ the Lord himself, all that is needed for holy and happy living and for the right maintenance of ecclesiastical ministries, it must be his utmost and most earnest concern to establish and preserve for the churches a sure income and the holy patrimony of their spouse. And if it still seems good to take something from church property for the uses of the realm (for nothing can rightly be yielded from this source to any private persons, except what is due them for faithful service to the churches or what is needed for study in preparation for these ministries or for poor relief), let it be taken, but with that moderation which will find approval from the Lord, the King of all the earth and our supreme Savior, who gives us all things; the rest must be put to the use for which it was consecrated, the use of the Crucified One, our only Redeemer, and dedicated to the necessary ministries of the churches, to schools, and the support of the needy. Hence there must be a severer punishment of anyone who by cunning, artifice, or fraud takes and claims for himself something from this patrimony of the Crucified (for this is a sacrilege) than of one who is guilty of any other theft or robbery, to the extent by which the right of Christ our Savior and his Church should be closer to our hearts than any public or private rights of men.

Once the Kingdom of Christ has been restored for his citizens in this responsible spirit, Your Majesty will also seek to make them ready for it with all his royal strength and power; and he will bring it about both by legislation and a faithful and constant enforcement of the laws, first, that all private homes are kept holy, that those whom God wills to be joined are joined in marriage piously and religiously, and that having been joined, they cultivate this divine social order in a most holy way, and once united by this yoke never turn from each other, unless this is necessary both for their own well-being and that of society. Next, every child which the Lord gives to the commonwealth shall be most exactingly educated, instructed, and trained for Christ the Lord and his Church, each being assigned to those skills and duties of life for which he seems to have been made and destined by the Lord. No place at all is to be provided in his realm for idlers, but everyone is to be used for worthy endeavors and tasks advantageous to the commonwealth.

And in order that these things can be perpetually and constantly preserved, Your Majesty will take care that laws be written to cover all the activities and affairs of his subjects, and that those written be amended and elucidated so that they are clear and wholesome for his citizens, steady shining lights for all their life and activities and not deceitfully designed illusions of the godless for gain or wrongdoing, or nets and snares for the capture and overthrow of the innocent.

And since neither written laws nor the ordering and constitution of the commonwealth, however accurate and careful, can long be of usefulness or preserve anything good, if men lack living laws, wise, pious, and vigilant magistrates and responsible and just judges, and also just and severe punishments for malefactors Your Majesty will endeavor to provide such magistrates and judges for his people everywhere, and he will establish and enforce punishments for all crimes and wickedness so that nothing will be lacking for the full and complete manifestation of the Kingdom and the judgment of God.

When Your Majesty will have laid these foundations and estab-

lished them and as he will strive to complete these things more
and more, day by day, he will know that Christ the King and Giver
of eternal life will always be present with his citizens and subjects,
and all evils will be so reduced and all good things so accumulated,
that this realm will be happy and successful in all things. For
Christ our King cannot fail to add most abundantly and liberally
all other things which are asked for by those who are seeking first
his Kingdom and his righteousness (cf. Matt. 6:33) .

And so Your Majesty will not let himself be disturbed that he
has the company of very few kings and that he acts almost alone in
exerting himself in this great task which is impossible for the flesh,
the perfect restitution of the Kingdom of Christ. Since he has in
Christ Almighty a helper and leader in this, what part of his aim
will he not accomplish, whatever the world and the flesh attempt to
the contrary? Nor will it cast down his spirits that so far not many
faithful ministers have appeared in his realm for this undertaking;
for Christ is accustomed to restore his Kingdom gloriously for his
people and to put their enemies under their feet even by the use
of the ministry of a very few men who are very weak and contemptible in the eyes of the world (I Cor. 15:25; 1:27-28) . Nor
will Your Majesty delay because there are at this time no examples
of the full restoration of the Kingdom of Christ: for he has the
orders of his God; he has the examples portrayed in his Scriptures
and they are abundantly sufficient for every pious prince for any
degree of zealous imitation. And finally, whatever objections are
made by Satan, personally or through those enslaved to him, Your
Majesty will strengthen himself with the very ample promises of
God which we should hold to be more certain than anything we
have experienced just as the Word of God is more certain than the
feeling of men.

There are not lacking illustrious examples, not only ancient
ones (which nevertheless alone would be abundantly sufficient,
since they are provided for us by the Holy Scriptures) , but also of
our own period, in which it is very clearly evident that Christ our
King is wonderfully and powerfully present with all his servants,
and with kings and princes and that it is he who gives the success
they hope for to those who have undertaken the full restoration
of his Kingdom among us. And whenever matters fall out otherwise, one can find that the cause has been impurity of effort and
the manifest offense of insincere zeal: as in the time of the Maccabees, so also now in the disaster of Germany.[89] For Christ our

[89] This is an allusion to the defeat of the German Lutherans in the Smalcaldic War.

King lives and still acts in every way characteristic of himself (cf. Heb. 13:8).

Therefore, Your Majesty may expect to receive from God in this task a no less magnificent support and happy outcome of his efforts than God has ever given to and provided for any of his servants, responsible princes,[90] as with his whole heart he seeks to show forth God's glory and obtain the total salvation of his subjects according to His words and commandments. This will be done; indeed, it will be done by our Lord Jesus Christ, the "King of Kings and the Lord of Lords" (Rev. 17:14), as Your Majesty gets these undertakings under way, no less than in the case of David, Asa, Jehoshaphat, Hezekiah, and Josiah, with a daily increase of magnificent prosperity, as he manifests himself to his subjects as a king altogether saving and successful, formidable and unconquered in the face of both his external and internal enemies, who will never be lacking so long as there has not been a unanimous acceptance of Christ in this realm. And since there must be some risk and labor, as there will be, Your Majesty will keep in mind the infinite and eternal rewards which await him for these slight dangers and labors of such a brief and momentary duration, and that the Son of God has prepared these rewards for him by his infinite sorrows and his most cruel sufferings.

May the same Lord, our Savior Jesus Christ, as he has given to Your Majesty an outstanding understanding and desire for all these things, so also reveal and unite to him as soon as possible those through whom he may as effectively as possible begin and inaugurate and ever further and perfect this restoration of his Kingdom. Amen, Amen, Amen.

I pray that Your Majesty will favorably accept this my little work of suggestion and advice on these matters; and if Your Majesty or anyone else should be of the opinion that I have proposed anything not in agreement with the eternal Word of God, I beg to be advised of this admonition, as I am always prepared in all things to follow the pure Word of God itself and to consecrate my total self to it.

This writing, begun early, I have completed late; this is due to the fact that my health was weakened by sickness and old age, and there were also the demands of the office of the ministry entrusted to me by Your Majesty. May Your Majesty regard and hold me, his unworthy servant and minister, as commended to the Lord and as one who prays and will always pray that God, our heavenly Father, through our Lord Jesus Christ, will preserve Your Majesty

[90] *Religiosis principibus.*

and give him success in all things, for the increase of His own glory and for the wonderful consolation and salvation of all the people who are his, in this and other realms. Amen, Amen.

End

of the Book on the Kingdom of Christ.

To God be the glory! [91]

[91] τῷ Θεῷ δόξα·

SELECTED BIBLIOGRAPHY

I. Melanchthon

Erasmus, Desiderius Roterodamus, *Ausgewählte Werke,* ed. by Hajo Holborn. München, 1933.

—— *Opus Epistolarum Erasmi,* ed. by P. S. Allen. Oxford, 1906 ff.

Kolde, Th., *Die Loci communes Ph. Melanchthons,* 4th ed. Leipzig, 1925.

Melanchthons Werke in Auswahl, ed. by Robert Stupperich, Vols. I and II. Gütersloh, 1951–1952.

The Loci Communes of Philip Melanchthon, ed. and tr. by Charles L. Hill, 2d ed. Boston: The Meador Press, 1944.

Bizer, Ernst, *Theologie der Verheissung. Studien zur theologischen Entwicklung des jungen Melanchthon* (1519–1524). Neukirchen, 1964.

Breen, Quirinus, *Christianity and Humanism: Studies in the History of Ideas,* ed. by Nelson P. Ross. Grand Rapids: Wm. B. Eerdmans Publishing Company, 1968.

Elliger, Walter, ed., Philipp Melanchthon, *Forschungsbeiträge zur 400. Wiederkehr seines Todestages.* Göttingen, 1961.

Hannemann, Kurt, *Reuchlin und die Berufung M.'s nach Wittenberg,* in *Festgabe Joh. Reuchlin* (Pforzheim, 1955), pp. 108–138.

Herrlinger, A., *Die Theologie Melanchthons in ihrer geschichtlichen Entwicklung.* Gotha, 1879.

Joachimsen, Paul, *Loci communes. Eine Untersuchung zur Geistesgeschichte des Humanismus und der Reformation,* in *Lutherjahrbuch* 8 (1926), pp. 27–97.

Lohse, B., "Die Kritik am Mönchtum bei Luther und Melanchthon" in Vilmos Vatja, ed., *Luther and Melanchthon in the*

History and Theology of the Reformation (Philadelphia: Fortress Press, 1961), pp. 129–145.

Manschreck, Clyde L., *Melanchthon: The Quiet Reformer.* New York: Abingdon Press, 1958.

Maurer, Wilhelm, *Melanchthon-Studien.* Gütersloh, 1964.

—— *Melanchthons Loci communes von 1521 als wissenschaftliche Programmschrift* in *Lutherjahrbuch* 27 (1960), pp. 1–50.

—— *Zur Komposition der Loci Mel. v. 1521. Ein Beitrag zur Frage Melanchthon u. Luther* in *Lutherjahrbuch* 25 (1958), pp. 146–180.

—— *Der junge Melanchthon zwischen Humanismus und Reformation.* Göttingen 1967.

Neuser, Wilhelm H., *Der Ansatz der Theologie Ph. Melanchthons.* Neukirchen, 1957.

Pauck, Wilhelm, "Luther and Melanchthon," in Vatja, ed., *Luther and Melanchthon,* pp. 13–31.

Pelikan, Jaroslav, *From Luther to Kierkegaard.* St. Louis: Concordia Publishing House, 1950.

Schäfer, R., *Christologie und Sittlichkeit in Melanchthons frühen Loci.* Tübingen, 1960. (See the criticism by E. Bizer in *Theologie der Verheissung,* pp. 9–33.)

Schwarzenau, P., *Der Wandel im theologischen Ansatz bei Melanchthon.* Gütersloh, 1956.

Sperl, Adolf, *Melanchthon zwischen Humanismus und Reformation.* München, 1959.

Stupperich, Robert, *Melanchthon.* Berlin, 1960 (English translation, Philadelphia: The Westminster Press, 1965).

II. BUCER

Bucer, Martin, *Deutsche Schriften,* ed. by Robert Stupperich. To date, Vols. I, II, III, VII; Gütersloh, 1960 ff.

—— *De Regno Christi* (Vol. XV of *Martini Buceri Opera Latina*), ed. by François Wendel. Paris, 1955.

—— *Scripta Anglicana.* Basel, 1577.

Anrich, Gustav, *Martin Bucer.* Strassburg, 1914.

Bornkamm, Heinrich, *Martin Bucers Bedeutung für die europäische Reformationsgeschichte.* Gütersloh, 1952.

Bromiley, G. W., *Thomas Cranmer, Theologian.* London: Lutterworth Press, 1956.

Clebsch, William A., *England's Earliest Protestants, 1520–1535.* Yale University Press, 1964.

Constant, Gustave, *The Reformation in England*. 2 vols., London, 1939–1942.

Corpus Iuris Civilis, English translation, *The Civil Law*, by S. P. Scott, 17 vols., Cincinnati, 1932.

Courvoisier, Jaques, *La notion d'Église chez Bucer dans son développement historique*. Paris, 1933.

Dickens, A. G., *The English Reformation*, London: B. T. Batsford, Ltd., 1964.

Eells, Hastings, *Martin Bucer*. New Haven, 1931.

Fisher, H. A. L., *The History of England from the Accession of Henry VII to the Death of Henry VIII*. London, 1906.

Gairdner, James, *The English Church in the Sixteenth Century*. London, 1904.

Holl, Karl, "Die Kulturbedeutung der Reformation" in *Luther* (Vol. I of *Gesammelte Aufsätze zur Kirchengeschichte*), 2d ed. Tübingen, 1923.

Holstein, Hugo, *Die Reformation im Spiegelbilde der dramatischen Litteratur des sechzehnten Jahrhunderts*. Halle, 1866.

Hopf, Constantin, *Martin Bucer and the English Reformation*. Oxford: Basil Blackwell & Mott, Ltd., 1946.

Hughes, Philip, *The Reformation in England*, 3 vols. London: Hollis & Carter, Ltd., Publishers, 1950–1953.

Hughes, Philip E., *The Theology of the English Reformers*. London: Hodder & Stoughton, Ltd., 1965.

Koch, Karl, *Studium Pietatis. Martin Bucer als Ethiker*. Neukirchen, 1962.

Köhler, Walther, *Zürcher Ehegericht und Genfer Konsistorium*, Vol. II. Leipzig, 1942.

Kohls, Ernst-Wilhelm, *Die Schule bei Martin Bucer in ihrem Verhältnis zu Kirche und Obrigkeit*. Heidelberg, 1963.

Lang, August, *Der Evangelienkommentar Martin Butzers und die Grundzüge seiner Theologie*. Leipzig, 1900.

——— *Puritanismus und Pietismus*. Neukirchen, 1941.

Leach, Arthur F., *English Schools at the Reformation*. Westminster, 1896.

Leonard, E. M., *The Early History of English Poor Relief*. Cambridge, 1900.

Levy, Max, *Der Sabbat in England. Wesen und Entwicklung des englischen Sonntags*. Leipzig, 1933.

Liljegren, S. B., *The Fall of the Monasteries and the Social Changes in England*. Lund, 1924.

McConica, James K., *English Humanists and Reformation Poli-*

tics Under Henry VIII and Edward VI. London: Oxford University Press, 1965.

Milton, John. *Complete Prose Works of John Milton,* Vol. II, ed. by Ernest Sirluck. New Haven: Yale University Press, 1959.

More, Sir Thomas, *Utopia,* Vol. 4 of *The Complete Works of St. Thomas More,* ed. by Edward Surtz and J. H. Hexter. New Haven: Yale University Press, 1965.

Müller, J., *Martin Bucers Hermeneutik.* Gütersloh, 1961.

Nottingham, W. J., "The Social Ethics of Martin Bucer." Dissertation, Columbia University, 1962.

Oman, C. W. C., *The Tudors and the Currency* (Transactions of the Royal Historical Society, New Series, Vol. IX). London, 1895.

Parker, T. H. L., ed., *English Reformers* (LCC, Vol. XXVI). Philadelphia: The Westminster Press, 1966.

Pauck, Wilhelm, *Das Reich Gottes auf Erden. Utopie und Wirklichkeit. Eine Untersuchung zu Butzers De Regno Christi u. der englischen Staatskirche des 16. Jahrhunderts.* Berlin, 1928.

—— *The Heritage of the Reformation,* rev. ed. New York: Oxford University Press, Inc., 1968.

Pollard, A. F., *England Under Protector Somerset.* London, 1900.

—— *Thomas Cranmer and the English Reformation.* London, 1904.

Porter, Harry C., *Reformation and Reaction in Tudor Cambridge.* Cambridge: Cambridge University Press, 1958.

Rott, J., "Le sort des papiers et de la bibliothèque de Bucer en Angleterre," *Revue d'Histoire et de Philosophie Religieuses,* Vol. 46 (1966), pp. 346–367.

Skopnic, Günter, *Das Strassburger Schultheater.* Frankfurt, 1935.

Smyth, Charles H., *Cranmer and the Reformation Under Edward VI.* Cambridge, 1926.

Strohl, Henri, *Bucer, humaniste chrétien.* Paris, 1939.

Stupperich, Robert, "Die Kirche in M. Bucers theologischer Entwicklung," *Archiv für Reformationsgeschichte,* Vol. 35 (1938), pp. 81–101.

—— "Bibliographia Bucerana" in H. Bornkamm, *Martin Bucers Bedeutung,* pp. 39–96.

Tawney, Richard H., *The Agrarian Problem in the Sixteenth Century.* London, 1912.

Torrance, T. F., *Kingdom and Church: A Study in the Theology of the Reformation. The Eschatology of Love: Martin Bucer,* pp. 73–89. Edinburgh: Oliver & Boyd, Ltd., 1956.

Trevelyan, G. M., *Illustrated English Social History*, Vol. I. London: Longmans, Green & Co., Ltd., 1954.

Vogt, Herbert, *Martin Bucer und die Kirche von England*. Dissertation, University of Münster, 1966 (published in typescript, 1968).

Wendel, François, *Le mariage à Strasbourg à l'époque de la Réforme*, Strassbourg, 1928.

────── *L'Église de Strasbourg, sa constitution et son organisation*. Paris, 1942.

────── "Un document inédit sur le séjour de Bucer en Angleterre," *Revue d'Histoire et de Philosophie Religieuses*, Vol. 34 (1954), pp. 223–233.

White, Helen C., *Social Criticism in Popular Religious Literature of the Sixteenth Century*. New York: The Macmillan Company, 1944.

Winckelmann, Otto, *Das Fürsorgewesen der Stadt Strassburg*. Leipzig, 1922.

Zeeveld, W. G., *Foundations of Tudor Policy*. Cambridge, Mass.: Harvard University Press, 1948.

INDEXES

I. *Melanchthon*

II. *Bucer*